PRINCIPLES OF
DATA STRUCTURES AND
ALGORITHMS WITH PASCAL

PRINCIPLES OF DATA STRUCTURES AND ALGORITHMS WITH PASCAL

ROBERT R. KORFHAGE
Southern Methodist University

NORMAN E. GIBBS
Software Engineering Institute/Carnegie-Mellon University

WM. C. BROWN PUBLISHERS
DUBUQUE, IOWA

Book Team

Developmental Editor   Nova A. Maack
Designer   Carol S. Joslin
Production Editor   Diane S. Clemens
Permissions Editor   Vicki Krug
Product Manager   Matt Shaughnessy

wcb group

Wm. C. Brown   **Chairman of the Board**
Mark C. Falb   **President and Chief Executive Officer**

wcb
Wm. C. Brown Publishers, College Division

G. Franklin Lewis   **Executive Vice-President, General Manager**
E. F. Jogerst   **Vice-President, Cost Analyst**
George Wm. Bergquist   **Editor in Chief**
Edward G. Jaffe   **Executive Editor**
Beverly Kolz   **Director of Production**
Chris C. Guzzardo   **Vice-President, Director of Sales and Marketing**
Bob McLaughlin   **National Sales Manager**
Marilyn A. Phelps   **Manager of Design**
Julie A. Kennedy   **Production Editorial Manager**
Faye M. Schilling   **Photo Research Manager**

Cover illustration by Tom Kovacs, Electronic Imaging Lab, School of Art and Design, University of Illinois, Urbana-Champaign

Lotus 1-2-3 is a registered trademark of Lotus Development Corporation.

VisiCalc is a registered trademark of Paladine.

CalcStar and WordStar are registered trademarks of MicroPro International.

TurboPascal is a registered trademark of Borland International.

Library of Congress Catalog Card Number: 86–70711

ISBN 0–697–00123–7

Printed in the United States of America
10 9 8 7 6 5 4 3 2 1

Dedicated to our families
Barbara, Karen, and Jennifer Gibbs
Ann, Willard, Margaret, Lisa, and David Korfhage

Contents

Preface

The goal of this text is to present a rigorous and clear exposition of abstract data types, algorithms, and data structures for undergraduate computer science students. The ACM curriculum recommendations for the courses CS1[1] and CS2[2] and the report on a Model Curriculum for Liberal Arts Programs[3] dictate the need for a text emphasizing abstraction that is at the same time both rigorous and readable.

The idea for this book grew out of a course, Algorithms and Data Structures, that was originally written and taught by Jon Bentley of Carnegie-Mellon University for the IBM Corporation under its University Level Computer Science Program. We attended pilots of the course taught by Jon and later revised it when Jon left Carnegie-Mellon for AT&T Bell Laboratories. Our revised notes and lectures form the basis of this textbook.

In the course of developing this text, we have examined every text in data structures and algorithms that we have found, from Knuth's *The Art of Computer Programming,* Volumes 1 and 3, to Aho, Hopcroft, and Ullman's *Algorithms and Data Structures,* and taught from many of these texts. Some of these texts are excellent, but aimed at a more advanced student of computer science; others are fine in parts, but lack adequate presentation of certain topics. However, we feel that few, if any, texts demonstrate to the student how the ideas and abstractions of theory can be used in concrete applications in the form of programs. The classic texts in this area are riddled with programs that will not work when keyed into the computer.

1. Koffman, E. B., Miller, P. L., and Wardle, C. E. Recommended curriculum for CS1, 1984: A report of the ACM Curriculum Committee Task Force for CS1. *Communications of the ACM* **27**, 10 (Oct. 1984), 998–1001.

2. Koffman, E. B., Stemple, D., and Wardle, C. E. Recommended curriculum for CS2, 1984: A report of the ACM Curriculum Committee Task Force for CS2. *Communications of the ACM* **28**, 8 (Aug. 1985), 815–818.

3. Gibbs, Norman E. and Tucker, Allen B. A model curriculum for a liberal arts degree in computer science. *Communications of the ACM,* **29**, 3 (Mar. 1986), 202–210.

Many authors stop short of actually implementing algorithms in code, or leave implementations to students. Many texts fail to present more than cursory documentation for any algorithms or programs. At least one famous author uses single character identifiers in complex Pascal programming examples, rendering them nearly unreadable.

In the nearly four decades of teaching experience between us, we have taught this material to students at Purdue University, Southern Methodist University, The College of William and Mary, Arizona State University, Bowdoin College, IBM practitioners, and secondary school teachers of computer science. We believe that given a proper presentation, this material is thoroughly comprehensible to students with a good introductory computer science course based on Pascal or some other block-structured language.

The first course in data structures and algorithms tends to be difficult for students who are forced to reason abstractly about algorithms and the programming process for the first time. Faculty folklore tells how this course is an excellent predictor of a student's potential success in computing because of the intellectual growth that students must undergo to gain mastery of the material. Student folklore describes this material as difficult because of the lack of adequate teaching and the lack of texts which explain the ideas and make them less abstract and more palatable.

This text is student oriented. We have drawn on our experience as teachers to design and develop a student-readable text with clear and understandable programming examples. We strive to take abstract ideas and notions and where appropriate implement them as Pascal programs and procedures. All programs in the text have been checked using Turbo Pascal, the IBM PC Pascal compiler, and two Pascal compilers on mainframe computers. Outside of idiosyncratic input/output conditions, all of the programs should work properly. We will make copies of the source code available at cost to instructors who adopt the text through the publisher.

The book begins with an overview and review of good programming practices and style which now should be a part of every introductory course. Although after Chapter 1 was written Congress changed the income tax laws, we chose an example based on the US 1040EZ Federal Income Tax form as one familiar to most teachers of the material, and to many students. Hints are given for good program design, and an overview of the nature and use of abstract data types and their relation to data structures is presented.

Chapter 2 discusses assertions, invariants, program checking, correctness, and a topic many students and teachers find difficult—computational complexity. We believe the material to be central to any contemporary presentation of algorithms and data structures. The amount of time an instructor spends on this material will, of course, vary depending on the background and maturity of the students. We urge that the instructor not gloss over the material, either because of a fear of it, or because of a belief that students cannot handle it; we have had good success in presenting the material to the students whom we have taught. For students to develop a thorough and comfortable understanding of this material, it is necessary to revisit it throughout the course, either explicitly or implicitly via exercises and programming assignments.

The chapter on Fundamental Data Types, Chapter 3, gives the student and instructor an opportunity to apply abstract data types to such computing primitives as characters, reals, booleans, integers, records, and strings. Most people do not think of these primitives in abstract terms; an attempt is made here to show that even in courses like "Introduction to Computing" or "Computer Organization," abstract data types are heavily used and are important. This chapter should also give students an idea of what questions about implementation should be asked when converting to a new compiler or computing system. The instructor should not view this chapter as "hacking" bits and bytes, but rather as an opportunity to reinforce the widespread implicit use of abstract data types. The opportunity here is to show students that abstract is not synonymous with impractical or theoretical.

Chapters 4 and 5 on Sets and Their Representations are an approach to presenting data structures and algorithms material that was inspired by Jon Bentley. Sets are viewed as being as important and fundamental to computing as they are to mathematics. The idea here is that as an abstraction, nearly everything may be thought of as a set. Programmers do not often think about sets—the chapter on sets in introductory Pascal-based texts is usually self-contained and independent of the other seemingly more important material like arrays. But arrays are just ordered multisets! These chapters form a basis for applying complexity to an exposition of searching and establish the tone for the presentation of the more traditional course material that follows.

Chapter 6 on Stacks and Queues is indicative of our approach to presenting traditional data structures material from an abstract data type point of view. Stacks and queues are viewed as special kinds of sets, not as seemingly random phenomena useful in computing for recursion and evaluating expressions. Chapter 7's exposition of hashing is also presented from the set point of view, again relying on implementations in Pascal of abstract data types from earlier chapters to make the notions concrete.

Chapter 8 on Tables and Other Complex Structures also represents a different approach to presentation of traditional material. The idea is to try to make students aware that tables are an important abstraction to consider using when exploring the design space for implementing problem solutions. The problem of locating information in tables and the associated complexity are emphasized.

The chapter on Iteration and Recursion in Algorithms and Data Structures, Chapter 9, is self-contained and optional. It is placed here so that the instructor may review or reinforce the material before plunging into trees, sorting, and graph algorithms where these tools inspire elegant algorithms and data representations. Our experience with this material is that it cannot be taught too often, nor reviewed too many times with students. Even the best students and instructors remain a little in awe of the power and elegance of recursion.

Chapter 10 on Trees starts with binary trees and tree traversals. Later, searching issues and the associated complexity are shown. We conclude the chapter with tree balancing issues and B-trees. These structures are the basis for understanding much of the material that follows in more advanced computing courses. This chapter should rarely be omitted by instructors.

Chapter 11 on Basic Sorting Techniques gives an overview of our favorite topic for the presentation and reinforcement of computational complexity to students. Probably nowhere else in computing are the ideas of abstract data types, complexity, data structures, and associated design tradeoffs so well demonstrated. Instructors may find it amusing that bubble sort is relegated to the exercises where, at best, it belongs. All of the Pascal implementations presented have been extensively tested and used in our own work.

The chapter on Graphs, Chapter 12, presents two important implementation tools that all students of computing should master—depth first search and breadth first search. These tools are applied to graphs which are widely used general data structures. Both directed and undirected graphs are presented and important graph algorithms are discussed. If time does not permit, this chapter is amenable to being pruned or omitted without destroying the consistency of course presentation.

We gratefully acknowledge the IBM Corporation for bringing us together with Jon Bentley and giving us the opportunity to use this material with practitioners. The students at Bowdoin College and Southern Methodist University who gave us many helpful comments on earlier drafts of this work are also acknowledged. We must thank Bob Stern and his editorial successors at William C. Brown Publishers for having the faith to get this work started, and the Brown staff for their able assistance in bringing the book to publication. Most particularly, we wish to thank John Forsyth, Pentti Honkanen, Emil Nue, Nilo Niccolai, Dan Olsen, Jr., Evelyn Rozanski, Charles Williams, Joe Turner, Stephen Allan, Bob Leeper, Grady Early, Ed Desautels, John Cowles, and any others whom we do not know explicitly, who so thoughtfully reviewed the manuscript in its various stages, and Jennie Lightner who patiently endured the unenviable task of locating and correcting the linguistic flaws in our presentation. Any errors that remain, whether grammatical or technical, are, of course, our responsibility, and not the fault of these fine people.

Finally, we express our appreciation for the encouragement and forebearance of our families, Barbara, Karen, and Jennifer Gibbs, and Ann and David Korfhage, in their patient understanding of our need to spend time on this work instead of with them. The successful completion of this project is as much due to their patience as it is to our modest but time-consuming efforts.

PRINCIPLES OF
DATA STRUCTURES AND
ALGORITHMS WITH PASCAL

1

Algorithms, Program Structure, and Data Structure

Introduction

A computer is a tool that can aid in solving problems. Specifically, a computer is an excellent tool for use with any problem that involves the transformation of data from one form to another. In this book we examine the shapes of data, the process of data transformation, and some techniques that can be used to make the data transformation process more efficient and comprehensible.

Our examination proceeds on two levels, the abstract and the concrete. In this chapter we introduce the two principal abstract components, the algorithm and the abstract data type, and their concrete counterparts, programs and concrete data types. Our discussion of some of the principles that are important to the correct and efficient use of a computer in problem solving provides a foundation for more detailed discussions in succeeding chapters.

1.1 The algorithm

Data transformation is the process of changing data from one form to another. This process may involve mathematical or statistical operations on the data, such as determining averages or computing paychecks from the hourly data on time cards. It may involve text manipulation through use of a word processor to create and edit text, or an information retrieval system to extract specific references from a large body of text. Or it may involve the analysis of data from various sensors to control an industrial process. In each situation, data enter the process in one form and are analyzed, yielding data in another form as the result of the process. Thus the process, whatever its details, is fundamentally one of transforming data from one form, the **input,** to another, the **output.**

Solving a problem involving data transformation involves two major components: the data themselves, and the method used to transform the data, thus solving the problem. The technical name for a well-defined method of data transformation is **algorithm.** For our purposes, an algorithm consists of a finite number of definite instructions. The term "definite" means that each instruction produces a single, well-defined result. For example, the instruction "Pick a number greater than zero" is not a suitable instruction for an algorithm, since the result is not definite. One person may pick one number, and another person a different number, and still claim to be following the same instruction. However, the instruction "For a given number, produce a number that is three larger than twice the given number" is suitable for an algorithm. If two different people follow this instruction using the same given number, they will produce the same final number.

An algorithm also has two other properties. First, the instructions are followed in some definite order. This means that once a given instruction has been completed, there is no choice about what to do next: either the algorithm stops or one specific next instruction is executed. This "next instruction" is not always predetermined. The current instruction might be one that identifies the proper instruction to do next, as in "If $A > B$, then do instruction 3 next; otherwise do instruction 5 next." Furthermore, a given instruction may be used several times in the course of executing an algorithm.

Second, an algorithm always stops. If the input data are correct and the algorithm has been correctly specified and written, then the output data will be the values the algorithm is expected to produce. If the input data are incorrect, then a properly written algorithm will halt with some indication that there is an error in the data.

1.2 The data

The other principal component in this problem-solving process is the set of **data,** or the objects to be transformed. Most of the problems we are concerned with involve more than one datum. We may have, for example, a list of names or a set of timecards or a group of sensor readings sent back by a satellite.

The fundamental organization of multiple input data is the mathematical **set.** However, a set has very little structure, and we often think of the data as having more structure associated with them. For example, rather than think of the set of officers and managers running an industrial company, we are likely to think of these people arranged in a corporate organization chart. Rather than think of the set of players on a football team, we think of the quarterback, the halfbacks, the ends, the center, and so forth. Sensor data frequently have a time sequence associated with them rather than being merely a set of numbers.

Furthermore, the computers we commonly use impose a structure on a data set. Each datum in the set is stored in some specific location, and the numerical addresses of these locations impose an ordering on the set that is not fundamental to the concept. We shall see that at times this ordering can be helpful in manipulating the data, while at other times it gets in the way of efficient computations. In any case, by focusing on the data as a *set* we can examine those operations that are common to all data, regardless of any extra structure we might impose.

When we begin to solve a problem, our thinking is likely to be quite abstract. We have a list of names, and we want to construct a mailing list of all those having certain ZIP codes. Perhaps we also want the list arranged alphabetically. Or we have a list of the secretaries in a company, and an opening has occurred. We want to find the secretary best qualified to fill that opening. If we had a brilliant "electronic brain," we could perhaps pose these problems in this way and expect to have them solved. However, present computers are quite dumb and uninspired, and need to have a more thorough specification of their instructions, along with a more thorough description of the form of the data. But when we are thinking about the basic process needed to solve the problem, we should not be constrained by the needs of the computer. We focus first on the problem-solving process and *then* see what must be done to implement this process.

An **abstract data structure** consists of a conceptual organization of data without regard to how this organization may be represented in a computer or some other device. Thus we may think of a **list** of names. We have some concept of the properties of a list—one name following another—but we are not concerned with the representation of this list. Similarly, we may think of a **map** of the United States without knowing how the map is represented in a computer.

An **abstract data type (ADT)** consists of an abstract data structure together with a set of basic operations to be performed on the data in the structure. For a list of names, our basic operations might include counting the names on the list, sorting them, finding a specific name, and inserting or deleting names. For the map, the operations might include locating a city and finding distances between cities, along with some other operations. In either case, we can discuss the solution of problems relating to the abstract data type without being concerned about how the data and operations are implemented.

Suppose that we have a map of the United States, and we wish to find the shortest route from Dallas to New York City via the interstate highway system. One way to solve this problem is to determine first the general direction of New York from Dallas (northeast). Having determined that, find all interstate highways leading north or east from Dallas (I-20, I-30, I-35). For each of these routes, find the distance from Dallas to the first point of intersection with another interstate highway leading north or east. At that point, repeat the process; that is, find all interstates leading north or east (including the one we are on), and for each find the distance from the current intersection point to the next intersection point. By repeating this and adding up the distances, we will eventually find the shortest distance to New York City. (It may not be clear that this process will solve the problem. How would you satisfy yourself that it does?)

This scenario seems quite clear; probably anyone who knows how to read a map and add distances could follow it. But we have never discussed *how* the map is represented, or the process we follow to locate each of the interstates and intersections. Thus our method is an abstract one, which might be implemented in several ways.

Similarly, in an abstract data type, we keep the structure and process definitions conceptual, permitting a variety of later implementations, each of which is perhaps suitable for a particular group of problems.

1.3 Implementing the algorithm

If we wish to use a computer to help solve a problem, we must at some time map the abstract process definition, or algorithm, into a program that the computer can use. One method of doing this involves the concept of **top-down design.** For this we organize the algorithm into a hierarchy of **blocks,** each consisting of a logical group of instructions. The hierarchy permits us to consider the program at different levels of resolution.

At one level we might have a rather broad instruction, which is well defined in our minds but too complex to correspond to a single instruction in the computer. For example, the instruction might be "Sort the list" or "Find the nearest intersection." Then at the next level we would expand these instructions into finer instructions that are closer to those that the computer can handle. As we continue to do this, we can alternate between the abstract definition and the more concrete, computer-oriented implementation. We can define the algorithm at the "Sort the list" level and then write a program that implements this. Of course, the program might only "pretend" to implement the algorithm, printing out "The list is sorted" rather than actually sorting the list. Then we can return to the abstract level, considering some of the details of how to sort the list. Finally, we implement these details concretely in the computer.

Figure 1.1   The software life cycle

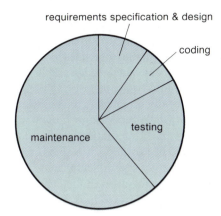

requirements specification & design

coding

testing

maintenance

1.4 Implementing the ADT

Implementing an abstract data type is an extension of implementing an algorithm. In an ADT we have both the data structure and the algorithms that correspond to the basic processes defined in the ADT. As we shall see later, there is a close relationship between the data and the program. A specific data structure implementation might permit efficient implementation for one algorithm but result in a program for another algorithm that is not very efficient. Another data structure implementation might permit a better implementation of the second algorithm at the cost of a poorer implementation of the first one.

Thus, as we develop our subject, we shall discuss several implementations for a given ADT, comparing the trade-offs in processing efficiency as we switch from one implementation to a different one.

1.5 Review of software design principles

While many programmers like to "jump right in" and begin writing code to solve a problem, sound programming practice dictates that we think about a problem before beginning to program it and that we do the actual programming in an orderly sequence of steps, with ample checking along the way. This process may seem overbearing for small, simple programs, but it is vital for the efficient design of the large programs that are commonly encountered in practice.

Experience throughout the computing industry has shown that large software projects follow a typical **life cycle.** The bulk of the effort on any large software project is devoted to maintenance of the software after its development and release (fig. 1.1). Adding to this the testing of the software during development, we observe that over 80 percent of the effort on a software project is devoted to correction and modification of the software and less than 20 percent of the effort is devoted to the initial design and construction. It is clear that sound design and development techniques for software will have a major impact on the effort needed to keep the software in good operating condition.

Over the years, a number of **design principles** for creating good software have been developed. These precepts of sound design and implementation are few and easily understood. They fall into two categories: those applicable to the process as a whole, and those specifically directed at the programming task. The design principles applicable to the whole process are presented as a series of discrete steps, but in reality there is much interaction among them. If a difficulty arises that cannot be solved at one of the steps, it is good practice to back up to the previous step, where resolution of the difficulty may be more apparent. Occasionally it may be necessary to back up even further to resolve a difficulty. Once the difficulty has been overcome, forward progress in the design and implementation can be continued. The main steps in this process are these:

1. Determine the needs and requirements for solving the problem.
2. Write detailed specifications for the solution of the problem.
3. Design a problem solution matching the specifications.
4. Code the program to solve the problem.
5. Test the program units individually.
6. Integrate the program units into a single system and test it.
7. Install the system.
8. Maintain the system.

A key point in this entire process is that coding does not take place until the fourth step of the process. The first step is to determine as best we can what results are wanted and what will be needed to provide these results. That is, we need to agree upon the final outputs and determine what inputs are needed to produce the outputs. This step is frequently a very difficult one for large projects, since it requires working with users who may not know exactly what they want, and may not be aware of what can and cannot be done to produce the desired results.

The second step is to write clear specifications of the needs and requirements. If the task is to produce a mailing list from a set of names, at this step we examine such questions as how many names are to be on the list, what information will be provided with each name (address, phone number, other data), how rapidly we may expect the list to change, what is to be done about purging names from the list, and so forth. Thus we provide detailed data specifications.

Once the specifications for the problem and its solution have been formulated, the next task is to design a solution that meets the specifications. From an examination of the data and the task to be done, we can determine the type of algorithm needed for each step in the processing. For example, there are several different sorting algorithms. Some of these perform very well if the input is already nearly sorted into order; other algorithms do poorly on such data. Again, the nature of the data may be such that we cannot use an efficient search process but must resort to one that is less efficient. The job at this stage is to choose appropriate algorithms and organize them into a model for the solution system.

It is next the task of the programmer to code a solution that meets the specifications and the design. We will discuss this in more detail in section 1.6. For the moment, it suffices to note that for large problems the program code is frequently broken into smaller units that can be tested separately and then assembled into a complete system.

One key to successful software design is to minimize the number of defects that must be eliminated from a large and complex system. This is done by attempting to identify and correct these defects before the system gains its final complexity. Indeed, a major reason for the first four stages in this software development scheme is to provide ample opportunity to detect any flaws before the full system is coded. The final opportunity to do this comes at the fifth stage, when the program units are individually tested. At that stage, well-written program modules are still relatively simple and can be tested under a wide variety of input conditions. Some additional work is needed to write simple driver programs to test each unit, but this work pays off in reducing the time and effort needed to test the full system.

When the individual software units have passed their tests, the time has come to integrate the units into a single system. It is hoped that this system solves the problem as specified. But there is always the possibility that the units have been erroneously assembled, along with the possibility of some undetected flaw in an individual unit. Hence there is a requirement to test the operation of the system as assembled. Errors detected at this stage may be difficult to correct. Those that cannot be traced to simple data communication problems between modules may require extensive redesign of individual program units. Careful work in the early stages of the design process helps to avoid this difficulty.

The last two stages of development, installation and maintenance, are frequently overlooked by programmers who have little experience with large systems. Experience shows that the environment in which the system is expected to function may differ from the development environment in several subtle ways. Hence a final test of the installed system is imperative. Experience also shows that an active maintenance program is needed for software that is expected to function for some time. Changes in computer hardware or the operating system may mean that a program that has been working well must be modified to continue functioning. And changes in project goals, or a better understanding of these goals, frequently mean that a software product, while still functioning according to the original specifications, no longer meets the currently desired level of performance.

1.6 Programming principles

We turn now to a more detailed examination of step 4 in the above process, the writing of program code. We have indicated that large programs should be broken into smaller units for coding. While this is being done, it is important to keep in mind the overall organization of the program, so that the individual units fit together well. There are seven guiding principles.

1. Design the program from the **top down.** Look first at the major tasks the program must do. While a breakdown of the form

   ```
   BEGIN
      read input;
      compute;
      print output
   END
   ```

   is not very helpful, the first pass at program development should probably involve no more than six or seven steps. These steps will include input, computation, and output, but will probably also include some of the major decisions to be made in the course of the program.

2. Design in small, logical **modules.** Some experts suggest that no program unit should contain more than one page or one screen of information, for ease of reading and comprehension. Strict adherence to this rule may be difficult, but it is nevertheless a good guideline. It is not unusual to find that we can define a logical module that fits easily onto a single page in a listing, or can be displayed fully on a terminal screen.

3. Use **subprograms,** such as Pascal PROCEDUREs and FUNCTIONs, wherever appropriate. Frequently, when modules have been properly defined, it is relatively easy to write these as distinct procedures and functions. Doing so simplifies the calling program and makes it easier to read. More important, the coding and checking of a large program are made simpler and more efficient through the definition of procedures and functions. These can often be checked independently of the main program by defining simple, special purpose **drivers** that will call up the routines individually with appropriate test data.

4. Use the standard **control structures** for sequencing, branching, and looping. For sequencing of instructions, the best control structure is the simplest one: place the instructions in sequential order as much as possible. For branching and looping, a small number of control structures have been used over the years and have become a standard library of structures. These include the constructs IF . . . THEN . . .

ELSE, IF . . . THEN, CASE . . . END, FOR . . . DO, WHILE
. . . DO, and REPEAT . . . UNTIL. These structures are known to
be adequate for all standard programming needs. Be aware that in
different languages these same constructs may have slightly different
forms.

5. Avoid the use of GOTO. The GOTO statement in itself is not an evil,
but free and unbridled use of it quickly leads to programs that are
muddled and difficult to understand. Since the control structures listed
above provide the means to organize a computation without the use of
GOTO, many serious programmers argue that we should never use
GOTO. However, there are a few occasions when the avoidance of this
statement obscures the intent of the program. Most of these are due to
error handling. In a large program with much error checking, trying to
avoid the use of GOTO can involve the setting of many error flags and
the development of a control structure that does not clearly separate
the error handling from the main flow of the code. Aside from error
handling, however, occasions for the effective use of GOTO are so rare
that we should think, not twice, but several times, before including a
GOTO statement in a program.

6. Use **mnemonic names** liberally. Pascal and most other modern
programming languages allow great flexibility in the choice of names
for programs, procedures, functions, and variables. Take full advantage
of this and choose names that reflect directly the purpose of the
program and procedures, and the content and meaning of the variables.

7. Write meaningful and accurate program documentation.
Documentation for a program includes the comments within the
program and any reports that are prepared to explain the program to
someone else. These reports often include user documentation
(describing how to use the program), programmer documentation
(enabling a programmer at some future time to correct any flaws in the
program or to modify it for different situations), and system
documentation (describing how the program fits into a larger system
context). It is important that this documentation be accurate, complete,
clear, and meaningful.

User documentation should describe the conditions assumed for correct
operation of the program, the procedure for using the program, the
input expected, the output generated, and the meaning of the possible
error messages. Its purpose is to provide the user with an accurate
guide to the operation of the program.

Program documentation should describe the purpose of each section of
the program, any special conditions assumed in each section, and, if the
section is complex, something about the operation of the section. Often

it is helpful to give references to the literature, if a particular algorithm has been taken from such a source. Mnemonic names form an important part of the program documentation. Within the program, documentation should precede the section that it describes rather than follow it. The use of indentation and blank lines helps to delineate the organization of a program. This documentation is an aid to the programmer who must maintain and possibly alter the program at some future date.

System documentation describes the assumptions made about the system on which the program is to run—memory size, particular languages used, special input and output devices, and so forth. This documentation also is for the programmer rather than the user, particularly the programmer who needs to adapt the program to a system environment different from that in which it was written.

While these principles apply to all programming tasks, some of them, such as the use of procedures and functions in defining a program, have greatest impact with large programs. Others, such as the use of mnemonic names and the proper use of comments, apply equally well to all programs. We shall follow these principles throughout this text, only occasionally making specific reference to them.

1.7 An example of program development

The use of these principles is illustrated by following the development of a moderately complex program. For our example, we choose the problem of income tax computation.

As the general nature of this problem is quite familiar to everyone, it is not too difficult to determine the needs and requirements. We know that to solve the problem we must have data about the amount of income involved, the various deductions and exemptions that will be claimed, and the current tax laws that apply. We will also need to know what income tax has already been paid. From these data we are required to produce an accurate statement of the total amount of tax and the amount still owed.

If the foregoing is an adequate statement of the needs and requirements involved, we can direct our attention to writing the specifications for the problem solution. First, we must specify the scope of the project. Are we considering both individual and corporate taxes? Are there limits on the amount of income to be considered? Do we need the full set of tax laws?

Let us specify that we are considering only individual incomes and that we will handle any kind of individual tax return. This specification requires that we need all income tax laws that apply to individuals, but no others. Note that it means that we will have a fairly large number of different tax forms to handle.

We must also specify the data sources and the forms the data will take. Here is a typical list:

data requirement	source	form
taxpayer name	taxpayer	up to 30 characters
taxpayer number	taxpayer	social security no.
taxpayer address	taxpayer	up to 60 characters
campaign deduction	taxpayer	a yes/no decision
amount of income	employer	W-2 form (in dollars)
supplemental income	taxpayer	dollars
sources of income	taxpayer	up to 30 characters
number of exemptions	taxpayer	integer
tax withheld	employer	W-2 form (in dollars)
tax form used	derived	various IRS forms
deductions	taxpayer	up to 30 characters
deduction amounts	taxpayer	dollars
calculated amounts	derived	dollars

We may also wish to put limits on the amount of income, the number of exemptions, and the amount of tax withheld. These limits could be used to check data validity and by the program to decide among the different tax forms. The limits of thirty characters that we have placed on different descriptive data may not be sufficient. At this stage in the process, such limits should be discussed and the best estimate used, with an awareness that it may be necessary later to return to the specifications and modify them. We should also decide whether "dollars" means "dollars and cents," "rounded dollars" (as the IRS permits), or whichever meaning the taxpayer decides it should have. If the latter, then another piece of data must be the taxpayer's choice in this.

The third step is to design a program. Top-down design of a solution to this or any other problem calls first for formulating the main features of the problem, which will be reflected in the structure of the main or driving program, then for examining each of these features in more detail. The program design process is kept separate from the program coding process, in the sense that many of the details actually necessary to develop a working program are omitted in the design process and only filled in during coding.

One key characteristic at the design stage is that the syntax of the programming language is of very little concern. Indeed, for many projects the choice of programming language is not made until the design has been done. There is, however, a need for some language in which to describe the design. This **program design language,** or **PDL,** is generally a language that is intermediate between natural language (English) and a structured programming language. Different designers have different preferences for how close to an actual programming language the PDL should be.

Since Pascal is the programming language we use in this text, we do not violate design principles by choosing a PDL that is very close to Pascal. To avoid introducing yet another language into this text, we choose to do our design in the form of a Pascal program consisting largely of comments. Note that in a realistic situation with several programming languages available, we would not do the design in a language that was this close to one of them.

For the income tax problem, the first main feature of the program is deciding which income tax form to use. Once this has been decided, the process of filling in the form can begin. We also observe that some information, such as the tax-payer's name, address, and social security number, is common to all the various tax forms. Thus the design concept can be summarized as follows:

Get the common information.

Get the information for making the form decision.

Decide which tax form to use.

Using the chosen form, compute the income tax.

Suppose that we decide to use the three different forms, 1040, 1040A, and 1040EZ. The next task is to decide how to distinguish among them. An obvious choice is a multiway branch. But in examining the tax rules, we find that there are certain cases in which forms 1040A and 1040EZ are permitted; otherwise, form 1040 must be used. In fact, certain conditions, such as itemizing deductions, require that form 1040 be used, independent of any other considerations. Thus we can expand our design:

Get the common information.

Get the information for making the form decision.

Decide which tax form to use.

   If 1040 is required, use it. If not, . . .

   If 1040EZ is permissible, use it. If not, . . .

   If 1040A is permissible, use it. If not, . . .

   Otherwise use 1040.

Using the chosen form, compute the income tax.

Note that the order of choice of the permissible forms is somewhat arbitrary, but the order we have chosen picks the simplest permissible form first.

We now have the option of expanding this design further or pausing to see how it works as a program. Let us do the latter. The program initially takes the form shown in figure 1.2.

Figure 1.2   Skeleton program for income tax

```
PROGRAM IncomeTax;

{ Since the name, address, social security number, and campaign fund
information are needed for all three tax forms, we will assume that
these are obtained by a procedure called "Header." Note that this
procedure must be included in the program and called before any of
the three procedures that compute the tax. Note also that we must
define a data structure for this information and decide how to
transmit it to the procedures that require it. }

PROCEDURE Header;
  BEGIN
  END; { Header }

PROCEDURE EzForm;
  BEGIN
  END; { EzForm }

PROCEDURE ShortForm;
  BEGIN
  END; { ShortForm }

PROCEDURE LongForm;
  BEGIN
  END; { LongForm }

{ Main program. }

BEGIN
  Header;
  IF { test for 1040 } THEN LongForm
  ELSE
    IF { test for 1040EZ } THEN EzForm
    ELSE
      IF { test for 1040A } THEN ShortForm
      ELSE LongForm
END. { IncomeTax }
```

In this very skeletal form, the program cannot be run, because there are no tests provided within the IF statements; but since we are in the *design* stage, we need not worry about actually running this skeleton. Four good programming practices have already been demonstrated. First, mnemonic names have been used for the program and its procedures, names that identify what is supposed to be done. Second, indentation and blank lines have been used to display the program structure. Third, the program has been broken down into four major components, with a relatively simple main program to drive them. And fourth, comments have been inserted at points where specific tests are to take place. These comments will remain as program documentation when the program is coded and the tests have been introduced.

We now have the program outlined, with seven major subtasks to do: four procedures and three tests. Since these subtasks are largely independent, we can choose to work on them in any order. Developing the tests first will enable us easily to turn this skeleton into a program that will compile and run, although it may do very little. This option has the advantage that as individual parts of the program are developed, they can be "exercised" to see if they are working correctly.

Here we come to a difference between large programs and small programs. We have discussed the concept of developing individual program modules and then testing them by developing a driver to supply data for each one. This driver simply generates some data, calls the module, and then prints out the results. The data can be built into the driver, generated randomly, or supplied by the programmer as input during a test run. In any case, the driver is a very simple program. But if the main program itself is quite small and simple, then writing a separate driver for each procedure and function may not be worth the effort: the program itself can serve as the driver.

If we choose to use the program as the driver, the next step in program development is to turn the program skeleton into something that works. Two things are necessary for this. First, we must provide the tests for the three forms; second, we must provide something for the procedures to do. The latter is very simple: we will make each procedure print out its role. Such a procedure, that only prints its purpose, is called a **stub.** It provides a completion to the program so that the program can be tested and at the same time warns the programmer that this section of the program needs to be finished. Observe that if we do not make at least this change we might call a procedure and never know it has run, simply because the procedure does nothing.

A very simple set of tests can be built by asking the user to enter the name of the form to be used, and testing for that. But a change this simple does not really advance program development much, and we shall omit it.

Providing realistic tests to determine which form to use is more difficult and depends on studying the income tax regulations. For this, we return to the design process and list the information that is needed for each of the three tests. This information must be supplied as input from the user.

Test for 1040 (a check of the IRS regulations would reveal that there are over a dozen different conditions, several of which have exceptions, that require the use of form 1040; we include only three of them in this example):

deductions are itemized,

there are nontaxable dividends,

an estimated tax was filed.

Test for 1040EZ (again simplified for our example):

the taxpayer is single,

all income is wages, salary, or tips,

the gross income is under $50,000.

Test for 1040A (simplified):

all income is wages, salary, or tips,

the gross income is under $50,000.

With the tests identified, we see that there is a different and probably better organization to the solution:

Get the common information.

Get the information for making the form decision.

Test for 1040:

deductions are itemized,

there are nontaxable dividends,

an estimated tax was filed.

If 1040 is required, use it. If not, . . .

Test for 1040EZ or 1040A:

all income is wages, salary, or tips,

the gross income is under $50,000.

If test is passed, test for 1040EZ:

the taxpayer is single,

If 1040EZ is permissible, use it. If not, . . .

Use 1040A.

Otherwise (neither 1040EZ nor 1040A permissible) use 1040.

Using the chosen form, compute the income tax.

This change in design requires a change in our skeleton program. The lines

```
ELSE
   IF { test for 1040EZ } THEN EzForm
   ELSE
      IF { test for 1040A } THEN ShortForm
      ELSE LongForm
```

become

```
ELSE
   IF { test for 1040A or 1040EZ } THEN
      IF { test for 1040EZ } THEN EzForm
      ELSE ShortForm
   ELSE LongForm
```

We can now expand the modified skeleton program into a working version. The data we need include:

How much income is there?

Is all income from wages and salary?

Are there nontaxable dividends?

Is the taxpayer single?

Does the taxpayer itemize deductions?

Was an estimated tax paid?

While we provide for this input so that we can test the program, we may later want to change the form of the input to make it simpler for the user. For now, we concentrate on the tests themselves. The result is the program of figure 1.3.

Observe that the step of transforming the design into a working program, even a skeleton one such as this, requires many decisions on detail that are not needed for the design. In addition to carefully observing the syntax of the programming language, we have had to specify types for all the variables, decide on messages to the user, and decide how the user should answer any questions. All of this is part of the software development process, but we cannot let it dominate the process. We must steer a course between two dangers. If we focus entirely on the design, we may develop a design that looks terrific but is very difficult to implement. If, however, we expend too much effort in verifying that various parts of the design can be easily implemented, we may unwittingly bias the design by the implementation, and miss a very elegant and efficient end product.

Figure 1.3, Part 1   Stubbed program for income tax, header and procedures

```
PROGRAM IncomeTax;

{ Since the name, address, social security number, and campaign fund
information are needed for all three tax forms, we will assume that
these are obtained by a procedure called "Header." Note that this
procedure must be included in the program and called before any of
the three procedures that compute the tax. Note also that we must
define a data type to hold this information and decide how to
transmit it to the procedures that require it. }

VAR
   Estimated       : char;
   Income          : real;
   Itemized        : char;
   NonTaxDividend  : char;
   Single          : char;
   WagesOnly       : char;

PROCEDURE Header;
   BEGIN
     writeln ('This procedure requests the taxpayer''s name, ',
              'address, social security number, and campaign fund ',
              'contribution information. ')
   END; { Header }

PROCEDURE EzForm;
   BEGIN
     writeln ('This procedure computes the tax by form 1040EZ. ')
   END; { EzForm }

PROCEDURE ShortForm;
   BEGIN
     writeln ('This procedure computes the tax by form 1040A. ')
   END; { ShortForm }

PROCEDURE LongForm;
   BEGIN
     writeln ('This procedure computes the tax by form 1040. ')
   END; { LongForm }
```

Figure 1.3, Part 2   Stubbed program for income tax, main program

```
{ Main program. }

BEGIN

   { Gather input information to decide if form 1040 must be used. }

   write ('Did you itemize deductions? (Y/N) ');
   readln (Itemized);
   write ('Did you have nontaxable dividends? (Y/N) ');
   readln (NonTaxDividend);
   write ('Did you file an estimated tax? (Y/N) ');
   readln (Estimated);

   { At this point, we should echo the input back, to give the user
   the opportunity to verify it. }

   { Decide on the proper form. Is 1040 required? }

   IF
      (Itemized = 'Y') OR (NonTaxDividend = 'Y') OR
        (Estimated = 'Y') { or any of the other requirements }
      THEN LongForm
   ELSE

      { Form 1040 is not required, so we need more information to
      decide if a shorter form can be used. Note: The test conditions
      are simplified for purposes of this example. }

      BEGIN
         write ('Are you single? (Y/N) ');
         readln (Single);
         write ('Does your income consist only of wages, salary, ',
                'and tips? (Y/N) ');
         readln (WagesOnly);
         write ('What is your gross income ?');
         readln (Income);

         IF { Test for 1040A or 1040EZ. }
           (WagesOnly = 'Y') AND (Income < 50000)
            THEN { Test for 1040EZ }
              IF Single = 'Y' THEN EzForm
              ELSE ShortForm
         ELSE LongForm
      END
END. { IncomeTax }
```

We can now run this program. It will ask the user several questions, and on the basis of the answers it will activate one of the three procedures and print out the corresponding statement. Thus the program is at its first testable stage. It clearly will not compute the tax correctly, but we are able to demonstrate that it can determine which income tax form to use for the computation. This is a "unit test," where the unit being tested is the main program.

A major question should now become evident, if we have not already thought through the problem in more detail than is shown here. We ask for input from the user. An algorithm is always supposed to halt for any input. But what will happen, for example, if the user ignores the "(Y/N)" hint and provides some other response to the first two questions? A user might, for example, respond "yes" to the question about being single. Here is a major design flaw: we should design the program to accept any reasonable response and to provide a graceful way around any unreasonable input, preferably by giving the user some clue as to what is wrong, together with the opportunity to correct it. As the procedure is written, any response other than "Y" is taken to be "N." We leave it as an exercise to correct this flaw.

Observe that we have slid quietly from program design through coding into unit test, at least for one portion of the program. On small projects involving a single programmer, this is one way of working. The next step is to back up to program design for another unit of the system. An alternative way to proceed is to stay in program design until all units have been more fully designed, and then advance to coding and unit test.

On large projects with several people involved, various pieces of the work are frequently assigned to different people. In this environment it makes good sense to carry the main program development forward as we have, so that individual pieces can be fitted in as they are developed and tested. At the same time, if the overall design is carefully established, the data that must be communicated from one process to another can be determined and plans for this communication can be built in before the various pieces are developed.

The next stage is to develop the header procedure and each of the three procedures for computing the tax. Note that these procedures can now be developed in any order, since the development of one does not affect the operation of either of the others. Since form 1040EZ is the simplest, we shall demonstrate development of the program for that. The development of the header procedure is left as an exercise.

Form 1040EZ (fig. 1.4) requires very few data from the user. We need name, address, social security number, and a decision on whether some of the tax money should go into the campaign fund. In addition, we need wages, interest income, and charitable contributions. The rest of the computation is done by the procedure, following the computation shown on the tax form. As we plan the design, we note that two more subprograms are needed—a function that will return the amount of tax due on the given income, and a routine to properly print all the information onto a tax form. We assume that those routines will be written later.

Figure 1.4   Income tax form 1040EZ

Department of the Treasury - Internal Revenue Service	

Form
1040EZ

Income Tax Return for
Single filers with no dependents   (O)   **1985**

OMB No. 1545-0675

Name &
address

Use the IRS mailing label. If you don't have one, please print:

▶

Print your name above (first, initial, last)

Present home address (number and street)

City, town, or post office, state, and ZIP code

Please print your numbers like this.

1234567890

Your social security number

Yes No

Presidential Election Campaign Fund
Do you want $1 of your tax to go to this fund?   ▶

Dollars   Cents

Figure
your
tax

1 Total wages, salaries, and tips. This should be shown in Box 10
   of your W-2 form(s). (Attach your W-2 form(s).)   1

2 Interest income of $400 or less. If the total is more
   than $400, you cannot use Form 1040EZ.   2

Attach
Copy B of
Form(s)
W-2 here

3 Add line 1 and line 2. This is your **adjusted gross income.**   3

4 Allowable part of your cash charitable contributions.
   See instructions for line 4 on back of this form.   4

5 Subtract line 4 from line 3.   5

6 Amount of your personal exemption.   6 | 040 00

7 Subtract line 6 from line 5. If line 6 is larger than line 5,
   enter 0 on line 7. This is your **taxable income.**   7

8 Enter your Federal income tax withheld. This should be
   shown in Box 9 of your W-2 form(s).   8

9 Use the **single** column in the tax table on pages 31-36 of
   the Form 1040A instruction booklet to find the **tax** on
   your taxable income on **line 7.** Enter the amount of tax.   9

Refund
or
amount
you owe

10 If line 8 is larger than line 9, subtract line 9 from line 8.
    Enter the **amount of your refund.**   10

Attach tax
payment here

11 If line 9 is larger than line 8, subtract line 8 from line 9.
    Enter the **amount you owe.** Attach check or money order
    for the full amount, payable to "Internal Revenue Service."   11

Sign
your
return

I have read this return. Under penalties of perjury, I declare
that to the best of my knowledge and belief, the return is true,
correct, and complete.

Your signature   Date

For IRS Use Only—Please
do not write in boxes below.

12345

Form **1040EZ** (1985)

Figure 1.5, Part 1   Procedure EzForm, declarations

```
FUNCTION TaxTable (Income : real) : real;

{ Computes, as in a tax table, the tax due on Income. }

   BEGIN
     writeln ('TaxTable function called for income ', Income);
     TaxTable := 1000.00
   END; { TaxTable }

PROCEDURE PrintOut (TaxForm : FormType);

{ Prints the appropriate tax form from the input and computed
values. }

   BEGIN
     writeln ('PrintOut called for tax form ', TaxForm)
   END; { PrintOut }

PROCEDURE EzForm;

{ Computation of income tax by form 1040EZ. }

   VAR
      Charity        : real;
      Due            : real;
      GrossIncome    : real;
      Interest       : real;
      Payment        : real;
      Refund         : real;
      TaxableIncome  : real;
      Wages          : real;
      Withheld       : real;
```

Since the computation and the printing will probably be useful for all three tax forms, we place these routines outside the EzForm block. If we later decide that the differences among the three forms are sufficient to make the computations largely distinct, we may redesign the system, moving one or both of these routines back into the computations for the three individual forms.

Figure 1.5 is the expanded form of the procedure. Note once again that much detail needs to be added as we move from the design concept into the actual program segment.

Figure 1.5, Part 2   Procedure EzForm, procedure body

```
BEGIN
  write ('Enter the total amount of your wages, salaries, and ',
         'tips. ');
  readln (Wages);

  IF Wages < 50000 THEN
    BEGIN
      write ('Enter the amount of your interest income. ');
      readln (Interest);
      IF Interest <= 400 THEN
        BEGIN
          GrossIncome := Wages + Interest;
          write ('Enter your charitable contributions. ');
          readln (Charity);
          IF Charity > 25 THEN
            BEGIN
              writeln ('Maximum charitable deduction is $25. ');
              Charity := 25
            END;
          TaxableIncome := GrossIncome - Charity - 1000;

          { We assume that "TaxTable" is a function that returns
          the tax on a given income. This also must be put in the
          program before any of the three procedures that will call
          it. }

          Payment := TaxTable (TaxableIncome);
          write ('Enter your withholding tax. ');
          readln (Withheld);
          writeln ('Your tax is ', Payment : 6 : 2);
          IF Withheld > Payment THEN
            writeln
              ('You get a refund of ', Withheld - Payment : 6 : 2)
          ELSE
            writeln ('You still owe ', Payment - Withheld : 6 : 2);

          { Again, we assume a procedure, called "Printout,"
          included in the program, to print out the tax form. }

          Printout (Form1040EZ)
        END
      ELSE { Interest too high. }
        writeln ('High interest: you should use form 1040A. ')
    END
  ELSE { Wages too high. }
    writeln ('High wages: you should use form 1040. ')
END; { EzForm }
```

Note that the procedure should print out what it is supposed to do but that the function must return some numerical value that can be used for testing. At this stage, the particular value is not important since we are interested simply in showing that the program is going through the proper sequence of steps.

One problem is evident, now that we have developed the program to this point. We observe that the procedure "EzForm" checks the input for validity and then issues warning messages if the input values do not permit use of form 1040EZ. However, this version of the program and procedure does not leave the user with any choice. The user must restart the program. It would be much better to redesign the system, extending the procedure in two ways. First, give the user the opportunity to correct the input if there has been an error so that form 1040EZ can be used. Second, assuming that the input data are correct, pass some signal out to the main program so that the correct procedure ("LongForm" or "ShortForm") can automatically be called. Here we see the cyclic nature of the software development process. Having written and tested some of the software, we have discovered problems that lead us back to the program design step again. Once the design modifications have been made, we move forward again, through coding and unit test.

The income tax program is far from complete, and certainly not very elegant. However, as a program it follows good programming principles:

The design of the program is from the top down—first the overall structure of the program is determined, and then the details are worked out.

This design is being accomplished in small, easily manageable modules, because of the way we have broken the program tasks into procedures and functions.

The program relies entirely on sequential ordering of the statements and on the IF . . . THEN . . . ELSE type of structure for decisions. Nothing more exotic is needed. The program does not use GOTO and does not require any special flags for error conditions. (Note that the procedure "EzForm" includes two error checks for excessive income.)

Throughout the program we have used names that relate directly to the meanings of the variables. These are longer than names we could have chosen, but when someone needs to read the program several months from now, the meaning of each variable should be clear.

Finally, we have included in the program several comment statements that explain what is being done or what is expected of those portions yet to be written.

1.8 Building a data structure

Programming has two facets. One is the development of a method or algorithm to accomplish a given task. The other is the organization of the data for the task. For many simple problems, data organization is almost trivial. Pascal and other languages provide the programmer with a good stock of data types—integer, real, boolean, character, and so forth—that serve the basic needs of the data organizer. However, as more complex problems are tackled, and more intricate programs developed, it becomes important to examine how the data are organized. Frequently the choice of an organizational structure for the data can greatly affect the efficiency of a program.

Before we tackle the questions of what types of data structures to develop and how to design these more complex data structures, we shall, in this chapter, consider the general problem of what operations we would like to do on a data structure. We consider the operations that relate to the structure itself—creating and manipulating it, adding or deleting data—rather than the operations (such as arithmetic) that we would apply to the data within the structure. We shall see that many of these operations are conceptually independent of the structure, although of course their implementation depends heavily on the particular structure being used. The operations we consider are common to most data structures; other operations, more specifically related to certain structures, will be considered in the discussion about each structure.

A key concept in designing a problem solution is the abstract data type. A **data structure** is the form in which we have the data organized—as a set, an array, or some more complex form. A **data type** consists of the structure together with the basic operations on it. An abstract data type is a data type designed without regard to any particular implementation. For example, when we consider a set of elements, there are certain operations we would like to do, regardless of the specific representation of the set. These may include building the set, determining its size, finding whether a particular element is in the set, taking the intersection of two sets, and so forth. For any data structure, we shall define the basic operations abstractly. Then, when we implement the data type, we will implement both a structural representation and procedures for each of the basic operations. Here, then, are some of the operations that we will find are common to many data types.

The first operation on any structure is to **build** or **create** the structure from given data. We generally assume that the data are accepted sequentially, one at a time, and placed in the structure according to the rules we decide to use. For example, in creating a one-dimensional array, we may simply enter the data into the array in the order in which they are given; or we may decide to sort the data by some criterion as they are entered. For a two-dimensional array, we may decide to enter the data row by row, or column by column; or we may examine some property of each datum and decide, on that basis, where to place it in the array. As we create a data structure, we shall find that this process itself involves several of the other operations we shall define. In effect, we shall at times think of the partially completed data structure as an entire structure and treat the creation process as an updating.

Three basic decisions must be made in building a data structure: its size (that is, how large it should be and whether that size should be fixed), its shape (that is, what the structure should look like), and its initial contents (that is, whether we should start with an empty structure or one preloaded with data).

The size

The size of the data structure may be either **static** or **dynamic.** That is, the size may be determined and fixed at the time the structure is built, or it may be flexible and allowed to change during use of the structure. Both of these possibilities have their uses. Sometimes we know in advance how many data we must place in the structure, but in other situations the number of data we must eventually handle is unknown.

Completely static data structures are relatively rare. However, there are many structures that can be regarded as static, since they change very rarely. Typical of these structures would be NFL team rosters, a congressional database (senators and representatives, not the legislation they consider), a city council database, basic data about the solar system (size, orbit of each planet, and so forth), a list of bird species found east of the Mississippi, the list of Pascal reserved words, and so forth. For each of these examples, we would probably be safe to use a static structure that allows for perhaps 5 to 10 percent growth over the present number of data.

However, there are also many situations in which we do not know beforehand how many data must be placed in the data structure. For example, a word processor must be able to handle words and documents of any reasonable length. We would obviously waste much storage were we to decide arbitrarily that enough storage space for 10,000 words should be set aside for each memo or letter. At the same time, such a decision would cause problems as soon as we tried to enter a report or book that was longer than that. This situation, then, is much better suited to a dynamic data structure, one that can expand or contract as the size of each particular memo, letter, or technical report requires.

In deciding on size, we need to consider two factors. First, we must decide on the basic data unit—a word, a number, a letter—allowing for one data **cell** per unit. Within this cell, however, we may also need to store some auxiliary information that is needed to organize the data structure and find paths through it. Thus an individual data cell might be quite large and have much information within it. The second factor that must be considered is the amount of computer memory available. If our proposed data structure is large enough that it will not fit conveniently into the available memory, we may want to rethink the problem and find another solution.

Computer memory sizes are commonly given in terms of **bytes** and **kilobytes.** A byte is a group of eight bits, and thus holds one **ASCII** or **EBCDIC** character. (These are methods of encoding data. See appendix A.) For many microcomputers, the memory size is described as "16K bytes" or "64K bytes." The "K" stands for "kilo." In ordinary use kilo means 1000, but in computer use it means 2^{10}, or 1024. Thus a 64K byte memory actually can hold 65,536 characters. (In practice, some of this space is used for the computer's operating system and hence is not available to the user.) Similarly, disk sizes are measured in **megabytes,** where "mega" means 2^{20}, or 1,048,576, rather than its customary 1,000,000. Thus a 10M byte disk will hold nearly 10.5 million characters.

Suppose that we are building a library and wish to develop an on-line card catalog for it. The basic information we need for each book includes the title, the names of each of the authors, and the call number or identification number. Book titles vary widely in length, and perhaps we should worry about that; but let us assume that we can represent each title by no more than forty characters, abbreviating the title if necessary. Similarly, let us assume that we can represent each author's name by twenty characters and that there will be a maximum of two authors per book. With these assumptions, we can allocate 100 bytes of memory for each book, which allows plenty of room for the call number. Thus we see that, if we are using a microcomputer with 64K of main memory, we can only handle a few books at a time. Memory has enough space for 640 or 650 books, but we must remember that the program itself must also fit into this space along with some of the operating system. So it is likely (without digging deeper) that we can only handle 100 or 200 books at a time. However, a 10M byte disk would have enough space to store the records for 100,000 books. This is very small for a public library but far more than most personal libraries hold. Thus we could quite easily develop an on-line catalog on a microcomputer for an individual's library.

Now suppose that we want to have more information on the "catalog card." In a public library, the card has quite a bit of other information—publisher, date of publication, number of pages, key words, and so forth (fig. 1.6). We could easily include another 200 characters of data in the record for each book. The 10M disk would now hold the records of only 34,000 books (still more than most personal libraries), but more important, the main memory space available would now only be enough for the records of 35 to 65 books. This means that we would need to access the disk about three times as often for any search or update, and that hence the program would be considerably slower. It might be slow enough that we would want to organize the data differently, to speed up the processing.

Figure 1.6   Typical library catalog card

> **Lindesmith, Alfred Ray,** 1905-
>   Social psychology / Alfred R. Lindesmith. Anselm L. Strauss.
> Norman K. Denzin. — 5th ed. — New York : Holt. Rinehart and
> Winston. c1977.
>   xiii. 576 p. : ill. : 24 cm.
>
>   Includes bibliographies and index.
>   ISBN 0-03-039861-4 : $13.95
>
>
>   1. Social psychology.   I. Strauss. Anselm L., joint author.   II. Denzin. Nor-
> man K., joint author.   III. Title.
> HM251.L477   1977   301.1   77-90837
>   MARC
>
> Library of Congress   77

The shape

The second basic decision we must make in building a data structure is the shape it is to take. Frequently, the operations we intend to carry out on the data dictate the organization of the data in memory. If possible, it is efficient to have the data structure match closely the problem for which it will be used.

The most common data structures are lists, tables, and trees. Lists, such as lists of names or book titles, are very familiar and have a very simple structure. Lists will often contain sets of two or three associated items, such as a list of people that includes their addresses and phone numbers.

Such lists are really simple tables. Tables like these are familiar, but a table may have a more complicated structure, as many people discover when looking at the income tax tables. Nevertheless, people use tables quite regularly as a means of organizing data.

Trees are perhaps not as familiar to the average person, although they too are common. Genealogical information is often presented in the form of a family tree. Play-off systems for football and basketball are tree structures. And most corporate management structures are organized as trees.

The list or **roster** is probably the most common structure used for data. We find lists in dictionaries, telephone directories, address books, and many other places. The library card catalog is basically a list, with perhaps some cross-references added to it. While these lists are in alphabetical order so that locating information in them is easy, a grocery shopping list is often not so well organized

Figure 1.7   Corporate organization chart

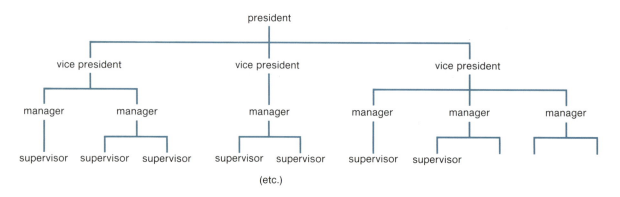

(etc.)

but is written down as the shopper thinks of various items to add. Another list structure is an appointment calendar, where the ordering is by time of occurrence. Lists are very useful when we want to keep items in sequence but have little need otherwise to relate one item to another.

When we have a number of pieces of information associated with a particular data entry, a **table** or **array** is often useful. For example, in a household budget book the data are arranged in tabular form. For each month, a row of the table represents a specific day and the columns of the table represent different budget categories—rent, food, telephone, and so forth. Many business data are easily represented in tables, and an array of numerical data is encountered frequently in engineering or scientific problems. The financial pages of a newspaper contain many different tables.

Tables, as well as lists, frequently have a sequential flavor to them; but in addition, in a table we have the ability to associate many data items with a specific entry and to organize the table entries in several different ways. Thus a table is more appropriate when we have clusters of data that relate to a specific event or when we want to examine the data in more than one way.

There are other problems for which neither the list nor the table is the appropriate data structure. For many of these, a **tree** is very useful. Whenever the data relate to a natural hierarchy, organization of them into a tree is a good idea. For example, the organizational charts for most businesses and industries are hierarchical, with the president at the top, several vice presidents just below, and other ranks of managers and workers further down in the structure (fig. 1.7). A family tree is another common example of the use of a tree to structure the data associated with the situation (fig. 1.8).

In each of these situations, the operations of most interest pertain to the hierarchical relationships among the data. Thus it is useful to mirror this hierarchy in the computer with a tree as the data structure.

Figure 1.8   Family tree

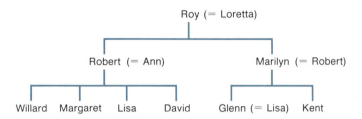

Figure 1.9   Data arrays

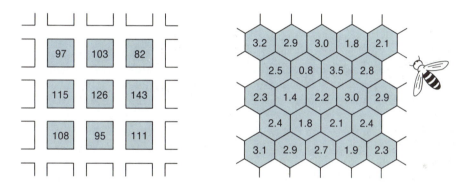

However, data structures can have other shapes as well. The decision on shape is often crucial for many operations which may be applied to a data structure. If the data structure is inappropriately organized, we may need to examine a substantial fraction of the data entries to find a desired one; if the structure is appropriately organized, we can often find the correct entry with just a few probes into the structure.

Just because a particular data structure is useful for one kind of problem does not mean that that structure will fit a different type of problem equally well. For example, a rectangular array matches well with many street maps, where we can go in any of four directions from a given corner to an adjacent one. We frequently give directions from one corner to the next; rarely do we advise cutting through the middle of a block. However, if we were working with a honeycomb structure, possibly in studying bees, where each cell in the natural honeycomb has six neighbors, a rectangular data structure might not fit the problem as well. In a honeycomb each cell has right and left neighbors, but there is not really a neighboring cell directly above or below it (see fig. 1.9).

The contents

Finally we must decide what the initial contents of the data structure we are building are to be. We can either fill the structure with input data, fill it with some recognizable constant, or leave it as we happen to find it and only enter data when we must. The danger of the third choice is clear. We might try to use the data in some position before we have put anything there. Who knows what answer would result from that!

Initialization of a data structure is closely related to the algorithms or processes that we intend to apply. In some situations the particular process may generate data for the structure independent of what is already there. In this case, filling the structure with specific initial values is of little use: they will just be replaced when we start the process. In other situations, the algorithm may seek to modify the data present in a structure. For such algorithms it may be necessary to initialize the structure, using either original data or a fixed constant, to avoid considering the first pass through the algorithm as a special case.

Using original data to fill the structure is generally the better choice if we know we have enough data to fill the structure immediately. This is often the case when the structure size is dynamic, so that its initial size can be just large enough for the data on hand. It may even be the case when the size is fixed beforehand.

The other choice, filling the structure with some constant, may be better if we are not sure the data on hand will fill the structure or if we want to be absolutely certain we know what is in each cell within the structure. For example, in working with numerical arrays, it is fairly common practice to "zero the array"—fill it with zeros—before putting any data into it. In this way, even if there is no datum to place in a particular cell, we know that that cell contains a valid number, zero. The danger in doing this is that if we inadvertently calculate using these initial data, the answers may be so reasonable that we do not realize that no real data have been used. Leaving random values in the structure may (or may not) give rise to outrageous answers that clearly signal trouble.

1.9 Navigating a data structure

The concept of **navigating** or **traversing** a data structure is fundamental to all other operations. To place a data element into the structure, we must first traverse the structure to find the proper location for the element. To operate on a datum already in the structure, we must traverse the structure to find it. To determine whether a given datum is in the structure, we must hunt for it throughout the structure. The organization of a data structure strongly affects this traversal process.

Figure 1.10   Circular traversal

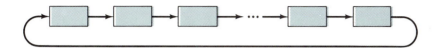

One obvious way to traverse a data structure is to start at one end and systematically work our way through the structure. Clearly this can take a long time if the structure contains large numbers of data, but sometimes it is the best way to proceed. In some data structures, however, there are better ways. For example, we do not find a name in the telephone directory by starting at the front of the "A" section and looking at each name. Similarly, we do not look up a word in the dictionary by starting at the front and reading all the definitions. In each of these situations, because the data structure is sorted into some order, we can very quickly plunge into the middle of it, and find the name or word we need. On a computer, if we have an array stored, we may be able to calculate the location of a given element of the array and go directly to it without having to examine each element preceding it.

Even if we must navigate a data structure sequentially, we have several choices. Normally we think of moving forward through the structure—looking at the first cell, then the second, and so forth. But we could equally well move backward through the structure, starting with the cell at the end of it. Moving in either direction, there are two more choices. Once we have found a particular element, we could begin hunting for the next one right there or go back to the end where we started. Also, once we have come to the other end of the structure, we face the problem of where to go next. In some situations, we want to quit. For example, if we have started to search at the front of the structure and are now at the end without having found the datum we want, we can quit, realizing that it is not there. However, if we started somewhere in the middle and are now at the end, then the datum might be in the front portion which we have not examined. In this case, we would want a **circular traversal,** one that would immediately return to the front of the structure and continue searching from there (fig. 1.10).

Circular traversals also arise in many service situations, such as the rounds of a night watchman or of an armored car delivering money to branch banks.

Finally, we must consider traversal of more complex structures. With a multidimensional array, a tree, or other complex structure, we frequently have a choice of several paths through the structure. As we discuss the various structures, we shall examine the choices we have. The problem of making sure that we traverse the structure efficiently and completely may involve following some path through the structure and then backing up to follow another path.

Figure 1.11   Identifying set elements

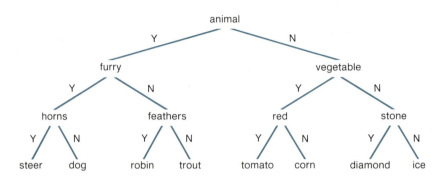

1.10 Searching a data structure

While we may traverse a data structure simply for the purpose of printing out
its elements, traversal is often a **search** for a datum within the structure, or at
least for the position the datum would occupy, were it there. We may find that
the datum is already in the structure or that it is missing. What we do next depends on whether the datum was found and why we were searching for it. In any
situation, we would like to be "smart" about the search and not look needlessly
at a great number of data cells. This we do for the telephone directory or the
dictionary by avoiding all names or words beginning with the wrong letter, and
going directly to those that begin with the letter of the word for which we are
looking. Being smart about this search process can save much time and effort.

Suppose we think of the game of "twenty questions." The game is to identify
something which is either "animal," "vegetable," or "mineral." To do so we are
allowed to ask up to twenty questions that can be answered yes or no. How many
different things could we identify by asking only twenty questions? The first
question will divide the set of things into two parts—equally if we are lucky. If
we focus on one of these parts, the second question will divide *it* into two parts.
Similarly, the third question can be used to divide one of these parts into two.
Thus, if we had started with only eight things, by the end of three questions, we
would have identified one (fig. 1.11).

If we had started with sixteen things, we would now have narrowed the choice
down to two, and by asking a fourth question, we could decide which one we
wanted. For each additional question, we can double the size of the set of objects
that we are examining. Asking twenty questions will double the size twenty times,
so that we could distinguish one among 1,048,576 objects. If we didn't use this
technique, on the average we would need to examine over half a million objects
to find the one we wanted. Asking just twenty questions is much quicker!

Although we are not always in the happy position of being able to do this well, we can use other techniques and avoid examining large masses of data. Sometimes, with proper organization, we can do even better and find what we want after just two or three probes.

A key question in any search process is how the datum sought relates to previous data. In many instances, we are looking for a new datum "at random"— we are looking for a datum that has no relationship to previous data. For example, in a set of examination papers for a course, the name of the student on a given paper will generally bear no relationship to the name of the student on the next paper, unless we have sorted the set of papers. But in other instances, for example with a sorted set of papers, we can expect to find the next datum immediately following or in front of the current datum. This type of knowledge is so useful when searching a data structure that it often pays to go through the extra work of sorting a data structure when we expect to be searching frequently for a data element near the previous one.

1.11 Ordering a data structure

One of the reasons that twenty questions can identify an object in such a large set is that the set is organized so that each question we ask eliminates roughly half of the possible answers. For many purposes, the key to efficient use of a data structure lies in the organization of the data within that structure. The most common organizational process we have is that of **ordering** or **sorting** the data. The large number of sorting methods that are known fall mainly into five classes, according to how data elements are chosen and placed into the sorted data set.

Insertion sorts focus on finding where the next incoming datum belongs in the sorted set and putting it there. **Selection sorts,** in contrast, look among the incoming data for the datum that should be next in the sorted set. **Exchange sorts** concentrate on switching data elements around until they are in the proper order. **Placement sorts** begin with space allocated for every potential datum and then place the incoming data in their proper positions. And **merge sorts** work by merging or blending together smaller subsets of the data that have already been sorted.

All these sorting techniques assume that there is a **linear arrangement** of the elements—we can determine a first, a second, and so forth. In some situations, we cannot easily find a linear arrangement. This may happen simply because not every pair of elements can be compared on the same basis. Such situations call for special techniques. A full discussion of sorting is given in chapter 11.

1.12 Updating a data structure

Most uses of data structures involve modifying or **updating** the data within the structure at one time or another. In a personnel file, for example, we need to change addresses, phone numbers, wages, names, and so forth. The concept of updating the data is not a difficult one. However, organization of the data structure may lead to some problems. For example, if we have a file sorted on names and someone changes his or her name, then the data record for that person must be moved to another part of the file to keep it sorted. If we have a data structure that tightly fills the memory space and we want to add more data, then we may have to move some of the present data to make room. Conversely, if we want to delete some data and still maintain the tight organization, we may have to move some data to fill in the gap.

One other problem that occurs during updating relates to the question of how many people are using the data. It would be bad, for example, to change a data value while someone else was using it. The results of the other person's work would probably be invalid. We also would not want to delete a data item even if we were through with it until we could be sure that nobody else was depending on that datum being present in the data structure.

1.13 Retrieving an element from a data structure

Searching for a data element involves merely locating it, not doing anything with it. Updating a data element, on the other hand, involves changing or deleting it. Generally, we must search for an element before we can update it. However, there are other reasons for searching for an element. We may simply want to examine it or copy it without changing or deleting it. This **retrieval** operation is an important one for many applications. Even when we wish to change a data element, we often retrieve a copy of it, modify the copy, and then replace the original element with the copy.

The retrieval or selection operation can be extended in a number of ways. We may search for some identifier and then retrieve a large number of data, called the **record,** associated with the identifier. Or we may search for two special indicators, such as the beginning and end of a paragraph, and retrieve all the information between them.

Many times we do not have an accurate description of the item we wish to retrieve, only an approximate description. For example, we may not know exactly how to spell a person's name, yet we need to obtain information on that person. In such situations, the selection or retrieval process must allow some flexibility. For example, if we search for "Ann?", where the question mark indicates some unknown character (including a blank), a good selection process would find the information about "Ann", "Anna", and "Anne". It would also find the information on "Annb", "Annc", . . . , if these strings of characters occurred. Note that most retrieval operations are quite precise about matching the given string exactly. Thus this particular query would also pick up the "Anni" in "Anniversary" but would miss "anniversary" because it begins with a lowercase "a."

1.14 Merging data structures

We frequently need to **merge** two or more data structures into one. We have already suggested doing this for one class of sorting techniques, the merge sorts. We may also do this when combining several procedures into a single program, when combining a form letter with a mailing list, or when adding new data, say from new experimental results, to already known data. Sometimes this combining can be done easily by adding each new datum individually to a given structure, updating it. Sometimes it is more efficient to organize the new data into their own structure and then merge this structure as a unit with the original structure. For example, we may have a large dictionary that is organized alphabetically. When we come across a new word, it may be more efficient to keep this in a separate list than to add it immediately to the dictionary. Then, once we have accumulated a reasonable number of new words, perhaps a hundred or so, we might organize these alphabetically and merge this new, smaller dictionary with the old, larger one.

1.15 Reshaping a data structure

Reshaping or **reformatting** a data structure is an operation that occurs commonly in text processing. We may write a paper and then for various reasons change the format of it by changing the spacing, the margins, the type style, the placement of page numbers, and so forth.

A similar process can occur as data structures grow with time. If a structure has some particular property, perhaps a special shape, then adding new data to the structure may destroy that property. Thus the structure must be reformatted to reestablish the initial property. For example, if data are organized in a tree structure, the tree may be quite symmetrically shaped ("balanced") or quite uneven (fig. 1.12). (Don't worry about the specific data. The shape is the important thing.)

If the unevenness reflects some property of the data, such as family ancestry, then it should be retained. But we may have arranged the data into a tree for ease of manipulation rather than because of properties inherent in the data. In this case, keeping the tree balanced by frequently reshaping it allows more efficient processing of the data.

Figure 1.12   Balanced and unbalanced trees

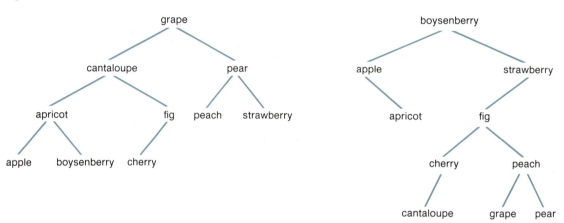

1.16 Combining data structures

Another type of merging, perhaps less common, occurs when we replace each single element of a data structure by a more complex substructure. This **combining** of two or more structures occurs in top-down program design, with the relatively simple "stub" replaced by a more complex structure that has been independently developed to fit into that position. It may also occur in data structures. For example, we may have a file of book titles and decide to replace each title by a record containing the title, the author's name, an abstract, and additional information. When we examine the data structure called a "record," we shall see that its component parts frequently have different structural properties. Several components may be strings of characters, while others are arrays or trees. We try to organize the data to take best advantage of each type of substructure.

1.17 Practical considerations

In this text we often discuss operations and the data structures to which they apply in isolation. We will talk about sorting, for example, as though that were the only operation. Or we will discuss some feature of a tree with the tacit assumption that that is the only structure we need consider at the time. This is necessary for a clear examination of the advantages and disadvantages of each technique and structure.

In practice, however, life is not so simple. The operations we do on a structure are many, and the mix of them differs depending on the application. Some applications require much updating and sorting, with relatively little retrieval. Others require primarily retrieval. The datum we think of as a unit in a tree or an array may in fact have a complex structure itself, so that we have a tree of lists or an array of trees. The practicing computer programmer or engineer must consider the full structure of the data, and the specific mixture of operations to be done on it, to arrive at a data structure that is highly efficient in a particular situation.

Summary

This chapter has been a review of the programming practices and techniques that we intend to follow throughout this book. In addition to the practices explicitly discussed here, we have adopted a specific program writing style, which is given in appendix B.

The operations we have discussed in this chapter are typical of those that are performed on a data structure. Not all of these operations will be used with every data structure; and each structure will most likely involve a few operations that are not in this general group. In each situation, however, we should aim at defining the structure and its operations—the data type—abstractly, before considering possible implementations. The term **information hiding** refers to the practice of keeping the exact implementation hidden from the user. By allowing the user only the abstract definitions, the system designer can then change and improve the data implementations without directly involving the user.

Vocabulary

abstract data structure
abstract data type
ADT
algorithm
array
ASCII
block
build
byte
cell
circular traversal
combine
control structure
create
data
data structure
data transformation
data type
design principles
documentation
driver
dynamic structure
EBCDIC
exchange sort
information hiding
initialization
input
insertion sort
kilobyte
life cycle
linear arrangement

list
map
megabyte
merge
merge sort
mnemonic name
module
navigation
order
output
PDL
placement sort
program design language
record
reformat
reshape
retrieval
roster
search
selection sort
set
sort
static structure
stub
subprogram
table
top-down design
traversal
tree
update

Problems

1.1. In the library card example, we made assumptions that forty characters would be enough to represent a title and that twenty characters could be used for each author's name. Check a sample of twenty to fifty books in your library to determine how reasonable these assumptions are. Do we really need more space, or could we have allowed less? Is our assumption of two authors per book appropriate, or will it cause quite a bit of trouble?

1.2. Indicate whether a fixed or dynamic data structure would be preferred when implementing the following (on-line):
  A. a library card catalog
  B. the name, address, and telephone number of an employee
  C. the examination grades of students in this course
  D. a student transcript
  E. the FBI's "ten most wanted" list
  F. a table of Pascal reserved words
  G. a trip itinerary
  H. the football team's fall schedule
  I. a list of seniors
  J. a telephone directory

1.3. Identify which structure (list, table, or tree) appears most natural to implement the following:
  A. the children in your town who own a Cabbage Patch doll
  B. postal rates for overseas mail
  C. the current prices of stocks on the NYSE
  D. foreign currency exchange rates
  E. the U.S. Open tennis championship play
  F. the salaries and uniform numbers of the Pittsburgh Steelers
  G. the past presidents of the United States
  H. an organizational chart for IBM
  I. a final grade report sheet
  J. an index for your tape collection

1.4. Rank the likelihood of each of the operations—updating, sorting, searching, or traversal—occurring on each of the following sets. Use the scale: often, occasionally, rarely, once, never.
  A. a telephone directory
  B. a list of the class of 1960
  C. a class roll
  D. the text of a book
  E. an employee record

1.5. Construct a tree containing the first ten words in the vocabulary list preceding these problems so that if you traverse the tree, taking always the leftmost branch that you have not yet traversed, the words will be encountered in alphabetical order. (Hint: see fig. 1.12)

1.6. Construct a tree as in problem 1.5 but using the first ten words in the present problem.

1.7. How many kilobytes of main memory does your computer have? How many megabytes of disk storage are available?

Programs

1.1. Test the program in fig. 1.3. Devise a set of test cases that exercise each possible branch of the program.

1.2. Rewrite the '(Y/N)' tests in the Income Tax program to accept 'Y', 'y', 'YES', 'Yes', or 'yes' as positive responses, 'N', 'n', 'NO', 'No', or 'no' as negative responses, and to prompt the user for one of these if some other answer is given.

1.3. Write the procedure "Header" as described in the income tax program. See fig. 1.3.

1.4. Modify the procedure "EzForm" (and the main program if necessary) to allow the user to correct erroneous input data or to transfer directly to one of the other procedures in case the data do not permit use of form 1040EZ.

1.5. Rewrite the following Pascal code fragment without using any GOTOs:

```
        .
        .
        .
read (N);
FOR I := 1 TO N DO
   BEGIN
      read (Score[I]);
      IF Score[I] < 0 THEN GOTO 300
   END;
writeln (N,' scores were read.');
GOTO 600;
300: writeln ('Bad data--score is negative.');
600: writeln;
     .
     .
     .
```

Observe that avoiding the GOTO in this situation requires more complicated testing for end conditions. How much extra work do you think this involves?

2

Programming Practices;
Program Complexity

Introduction

One programming adage is that if a program isn't correct, then it doesn't matter how efficient it is. This chapter extends the concepts of structured programming and design by introducing program assertions and invariants. It then examines the concept of algorithm and program complexity.

An assertion is a statement that describes an aspect of the program at some point. The programmer uses the assertion to check the program's operation at that point. If the assertion is false, then there is an error in the program; but if the assertion is true, then the program is probably (although not necessarily) correct to that point. Similarly, an invariant is a quantity which is supposedly left unchanged by a given operation or group of operations, providing the programmer with another check on the proper operation of the program.

The complexity of an algorithm or a program can be measured in terms of the amount of time that is required to process a certain number of data or the amount of storage that is used during the processing. The basic mathematics for both measurements is the same; since time constraints are generally the more critical in practice, our discussion will be largely in terms of the amount of time required. We distinguish between algorithm and program complexity because it is possible to make an elegant algorithm operate inefficiently simply by programming it poorly.

2.1 Assertions

Assertions are statements we place in a program that describe facts about the program. These facts should be simple to check and should relate directly to the operation of the program at the point at which the assertion is made. Each assertion should be a logical proposition that is either true or false. While some compilers provide for automatic checking of assertions, most do not. Nevertheless, assertions are important tools for the programmer to use in the course of developing a program.

In addition, assertions provide invaluable guidance for program maintenance during the life of the program. It often happens that the person or team in charge of maintaining a program is not the same one that developed it. Even when the maintenance staff is the program development staff, it is possible that comments added during program development will not be sufficient to guide maintenance several months later. An assertion definitely stating that some condition holds or does not hold at a particular point in the program is very helpful in the maintenance process, since it provides a semiautomatic checkpoint in the program.

We cannot at any one point in the program state everything that is true about the program at that point, not because we may not know what is true, but rather because there are too many facts that are true, many of which are not relevant to the present situation. For example, when we perform a test in a program, the important fact at that point is the result of the test. It is generally true that performing the test has not changed any of the data in memory, but we do not want to state that every time. Thus we have a universal **default assertion,** that any datum that is not mentioned in a given assertion either is unchanged from its previous value or is irrelevant.

Suppose that we have a small loop that sums several values in an array:

```
Sum := 0;
FOR I := 1 TO N DO
   Sum := Sum + A[I];
```

At the end of the loop we may wish to assert that the sum has a certain value. It is also true that N has a certain value, but since its value has not been changed from what it was before the loop, we do not specifically assert that. It is further true that I has a value, usually $N + 1$. But since many programming languages, including Pascal, do not permit access to the loop control variable outside of the loop, the value of I is irrelevant. Hence it is also pointless to assert that. Thus our assertion would take the form

```
{ Assert: Sum has the value .... },
```

with the facts about N and I left to the default assertion.

The most convenient assertions to make are those that describe the condition of a program and its data immediately before and after some block of operations. These are called **preconditions** and **postconditions.** If the programmer cannot satisfactorily demonstrate that these conditions hold, then chances are good that there is an error in the program at that point. The assertion about Sum is a postcondition, while the precondition for the loop, which is guaranteed by the assignment Sum := 0, is that Sum has the value zero.

Some programmers think of preconditions and postconditions as forming contracts. If there is a guarantee that the precondition for a given block of code holds, then the programmer contracts that the corresponding postcondition following that block of code will also hold. Note that in our loop example, if we cannot guarantee that Sum has the value zero when we enter the loop, then we cannot guarantee that its value upon leaving the loop will be what we desire.

To distinguish between assertions that can be verified and expository comments, we shall follow the practice of beginning each assertion with the word "Assert" followed by a colon, as in

```
{ Assert: 0 < X ≤ 100 }.
```

Typical points for the placement of assertions are before and after a loop, and before and after a branching operation. For example, in the income tax program we developed in chapter 1, we have several branching operations that select the correct procedure to use. Let us examine the first of these.

```
{ Decide on the proper form. Is use of 1040
required? }

IF (Itemized = 'Y') OR (NonTaxDividend = 'Y')
   OR (Estimated = 'Y')

   { or any of the other requirements }

   THEN LongForm
ELSE

   { Form 1040 is not required, so we need more
   information to decide if a shorter form can
   be used. }
   ...
```

In this IF statement, we are checking the values of three variables. We can place assertions before the test and after each branch of the test. Before the test, an appropriate assertion would be that "Itemized," "NonTaxDividend," and "Estimated" all have character values. Following the test, we need assertions on the IF branch and on the ELSE branch. On the IF branch we know that at least one of the three variables in question has the value "Y" (but not which one), while on the ELSE branch we know exactly the opposite—that none of these variables has the value "Y." Thus, with assertions in place, this piece of code might look like this.

```
{ Decide on the proper form. Is use of 1040
required? }

{ Assert: Itemized, NonTaxDividend, and
Estimated have character values. }

IF (Itemized = 'Y') OR (NonTaxDividend = 'Y')
   OR (Estimated = 'Y')

  { or any of the other requirements }

  THEN

      { Assert: At least one of the values of
      Itemized, NonTaxDividend, or Estimated is
      "Y" }

      LongForm
  ELSE

      { Assert: None of the values of Itemized,
      NonTaxDividend, or Estimated is "Y". }

      { Form 1040 is not required, so we need
      more information to decide if a shorter
      form can be used. }
      . . .
```

Note that these assertions are included as comments, since most Pascal compilers cannot check assertions. Thus we must check them manually. If the compiler or interpreter is one that can check assertions, then these can be included as program statements rather than comments and checked automatically at run time.

The value of assertions lies in the fact that they point out to the programmer conditions that are supposed to hold. If the conditions are trivial, then the assertions have little value; but if the conditions are more complex, then they have great value. Pascal requires that all variables be defined and given types before the program is compiled. Hence, in this example, the first assertion is simply a reminder of the type that is assumed for these variables. While this assertion may thus seem useless, it is nevertheless frequently useful to have this reminder handy rather than to require checking of the VAR declarations. The other two assertions have a little more meat. The first one reminds us that one of the variables has the value "Y" but that we do not know which one. The final assertion reminds us that at this point none of the variables has the value "Y"—but does not say which values they do have.

Assertions thus provide points within a program at which the correctness of the program and the data can be checked. If the fact that an assertion holds is critical at some point but not obvious, then this is a good point for an explicit test to verify the assertion. If the assertion does not hold, something is wrong and corrective action must be taken. Note that in production programming the proper corrective action is generally *not* to halt the program. Doing this would only frustrate the user, since he or she may not know what is wrong. Furthermore, if the error lies in the program rather than in the data, the user is in no position to correct it. The correct action might be to print out an error message, abort this particular run, and continue with the next set of input or the next program. In an interactive environment, the correct action might be to print the error message and give the user the option of entering new data (if that is the source of the error), continuing with the next run, or quitting.

In addition to before and after a branching operation, assertions are commonly found surrounding a loop. In this case, the precondition assertion is often a very general one, stating, for example, that any sequence of values for use in the loop can be expected or that the length of the sequence is the value of the loop exit variable or, as in the Sum example, that appropriate variables have been properly initialized. Following a loop, the assertion commonly is that a particular value has been computed or that a particular arrangement of variables has been achieved. For example, in a sorting routine, the precondition might be that we have a non-empty set of words to sort and the postcondition might be that the words have been sorted into alphabetical order. We shall see many examples of these types of assertions in the course of our work.

Assertions are particularly useful in controlling **side effects.** A side effect of a program segment is a change in the value of variables other than those at which the program segment is directed. A procedure or function, for example, may change the value of one or more global variables, in addition to the values of those variables that are explicitly passed as parameters. In languages that allow a loop control variable to retain a value outside of the loop, the loop obviously changes the value of that variable and may leave an unexpected value if the loop terminates abnormally. Assertions provide a means of monitoring and controlling these side effects.

Just as with comments in general, we should be judicious in the use of assertions. Rather than clutter up a program with many trivial assertions, it is better to have a small number of significant assertions. The important thing to remember is that assertions are meant to aid in program design and maintenance.

Hence they should be meaningful and at the same time easily checked and verified. An assertion that is trivial lacks meaning; on the other hand, an assertion that claims that seventeen variables have changed their values is very hard to check and probably indicates that some of the changes should be separated out into other, earlier assertions.

2.2 Invariants

An **invariant** is a quantity that remains unchanged during a particular operation. A large program has a great many variables. However, any given section of the program will use only a small number of those variables. The other variables, those that are not mentioned in a section, are invariant with respect to that section of the program. (These are the variables whose values are left to the default assertion.)

We are interested in the effect a program section has on those variables that it does reference and on combinations of them. If the section is incorrect, then some variables or combinations may be left with invalid values. Some of these are specific values. For example, in a FOR loop, we normally want the final value of the loop variable to remain unchanged—be invariant—as we execute the loop. Or we may require that the sum of several variables be the same leaving the program section as it was entering it, even though the values of the individual variables may have changed.

Other invariants relate to properties of data structures. For example, most sorting algorithms have the property that they do not "unsort" that part of the set which has already been sorted. Hence the property that the part of the set which has been examined is sorted becomes an invariant for this type of program.

A statement about an invariant is a special kind of assertion, since it states that something does *not* happen during the operation of a program segment. This becomes important in program segments which might modify the value of the variable. Suppose that we are performing a numerical calculation that could modify the value of an angle, but that it is important that the original value of the angle be preserved following the calculation. This value then becomes an invariant, and the program should be checked to verify that it indeed remains unchanged. If the segment does change the value and does so legitimately, then there are two possible remedies. Either preserve the original value and restore it following the calculation or (better) define a new variable, give it the original value of the angle, and do the calculation using this new variable.

To demonstrate the use of an invariant, suppose that we have an integer array called Count, indexed from 0 to M, and suppose that every location in the array contains a value. Suppose further that our program contains the following loop:

```
FOR I := 1 TO M DO
    Count[I] := Count[I] + Count[I - 1];

{ End of FOR loop }
```

We want to be certain that this loop does its intended function. First, we must determine exactly what it does. Let us take a small example. Take M = 5, and let the array have the values

```
Count[0] = 4
Count[1] = 5
Count[2] = 1
Count[3] = 2
Count[4] = 9
Count[5] = 6
```

Now simulate the loop operation. Count[0] remains unchanged, and then we sequentially change all other values:

```
Count[0] =   4
Count[1] =   9
Count[2] =  10
Count[3] =  12
Count[4] =  21
Count[5] =  27
```

As we follow this simulation, it appears that the operation simply sums up all the values, leaving Count[I] with the sum of all the original values up to and including its own. Let us put in appropriate assertions. In the assertions we shall use the convention that Count[I] refers to the original value and Count'[I] refers to the new value.

```
{ Assert: M >=1 and the Count values have been
assigned. }

FOR I := 1 TO M DO

    { Assert: 1 <= I <= M and for J = 1 to I - 1,
    Count'[J] = Count[0] + ... + Count[J]. }

    Count[I] := Count[I] + Count[I - 1];

    { Assert: 1 <= I <= M and for J = 1 to I,
    Count'[J] = Count[0] + ... + Count[J]. }

{ End of FOR loop }

{ Assert: I = M + 1 and for J = 1 to I - 1,
Count'[J] = Count[0] + ... + Count[J]. }

{ Assert: Count[M] contains the sum of the
original values in the array. }
```

We have placed five assertions in here, more than we would in normal practice. The important thing to note is that the statements about J and Count' are the same in the second and fourth assertions. This is our invariant: for $J = 1$ to $I - 1$, Count'[J] = Count[0] $+ ... +$ Count[J]. It is this invariant that allows the final assertion to be made. Note also that the first assertion states that $M \geq 1$. If this is not true, then the loop will not be executed and the values in the array will not be changed. Thus we have a contract: the final assertion cannot be guaranteed if the initial assertion is not true.

The process of defining good invariants, and good preconditions and postconditions surrounding a particular operation, is a complex one that requires considerably more discussion than we have so far presented. Further discussion will take place throughout the rest of the text, as appropriate programming situations arise. For the present, it is sufficient to know that good invariants and conditions can be defined, and that they are useful in establishing that a program is properly designed and written.

We caution the reader, however, that the invariants and other assertions we include with our programs are to be taken seriously, and that every effort should be made to understand them and understand why they are included. Skimming lightly over the assertions courts the danger of missing, or misunderstanding, some of the succeeding material.

2.3 Program correctness

Given that we have an unlimited variety of data that may be presented to a given program, the only way we can firmly establish that the program is correct is to prove formally that it is. While assertions and invariants are used as an aid in correct program design and maintenance, they also provide a set of tools that can be used in proving that a program is correct. Unfortunately, even with these tools, presenting a formal proof of correctness for a program is exceedingly difficult. In fact, no program of more than a few thousand lines has ever been formally proven to operate correctly for all possible input values.

Nevertheless, the concept of making formal, or at least semiformal, arguments that a program is indeed correct is an important one, since if these arguments are valid, then there is no need to test the program further. The extreme difficulty of arguing about large programs is yet another reason for organizing a program into small modules. If we can prove that each module is correct, then the correctness of the entire program hinges on the manner in which the modules are put together. This focuses our program testing.

We will demonstrate an at least semiformal argument of program correctness for the small loop that adds up the values of the Count array. We will do this by discussing each of the five assertions in turn. Here is the loop:

```
{ Assert: M >= 1 and the Count values have been
assigned. }

FOR I := 1 TO M DO

    { Assert: 1 <= I <= M and for J = 1 to I - 1,
    Count'[J] = Count[0] + ... + Count[J]. }

    Count[I] := Count[I] + Count[I - 1];

    { Assert: 1 <= I <= M and for J = 1 to I,
    Count'[J] = Count[0] + ... + Count[J]. }

{ End of FOR loop }

{ Assert: I = M + 1 and for J = 1 to I - 1,
Count'[J] = Count[0] + ... + Count[J]. }

{ Assert: Count[M] contains the sum of the
original values in the array. }
```

The first assertion is the hypothesis upon which our entire argument must be based. Since it refers to prior program segments, there is nothing in the loop that can be used to prove this first assertion true or to demonstrate that it is false. We must accept it as given.

The second assertion comes within the loop and consists of two statements. From our knowledge of the operation of FOR, we argue that the first statement, $1 \leq I \leq M$, is true: otherwise we would not be within the loop. The argument for the second statement breaks into two parts, for $I = 1$ and for all other values of I.

For $I = 1$, the second statement asserts only that Count'[0] = Count[0]. At this point in the program operation, all that has been done since making the first assertion is to set the value of I to 1. The values within the Count array have not been changed. Hence, for $I = 1$, the second part of the second assertion is true.

Now we must consider this same statement for $I > 1$. We observe that the claim being made here is exactly the same as the claim for the third assertion on the previous pass through the loop. That is, this statement is true if and only if the second statement of the third assertion was true on the previous pass. Thus we defer judgment on this statement until after we have examined the third assertion.

The third assertion also contains two parts, the first of which is the same as the first part of the second assertion. We had decided that this part was true in the second assertion. Since the assignment statement does not change the value of I, it is also true here.

The second part of the third assertion looks much like the second part of the second assertion. In fact, all it says is that the statement about Count'[J] holds for J = I as well as for all the previous values. Let's assume that the second part of the second assertion holds. (We'll come back to this later.) We examine the assignment statement carefully. On the right-hand side we find two values, Count[I] and Count[I − 1]. Since this is the first time within the loop that we have met Count[I], it still has the original value. But since we have already been through the loop for lesser values, Count[I − 1] in the assignment statement has been changed to the value that we call Count'[I − 1] in the assertion. (Note that this is true even for I = 1, since Count'[0] = Count[0].) Thus, in the notation of the assertion,

```
Count'[I] = Count[I] + Count'[I - 1]
          = Count[I] +
            Count[0] + ... + Count[I - 1].
```

That is, Count'[I] is the sum of all the original values of the Count array, up to and including the value of Count[I], as is asserted.

Now we come back to the interplay between the second and third assertions. Recall that we deferred judgment on the second part of the second assertion until we had examined the third assertion; but then in the third assertion our argument is based on the assumption that the second assertion is true. On the surface, this seems to be a circular argument. What breaks the circle for us is the fact that the second assertion is true for I = 1, without considering the third assertion. Hence we find the following line of reasoning:

For I = 1, the second assertion is true.

Hence, for I = 1, the third assertion is true.

For I = 2, the second assertion is true, because the third assertion is true for I = 1.

Hence, for I = 2, the third assertion is true.

For I = 3, the second assertion is true, because the third assertion is true for I = 2.

Hence, for I = 3, the third assertion is true.

. . .

Thus, on each pass through the loop, both the second and the third assertions are true. We can keep this line of reasoning up as long as needed. It finally breaks down because the first part of the second assertion, $1 \le I \le M$, becomes false. That happens when I = M + 1; it is time to examine the fourth assertion.

The fourth assertion again has two parts. The first of these asserts that $I = M + 1$. This is true; in fact, it is this which has broken us out of the loop. (We need not worry about the fact that in Pascal we can't really access the value of I, since this is an argument about how the program operates rather than an attempt to use this value within the program.) The second part of the fourth assertion is identical to the second part of the second assertion. Since leaving the loop does not change the array values, this part is also true and the fourth assertion has been established.

The fifth assertion is easy to prove. It simply picks out the one value in the fourth assertion that we really want to use and focuses our attention on that. Note that, if we want to use any of the other values in the Count array later in the program, we must remember that they are all partial sums rather than the original array values.

We have been discussing a very simple one line loop, and it has taken us many paragraphs of argument to establish that this really does what the postcondition (the fifth assertion) states. This gives us some idea of the amount of effort that would be required to prove a large program correct.

2.4 Program checking

It is almost a tradition in computing that one cannot write a program that is error-free. Certainly we have seen a small example of the effort required to establish that a program is completely correct. Given the extent of this effort, it is reasonable to examine other ways of trying to convince ourselves that we have written a good program. **Debugging** a program is the process of testing a program to identify and correct the errors in it. Many techniques for doing this exist; all are made simpler by starting with a program that is clearly written and has good structure, and by using built-in debugging aids such as the assertions and invariants we have discussed. This section reviews some of the basic methods of program checking and verification, including the choice of proper test data.

The ideal, of course, is to write a program that is error-free. The chances that this will happen are greatly improved by using a good structured language, like Pascal, and carefully following the design and programming concepts we have been discussing. Nevertheless, we may ultimately be faced with the problem of correcting a program that is not doing exactly what we expect of it. Good debugging techniques can simplify this task.

We should recognize immediately that errors fall into four broad classes. (We ignore the "fat fingers" errors, that are simply a matter of typing mistakes.) First, there are **syntactic errors**. These are "grammatical" errors in the use of the programming language—undefined variables, improper constructs, and so forth.

Next, there are **semantic errors**, which arise because of a misunderstanding of the meaning of constructs in a language rather than because of grammatical errors. Such errors may arise if the programmer fails to understand exactly what some procedure or function does. Sometimes, for example, Pascal programmers have problems trying to read past the end of a data file, not because reading is the wrong thing to do, but rather because they do not fully understand what "read" does at the end of a file.

Third, we have **logic errors**. Logic errors relate, not to the syntax or semantics of a language, but to a misunderstanding of how to solve the problem. The programmer thinks he or she has written an algorithm that will solve the problem, but perhaps has forgotten to divide by some constant at one point or has multiplied values that should have been added.

The final type of error we consider is a **boundary error**. A program is likely to have this type of error if it works correctly most of the time but fails for certain combinations of input. Typically these input values fall at one end or another of the admissible range of values.

Virtually all the syntactic errors will be caught automatically by the compiler or interpreter. However, there are frequently two difficulties that arise in locating syntactic errors. First, such an error may not be caught immediately but only at some later point in the program, where its effect is noticed. Thus we need to hunt back from the point of error detection to determine what is wrong. Fortunately, the error is usually found close to the point of detection.

The second difficulty is that one syntactic error can induce many more. For example, if the compiler cannot find the end of one statement, then many of the following statements may be misinterpreted. Thus we are faced with a program that appears to have a great many errors, when in fact correction of two or three will clear up all the remaining ones. Experienced programmers become used to this and are generally able to identify the few crucial errors that will clear up most of the problems.

A key tool in correcting syntactic errors is a good **grammar** or **syntax** for the language. This syntax is most frequently defined by use of **Backus-Naur Form (BNF)** rules, or **syntax diagrams,** which specify exactly how a language construct, such as an assignment statement, can be developed from simpler constructs. Most programming language books present the syntax of the language in one or both of these ways. Difficult errors can be located quite easily by carefully tracing the syntax using one of these tools.

Figure 2.1   Syntax for Pascal variable declaration

As an example of these syntactic tools, here is the definition of the variable declaration for Pascal, first using a syntax diagram (fig. 2.1) and then in BNF.

<identifier string> ::= <identifier> |
      <identifier> , <identifier string>

<identifier declaration> ::= <identifier string> : <type> ;

<identifier declaration string> ::= <identifier declaration> |
      <identifier declaration> <identifier declaration string>

<variable declaration> ::= VAR <identifier declaration string>

In the BNF we assume that the two definitions for <identifier> and <type> have been made. (The angle brackets < ... > are used to denote names of defined symbols.)

First, an <identifier string> is defined (::=) to be a single <identifier> or (|) several <identifier>s separated by commas.

Second, an <identifier declaration> is defined to be an <identifier string>, followed by a colon, followed by a <type>, followed by a semicolon.

Third, an <identifier declaration string> is defined to be a sequence of one or more <identifier declaration>s.

And finally, a <variable declaration> is defined to be the symbol VAR followed by an <identifier declaration string>.

All the information contained in the BNF definition of a variable declaration is contained in the syntax diagram. Since this is more compact and visual, it is somewhat easier to understand. The great advantage of BNF is that it can be used directly by a compiler for syntax checking.

The remaining three kinds of errors are much more difficult to detect and correct, because they generally result in a program that will compile correctly and that may even run for quite some time before a particular combination of data occurs that will trigger the error.

Semantic errors involve a misinterpretation of an operation within a program. A program may be syntactically correct—that is, make good sense to the compiler—yet not work according to the intentions of its designer, because the programmer has not correctly understood the language constructs. These errors are frequently very difficult to detect, because when the programmer studies and reexamines his or her code it appears to be entirely correct. The programmer is, in essence, mistakenly affirming the correctness of an earlier error, without even considering that the interpretation of a given operation may be wrong.

Logic errors, which do not relate to the programming language, are also difficult to detect. Such errors occur when the program is a correct implementation of the algorithm—but there are errors in the definition of the underlying algorithm. Correcting these errors requires carefully rethinking, and perhaps extensively reworking, the underlying algorithm, and then revising the program to correspond to the new version of the algorithm. Structuring the program in relatively small modules and placing assertions carefully within the program help to minimize both the number of logic errors and the effort required to locate them.

One common type of logic error is the **off-by-one error,** which occurs when a loop is executed either one less time or one more time than the algorithm requires. This type of error is also called a **fence post error,** alluding to the fact that $n + 1$ fence posts are needed for a fence of n segments.

The final type of error, the boundary error, is the most insidious. Here we find that the syntax and semantics of the program are correct, and generally that the logic of the algorithm is also correct. A prime cause of this type of error lies in the characteristics of the computer itself. Perhaps too large or too small a value for a variable will cause the malfunction. For example, if the computer cannot handle numbers larger than 10^{20}, then squaring a variable will cause trouble if the value of the variable is 10^{11}, even though squaring the value may be logically correct. Similarly, subtracting two supposedly identical values may result in a nonzero difference simply because of the limited accuracy of the computer.

The first problem in locating a semantic, logic, or boundary error is determining that the error exists. In some cases, programs will run for several years before a particular combination of data triggers an erroneous calculation. For this reason, it is important to choose test data carefully when a program is first run. Typically, we try to choose data that will check out all possible paths through the program and that will check all error conditions. For example, in the income tax program, different data should be tried, to force the program into all its various procedures. The assertions play a role in this. Since we have asserted that it is only necessary for one of the variables "Itemized," "NonTaxDividend," or "Estimated" to have the value "Y" to trigger use of the LongForm procedure, a thorough test will check to see that each of these three variables triggers that particular path through the program.

Figure 2.2   Fencing the wolf

If we find a nonsyntactic error, the next problem is to isolate it as much as possible. If the error occurs during a well-designed testing program, there is not too much of a problem. But if the error has escaped detection during testing and shows up only once the program is in service, then isolation of the cause of the error can be more difficult. As with many diseases, the symptom that indicates an error in the program may bear little direct relation to the error itself.

A tedious way to locate these types of errors is to trace through the program, following the calculation in great detail to see where the error first occurs. A better technique involves the use of a **wolf fence.** For this, **modular design** of a program pays off. If we can check the calculation at selected points in the program, it is often possible to isolate the section of the program which must contain the error. Then we can examine this section in more detail, tracing it without needing to trace the entire program.

Isolating an erroneous section is done by constructing a wolf fence—a checkpoint in the program where we can determine if the error has occurred or not. Having determined this, we can then construct a second fence in that portion of the program known to contain the error, to narrow down still further the location of the error (fig. 2.2). Natural points for these fences are at branch points within the program, or at the entrances and exits for procedures and functions.

For example, the income tax program we outlined in chapter 1 involved four major procedures, for the header and each of the three different income tax forms. If testing reveals an error in the program, then the first step is to try to isolate the error into one of the procedures or into the main program itself. This can be done with five or six well-chosen test cases. If the error occurs whenever the procedure EzForm, say, is called but not when the other tax form procedures are called, then we have fenced off the EzForm procedure as the one most likely to contain the error. The main control structure used in that procedure (fig. 1.5) is the IF ... THEN ... ELSE ... structure. By running a series of test cases designed to take different branches of these conditional statements, we can further fence off the error into one of the branches. At this point, we have a small number of lines of code to examine for the error.

Because the error which appears in program output may not be the real error but only a symptom of an error earlier in the program, a thorough knowledge of the program and a good set of test data are important. The experienced programmer may be able to examine the data that caused the error, and to modify these data in a variety of ways that will help define the actual error and its location. The primary caution when doing this is to modify the data carefully and slowly, not changing more than one value at a time.

Error correction is often simple if it arises during modification of a program. Suppose that we have a program that works and that we wish to modify it, perhaps to add a new feature to it, perhaps to improve its operation, perhaps to extend the range of values to which it applies. In this situation, test cases can be run using the old program, which presumably yields good results, and the new program. If there is a difference in the results, then we can check for an error, reasonably certain that the error is related to the section that has been modified.

2.5 Complexity

If we are writing a program that will do simple calculations on a small number of data, then the efficiency of the program is of little importance. Not much storage will be required, and the program will probably have finished running before we know it. However, if the computations are rather complex and we have huge numbers of data to process, then any savings in time or space we can achieve may be critical to the success of the program. Jon Bentley, in section 8.3 of his book *Writing Efficient Programs,* writes that processing a million searches through one database using a simple search program required six minutes when there were 100 items in the database but ten hours when the database contained 10,000 items. Changing the algorithm produced a program requiring twenty-eight minutes on the small database but only fifty-seven minutes on the large one. Subsequent fine-tuning of this second program resulted in run times of six seconds for the small database and twelve seconds for the large one.

This example shows two things. First, while a change of algorithms may produce good gains for large numbers of data (a 10 to 1 improvement), it can actually be detrimental for small numbers of data. Second, fine-tuning a program can itself make a significant contribution to the efficiency of a computation. In the example, the combination of a better algorithm and better implementation of it resulted in a 60 to 1 time reduction for the small database and a 3000 to 1 improvement for the large one!

We see that there are two components to writing efficient programs: choice of the proper algorithm, and careful programming to avoid introducing inefficiencies. The first component, algorithm choice, is the more important one, as it places definite limits on the amount of improvement that can be achieved by the second, fine-tuning. We wish to examine the mathematics behind judging the efficiency of an algorithm.

As we have already mentioned, two of the key parameters used to measure a computer program after it has been written are the amount of time required to process a given number of data and the amount of memory required for the processing. While we would expect that most programs require more time and memory to process larger numbers of data, we are concerned that the requirements not grow so rapidly that it becomes impossible to process very large data files. More specifically, we are concerned with finding the most efficient and quickest means of processing data. In this section we discuss the elements of **computational complexity theory.** Later, as we discuss each algorithm throughout the book, we shall examine its complexity more carefully.

The term **complexity** refers to the impact that the data set size has on the processing time and space requirements. This impact can be measured in terms of the behavior of an algorithm in the worst case, the best case, or the average case. For obvious reasons, we are most concerned with what happens in the worst case—the upper limit on the amount of time or storage that a particular process will require. Thus, in our complexity discussions, we will be examining worst case behavior unless we specifically state otherwise.

Our basic concern is what happens to the operation of a given algorithm when we increase the size of the data set by one element. We must first note that the time required to process a set of elements depends on three main factors. One of these, the size of the set, will be our focus. The other factors are the particular processing being done and computer being used. While these factors are important in the final analysis, they do not have much significance when we are comparing one procedure to another: the organization of the procedures themselves is much more important.

It may be surprising that the time required for some processes does not depend on the number of elements processed. Suppose that we have a long list of names. How much effort is required to find the first name on the list? If we know where the first name is stored, a reasonable process is to go directly to it. Thus the time to find it is independent of the length of the list—it does not matter whether we have a hundred or a million names on the list. We say that this process is **constant,** or **order 1 complexity** or $O(1)$**,** in time.

Here is an example of how implementation can affect the time of an operation. Finding the last name on our list is also an $O(1)$ process if we have written the algorithm to go directly to it. However, if our algorithm always starts at the first name on the list, then finding the last name will clearly depend on how long the list is and could take much longer for a long list.

Saying that a process is $O(1)$ does not mean that we can always do it in a fixed number of microseconds, independent of the computing environment. The actual time depends on the cycle time of the computer being used, on whether the list is in main memory or on disk, and on similar factors. The *key idea* is that we do not change this time (whatever it is) by increasing or decreasing the number of data.

Thus, changing the number of names on the list does not affect the amount of time needed to find the first name. Note also that we are discussing only the *time* required to find the name. Obviously, it will require more *space* to store a longer list.

It is also true that an $O(1)$ process may take a very long time. Frequently we can process a set of data in $O(1)$ or constant time simply by designing the algorithm to consider all possible data items. Suppose, for example, that the number of students at a college is constant, say 10,000, but that the number of computer science majors varies from year to year, with a maximum of about 500. We can find the average grades for all computer science majors by processing the data for every single student and using only the grades of the computer science students. That is, for each student compute the average grade and then decide whether to keep it (because the student is a computer science major) or discard it. This would be an $O(1)$ process, since the total number of students is constant. Or, if the students were classified by major, we could compute the average grade for computer science students by looking only at that group of students. This method would not be $O(1)$ but would depend on the number of computer science students each year. If we used the same basic computation process in each method, then the $O(1)$ method could take twenty times as long as the method whose complexity depends on the number of computer science students, since the former method must handle at least twenty times as many students. Despite this time difference, the first method might be more desirable for some other reason.

The important thing to remember is that $O(1)$ means constant time, independent of the number of data, *not* short time.

Consider next the process of constructing a list of names. As long as we do not have to change storage media (from main memory to disk, say), the amount of time required to add one name to the list will have two components. First, we must decide where to put the name. Second, we must actually place the name there. Deciding where to put the name can be time-consuming, depending on whether we want the list in some particular order, whether space is available, and other factors. Let us suppose that we will add names to the list in the order in which they are received and that there is always space available. Then the time required to add one name to the list will be constant. Thus the amount of time needed to build the entire list is proportional to *n*, the number of names on the list. We say that this process is **linear,** or **order *n* complexity,** or $O(n)$. Again, observe that the actual time needed to build the list depends on the computer being used. A fast computer might require 0.0000002 seconds per name. For this computer, the time needed to build a list of n names is $f(n) = 0.0000002n$. An extremely slow computer might require a full second per name, so that its list construction time would be $g(n) = n$. Making the list by hand and writing down each name might require even longer, say 25 seconds per name. Thus the list

Figure 2.3   Time to build a list of names

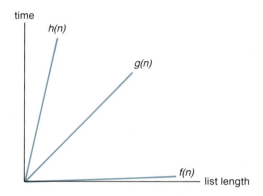

Table 2.1   Examples of time complexity

$O(1)$	Locating the first element in a list of length n
$O(\lg n)$	Locating an element in a sorted list of length n by binary search
$O(n)$	Building a list of length n; locating an element in an unsorted list of length n
$O(n \lg n)$	Sorting a list of length n using comparisons
$O(n^2)$	Adding two square matrices of size n
$O(n^3)$	Multiplying two square matrices of size n
$O(2^n)$	Listing all subsets of a set of size n
$O(n!)$	Listing all permutations of a set of size n

construction time for this "computer" would be $h(n) = 25n$. The important thing is that each of these times is proportional to n: one can be derived from another simply by multiplying by a constant (see fig. 2.3).

Different processes require different amounts of time and space for a given size of data set. Table 2.1 contains some examples of these time requirements for different operations. As is common in computing, we use "$\lg n$" to denote $\log_2 n$. Recall that for any numbers a and n, $\log_a n = b$ is equivalent to $a^b = n$. During the course of our discussion we shall come back to each of these formulas and show why the process has the time complexity given in the table.

One of the most common complexity calculations involves summing the integers from 1 to n. Suppose that we are building a set of n elements, one at a time, and that we may possibly have some duplicate elements in the input stream. If we have no idea of the order in which the elements arrive, then we must check each new element against the preceding ones to be sure it is different. Processing the first element requires one step: no check, just add it. Processing the second requires two steps: check against the first; then add it. Similarly, we need three steps for the third (assuming that it is different), four steps for the fourth, and so on. The total number of steps is the sum $1 + 2 + \ldots + n$. This sum has the value $n(n + 1)/2$.

Figure 2.4   Various orders of complexity

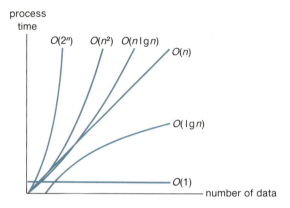

The classic proof of this, due to Karl F. Gauss, is to observe that the first and last terms add to $n + 1$, as do the second and next-to-last terms. The same is true also for the other term pairs. Thus, letting S denote the sum, we have

$$
\begin{aligned}
S &= 1 + 2 + \ldots + n - 1 + n, \\
S &= n + n - 1 + \ldots + 2 + 1,
\end{aligned}
$$

adding,

$$
\begin{aligned}
2S &= (n + 1) + (n + 1) + \ldots + (n + 1) + (n + 1), \\
2S &= n (n + 1),
\end{aligned}
$$

and finally,

$$
S = n (n + 1)/2.
$$

The value can also be established through mathematical induction (problem 2.2), or by observing that a quadratic polynomial fits the values and determining its coefficients.

As figure 2.4 and table 2.2 show, the order of complexity of a process can have a significant impact on the time required to execute the process, particularly for very large data sets. A similar remark can be made about the space requirements, although in practice the space requirements are of lower complexity and thus do not have such a dramatic effect.

Table 2.2 Values of complexity orders

	n						
	10	100	500	1000	10,000	100,000	1,000,000
1	1	1	1	1	1	1	1
$\lg n$	3.32	6.64	8.96	9.96	13.3	16.6	19.9
n	10	100	500	1000	10,000	100,000	1,000,000
$n \lg n$	33.2	664	4480	9960	133,000	$1.66 \cdot 10^6$	$1.99 \cdot 10^7$
n^2	100	10^4	$25 \cdot 10^4$	10^6	10^8	10^{10}	10^{12}
n^3	10^3	10^6	$125 \cdot 10^6$	10^9	10^{12}	10^{15}	10^{18}
2^n	1024	10^{30}	10^{151}	10^{301}	10^{3010}	10^{30103}	10^{301030}
$n!$	$3.6 \cdot 10^6$						

Table 2.3 Time for n calculation steps, different complexities (ns = nanoseconds, μs = microseconds, ms = milliseconds, s = seconds, c = centuries)

	n			
	10	100	500	1000
$\lg n$	332ns	664ns	893ns	996ns
n	1μs	10μs	50μs	100μs
n^2	10μs	1ms	25ms	100ms
n^3	100μs	100ms	12.5s	100s
2^n	102μs	$4.0 \cdot 10^{13}$c	$1.0 \cdot 10^{135}$c	$3.4 \cdot 10^{285}$c

To place these large numbers in a more understandable context, suppose that it takes 100 nanoseconds (10^{-7} seconds) to perform one step of a calculation. Then table 2.3 shows the time required for different numbers of calculations and different complexities.

This table demonstrates why proper choice of an algorithm is so important. Fine-tuning a program may make it run hundreds of times faster, but changing to a more efficient algorithm may change processing time from centuries to minutes or seconds.

The impact of the high orders of complexity on our ability to solve a very large problem can also be demonstrated by considering what happens if we can build faster computers. In table 2.4, the N_i represent the size of a problem that can be solved in a given time, say one hour, using the best present computers. Observe that for exponential and higher order time complexities, large increases in computer speed do not materially change the size of the problems we can solve: we can only process another four or five data elements.

Table 2.4   Interaction of computer speed and complexity

	computer speed			
$O(n)$	present	×10	×100	×1000
n	N_1	$10N_1$	$100N_1$	$1000N_1$
n^2	N_2	$3.2N_2$	$10N_2$	$31.6N_2$
n^3	N_3	$2.2N_3$	$4.6N_3$	$10N_3$
2^n	N_4	$N_4+3.3$	$N_4+6.6$	N_4+10
3^n	N_5	$N_5+2.1$	$N_5+4.2$	$N_5+6.3$

Three basic rules apply to computing the order of complexity of a function or algorithm.

1. Multiplicative constants do not matter. To say that an algorithm is $O(kf)$, where k is a constant, is the same as saying that it is $O(f)$.

2. Addition is done by taking the maximum. To say that an algorithm is $O(f + g)$ is the same as saying that it is $O(\max(O(f), O(g))$. This type of computation occurs when an $O(f)$ process is followed by an $O(g)$ process, and the computation simply says that the longer of the two processes (the larger of the two complexity functions $O(f)$ and $O(g)$) dominates the order of the combined processes.

3. Multiplication remains multiplication. That is, $O(f) \cdot O(g) = O(f \cdot g)$. This type of computation arises most frequently when a loop is involved. For example, a FOR loop from 1 to n is $O(n)$. But if the loop contains an embedded process of $O(f)$, then the complexity of the full process is $O(n) \cdot O(f) = O(nf)$.

This **order arithmetic** is used to simplify estimation of the complexity of an algorithm. For example, we may be able to show that a particular computation takes $n(n - 1)/2$ steps. Thus the process is $O(n(n - 1)/2) = O(n^2/2 - n/2)$. By the second rule this is equivalent to $O(n^2/2)$, and by the first rule this in turn is equivalent to $O(n^2)$, a much simpler expression. This simplification is justified because we are just making order of magnitude estimates of the efficiency of an algorithm. As we have seen in Bentley's example, the details of a program implementation can have a large impact, overshadowing the simplifications that have been done in making the complexity estimate.

Here are a few examples of order arithmetic:

$O(2n^3 + 1000n) = O(n^3)$, because eventually (for $n > 25$) $2n^3$ dominates $1000n$, and the constant "2" can be dropped by the first rule.

$O(5n^2) + O(3n\lg n) = O(n^2)$, because $5n^2$ dominates $3n\lg n$ beyond $n = 1$, and again the constant can be dropped.

$O(n) \cdot O(n - 1) \cdot O(n\lg n) = O(n^3\lg n)$. This example is a little more complex. By the multiplication rule, the product is

$$O(n(n - 1)n\lg n) = O(n^3\lg n - n^2 \lg n).$$

The first term dominates, so the second may be dropped. This type of computation might occur during sorting within a double loop.

Summary

This chapter has introduced the concepts of assertions and invariants as tools to help assure that a program is correctly written and will correctly solve the specified problem. The development of good, helpful assertions and invariants requires practice and thought. We suggest that you read the series of papers by Jon Bentley for suggestions on these topics, and on sound programming practices in general.

In addition, we have discussed the various classes of errors that can occur in programming, and some of the methods for detecting and correcting these errors.

We have also introduced the notion of the complexity of a computation. We have discussed how to estimate the order of magnitude of time that a computation will require, as the number of data is varied. Two key points to remember are that this estimate can be made on the basis of the dominant process only, which corresponds to the dominant term in the order calculation, and that $O(1)$ means constant time but not necessarily a short time.

Vocabulary

assertion	$O(1)$
Backus-Naur Form	$O(n)$
BNF	off-by-one error
boundary error	order 1 complexity
complexity	order arithmetic
computational complexity theory	order n complexity
constant complexity	postcondition
debugging	precondition
default assertion	semantic error
fence post error	side effect
grammar	syntactic error
invariant	syntax
linear complexity	syntax diagram
logic error	wolf fence
modular design	

References

Bentley, Jon. "Programming Pearls—Writing Correct Programs." This is a bimonthly series of articles on writing good programs appearing in the *Communications of the ACM* beginning in Vol. 26, No. 12 (December 1983).

Bentley, Jon. *Writing Efficient Programs.* Prentice-Hall, Englewood Cliffs, N.J., 1982.

Problems

2.1. Classify each of the following errors as syntactic, semantic, or logic. More than one category may apply.
   - A. A negative number was printed where a positive integer was expected.
   - B. A semicolon appears before an ELSE in a conditional statement.
   - C. An infinite loop occurs in the vicinity of the following statements:

```
Sum := 0;
N := 1;
WHILE N < 10 DO;
    BEGIN
        Sum := Sum + N;
        N := N + 1
    END;
```

   - D. The Pascal program compiles and terminates without error indication, but the user receives no output.
   - E. When PROCEDURE Sort (List, ListSize) is called, the list is sorted when printed out inside PROCEDURE Sort, but the list is in the same order before and after transferring control to the PROCEDURE Sort.

2.2. Prove by mathematical induction that $\sum_{i=1}^{n} i = n(n + 1)/2$ for all n and hence that this sum is $O(n^2)$.

2.3. Show that $\sum_{i=1}^{n} i^2$ is $O(n^3)$.

2.4. Compute another column for table 2.2 showing the complexity values for $n = 20$.

2.5. Assuming that it takes 100 nanoseconds for one calculation step, how long will it take to do thirty such calculations if the number of steps is n^3? To do fifty such calculations if the number of steps is 2^n?

2.6. Assuming that it takes 100 nanoseconds for one calculation step, how many calculations on a data set of size n can be done in 1 day, and in 1year, if the number of steps in a calculation is n, n^2, or 2^n? Solve for n = 10, 20, 50, 100, and 1000.

2.7. In discussing the list of names in section 2.5, we learned that the amount of effort required to find the first name is $O(1)$. How much effort is needed to find the twenty-fourth name? The last name? The longest name?

2.8. Suppose that we have two programs, A and B, which result in the same output when applied to a given set of data. Suppose that program A requires $44n\lg n$ steps to process a set of n data and program B requires $164n$ steps to process the same set. If the amount of time required per step is the same for both programs, when should program A be used and when should program B be used? If each step in program A requires 5 time units and each step in program B requires only 2 time units, now when should each program be used?

2.9. Give the complexity in order notation for each of the following tasks:
    A. Adding up a list of n numbers
    B. Reading in a list of twelve examination scores
    C. Setting all the elements of an $m \times n$ matrix to zero
    D. Printing out the sixteenth element of an array
    E. Determining whether or not the value 32 is present in a list of n
       integers
    F. Setting all the elements of a 10×10 matrix to zero
    G. Finding the largest or smallest value on a list of n reals
    H. Finding both the largest and smallest values at the same time on a list
       of length n
    I. Adding the elements of two lists of lengths m and n
    J. Printing out all the subsets of a set of n elements

2.10. Show that for any numbers a and n, $\log_a n = \log_a 2 \cdot \log_2 n$. Hence show that a
function is $O(\log_a n)$ if and only if it is $O(\lg n)$.

2.11. Use order arithmetic to evaluate the following:
    A. $O(1) + O(n^2) =$
    B. $O(n \lg n) + O(n^2) =$
    C. $O(n \lg n) + O(\lg n) =$
    D. $O(n^2 \lg n) + O(n^3) =$
    E. $O(n^2) \cdot O(n \lg n) =$
    F. $400\,O(n^2) - O(n^3) =$
    G. $O(2^n) + O(n^{24}) =$
    H. $O(e^n) + O(n!) =$
    I. $O(n^2 - 15n + 16) =$
    J. $O(\lg n!) =$
    K. $O(2^n) + O(2^n) =$
    L. $O(2^n) + O(5^n) =$

Programs

2.1. Write a procedure named "Convert" that takes a pair of positive integers a, b
(where $0 < a \le 366$ and $0 < b$) and converts them into a standard calendar
date. For example, the pair 6, 1985 produces "January 6, 1985" as output, while
the pair 67, 1988 causes "March 7, 1988" to be printed. Include adequate
assertions in your procedure.

3

Fundamental Data Types

Introduction

While it is convenient, and even important, to treat complex data types such as lists, tables, and records in the abstract, at some point even the most abstract data type must be implemented on a computer for it to be useful to us. In this chapter we discuss several fundamental data types that underlie all work on data structures and data types. We begin with data types that are so close to the computer that users do not usually even consider them. From there we move on to the basic types of data that are used daily, such as characters and numbers. We may think of these as "atomic" data types, upon which all other types are built. Finally, we consider two types, records and strings, that are more complex, forming perhaps basic "molecular" data types.

3.1 Bits, bytes, and words

Very early in the history of computing and communication theory it was postulated that the basic data structure is the **bit,** which may take on only two values—0 and 1, yes and no, or true and false. The argument for this is that, on the one hand it is difficult to conceive of any unit of "information" that is more primitive than a simple two value unit, while on the other hand all more complex information structures can be constructed from bits. The result has been that every digital computer in use today has, as the basis of its functioning, the electronic or magnetic equivalent of the bit. Character sets are developed in terms of their representation in bits. While we may think of computer arithmetic as decimal based, it is in fact binary (or sometimes hexadecimal) arithmetic. Even the binary tree, which we shall study in chapter 10, reflects the "yes/no" nature of the bit.

Note that we take bit to be an abstract data structure having only two values. The *concrete realization* of a bit is something quite different. It may be a pair of voltage levels, a direction of magnetization, a light bulb being on or off, or whether or not your car is in the driveway. The important point is that we are considering only *two* states for the bit. If we are representing the bit by a car in the driveway, the salient fact is whether the car is there or not, not the direction in which it is pointing or its color or any other fact about it.

While bits are the fundamental building blocks, they are so primitive that building data structures and types directly from them would be an exceedingly tedious task. It is as if we tried to describe a chair in terms of electrons, protons, and neutrons. The significance of the structure "chair" would be lost in the details of the description.

Very early in computing, people developed the habit of grouping bits together so that it would be easier to understand and discuss how a computer handles data. The groupings chosen, octal and hexadecimal, provide a larger range of symbols than just 0 and 1, and also lead to arithmetics that are close enough to decimal arithmetic that people can develop some sense of the data manipulation internal to the computer.

An **octal** representation uses bits in groups of three. If we represent a bit by 0 or 1, then the octal representation has eight different symbols, usually considered to be

0, 1, 2, ... , 7

that denote the groups

000, 001, 010, ... , 111.

Hexadecimal representation uses groups of four bits, resulting in sixteen different symbols. These are written as

0, 1, ... , 9, *A, B, ... , F,*

representing the groups

0000, 0001, ... , 1001, 1010, 1011, ... , 1111.

Octal and hexadecimal representations of data are not used by most computer users but still are important to system developers, who must work close to the machine.

Still primitive, but at a sufficiently high level that we can make some use of the concept, is the **byte**, defined to be a group of eight bits. Since each bit can take on two different values, a byte can take on any of $2^8 = 256$ different values. Now consider the following. We have (in English) twenty-six letters, which we will probably want to represent as both upper- and lowercase letters. We also have ten digits, about fifteen or sixteen common punctuation marks, and several other symbols, such as $+$, #, $, %, $<$, $>$, @, and the blank space. In all, we have roughly eighty-five to ninety symbols that are commonly used. Thus we can assign a different byte value to each of our common symbols and have plenty left over for other symbols, such as italic letters and graphic symbols, and for various control codes, such as the carriage return and the line feed. In short, the byte has enough flexibility in its values that we can use it as a basic data structure.

The assignment of byte values to different symbols is called **encoding.** Several different codes for symbols exist, the most common being **ASCII** and **EBCDIC** (see appendix A). Since the common symbols and control codes use fewer than half the available values, there is general agreement only on the code values 0 through 127. The values 128 through 255 may be used for italics (as they are by Epson printers), for graphics (as they are by the IBM PC), or in some other way. Some systems permit the user to define his or her own code values. For international data transmission, some of the codes that are not used for numerals or upper- or lowercase letters, including code values less than 128, are available for letters and symbols that are specific to a non-English language, such as Danish, German, or Spanish.

One other common data structure is the **word.** A word is a group of one or more bytes, generally one, two, or four. While we will not be directly concerned with words (in this sense), we will be interested in them insofar as their exact definition is closely related to the design of a given type of computer. The word is generally the largest group of bytes that can be handled as a unit by all the computer components, such as the registers and data channels.

In summary, we have three fundamental data structures, the bit, the byte, and the word, upon which other structures are built. For our purposes, the byte is the most important of these, since it permits representation of all the characters we normally use, together with all the basic control codes for a computer. If we think of the byte as a *data type,* we must define operations for it. These are kept at a very primitive level. The only operations that we assume are the ability to set a byte to a given value and to compare two bytes for equality. All other operations are defined only for more complex abstract data types. These data are generally represented by grouping bytes together in various ways, much as a chemist constructs a molecule by grouping atoms together.

3.2 Boolean data

The most primitive data type beyond the bits and bytes level is the **boolean** or **logical** data type. The underlying data structure is the bit, since a boolean data type can take on only two values—"true" and "false," the values of a bit. However, even though a bit is the underlying structure, different systems may choose to implement the boolean data type as a byte or in some other way. Note that in this case, only two out of many possible values are really being used.

A data type consists of a data structure together with a set of operations. The operations we desire for the boolean data type are the usual logical operations—*and, or, not, implication,* and *equivalence.* In addition, we must have operations to build and destroy the data type. Here is an abstract data type (ADT) for boolean. Each operation returns an error if its boolean variables are undefined.

NewBoolean (BooleanName)—defines a boolean variable, with no assigned value.

MakeTrue (BooleanName)—assigns the value "true" to BooleanName.

MakeFalse (BooleanName)—assigns the value "false" to BooleanName.

IsItTrue (BooleanName)—returns the value "true" if the value of BooleanName is true, "false" if the value of BooleanName is false, and an error if the value of BooleanName is undefined.

IsItFalse (BooleanName)—returns the value "true" if the value of BooleanName is false, "false" if the value of BooleanName is true, and an error if the value of BooleanName is undefined.

Assign (BooleanName1, BooleanName2)—assigns the value of BooleanName2 to BooleanName1. It returns an error if either variable is undefined or the value of BooleanName2 is undefined.

Table 3.1   The Boolean ADT as implemented in Pascal

ADT	Pascal
NewBoolean (BooleanName)	VAR BooleanName : boolean;
MakeTrue (BooleanName)	BooleanName := true;
MakeFalse (BooleanName)	BooleanName := false;
IsItTrue (BooleanName)	BooleanName = true
(Alternatively, this can be implemented simply as BooleanName, since this has the value "true" if and only if BooleanName has the value "true.")	
IsItFalse (BooleanName)	BooleanName = false
(Alternatively, this can be implemented simply as NOT (BooleanName), since this has the value "true" if and only if BooleanName has the value "false.")	
Assign (BooleanName1, BooleanName2)	BooleanName1 := BooleanName2;
And (BooleanName1, BooleanName2)	BooleanName1 AND BooleanName2
Or (BooleanName1, BooleanName2)	BooleanName1 OR BooleanName2
Not (BooleanName)	NOT BooleanName
Delete (BooleanName)	No explicit operation

And (BooleanName1, BooleanName2)—returns the value "true" if both BooleanName1 and BooleanName2 have the value true, "false" if either has the value false, and an error if either value is undefined. This operation is called **conjunction.**

Or (BooleanName1, BooleanName2)—returns the value "true" if either BooleanName1 or BooleanName2 has the value true, "false" if both have the value false, and an error if either value is undefined. This operation is called **disjunction** or **inclusive or.**

Not (BooleanName)—returns the value "true" if the value of BooleanName is false, "false" if the value of BooleanName is true, and an error otherwise. This operation is called **negation.**

Delete (BooleanName)—deletes the variable BooleanName.

The definition of the other logical operators, **exclusive or, implication,** and **equivalence,** is left as an exercise.

Since we wish to use the type boolean in programming, each of the functions and procedures within the ADT must be implemented in proper code within the language we choose. In Pascal, boolean is one of the basic defined data types. Thus the translation is direct, with a single expression or statement corresponding to each of the ADT definitions. This correspondence is shown in table 3.1.

Creation and deletion are handled rather differently from the other operations. A (boolean) variable is created at compile time simply by declaring it. We have no way in Pascal of creating a new variable during program execution. In contrast, the other operations are set up at compile time but actually carried out during program execution.

Pascal also does not give us the ability to delete a variable explicitly. Deletion occurs only in the sense that local variables are not available outside of their defining routines. Thus we could take the view that if BooleanName is declared in procedure "FixUp," it is created whenever FixUp is called and deleted as soon as we exit from FixUp. This is, in fact, close to the way many Pascal systems operate, in terms of space allocation.

3.3 Characters

A **character** is one of the symbols we can represent in an encoding, and hence manipulate by programs. The exact definition of what is or is not considered a character is heavily implementation dependent. Here are some possible examples:

The set of all uppercase letters.

The set of all upper- and lowercase letters, and numerals.

The set of all upper- and lowercase letters, numerals, and punctuation marks.

The set of all uppercase Greek letters.

The set of all Roman numerals.

The above examples show a dependence on the user's concept and need. The set of all uppercase letters might be just exactly the character set needed to teach a preschooler how to write, while the set of all Roman numerals might meet the needs of a clockmaker. Here are two more character sets; these sets depend on knowing something about how characters are represented in a computer:

The set of all symbols that have ASCII representations from 32 to 126 (decimal). This includes upper- and lowercase letters, numerals, punctuation marks, the blank space, and such symbols as $, %, *, +,ˆ, <, and > (see appendix A).

The set of all symbols that have ASCII representations from 0 to 127 (decimal).

Whatever the set chosen, the encodings commonly used in computing have three properties:

The order of the numerals is preserved; that is, the encoding for 0 precedes (numerically) the encoding for 1, which precedes the encoding for 2, and so forth.

The order of the lowercase letters is preserved; that is, "a" comes before "b," which comes before "c," and so forth.

The order of the uppercase letters is preserved.

It may or may not be true that these encodings are kept separate. For example, in ASCII the numerals have codes from 48 through 57, the uppercase letters have codes from 65 through 90, and the lowercase letters have codes from 97 through 122. In EBCDIC, however, the encodings for the upper- and lowercase letters are split up, with other characters stuck in between (see appendix A).

Characters constitute a very primitive data type, since there is little that can be done with individual characters other than compare them. Here is the ADT.

NewChar (CharName)—defines a character variable, with no assigned value.

Assign (CharName1, CharName2)—assigns the value of CharName2 to CharName1. It returns an error if either CharName1 or CharName2 is undefined, or if CharName2 has no defined value. Note: CharName2 may be a character name or a specific, constant value, often represented in single quotes. Thus we might have **Assign** (CharName, 'a') or **Assign** (CharName, '*').

AreTheyEqual (CharName1, CharName2)—returns the value "true" if CharName1 and CharName2 have the same value, "false" if they have different values, and an error otherwise.

Encode (CharName)—returns the numerical code value (in a specific coding scheme) assigned to the value of CharName. It returns an error if CharName is undefined or has no assigned value.

Decode (CodeValue)—returns the character value corresponding to CodeValue. It returns an error if CodeValue is undefined or not a legitimate numerical code value (in a specific coding scheme).

ADT	Pascal
Table 3.2 The Character ADT as implemented in Pascal	
NewChar (CharName)	VAR CharName : char;
Assign (CharName1, CharName2)	CharName1 := CharName2;
AreTheyEqual (CharName1, CharName2)	CharName1 = CharName2
Encode (CharName)	ord (CharName);
Decode (CodeValue)	chr (CodeValue);
Precedes (CharName1, CharName2)	CharName1 < CharName2
Delete (CharName)	No explicit operation

Precedes (CharName1, CharName2)—returns "true" if Encode (CharName1) < Encode (CharName2), "false" if Encode (CharName1) $\geq$ Encode (CharName2), and an error otherwise.

Delete (CharName)—deletes the variable CharName and returns an error if CharName is undefined.

The Pascal implementation of this ADT is given in table 3.2.

3.4 Integers

Characters are fine for word processing and much of the work with databases. But since the ADTs do not include any arithmetic operations, we do not have the capability of doing such operations on characters. Obviously, we need some numerical data types to provide this capability. The first of these is the **integer** type.

We shall not immediately concern ourselves with the internal representation of integers: first, we must discuss the ADT. Thus we assume that we have a data structure called an integer, which for our purposes must be capable of representing whole numbers, positive or negative, whose absolute value is at most some highest value **MaxSize**. That is, if N is an integer variable, then we assume that the values of N have all the properties we associate with whole numbers (positive or negative) and that

$|N| \leq$ MaxSize.

Here is the ADT for finite integer arithmetic. It includes the standard arithmetic operations, along with tests for integer equality and inequality. Within this set of definitions the phrase **reduced to within range** means that, if the result of the operation (without size limits) is N, then the value used in the ADT is

N mod MaxSize if $N \geq 0$,

$-(-N$ mod MaxSize) if $N < 0$.

For example, if MaxSize = 100, then 22 * 40 = 80, and −53 + −69 = −22. Similarly, we say that N is **out of range** if $N >$ MaxSize or $N < -$MaxSize.

Create (IntegerName)—defines an integer variable, IntegerName, with an undefined value.

Assign (IntegerName1, IntegerName2)—assigns the value of IntegerName2 to IntegerName1. IntegerName2 may be either an integer name or a representation of a whole number, N (positive or negative), such that $|N| \leq$ MaxSize. The result is an error if either argument is undefined or the value of IntegerName2 or N is out of range.

AreTheyEqual (IntegerName1, IntegerName2)—returns "true" if the values of IntegerName1 and IntegerName2 are equal, "false" if they are unequal, and an error if either argument is undefined or has no assigned value.

IsLessThan (IntegerName1, IntegerName2)—returns "true" if IntegerName1 $<$ IntegerName2, "false" if IntegerName1 $\geq$ IntegerName2, and an error if either argument is undefined or has no assigned value.

Negative (IntegerName)—returns the negative of IntegerName. The result is an error if IntegerName is undefined or has no assigned value.

Sum (IntegerName1, IntegerName2)—returns IntegerName1 $+$ IntegerName2, reduced to within range. The result is an error if either variable is undefined or has no assigned value.

Difference (IntegerName1, IntegerName2)—returns IntegerName1 $-$ IntegerName2, reduced to within range. The result is an error if either variable is undefined or has no assigned value.

Product (IntegerName1, IntegerName2)—returns IntegerName1 $*$ IntegerName2, reduced to within range. The result is an error if either variable is undefined or has no assigned value.

Quotient (IntegerName1, IntegerName2)—returns the greatest integer less than or equal to IntegerName1/IntegerName2, reduced to within range. The result is an error if either variable is undefined or has no assigned value, or if IntegerName2 has the value zero.

Mod (IntegerName1, IntegerName2)—returns the remainder resulting from IntegerName1/IntegerName2, with the condition that

$$0 \leq \text{Mod (IntegerName1, IntegerName2)} < \text{IntegerName2}.$$

The result is an error if either variable is undefined or has no assigned value, or if IntegerName2 has the value zero.

Delete (IntegerName)—deletes the variable IntegerName. It returns an error if IntegerName is undefined.

The ADT definition is somewhat complicated as a concession to the fact that any computer has only a finite range of integer values that can be represented in a computer word. We could easily write an ADT for "genuine" integer arithmetic that does not have any limitation on the size of an integer. However, any implementation would then not be consistent with the ADT, since the implementation must address the maximum size limit. We have chosen instead to include the size limitation in the ADT. Then, while this limit may be different for various computer systems, any implementation can conform to the ADT.

The specific MaxSize limit depends on the computer manufacturer's choice of word size for its software. With a one byte word, the maximum size is $2^7 - 1 = 127$, since one bit of the eight must be reserved for the sign. (Alternatively, some software allows for representation of only non-negative integers, which would then fall within the range from 0 to 255.) A two byte word expands this range to $2^{15} - 1 = 32,767$. While this is a much more reasonable value for most computations and is used by some popular implementations such as Turbo Pascal, for some computations even this is too small. Thus some computers use three or four bytes to represent an integer. Others, particularly microcomputers, will use two bytes to represent an integer and then define an extended type, **long integer,** which has the same ADT as an integer but a word size limit of four bytes.

While the ADT for integer may seem complicated by the need to limit the size of the results of operations, this limitation is generally accomplished automatically, through the overflow mechanism of the computer, so that the programmer need not worry about it unless the program halts. For example, $101 + 175 = 276$ in normal arithmetic. Using binary numerals, this becomes

$$01100101 + 10101111 = 100010100.$$

Observe that the result has nine bits. The overflow mechanisms of the computer using a one byte word would automatically ignore the high order bit, producing the result 00010100, or $20 = 276 \bmod 256$. Be aware, however, that in some computers that extra bit is taken to be a sign bit, so that the result would be interpreted as -20.

The Pascal implementation of this ADT is given in table 3.3. The identifier maxint used in the table to denote the limit on the size of an integer is a standard identifier recognized by all Pascal compilers. However, its value depends on the particular implementation.

3.5 Real numbers

The ADT for the data type **real** is quite similar to that for integer. In fact, **Create, Assign, AreTheyEqual, IsLessThan, Negative, Sum, Difference, Product,** and **Delete** can be defined in exactly the same way, generally with a different value of

Table 3.3	The Integer ADT as implemented in Pascal
ADT	**Pascal**
MaxSize	maxint (a system-defined constant)
Create (IntegerName)	VAR IntegerName : integer;
Assign (IntegerName1, IntegerName2)	IntegerName1 := IntegerName2;
AreTheyEqual (IntegerName1, IntegerName2)	IntegerName1 = IntegerName2
IsLessThan (IntegerName1, IntegerName2)	IntegerName1 < IntegerName2
Negative (IntegerName)	−IntegerName
Sum (IntegerName1, IntegerName2)	IntegerName1 + IntegerName2
Difference (IntegerName1, IntegerName2)	IntegerName1 − IntegerName2
Product (IntegerName1, IntegerName2)	IntegerName1 * IntegerName2
Quotient (IntegerName1, IntegerName2)	IntegerName1 DIV IntegerName2
Mod (IntegerName1, IntegerName2)	IntegerName1 MOD IntegerName2
(Note that ISO Standard Pascal agrees with the ADT definition but that some implementations, notably the IBM Pascal compiler, define $(K * N)$ MOD N to be N, not 0.)	
Delete (IntegerName)	No explicit operation

MaxSize. The function **Quotient** is defined slightly differently, to mirror the usual arithmetic division of real numbers, and the function **Mod** is not defined for the data type real. In each case, there must be provision for keeping the result of an operation within the range limits of the computer.

Because of the close similarity between the integer and real ADTs, we could terminate our discussion at this point. However, it is useful to point out that a difference in implementation exists and that there is a reason for this difference.

We have discussed the MaxSize limitation on the integer data type. While this poses no problem for many calculations, it causes difficulties when the calculations involve very large numbers. Some alternative way of representing these large numbers is needed. Also, integer arithmetic suffers from the fundamental limitation that division does not always yield integer results. Hence some way must be found to represent non-integer values. The representation usually chosen for real numbers solves both these problems. It is capable both of handling very large (and very small) numbers and of representing non-integer values. However, since we must still contend with the reality of a finite word size in the computer, some accuracy is lost, since not all numbers within the allowable range can be represented. For example, if our representation range is limited to 1,000,000 but we have only four digits of accuracy, then we cannot distinguish among 356 214, 356 200, and 356 279: all must be represented as 356 200.

The usual computer representation of real numbers is in terms of a **mantissa,** or value part, and an **exponent,** or size part. The mantissa is generally taken as a value between 0 and 1 whose leading digit is not 0, and the exponent is used as a multiplying factor to make the value larger or smaller. Both the mantissa and the exponent may have positive or negative values. The first examples below are given in decimal notation with 10 as the base of the exponent (E = 10). The usual written representation is

<mantissa sign> . <mantissa> E <exponent sign> <exponent>

+.123E+2	= 12.3
+.123E−2	= 0.00123
−.421E+11	= −42,100,000,000
−.421E−5	= −0.00000421.

The next examples are given in binary form (E = 2):

+.110111E+101	= 11011.1
+.110111E−11	= 0.000110111
−.10101E+111	= −1010100
−.10101E−10	= −0.0010101.

On a typical microcomputer, real number representation may use three bytes for the mantissa and one byte for the exponent. Notice that the leading digit in the binary representation is always 1. Knowing this, we can omit that from the representation. This allows us to represent both positive and negative numbers without the need for an extra sign bit for the mantissa. To avoid a sign bit for the exponent we offset the exponent by half the allowable range of values. One byte allows us to represent values from 0 through 255. Offsetting by half the range (128), we interpret these as representing the exponents from −128 through +127. Here is how this works using a four bit exponent so that the offset is 8:

.010111E0011	= +0.00000110111
.010111E1100	= +1101.11
.110111E0101	= −0.000110111
.110111E1010	= −11.0111.

The values we can represent in this way are large enough for all except the most astronomical calculations. The largest mantissa we can represent contains a leading 0 followed by twenty-three 1's. Since we are counting on omitting the leading 1 from the number, the largest mantissa is

+0.1111   1111   1111   1111   1111   1111,

which has the value $1 - 2^{-24}$. Multiplying this by the exponential part, 2^{127}, we find that the largest number we can represent is

$2^{127} - 2^{103}$, approximately $1.701412\text{E}+38$.

With integer numbers we encounter a difficulty when the value of an operation, such as **Sum** or **Product,** exceeds the word size. This condition, called **overflow,** causes a reduction of the value to within range, by truncation of the high order bits. With real numbers the problem is somewhat different. The high order bits of the mantissa are always kept, with the low order bits truncated. Since the highest bit in the mantissa is used to carry the sign, the exponent is adjusted to maintain the second highest order bit of the mantissa as 1. This is called **normalization.** Normalization may cause a loss of accuracy.

For example, let us suppose that we have a four bit mantissa (just to keep the numbers small) and a three bit exponent. Let us consider multiplying 11 by 9. Here is the process (binary representation, mantissa and exponent):

11:          $+.1011\text{E}+100$

9:           $+.1001\text{E}+100.$

The product is 99, or 01100011 in binary notation. The real representation takes the four high order bits that start with a 1, and adjusts the exponent to compensate:

99:          $+.1100\text{E}+111.$

Observe that if we translate this directly back into a binary integer notation, 1100000, we have a representation of 96, not 99!

Thus we see that overflow does not occur for real numbers as it does for integer numbers but that there is a resultant loss of accuracy. This does not mean that we cannot have overflow. From the example we see that the value of the exponent has increased to accommodate the higher value of the number. Overflow for real numbers occurs when the value of the exponent exceeds the room allowed. On a typical microcomputer, the exponent value can be as large as $+2^7 - 1$ (allowing for a sign), so that the "real" exponent can be as large as 2^{127}. We can represent very large real numbers, with limited accuracy.

Real numbers also have a problem with **underflow,** when the exponent becomes too small. Since the exponent value can be as small as -2^7, the "real" exponent can be as small as 2^{-128}. If an operation generates an exponent smaller than this, we cannot represent it, and underflow occurs.

An exception to these rules is made for representing 0, since this is a very important number. Obviously, the mantissa of 0 contains no 1, so we cannot adjust the exponent to place a 1 in the second bit. The easiest way to represent 0 is to declare that it is represented by a mantissa and exponent of 0, and then check for a 0 mantissa whenever that is important, such as in division.

One final accuracy problem for real numbers must be mentioned. This is the loss of accuracy that can occur when operations result in nearly canceling numbers out. Here is an example:

Subtraction: $+.1011E-011 - +.1010E-011 = +.1000E-110.$

On the surface, this calculation appears to be perfectly correct. The problem arises from our not knowing how accurate the representations of the two original numbers are; hence we cannot guarantee that the three 0's in the resultant mantissa have any meaning. Remember that we have only four bits of each of the original numbers, and consider this. Suppose that the first number is really 0.00010110111 and the second number is really 0.00010100001. Then subtraction would yield 0.00000010110, which would be represented as $+.1011E-110$, not the value $+.1000E-110$ which we found. This type of inaccuracy is called **truncation error.**

Closely related to truncation error is **roundoff error.** This occurs when a user or a system rounds a number up or down, to maintain as much accuracy as possible. The dividing point is taken as half the maximum allowable truncated portion. For example, consider the numbers 0.1101011 and 0.1101101, and suppose that we can only store four bits. The remaining bits can be divided into the low half (000, 001, 010, 011) and the high half (100, 101, 110, 111). The remainder in the first number is 011, in the low half, so that the number is "rounded down" to 0.1101. The remainder in the second number is 101, in the high half, so that the number is "rounded up" by adding 1 to the fourth position, resulting in 0.1110. In both situations, roundoff error has been introduced.

The study of these errors and **error propagation** as they accumulate through several operations is part of the branch of mathematics called **numerical analysis.**

In summary, for real numbers the values at which overflow and underflow occur are very extreme, and unlikely to be encountered in most calculations. However, we do have accuracy problems that can be severe.

3.6 Records

A mathematician thinking of a set assumes that there is some way to distinguish the elements of the set from those entities not in the set. While this assumption does not imply any underlying **homogeneity** of the elements, in most cases such homogeneity is present. Thus the mathematician is likely to think of a set of integers or a set of real numbers, and is unlikely to use a set whose elements include some numbers, some geometric figures, and some arrays.

Yet, in computing, many of the data we handle have this mixed character. We want, for example, to deal with personnel records, which contain relatively fixed alphabetic information (name, address, office location, starting employment date, and so forth); free form alphabetic information (evaluative comments); numerical data which we use in computations (salary, number of dependents, age); and numerical data which are basically codes, not subject to computations (social security number, telephone number). In most programming languages, including Pascal, an array is not the proper structure for these data, because the data within an array are assumed to be homogeneous. The data structure that provides capabilities for handling **heterogeneous** data is often called a **record.** In this section, we treat the record as a data structure that will allow us to store mixed types of data. We introduce these (or any other) data structures to provide a logical picture of the data that corresponds more closely to reality in some situations.

A record is a set of fields, with each **field** in turn having its own structure. As with all structures on the computer, we assume that the number of elements (fields) is finite. We also assume that the order or sequencing of the fields is not significant. Because a record is a highly flexible structure, very few operations can be built into its ADT. Most operations defined on a record are dependent on the specific application and relate to the structure of the fields within the record. Here is the record ADT.

Create (RecordName, FieldName1, . . . , FieldNamen)—defines a record variable, RecordName, with fields specified by FieldName1, . . . , FieldNamen. Each field name must be a variable of a defined data type, with an error occurring if any one is not. The value of RecordName is undefined.

Assign (RecordName, FieldName, FieldValue)—sets the value of FieldName within RecordName to FieldValue, with an error occurring if FieldValue is not of the same type as FieldName. The result is an error if FieldValue is undefined or if FieldName is not the name of a field in RecordName.

Delete (RecordName)—deletes the variable RecordName.

Operations within a record are carried out on the fields of the record and derive their values directly from the data types pertaining to the fields. For example, two records are considered equal when they have the same defined fields and when each field in one record has the same value as its counterpart in the other record.

Because a record is constructed from several fields, it may exist in various states of semidefinition. On the one hand, when we create a record, we do not automatically supply values for its fields. Hence they are all undefined, and it is appropriate to consider the record value as undefined. On the other hand, we expect at some point in our work to have assigned values to each field in the record, at which time the record may certainly be considered to have a defined value. But there are intermediate states in which some field values are defined while others are not; and some of these states may persist over long periods of time. For example, an instructor may wish to create a student record containing all the grades on assignments and tests for a specific course. It is reasonable to create the record when the course starts, but the last value in the record cannot

Table 3.4   The Record ADT as implemented in Pascal

ADT	Pascal

Create (RecordName, FieldName1, . . . , FieldName*n*)	VAR
	    RecordName = RECORD
	                FieldName1 : Field1Type;
	                FieldName2 : Field2Type;
	                . . .
	                FieldName*n* : Field*n*Type
	    END;
	where the field types are defined data types.

Assign (RecordName, FieldName, FieldValue)	RecordName.FieldName := FieldValue;
Delete (RecordName)	No explicit operation

be supplied until some weeks later, when the course ends. For this reason, we usually assume that a record is "defined" once it has been created, but we acknowledge that a "defined" record may contain undefined field values. We match the record ADT to a Pascal implementation in table 3.4.

Suppose that we construct a record called "Biography." In Pascal, this record is defined by the statement in figure 3.1. As usual, we can also define a record TYPE and then define one or more variables of that type. The two significant points to note are that the number of fields is arbitrary and that each field has its own type definition. Thus the record concept allows us to gather together into one structure diverse types of data.

In particular, a field within a record can itself be a record. In this way we can build data structures consisting of records of records of... .

We note that Pascal requires that the type specifications of the fields be constants rather than computable values. Within that limitation, however, we are free to use both scalar and structured type specifications. We might, for example, use the RECORD definition in figure 3.2 in connection with a transportation study.

When we have several record types to define, with structured fields, it is good practice to define first a type identifier whose type is the desired structure. For example, figure 3.3 is a fuller definition of the variable "Biography." In this definition, the various character arrays are defined with appropriate sizes. If these sizes prove inadequate, then the definitions can be changed. Similarly, the use of subrange bounds on the number of dependents puts a reasonable limit on this value: the system will automatically reject any claim of more than ten dependents, which may catch some data entry errors. If there are legitimate claims for more dependents, then the upper bound on this subrange must be changed. The telephone and social security numbers are defined as characters, since no computation will be done with them. In contrast, both the number of dependents and the salary will be used in computations, so they are defined as numerical types.

Figure 3.1   Initial definition of "Biography"

```
VAR
  Biography : RECORD
                   Field1 : Field1Type;
                   Field2 : Field2Type;
                   . . .
                   Fieldn : FieldnType
              END;
```

Figure 3.2   Transportation record

```
VAR
  Transportation : RECORD
                       Vehicle   : (Car, Bus, Train, Bicycle);
                       Cost      : real;
                       Distance  : 1..100;
                       Direction : (North, South, East, West)
                   END;
```

Figure 3.3   Second definition of "Biography"

```
TYPE
  NameType    = PACKED ARRAY[1..25] OF char;
  AddressType = PACKED ARRAY[1..30] OF char;
  CityType    = PACKED ARRAY[1..15] OF char;
  StateType   = PACKED ARRAY[1..2]  OF char;
  ZipType     = PACKED ARRAY[1..5]  OF char;
  NumberType  = PACKED ARRAY[1..11] OF char;
  FamilySize  = 1..10;

VAR
  Biography : RECORD
                  RecordId             : integer;
                  Name                 : NameType;
                  SpouseName           : NameType;
                  Street               : AddressType;
                  City                 : CityType;
                  State                : StateType;
                  ZipCode              : ZipType;
                  Phone                : NumberType;
                  SocialSecurityNumber : NumberType;
                  NumberOfDependents   : FamilySize;
                  Salary               : real
              END;
```

Figure 3.4   Third definition of "Biography"

```
TYPE
  NameType     = PACKED ARRAY[1..25] OF char;
  AddressType  = RECORD
                   Street  : PACKED ARRAY[1..30] OF char;
                   City    : PACKED ARRAY[1..15] OF char;
                   State   : PACKED ARRAY[1..2]  OF char;
                   Zip     : PACKED ARRAY[1..5]  OF char
                 END;
  NumberType   = PACKED ARRAY[1..11] OF char;
  FamilySize   = 1..10;

VAR
  Biography : RECORD
                RecordId               : integer;
                Name                   : NameType;
                SpouseName             : NameType;
                Address                : AddressType;
                Phone                  : NumberType;
                SocialSecurityNumber   : NumberType;
                NumberOfDependents     : FamilySize;
                Salary                 : real
              END;
```

To show the use of records within records, let us redesign the Biography record, collecting together all the address information into one record. The result is figure 3.4. This definition of records within records has two uses. First, it tends to simplify and clarify the major record definition, reducing the number of distinct fields to be considered. In our example, we have one "Address" field rather than four separate ones for the address components. Second, since this address field is separately defined as a record type in its own right, that definition can be incorporated into other record specifications. We might, for example, have types MedicalRecord, EmploymentRecord, and CreditRecord, each of which contains a field of the type AddressType.

One important field in a record is an **identifier** or **index** field, a field that provides a label for the record. We often use records when dealing with large numbers of data. Under such circumstances we must be able to identify and handle individual records quickly. Some storage methods permit rapid access to any record, but most such methods still require a means of verifying that we have found the correct record. An identifier field provides a unique code for each record. This code can be used to locate the record or verify that it has been found. In our Biography records, the identifier field is called RecordId and is given as an integer in case we wish to do numerical comparisons of the identifiers for sorting or other purposes.

An index field serves much the same purpose but may also be thought of as a characteristic of a group of records, enabling us to reach a certain portion of the data structure quickly. The Biography records contain no index field. If we wanted one, we might break the Name field into FamilyName and FirstName, using FamilyName as the index field. This would identify all records belonging to members of the same family, assuming that people are related if and only if they have the same family name. We could then create an index into all these records.

A key factor in the successful manipulation of large numbers of large records is the use of index and identifier fields for most of the manipulation. Suppose, for example, that we have 30,000 records, each containing 300 units of data. (The unit might be a byte, a character, an integer, or some other unit.) This might be the situation in the personnel records of a large company or in the student records of a large university. In total, we have 9,000,000 units of data. Suppose that we wish to sort these records and that we choose an efficient sorting method that will operate in $O(n \lg n)$ time. Thus we can estimate that sorting the records will take $450,000k$ units of time, since $n \lg n$ is approximately $30,000 \times 15$. But what is k? It is basically the amount of time it takes to process a single record, that is, to compare and move 300 units of data. Using identifier and index fields can cut this time greatly. With the most compact coding, we need fifteen bits of data to identify each record uniquely, since this will allow identification of 2^{15} = 32,768 records. We also need another fifteen bits to identify the location of each record. Thus, in a byte-oriented computer, we would use four bytes for identification and location. Suppose that we have a table of identifiers for the set of records, each entry in the table consisting of an identifier and a location. We can effectively sort the entire set of records by sorting only on the identifier. Thus we would need to handle only four bytes of data per record, rather than 300 units, to sort the set of records. Assuming that each data unit requires one byte of storage, this cuts the value of k by a factor of 75. Let's look at a simple example.

Consider the Biography records in figure 3.5. Each record contains 124 characters of data, plus two integers (RecordId and NumberOfDependents) and a real number (Salary). Assuming that each character requires 1 byte of storage, each integer requires 1 byte, and each real requires 4 bytes, we need 130 bytes per record. With only ten records, there are still 1300 bytes of data to be moved in any sorting operation.

The first element in each record shown in figure 3.5 is the RecordId, which uniquely identifies it. Now consider the table of figure 3.6a. This contains each record identifier (RecordId) and social security number. Either will serve as a unique identifier for the record. The RecordId numbers have the advantage of following the storage order; the social security numbers, however, have meaning to the outside world. Therefore we may wish to sort and print the records in social security number order. By sorting the table instead of the records themselves, we arrive at a table in social security number order (fig. 3.6b) which identifies for us the order in which the records should be retrieved and printed. As we can see, sorting the index table requires manipulation of only 120 bytes of data—12 bytes per record.

Figure 3.5   Sample collection of Biography records

Record 1:   1
David Zichtermann
Annabelle Zichtermann
235 West Cedar Street
West Lafayette
Indiana
47906
317–427–3030
441–17–5208
3
4350.50

Record 2:   2
Clarabelle Schnozzle

. . .
763–24–0869 { social security number }
. . .

Record 3:   3
Archie Wingdinger

. . .
225–30–1007
. . .

Record 4:   4
Dennis DelNoche

. . .
545–45–4545
. . .

. . .

Record 10:   10
William Smith

. . .
235–71–1131

Figure 3.6   Index table for sample collection of records

RecordId	SocialSecurityNumber	RecordId	SocialSecurityNumber
1	441–17–5208	6	035–31–5764
2	763–24–0869	7	123–45–6789
3	225–30–1007	3	225–30–1007
4	545–45–4545	10	235–71–1131
5	812–49–7083	1	441–17–5208
6	035–31–5764	8	449–57–8321
7	123–45–6789	4	545–45–4545
8	449–57–8321	9	695–03–4817
9	695–03–4817	2	763–24–0869
10	235–71–1131	5	812–49–7083
(a)		*(b)*	

Pascal provides two methods for accessing individual fields within a record. The basic method is the **dot method,** which consists of specifying the full name in the form

```
RecordName.FieldName
```

Thus some of the fields of our Biography record would be Biography.Name, Biography.Address, Biography.Phone, and Biography.Salary. While this method is satisfactory for infrequent field accesses, it obviously becomes tedious when nearly every line of a program accesses a record field. As an alternative, Pascal provides the **WITH** operator, which can be used to name a record for subsequent use. The format is

```
WITH RecordList DO action;
```

where "RecordList" consists of one or more record identifiers separated by commas, and "action" consists of the program statements to be executed for the named records. Generally, "action" will be a compound statement, surrounded by BEGIN . . . END. This operator permits use of the various fields in the named records without explicit reference to the record name. For example, if we write

```
WITH Biography DO
   BEGIN
      .
      .
      .
   END;
```

then whatever action is specified between the BEGIN and the END can refer to Name, Address.Street, Address.City, Salary, or any of the other fields of the Biography record without the use of the prefix "Biography.". Similarly, if we also have a record called "Department," then we could write

```
WITH Biography, Department DO
   BEGIN
      .
      .
      .
   END;
```

and use fields from each of these records in our computation. Obviously, if the field names are not distinct, there is the possibility of confusion. Pascal has a set of **scoping rules** that determine when different variable names and operators are valid. These rules resolve this issue by declaring that the field name used by itself refers to the last named record in the appropriate list. Thus, if Department also has a field called "Salary," the use of Salary by itself within this code segment would refer to Department.Salary, not Biography.Salary. To refer to the latter, we would need to use the full specification, Biography.Salary, which includes the record name.

A typical application of WITH arises when dates are involved. We might define the data type Date by

```
TYPE
   Date = RECORD
            Month : (January, February, March,
                     April,    May,      June,
                     July,     August,   September,
                     October,  November, December);
            Day   : 1..31;
            Year  : 0..2000
          END;
```

If we define different variables of type Date, such as BirthDate and StartingDate, it would make sense to use the construction

```
WITH StartingDate DO
```

in a search of personnel records. Note, however, that if we want to examine one person's data in detail, then it may be necessary to use the full field specification, such as BirthDate.Month or StartingDate.Month.

Finally, we observe that just as the fields of records can be other structures, so also may records be used as components in different types of structures. We can define, for example, an array of records.

In summary, records may have an arbitrary (finite) number of fields, each having its own structure; and in turn, records can be used as components in other structured types, such as arrays and sets. Nested records (records of records) are useful when several fields can appropriately be grouped together, either for clarity in presentation or for use in a variety of different record definitions.

3.7 Strings

The data type **string** has as its base structure a concatenated group of characters, such as words in a sentence, letters in a word, or characters on a license plate. Thus one of the key properties of strings is that they tend to vary greatly in length. We have, for example, many very short words. But there are also some very long words, which occur in scientific disciplines or arise from non-English languages. For example, one of the longest words known is the name of a New Zealand mountain peak:

Taumatawhakatangihangakoauauotamateapokaiwhenuakitanatahu.

Similarly, sentences range from short ones to those with over 12,500 words, like the last sentence of James Joyce's *Ulysses*. Thus one of the practical problems to be addressed in handling strings is how to store them efficiently.

Before we address this problem, let us define an ADT for the data type "string." While we found little we could do with individual characters, there is a great deal we can do with strings. The operations we might like to do include comparison, finding a specified substring, deleting part of a string, inserting new characters in a string, and concatenating two strings. We might also be interested in determining the length of a string, that is, the number of characters it contains. Finally, we shall certainly be interested in sorting strings, for we shall want to put lists of names in alphabetical order, just to cite one use of strings. Here is an ADT for strings. We define the **null string** to be a string containing no characters. Note that the null string is a specific string constant, rather than a string with an undefined value.

NewString (StringName)—defines a string variable, with no assigned value.

AssignString (StringName1, StringName2)—sets the value of StringName1 to the value of StringName2. It returns an error if either StringName1 or StringName2 is undefined, or if StringName2 has no assigned value.

Concatenate (StringName1, StringName2, StringName3)—sets the value of StringName3 to be the string whose value is the characters of StringName1 followed by the characters of StringName2. It returns an error if StringName1, StringName2, or StringName3 is undefined or either StringName1 or StringName2 has no assigned value.

IsSubstring (StringName1, StringName2)—returns the location of the first (leftmost) occurrence of StringName1 in StringName2 if the value of StringName1 is a substring of the value of StringName2, 0 otherwise. It returns an error if either StringName1 or StringName2 is undefined or has no assigned value.

Replace (StringName1, StringName2, StringName3)—replaces the first (leftmost) occurrence of StringName2 in StringName1 by StringName3. It leaves StringName1 unchanged if StringName2 is not a substring of StringName1 and returns an error if StringName1, StringName2, or StringName3 is undefined or has no assigned value.

Length (StringName)—returns the number of characters in StringName. It returns an error if StringName is undefined or has no assigned value.

IsItNull (StringName)—returns "true" if StringName is the null string, "false" if it is a non-null string, and an error if StringName is undefined or has no assigned value.

Delete (StringName)—deletes the variable StringName. It returns an error if StringName is undefined.

Note that while we have not included an explicit operation to delete a substring from a string, we achieve this by Replacing the substring by the null string, a string of length 0.

Good string manipulation languages, such as LISP and SNOBOL, implement these ADT operations or similar ones as basic operations within the language, much as Pascal, FORTRAN, and BASIC implement arithmetic operations directly. Thus it is easy within a language such as LISP to concatenate strings, search for substrings, and perform general string replacements.

String is the first data type we have encountered which is not a basic data type for Pascal. Hence implementation of the string data type in Pascal requires the definition of appropriate procedures and functions. Unfortunately, Pascal places some severe constraints on the implementation of the string ADT. The most severe of these arises from the fact that in Pascal a string must be thought of as an array of characters: as such, a string is required to have a fixed length. Thus we must define a new type for each different length of string. Because of this, string operations range from cumbersome to painful.

Be that as it may, we present a Pascal string implementation in table 3.5. In the implementation we assume that StringLength is an integer denoting the maximal length of the string.

Table 3.5   The String ADT as Implemented in Pascal

ADT	Pascal

NewString (StringName)	`CONST`
	`    StringLength = UserSuppliedLength;`
	
	`TYPE`
	`    WordType      = ARRAY [1..StringLength] OF char;`
	`    StringSizeType = 0..StringLength;`
	`    StringType    = RECORD`
	`                        Size  : StringSizeType;`
	`                        Word : WordType`
	`                    END;`
	
	`VAR`
	`    StringName : StringType;`

AssignString (StringName1,
StringName2)
	`PROCEDURE AssignString (VAR StringName1 : StringType;`
	`                                         StringName2     : StringType);`
	
	`VAR`
	`    I : 1..StringLength;`
	
	`BEGIN`
	`    FOR I := 1 TO Length (StringName2) DO`
	`        StringName1.Word[I] := StringName2.Word[I];`
	`    StringName1.Size := StringName2.Size`
	`END; { AssignString }`

Concatenate (StringName1,
StringName2,
StringName3)
	`PROCEDURE Concatenate (StringName1,`
	`                                      StringName2     : StringType;`
	`                                      VAR StringName3 : StringType);`
	
	`VAR I : 1..StringLength;`
	
	`BEGIN`
	
	`{ Assert: Length (StringName1) + Length (StringName2) <= StringLength. }`
	
	`    FOR I := 1 TO Length (StringName1) DO`
	`        StringName3.Word[I] := StringName1.Word[I];`
	`    FOR I := 1 TO Length (StringName2) DO`
	`        StringName3.Word[Length (StringName1) + I] :=`
	`            StringName2.Word[I];`
	`    StringName3.Size:= Length (StringName1) + Length (StringName2)`
	
	`END; { Concatenate }`

IsSubString (StringName1,
StringName2)
	`FUNCTION IsSubstring (StringName1, StringName2 : StringType) : StringSizeType;`
	
	`VAR`
	`    Found       : boolean;`
	`    Pattern     : StringType;`
	`    PatternLoc  : StringSizeType;`
	`    PatternSize : StringSizeType;`
	`    Text        : StringType;`
	`    TextLoc     : StringSizeType;`
	`    TextSize    : StringSizeType;`

Table 3.5—*Continued*	
ADT	**Pascal**

	BEGIN
	  Found := false;
	  PatternSize := Length (StringName1);
	  TextSize := Length (StringName2);
	  IF TextSize >= PatternSize THEN
	    BEGIN
	      AssignString (Pattern, StringName1);
	      AssignString (Text, StringName2);
	      TextLoc := 0;
	      WHILE (TextLoc <= TextSize − PatternSize) AND NOT Found DO
	        BEGIN
	          TextLoc := TextLoc + 1;
	          PatternLoc := 0;
	          Found := true;
	          WHILE Found AND (PatternLoc < PatternSize) DO
	            BEGIN
	              PatternLoc := PatternLoc + 1;
	              Found := Text.Word[TextLoc + PatternLoc − 1]
	                  = Pattern.Word[PatternLoc]
	            END
	        END
	    END;
	  IF NOT Found THEN TextLoc := 0;
	  IsSubstring := TextLoc
	END; { *IsSubstring* }

Replace (StringName1,
          StringName2,
          StringName3)
	PROCEDURE Replace (VAR StringName1 : StringType
	                          StringName2 : StringType
	                          StringName3 : StringType);
	
	VAR
	  Difference : integer;
	  I : StringSizeType;
	  Location : StringSizeType;
	  SubstituteLoc : StringSizeType;
	
	BEGIN
	  Location := IsSubstring (StringName2, StringName1);
	  IF Location > 0 THEN
	    BEGIN
	      Difference := Length (StringName3) − Length (StringName2);
	      IF Difference = 0 THEN
	        FOR I := 1 TO Length (StringName2) DO
	          StringName1.Word[Location + I − 1] := StringName3.Word[I]
	      ELSE
	        IF Difference < 0 THEN
	
	        { *Make StringName1 shorter by the difference in lengths.* }
	
	        BEGIN
	          FOR I := Location + Length (StringName2) + Difference
	            TO Length (StringName1) DO
	            StringName1.Word[I] :=
	              StringName1.Word[I + abs (Difference)];
	
	        { *Move StringName3 to proper position in StringName1.* }

ADT	Pascal

	FOR I := 1 TO Length (StringName3) DO
	    StringName1.Word[Location + I − 1] :=
	      StringName3.Word[I];
	    StringName1.Size := StringName1.Size + Difference
	  END
	ELSE
	
	  { *Move the end of StringName1 to the right to make room.* }
	
	  BEGIN
	    FOR I := StringName1.Size DOWNTO
	            Location + StringName2.Size DO
	      StringName1.Word[I + Difference] :=
	        StringName1.Word[I];
	    FOR I := 1 TO StringName3.Size DO
	      StringName1.Word[Location + I − 1] :=
	        StringName3.Word[I];
	    StringName1.Size := StringName1.Size + Difference
	  END
	END
	END; { *Replace* }

Length (StringName)	FUNCTION Length (StringName : StringType) : StringSizeType; BEGIN Length := StringName.Size END; { *Length* }
IsItNull (StringName)	FUNCTION IsItNull (StringName: StringType) : boolean; BEGIN IsItNull := Length (StringName) = 0 END; { *IsItNull* }
Delete (StringName)	No explicit operation

Figure 3.7 presents a useful tool for working with strings. In creating a book index, it is customary to have each entry capitalized. The code in the figure checks the first letter of an entry and capitalizes it if it is not already an uppercase letter. The numbers involved correspond to the ASCII character codes. The numerical value of "A" is 65, and the code for "a" is 97. The difference between values for upper- and lowercase letters is $97 − 65 = 32$.

Many implementations of Pascal interpret a string as a **PACKED ARRAY.** Since PACKED ARRAYs can be treated as single entities, this permits simple relational or comparison operations. The key requirement for these operations is that the strings be compatible. That is, two strings must be of exactly the same length if we wish to compare them. With that limitation, we can test for equality or inequality, and we can test for **lexicographic order**—which string precedes the other alphabetically. Figure 3.8, for example, is a simple program to print out a short list of names in alphabetical order.

Figure 3.7   Code to capitalize a word

```
PROGRAM Capitalizer (input, output);

{ A program to capitalize an input word. }

CONST
  ArraySize       = UserSuppliedSize;
  AValue          =  97;
  ZValue          = 122;
  CaseDifference  =  32;

VAR
  Entry : ARRAY[1..ArraySize] OF char;
  I     : 1..ArraySize;

BEGIN
  write ('Enter a word: ');
  FOR I := 1 TO ArraySize DO
    read (Entry[I]);
  IF (ord (Entry[1]) >= AValue) AND (ord (Entry[1]) <= ZValue) THEN

  { Assert: Entry[1] is lowercase if ASCII character set
  is used. }

  Entry[1] := chr (ord (Entry[1]) - CaseDifference);
write ('The result is: ');
FOR I := 1 TO ArraySize DO
  write (Entry[I]);
writeln
END. { Capitalizer }
```

Figure 3.8, Part 1   Name-printing program

```
PROGRAM PrintName (input, output);

{ A program to print a list of names in sorted order. }

CONST
  ListSize = 10;   { The list size is ten. }
  NameSize = 12;   { The name length is twelve. }

TYPE
  NameType = PACKED ARRAY[1..NameSize] OF char;
  ListType = ARRAY[1..ListSize] OF NameType;

VAR
  ListIndex   : 1..ListSize;
  ListOfNames : ListType;

PROCEDURE ReadString (VAR NewWord : NameType);

  VAR
    I    : 1..NameSize;
    Temp : char;

  BEGIN
    FOR I := 1 TO NameSize DO
      BEGIN
        read (Temp);
        NewWord[I] := Temp
      END
  END; { ReadString }

PROCEDURE BuildList (VAR ListOfNames : ListType);

{ This procedure builds a list of names from input. }

  VAR
    ListIndex : 1..ListSize;

  BEGIN
    FOR ListIndex := 1 TO ListSize DO
      BEGIN

        { Strings are read from the standard file input. }

        write ('Next name, please. ');
        ReadString (ListOfNames[ListIndex]);
        readln
      END
  END; { BuildList }
```

Figure 3.8, Part 2   Name-printing program

```
PROCEDURE LocateAndPrint (VAR ListOfNames : ListType);

{ This procedure finds the first remaining name on a list, prints
and marks it. }

   CONST
      NameTaken = 'ZZZZZZZZZZZZ';   { Number of Z's = NameSize }

   VAR
      LeastLoc  : 1..ListSize;
      ListIndex : 1..ListSize;

   BEGIN
      LeastLoc := 1;
      FOR ListIndex := 2 TO ListSize DO
        IF ListOfNames[ListIndex] < ListOfNames[LeastLoc] THEN
           LeastLoc := ListIndex;

      { Assert: LeastLoc identifies the first (alphabetically)
      remaining name on the list. }

      IF ListOfNames[LeastLoc] <> NameTaken THEN
        writeln (ListOfNames[LeastLoc]);
      ListOfNames[LeastLoc] := NameTaken
   END; { LocateAndPrint }

{ Main program. }

BEGIN
   BuildList (ListOfNames);
   FOR ListIndex := 1 TO ListSize DO LocateAndPrint (ListOfNames)
END.
```

The algorithm in figure 3.8 is not an efficient one, but it is fine for a short list of names and illustrates the comparison of strings implemented as PACKED ARRAYs. Note that we search the entire list for each name. Hence, if we generalize this to handle a list of length *n,* we observe that it is an $O(n^2)$ algorithm. For long lists of names, it is better to use a more efficient sorting method and then print the resulting list.

Finally, it must be mentioned that some, but not all, Pascal implementations allow a definition of the null string. In IBM Pascal, for example, we cannot define a null string by ' ', but NULL is a predefined (constant) null string. In some versions of Pascal running on DEC equipment, it is permissible to define the null string by ' '. Because of the lack of any standard string type, it is important to check your particular implementation for its rules on strings.

Summary

In this chapter we have discussed several of the fundamental data types from which more complex types are built. The more primitive of these types are closely tied to the design and architecture of the computer system itself, and thus form a bridge between the complex data types that are commonly used and the basic capabilities of the computer. One of the types we have discussed, the record, permits great flexibility since it is a data type that is tailored toward combining other types within its structure. The purpose of this and other more sophisticated data types is to provide us with data models that more closely match reality, and that are easier and quicker to manipulate.

Vocabulary

ASCII
bit
boolean data type
byte
character data type
conjunction
disjunction
dot method
EBCDIC
encoding
equivalence
error propagation
exclusive or
exponent
field
heterogeneous
hexadecimal
homogeneity
identifier field
implication
inclusive or
index field
integer data type

lexicographic order
logical data type
long integer
mantissa
MaxSize
negation
normalization
null string
numerical analysis
octal
out of range
overflow
PACKED ARRAY
real data type
record data type
reduced to within range
roundoff error
scoping rule
string data type
truncation error
underflow
WITH
word

Problems

3.1. Give ADT definitions and a Pascal implementation for the boolean operators *implication, equivalence,* and *exclusive or.*

3.2. Look at the first twenty-five entries in your local telephone book. Are the entries in lexicographic order? How are spaces and special characters such as dashes handled? Make up a new entry which would appear first in *your* telephone book.

3.3. Assuming that a character takes one byte and integers and reals take four bytes of storage, how many bytes of storage are necessary to represent the variable Biography in figure 3.3?

3.4. Given the following record definition, give the type of the following expressions:

```
VAR
   A : RECORD
            A : integer;
            B : RECORD
                     A : real;
                     B : char
                 END
       END;
```

A. A.A
B. A.B
C. A.B.A
D. A.B.B
E. B

Note the possible confusion here caused by repeated use of the same variable names. Rewrite this declaration and the five expressions so that there is no confusion.

Programs

3.1. The PrintName program that we have written (figure 3.8) destroys the list of names. Modify this program so that the original list of names is preserved. How does this change affect the complexity of the program?

3.2. Write a procedure which finds the longest word in an input file of text. Print out the longest word and how many times it appears.

3.3. Write a program which counts the number of words, sentences, and paragraphs in a text file.

3.4. Set up a record structure for a personnel file, with four fields: employee name, employee number, and pointer fields for both name and number. Write a procedure to build a list of employees, keeping it sorted in both name and numerical order.

4

Sets: Sequential Representation

Introduction

The concept of a set is as fundamental to computing as it is to mathematics, for we think of our data as sets with some organizational structure superimposed. In this chapter we examine two basic representations of sets, the set data type as it is supported by Pascal and some other languages, and sequential representation of sets. We discuss forward, backward, and circular traversal of these structures; but because of the simple structure of these sets, there is no need for branching or other complex traversal methods. The basic operations are discussed for each of these structures. Algorithms are provided, together with the corresponding Pascal programs, and the previously defined concepts of order of complexity, invariants, and assertions are used as is appropriate.

Figure 4.1   The subsets of ⟨A, B, C⟩

```
    Ø                {A,  B}
   {A}               {A,  C}
   {B}               {B,  C}
   {C}              {A,  B,  C}
```

Figure 4.2   Venn diagram for two sets

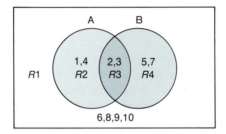

4.1 Sets: theory and abstract data type

Mathematically, a **set** is a collection of objects that are related simply by the fact of their being gathered together. While the objects may, and generally do, have some other properties in common, these other properties are immaterial in the context of set operations. A given set of n objects always has 2^n **subsets**, one of which is the set itself and another of which is the **empty set**, $\emptyset$ (fig. 4.1). We use the standard notation, $a \in S$, to indicate that a is an element of the set S.

Several basic set operations interest us. For any two sets A and B, $A \cup B$, the **union,** consists of all elements which are in either or both of the sets; $A \cap B$, the **intersection,** consists only of those elements that are in both of the sets; $A \triangle B$, the **symmetric difference,** consists of those elements that are in either one of the two sets *but not in both;* and $A - B$, the **difference,** consists of those elements that are in the first set but not in the second. $A - B$ is also called the **relative complement** of B with respect to A. Finally, all sets that we consider are subsets of some **universal set,** such as the set of all integers or the set of all names. The **complement** of a set A consists of all elements of the universal set that are not in A; it is denoted by $\overline{A}$.

As an example, let us take the universal set to be $\{1, \ldots, 10\}$, the integers from 1 to 10, and consider the sets $A = \{1, 2, 3, 4\}$ and $B = \{2, 3, 5, 7\}$. Figure 4.2 shows the **Venn diagram** representation of these sets, with each of the four regions of the diagram labeled. Table 4.1 gives the interpretation of each of the regions and combinations of regions, both in terms of set operations and in terms of the actual numbers contained in the regions.

Table 4.1.   Interpretation of Venn diagram

Regions	Contents	Set Operation
none	none	$\emptyset$
R1	6,8,9,10	$\overline{(A \cup B)}$
R2	1,4	$A - B$
R3	2,3	$A \cap B$
R4	5,7	$B - A$
R1, R2	1,4,6,8,9,10	$\overline{B}$
R1, R3	2,3,6,8,9,10	$\overline{(A \, \Delta \, B)}$
R1, R4	5,6,7,8,9,10	$\overline{A}$
R2, R3	1,2,3,4	A
R2, R4	1,4,5,7	$A \, \Delta \, B$
R3, R4	2,3,5,7	B
R1, R2, R3	1,2,3,4,6,8,9,10	$\overline{(B - A)}$
R1, R2, R4	1,4,5,6,7,8,9,10	$\overline{(A \cap B)}$
R1, R3, R4	2,3,5,6,7,8,9,10	$\overline{(A - B)}$
R2, R3, R4	1,2,3,4,5,7	$A \cup B$
R1, R2, R3, R4	1,2,3,4,5,6,7,8,9,10	universal set

When we consider a set as an abstract data type, we have basically two classes of operations to implement. One class consists of the general data structure operations: building, updating, searching, and so forth. The other class consists of operations that are specific to sets, such as union, intersection, and complement.

Two separate operations are involved in building a set: creating the set initially, and adding elements to the set. Thus we need an operation that creates an empty set and an operation that adds an element to the set. The first of these we shall call

NewSet (SetName),

and the second

AddElement (SetElement, SetName, AddedToSet).

NewSet will always return an empty set, while AddElement will return a new version of SetName, with SetElement included in it. The variable AddedToSet is to have the value "true" when SetElement has been added to the set or SetElement is already in the set, and "false" when we are unable in the particular implementation to add SetElement. This can happen, for example, if the amount of space available for representing the set is limited.

What happens if SetElement is not in the universal set for SetName? For example, suppose that SetName has been declared a set of integers and we try to add a name to the set. This is clearly an error that should be caught. In Pascal the result is failure. The type declarations are automatically checked, and any attempt to add an element of an incorrect type to a set is rejected at compile time.

AddElement should also signal an error condition if either SetName or SetElement is undefined. Note that this is a different type of error: it results from failure to define one of the arguments rather than from using a wrongly defined argument.

Similarly, we can define the remaining basic set operations and functions. In all of these default error conditions result whenever one of the arguments is undefined.

DeleteElement (SetElement, SetName, DeletedFromSet)—deletes the element from the set, generating the value "true" for DeletedFromSet if SetElement has been deleted, and "false" if we attempted to delete an element that was not there.

IsEmpty (SetName)—returns "true" if the set is empty, "false" otherwise.

IsElement (SetElement, SetName)—returns "true" if the element is in the set, "false" otherwise.

GetAnother (SetElement, SetName)—returns another element in the set SetName. If the set is empty, nothing is returned; if the set consists of one element, that element is returned; and if the set consists of more than one element, an element different from SetElement is returned. (Since a set is stored within a computer in some order (which the user may not know), the typical implementation of GetAnother returns the next element in that order, or the first element if SetElement happens to be the last in storage order. If SetElement is not in SetName, then GetAnother returns an element from SetName.)

Size (SetName)—returns the number of elements in the set.

Three of the operations that are specific to sets are fundamental: union, intersection, and complement. (Actually only one or the other of union and intersection is needed. See problem 4.4.) Union is defined abstractly in a simple way: **Union** (SetA, SetB, SetC) takes as input SetA and SetB, and returns as output SetC, the set union of SetA and SetB. **Intersection** (SetA, SetB, SetC) is similarly defined. Complement is a little more tricky, since **Complement** (SetA) is "everything that is not in SetA." Obviously, this must be interpreted with respect to some universal set.

One final note. Since we are interested in implementing sets on computers, we will always be handling finite sets. While we have not explicitly stated this in our discussion of the abstract types, it is implicit in our set-building operations. Using the operations we have defined, we cannot in any finite time build an infinite set.

4.2 Sets, using SET operations

There are basically two methods of representing a set in a computer. We can list each set element separately, or we can list all elements in the universal set and then indicate for each one whether it is in the desired set. Recall that a mathematician considers a set to be unordered and to have no duplicate elements, so that $\{a, b\}$, $\{b, a\}$, and $\{a, b, a\}$, for example, all represent the same set. Any computer representation must mirror these conditions.

If we list each set element separately, then the space required to represent a set is proportional to the number of elements in the set, provided that we maintain a check to assure that there are no duplicate elements. The fact that the elements can be listed in any order can cause severe computational strain unless something is done to assure that only one listing is used. For example, even with a set of ten elements there are 10! (over 3,000,000) ways to list the set. Thus, while the set concept does not require it, operational efficiency suggests strongly that some specific ordering of the set elements be established and maintained.

The other method of representing a set, by listing the universal set and indicating whether each element is in or out of the desired set, seems at first glance to be wasteful. If the universal set is large, and most individual sets are small, then this can indeed be wasteful. However, for small universal sets, this method can be used to advantage, provided that an efficient method of representing the universal set is used. Operational efficiency forces an ordering of the elements of the set represented in this way.

The common representation of a set using this latter approach is the **bit map.** The universal set is considered to be ordered (for example, in alphabetical order), and a single bit is assigned to each element of the universal set. For any set, the bits corresponding to its elements are set to 1 and all other bits are set to 0. For example, if the universal set is the alphabet, the set $A = \{b, c, f, h, k\}$ would be represented in twenty-six bits as

01100101001000000000000000.

This representation of a set allows us to use the logical operations of the computer to operate on many elements of the set in parallel. An alphabetic set, for example, requires twenty-six bits, one for each letter. Suppose, for example, that we define the set $B = \{a, c, e, g, i, k, m\}$ and represent it by a bit map:

10101010101010000000000000.

We can determine the intersection $A \cap B$ by comparing these two bit maps. Since each bit represents a different element, the comparisons can be done in parallel. Any element in the intersection will be represented by a 1 in both bit maps:

$$
\begin{aligned}
A: &\quad 01100101001000000000000000 \\
B: &\quad 10101010101010000000000000 \\
A \cap B: &\quad 00100000001000000000000000.
\end{aligned}
$$

We observe that twenty-six bits fit into four bytes. Thus, if the logical operations of the computer are defined on bytes, we can find the intersection of any two sets of letters by applying the "logical and" operator four times. If the logical operations are defined on two-byte words, we only need two applications of the operator.

Since the logical computer operations are usually defined to operate on an entire byte (eight bits) at once, it is reasonable to represent a set (in bit map representation) by a fixed number of bytes. The number of bytes chosen is generally a decision made by the person who implements the language processor. For example, whoever wrote the Pascal compiler may have decided to use eight bytes to represent a set. This would permit representation of any set of up to 64 elements. Or the compiler writer may have decided to use thirty-two bytes for set representation, allowing us to use sets of at most 256 elements. Whatever the decision, the key fact is that any permissible set is represented by the same number of bytes; hence set operations that use a constant amount of time per byte require a constant time, independent of the particular set.

One of the nice features of Pascal, in contrast to some other programming languages, is that it supports a SET type, which makes it very easy to program set operations. In many programming languages, assuring that a set does not contain duplicate elements, or that it is not represented in two different orderings, requires some effort; in Pascal, these are automatically handled by the SET type.

The representation used for the Pascal SET type is hidden from the user. That is, the user does not *know* how a set is represented when the SET type is used. The user may think of the representation as a bit map. However, be aware that the actual implementation of SET may not be done in this manner. (See problem 4.6.)

Suppose that we wish to store a set of elements in a computer. The simplest way to do this is to store the elements sequentially, as they are read. The *creation* of a set within the computer is then very simple, as the procedures in figure 4.3 show. For these procedures, "SetType" is defined to be "SET OF ElementType."

With this representation, NewSet is obviously $O(1)$, since its use is independent of the size of the set being created. If NewSet requires one time unit per byte and sets are represented by eight bytes, then NewSet requires eight time units, independent of the set being created. (Remember that $O(1)$ does *not* mean

Figure 4.3   First set-building procedures

```
TYPE
   ElementType = UserSelectedType;
   SetType     = SET OF ElementType;

PROCEDURE NewSet (VAR SetName : SetType);

{ This procedure initializes a set. }

  BEGIN
    SetName := []
  END; { NewSet }

PROCEDURE AddElement (SetElement    : ElementType;
                      VAR SetName    : SetType;
                      VAR AddedToSet : boolean);

{ This procedure adds one element to a set. The implementation as a
SET guarantees that there will be room to add the element, so
AddedToSet always has the value true. }

  BEGIN
    SetName := SetName + [SetElement];
    AddedToSet := true
  END; { AddElement }
```

that the operation takes only one time unit but, rather, that the time it takes is constant, independent of the number of data.) In using the procedure Add-Element we handle the new element once, independent of set size. That is, AddElement is also $O(1)$. To build a set, we apply this procedure for each of the elements of the set. Since each element is handled once, the time to create the data structure for a set of size n is $O(n)$. That is, the time to create a set is linearly proportional to the size of the set. Of course, if we forget that we have handled a given element, we may handle that element several times and end up with a less efficient program.

For this implementation, we need not check to determine whether an element is already in a set. Pascal does this automatically, through use of its set operations. Pascal also generates a compile time error message in the event that we try to add to the set an element that is not in the universal set.

Among the other operations, DeleteElement, IsEmpty, and IsElement are all easily defined for this implementation (fig. 4.4). Recall that the Pascal operator IN is a boolean operator yielding "true" if an element is in a set and "false" otherwise. These procedures make use of this. Each procedure is $O(1)$.

Figure 4.4   Additional set procedures

```
TYPE
  ElementType = UserSelectedType;
  SetType     = SET OF ElementType;

FUNCTION IsElement (SetElement : ElementType;
                    SetName    : SetType) : boolean;

{ This function determines if the element is in the set. }

  BEGIN
    IsElement := SetElement IN SetName
  END; { IsElement }

PROCEDURE DeleteElement (SetElement       : ElementType;
                         VAR SetName       : SetType;
                         VAR DeletedFromSet : boolean);

{ This procedure deletes the given element from the set. }

  BEGIN
    IF IsElement (SetElement, SetName) THEN
      BEGIN
        SetName := SetName - [SetElement];
        DeletedFromSet := true
      END
    ELSE
      DeletedFromSet := false
  END; { DeleteElement }

FUNCTION IsEmpty (SetName : SetType) : boolean;

{ This function determines if the set is empty. }

  BEGIN
    IsEmpty := SetName = []
  END; { IsEmpty }
```

The basic operation of *traversal* is not supported for the Pascal SET type, although some other languages do support it. Thus the instruction

```
FOR SetElement IN SetName DO
    { whatever must be done to SetElement }
```

is *not* available in Pascal, despite its obvious usefulness. If we had this capability, determining the size of a set and traversing it would both be simple. As it is, both require some detailed effort.

The functions GetAnother and Size make use of the ordering that is implicit in the Pascal SET. To define a general type of SET, we first define a data TYPE, which will be used to define the universal set. For example, we might define

```
TYPE
   WeekDay = (Sunday, Monday, Tuesday,
              Wednesday, Thursday, Friday,
              Saturday);
```

With this, we can then define

```
VAR
   Day      : WeekDay
   Vacation : SET OF WeekDay;
```

This definition says that Vacation is a SET of WeekDay, implying that the universal set is [Sunday..Saturday]. Pascal implements this kind of definition in the order given, so that Sunday is the first day, Tuesday is the third day, and so forth. Thus we can use the following Pascal functions:

ord (Day)—returns the ordinal number of the day;

pred (Day)—returns the day before the given one;

succ (Day)—returns the day after the given one.

In addition, we can define a FOR loop from Day1 to Day2 that will operate correctly—that is, really do something if and only if Day1 comes before Day2 in the defined order.

If the SET consists of directly represented characters, such as letters or numerals, then we can make use of the encoding of these characters in defining GetAnother and Size. For example, we can check all letters with a FOR loop running from "A" to "z," or all digits with a FOR loop from "0" to "9." For this to work properly, we must be sure that the code value for the initial character is not greater than the code value for the final character. In the ASCII code, for example, the numerical value of "A" is 65 and that of "z" is 122. Since all the letters (and some punctuation marks) have values between these two, the FOR loop will work correctly. However, a FOR loop from "a" to "Z" would not check any letters since the ASCII code for "a" is 97 and that for "Z" is 90. (See appendix A for the code values.)

The definitions for the functions Size and GetAnother are given in figure 4.5.

Figure 4.5, Part 1   GetAnother and Size for general SETs

```
{  These functions assume global definitions of Universe as
[FirstElement..LastElement], and of the elements themselves. }

CONST
  FirstElement = UserSelectedFirstElement;
  LastElement  = UserSelectedLastElement;

TYPE
  ElementType = FirstElement..LastElement;
  SetType     = SET OF ElementType;

FUNCTION GetAnother (SetElement : ElementType;
                     SetName    : SetType) : ElementType;

{  This function returns the element following the given one in the
set. }

  VAR
    CurrentElement : ElementType;

  BEGIN

    { Assert: SetName is not empty and SetElement is an element of
    SetName. }

    CurrentElement := SetElement;
    REPEAT
      IF CurrentElement = LastElement THEN
        CurrentElement := FirstElement
      ELSE
        CurrentElement := succ (CurrentElement)
    UNTIL IsElement (CurrentElement, SetName)
        OR (CurrentElement = SetElement);
    GetAnother := CurrentElement

    { Assert:  If SetName is a singleton set, then GetAnother
    returns SetElement. }

  END; { GetAnother }
```

Figure 4.5, Part 2   GetAnother and Size for general SETs

```
FUNCTION Size (SetName : SetType) : integer;

{ This function determines the size of the set. }

  VAR
    Count            : integer;
    CurrentElement : ElementType;

  BEGIN
    Count := 0;
    FOR CurrentElement := FirstElement TO LastElement DO
      IF IsElement (CurrentElement, SetName) THEN
        Count := Count + 1;
    Size := Count
  END; { Size }
```

Figure 4.6   The procedure for set intersection

```
TYPE
  ElementType = UserSelectedType;
  SetType     = SET OF ElementType;

PROCEDURE Intersect (SetA, SetB : SetType;
                     VAR SetC   : SetType);

{ This procedure produces SetC, the intersection of SetA and SetB. }

  BEGIN
    SetC := SetA * SetB
  END; { Intersect }
```

For this implementation of GetAnother and Size, we must traverse the entire universal set, either to traverse the entire given set or to count it. Thus these operations take constant time, regardless of the size of SetName. But if the universe increases in size, the time to perform these operations probably does also. Again, $O(1)$ may be large!

The operations of union, intersection, and relative complement are directly supported for the Pascal SET type, using the symbols $+$, $*$, and $-$, respectively. Figure 4.6, for example, is the implementation of Intersect. The procedure Intersect is also $O(1)$ in our model bit map SET implementation, which accomplishes this by a "logical and" of the bytes of the two sets in one operation. Note that we have used $+$ and $-$ in AddElement and DeleteElement without explicitly defining procedures for them.

Figure 4.7, Part 1   Building a set as an ARRAY

```
CONST
  MaxSize = UserSelectedSize; { Maximum size allowed. }

TYPE
  ElementType = UserSelectedType;
  SetType     = RECORD
                  SetItself : ARRAY[1..MaxSize] OF ElementType;
                  SetSize   : 0..MaxSize
                END;

PROCEDURE NewSet (VAR SetName : SetType);

{ This procedure initializes a set. }

  BEGIN
    SetName.SetSize := 0
  END; { NewSet }

PROCEDURE AddElement (SetElement      : ElementType;
                      VAR SetName      : SetType;
                      VAR AddedToSet : boolean);

{ This procedure adds one element to a set. }

  VAR
    Count : 1..MaxSize;

  BEGIN
    IF SetName.SetSize < MaxSize THEN
      BEGIN
        SetName.SetSize := SetName.SetSize + 1;
        SetName.SetItself[SetName.SetSize] := SetElement;
        AddedToSet := true;

        { Check for and eliminate a duplicate element. }

        Count := 1;

        { Count identifies the first location of SetElement. }

        WHILE SetName.SetItself[Count] <> SetElement DO
          Count := Count + 1;
```

Figure 4.7, Part 2   Building a set as an ARRAY

```
      { Assert: SetElement is in SetName. }

      IF Count < SetName.SetSize THEN
         SetName.SetSize := SetName.SetSize - 1
      END
   ELSE

      { Assert: SetName is full; no more elements can be added. }

      AddedToSet := false
   END; { AddElement }
```

4.3 Sets, sequentially stored

The "typical" computer is called a **von Neumann computer.** One of the characteristics of this class of computer is that main memory is ARRAY[0..(MemorySize−1)] OF MemoryElements (usually bytes). Any datum stored in the computer is stored as one or more of the elements in this array. Thus, while a mathematician thinks of a set as an unordered collection of elements, whenever we represent a set in a typical computer, the memory organization automatically imposes an order on the elements of the set. Storing the set elements sequentially in an array enables us to use this order in traversing the set.

Here are our set operations, using a linear array to represent the set. (This is the common way of implementing sets in FORTRAN or BASIC.) We begin in figure 4.7 with another pair of procedures to build a set. For these procedures, the basic structure we use for the set is ARRAY[1..MaxSize] OF ElementType.

We must now discuss a technicality. For the SET implementation of sets, we do not need to know the size of the set. Since each element has a specific location within the set, an element can be added, checked, or deleted without concern. However, for an ARRAY implementation, if we do not know the size of the set, then whenever we want to add an element to the set, we must first figure out where the end of the set is. Hence it is very useful in AddElement and the other procedures to know the size of the set.

Since the entries in an ARRAY must all be of the same type, we cannot generally keep the size of the ARRAY within it, nor is it good practice to do so even if we can. The RECORD provides the structure we want here:

```
SetType = RECORD
            SetItself : ARRAY[1..MaxSize] OF ElementType;
                          ElementType;
            SetSize   : 0..MaxSize
          END;
```

We must, of course, define MaxSize and ElementType also.

Note that we have given these procedures the same names as those used in section 4.2. This is deliberate. When we later use set operations in applications, it will make no difference in programming the application which group of procedures we choose. However, we must consistently choose one group or the other.

We make two observations on constructing a set as an ARRAY. First, the boolean AddedToSet is set to "true" if we have added the element to the set and to "false" if there was no room. Recall that in the SET implementation, AddedToSet is always set to "true," since by the nature of the implementation there was always room for the element. It is included in both, so that the same abstract data type definition holds.

Second, observe that we have built a **sentinel** into AddElement, for use in the loop that checks for duplicates. A sentinel is generally some marker whose presence we can guarantee. In this situation, we have added the new element, which serves as our sentinel. Since the WHILE statement only checks for the presence of the value of SetElement, if it were not present we could have an out of range error. But just before that loop we have put this value in at the end of the array, so we *know* that at least one copy is there. If we find its value before we reach the current end of the array, then the IF statement basically forgets that we have added it a second time. Since the new value was added at the end of the set, reducing Count by one effectively removes it from the set. By placing the value of SetElement into the array before entering the loop we avoid the need to check for the end of the array each time through the loop. Thus we save many checks, at the expense of one added check at the end, the "IF Count < SetSize" statement.

In this procedure we handle each element once to enter it, but we must also check each element against all previously entered ones to eliminate duplicates. Let us examine this in some detail. In the worst situation, each element entered is distinct from the previous ones, but we do not know this beforehand. Then we must check each new element against all the others to be certain. This requires much work, none of which results in any action. For the first element, there is no check since there is no previous one. For the second element, we must check against the one previous one. The third element must be checked against the two previous ones, and so forth. In general, the kth element must be checked against all $k - 1$ previous ones. Adding to this the one operation necessary to add an element to the set, we find that adding the kth element requires a total of k operations. Hence to create a set of n elements requires

$$1 + 2 + 3 + \ldots + (n - 2) + (n - 1) + n$$

operations. We observed in chapter 2 that this sum has the value

$$n (n + 1)/2 = n^2/2 + n/2.$$

The n^2 term dominates, so the time for completing the entire operation is $O(n^2)$.

Does it take more time to create a set in this implementation than in the SET implementation? Not necessarily. Recall that $O(1)$ means constant time, *not* a short time. If the SET implementation assumes very large sets and we are using very small ones, then it is possible (although not likely) that this implementation is quicker. You may want to investigate this on your system.

Recall that using the SET type of Pascal, DeleteElement, IsEmpty, and IsElement each require only one assignment statement (plus the error statement in DeleteElement). With an ARRAY implementation two of these require more work. The procedures are given in figures 4.8, 4.9, and 4.10.

The procedure DeleteElement initializes DeletedFromSet to "false" and then changes it to "true" if the procedure succeeds. Observe also that the procedure does not shuffle large numbers of data. Since the set elements are in no specific order (such as alphabetical), we fill the gap caused by deleting SetElement with the last element in the set and then reduce the size by one.

We see that for a set implemented as an ARRAY, both the procedure DeleteElement and the function IsElement require traversal of the entire set. Hence they are $O(n)$. In contrast, since we can determine IsEmpty by checking SetSize, that function is $O(1)$.

The next two basic functions, GetAnother and Size, require traversal of the entire universal set using a SET implementation. We find that for an ARRAY implementation, GetAnother requires a search to find the given element, but Size is $O(1)$, as in figure 4.11.

We now consider a typical set operation: forming the intersection of two sets. Recall that in the SET implementation, this can be accomplished by a single instruction, SetA * SetB. For the ARRAY implementation we must check each element individually, to decide whether it should be included in the intersection (fig. 4.12).

Figure 4.8   DeleteElement for an ARRAY set

```
CONST
  MaxSize = UserSelectedSize; { Maximum size. }

TYPE
  ElementType = UserSelectedType;
  SetType     = RECORD
                  SetItself : ARRAY[1..MaxSize] OF ElementType;
                  SetSize   : 0..MaxSize
                END;

PROCEDURE DeleteElement (SetElement         : ElementType;
                         VAR SetName         : SetType;
                         VAR DeletedFromSet : boolean);

{ This procedure deletes the given element from the set. }

  VAR
    Index : 0..MaxSize;

  BEGIN
    WITH SetName DO
      BEGIN
        DeletedFromSet := false;
        FOR Index := 1 TO SetSize DO
          IF SetItself[Index] = SetElement THEN
            BEGIN
              SetItself[Index] := SetItself[SetSize];
              DeletedFromSet   := true
            END;

        { Assert: DeletedFromSet is true if and only if SetElement
        was in SetName. }

        IF DeletedFromSet THEN SetSize := SetSize - 1
      END { WITH }
  END; { DeleteElement }
```

Figure 4.9   The function IsEmpty for an ARRAY set

```
CONST
  MaxSize = UserSelectedSize; { Maximum size. }

TYPE
  ElementType = UserSelectedType;
  SetType     = RECORD
                  SetItself : ARRAY[1..MaxSize] OF ElementType;
                  SetSize   : 0..MaxSize
                END;

FUNCTION IsEmpty (SetName : SetType) : boolean;

{ This function determines if the set is empty. }

  BEGIN
    IsEmpty := SetName.SetSize = 0
  END; { IsEmpty }
```

Figure 4.10   The function IsElement for an ARRAY set

```
CONST
  MaxSize = UserSelectedSize; { Maximum size. }

TYPE
  ElementType = UserSelectedType;
  SetType     = RECORD
                  SetItself : ARRAY[1..MaxSize] OF ElementType;
                  SetSize   : 0..MaxSize
                END;

FUNCTION IsElement (SetElement : ElementType;
                    SetName    : SetType) : boolean;

{ The procedure determines if SetElement is an element of SetName. }

  VAR
    Index         : 0..MaxSize;
    TempIsElement : boolean;

  BEGIN
    TempIsElement := false;
    WITH SetName DO
      FOR Index := 1 TO SetSize DO
        TempIsElement := (SetItself[Index] = SetElement)
                          OR TempIsElement;
    IsElement := TempIsElement
  END; { IsElement }
```

Figure 4.11   GetAnother and Size for an ARRAY set

```
CONST
  MaxSize = UserSelectedSize; { Maximum size. }

TYPE
  ElementType = UserSelectedType;
  SetType     = RECORD
                  SetItself : ARRAY[1..MaxSize] OF ElementType;
                  SetSize   : 0..MaxSize
                END;

FUNCTION GetAnother (SetElement : ElementType;
                     SetName     : SetType) : ElementType;

{ This function returns the element following the given one in the
set. }

{ Assert : SetElement is a member of SetName. }

{ Assert : If SetName is a singleton set then GetAnother returns
SetElement. }

  VAR
    Index : 0..MaxSize;

  BEGIN
    Index := 0;
    WITH SetName DO
      BEGIN
        REPEAT
          Index := Index + 1
        UNTIL (SetItself[Index] = SetElement) OR (Index = SetSize);
        IF Index < SetSize THEN
          GetAnother := SetItself[Index + 1]
        ELSE

          { Assert: SetElement has no successor in SetName. }

          GetAnother := SetItself[1]
      END { WITH }
  END; { GetAnother }

FUNCTION Size (SetName : SetType) : integer;

{ This function determines the size of the set. }

  BEGIN
    Size := SetName.SetSize
  END; { Size }
```

Figure 4.12   Procedure to compute set intersection

```
CONST
  MaxSize = UserSelectedSize; { Maximum size. }

TYPE
  ElementType = UserSelectedType;
  SetType     = RECORD
                   SetItself : ARRAY[1..MaxSize] OF ElementType;
                   SetSize   : 0..MaxSize
                END;

FUNCTION Size (SetName : SetType) : integer;

{ This function is defined in fig. 4.11 }

PROCEDURE Intersect (SetA, SetB : SetType;
                     VAR SetC   : SetType);

{ Procedure to compute SetC, the intersection of SetA and SetB. }

  VAR
    AIndex : 0..MaxSize;
    BIndex : 0..MaxSize;
    CIndex : 0..MaxSize;

  BEGIN
    CIndex := 0;
    FOR AIndex := 1 TO Size (SetA) DO
      FOR BIndex := 1 TO Size (SetB) DO

        { Assert: Any given element occurs at most once in SetA and
        at most once in SetB. }

        IF SetA.SetItself[AIndex] = SetB.SetItself[BIndex] THEN
          BEGIN
            CIndex := CIndex + 1;
            SetC.SetItself[CIndex] := SetA.SetItself[AIndex]
          END;

    { Assert: SetC is the intersection of SetA and SetB. }

    SetC.SetSize := CIndex
  END; { Intersect }
```

Figure 4.13   Skeleton of a vowel-finding program

```
PROGRAM FindVowels (input, output);

VAR

    . . .

BEGIN

  { Read the InputSet. }

  IF (IsElement ('a', InputSet)) OR
     (IsElement ('e', InputSet)) OR
     (IsElement ('i', InputSet)) OR
     (IsElement ('o', InputSet)) OR
     (IsElement ('u', InputSet)) THEN

    { Write that we found a vowel. }

  ELSE

    { Write that there is no vowel. }

END. { FindVowels }
```

The complexity of our version of Intersect, an ARRAY implementation, is rather high. The procedure involves two nested loops, each scanning one of the sets. Hence, if the sets are of size n, Intersect is $O(n^2)$. Observe that since we are dealing with three sets, this is not a good place to use the WITH statement.

4.4 Applications of sets

In this section we show how the procedures we have defined can be used in the solution of several simple problems. We begin with two problems involving a set of letters. For these problems, ElementType is char. Thus SetType is either SET OF char or ARRAY[1..MaxSize] OF char (as a field of a RECORD), depending on the set implementation we use. To simplify matters, we will assume that all the letters are lowercase. The first problem is to determine whether the set contains any vowels.

This problem is rather simple. We could ask individually if each vowel was in the set. This process would end either upon finding a vowel in the set or upon determining that there are none. Figure 4.13 is the skeleton of this program. Note that this program involves comparing each individual vowel with the entire input

Figure 4.14   A second program skeleton for vowel finding

```
PROGRAM FindVowels (input, output);

VAR
    . . .

BEGIN

    { Define the VowelSet. }

    { Read the InputSet. }

    IF Intersect (InputSet, VowelSet) is not empty THEN

        { Write that we found a vowel. }

    ELSE

        { Write that there is no vowel. }

END. { FindVowels }
```

set. If we use a SET implementation each of these comparisons is done in constant time, independent of the set size, but if we use an ARRAY implementation the amount of time needed for each comparison depends on the size of the set. Thus this program can be expected to run in $O(1)$ time with the SET implementation, or $O(n)$ time with the ARRAY implementation.

A different procedure is to define the set of all vowels, and then ask whether the intersection of this set and the input set is empty. The skeleton for this program is given in figure 4.14. The key operation in this algorithm is computing the set intersection. Recall that this is an $O(1)$ operation for the SET implementation but an $O(n^2)$ operation for the ARRAY implementation. A program written from this skeleton might be expected to run faster than one from the first skeleton if the SET implementation is used, since there is one intersection computation in contrast to five comparison computations. However, it might be expected to run more slowly in an ARRAY implementation, because it is an $O(n^2)$ algorithm rather than an $O(n)$ one (see program 4.5).

We shall implement this second program, leaving the first one as an exercise. Notice that except for the line defining SetType in the program (fig. 4.15), there is nothing to indicate whether we are using the SET implementation or the ARRAY implementation of the sets. In more recent languages, such as Modula-2, even this SetType definition is hidden from the writer of the program.

Figure 4.15, Part 1　　A program for vowel finding

```
PROGRAM FindVowels (input, output);

{  A program to determine whether a set of lowercase letters
contains a vowel. }

TYPE
  ElementType = char;
  SetType     = SET OF ElementType;

VAR
  AddedIt    : boolean;
  AnyVowels  : SetType;
  InputSet   : SetType;
  Letter     : ElementType;
  VowelSet   : SetType;

PROCEDURE NewSet (VAR SetName : SetType);

{ Procedure defined in fig. 4.3. }

PROCEDURE AddElement (SetElement    : ElementType;
                      VAR SetName    : SetType;
                      VAR AddedToSet : boolean);

{ Procedure defined in fig. 4.3. }

FUNCTION IsElement (SetElement : ElementType;
                    SetName     : SetType) : boolean;

{ Function defined in fig. 4.4. }

FUNCTION IsEmpty (SetName : SetType) : boolean;

{ Function defined in fig. 4.4. }

PROCEDURE Intersect (SetA, SetB : SetType;
                     VAR SetC    : SetType);

{ Procedure defined in fig. 4.6. }
```

Figure 4.15, Part 2   A program for vowel finding

```
PROCEDURE PrintLetterSet (SetName : SetType);

  VAR
    Index : ElementType;

  BEGIN
    write ('The input set is');
    FOR Index := 'a' TO 'z' DO
      IF IsElement (Index, SetName) THEN write (Index : 2);
    writeln
  END; { PrintLetterSet }

{ Main program. }

BEGIN

  { Define the VowelSet. }

  NewSet (VowelSet);
  AddElement ('a', VowelSet, AddedIt);
  AddElement ('e', VowelSet, AddedIt);
  AddElement ('i', VowelSet, AddedIt);
  AddElement ('o', VowelSet, AddedIt);
  AddElement ('u', VowelSet, AddedIt);

  { Read the InputSet. }

  NewSet (InputSet);
  REPEAT
    read (Letter);
    AddElement (Letter, InputSet, AddedIt)
  UNTIL eoln;

  PrintLetterSet (InputSet);

  { Check the intersection. }

  Intersect (InputSet, VowelSet, AnyVowels);
  IF NOT IsEmpty (AnyVowels) THEN
    writeln ('The input set contains a vowel.')
  ELSE
    writeln ('The input set does not contain a vowel.')
END. { FindVowels }
```

Let us calculate the complexity of this program. The program performs four computations in sequence: form VowelSet, form InputSet, form the intersection (AnyVowels), and check to determine whether the intersection is empty. By the rules of order arithmetic, the complexity of this program is therefore the maximum of the complexity of these four tasks. Suppose that the input set contains n letters. Forming VowelSet is independent of the size of the input set. Hence it is $O(1)$. Forming InputSet depends on the amount of input and on the representation of the set. We saw that if we use the SET implementation, forming InputSet is $O(n)$, whereas if we use the ARRAY implementation, forming InputSet is $O(n^2)$. Similarly, forming AnyVowels is $O(1)$ for the SET implementation and $O(n^2)$ for the ARRAY implementation. Finally, IsEmpty is $O(1)$ for either implementation. Putting this all together, we see that this program for vowel finding has complexity $O(n)$ if the SET implementation is used, and $O(n^2)$ if the ARRAY implementation is used. Note that the $O(n)$ complexity for the SET implementation comes entirely from the work involved in forming the SET initially, and that if the program were given the SET already formed, its complexity would be $O(1)$.

The second problem we examine is to count the vowels in a set of characters. Counting the vowels requires more work. First, we are considering a *set* of characters, not a string. Thus, if a vowel, say "a," occurs in the set, it occurs only once. For example, in "east avenue," we have just three vowels occurring: "a," "e," and "u." If we considered "east avenue" as a string of characters rather than a set, we would have a total of six vowel occurrences. Thus, in our example, we expect the result to be three. We will again assume that only lowercase vowels occur, leaving as an exercise a generalized program to deal with upper- and lowercase letters. The program (fig. 4.16) begins in the same way that FindVowels does: form both VowelSet and InputSet. The intersection, AnyVowels, will contain any vowels that are in InputSet. Then we need only check the size of AnyVowels.

If we calculate the complexity of this program, we find that it is the same as for finding vowels—$O(n)$ for the SET implementation and $O(n^2)$ for the ARRAY implementation.

Updating a data structure involves changing an element in the data structure, adding a new element, or deleting a current element. When an element is changed, if the altered element occupies the same amount of space as the original element, then there is no great problem. However, if the altered element uses a different amount of space, then there can be some difficulties.

For example, let's consider the set of names of the ten most wanted criminals in the United States. Note first that the FBI in fact keeps this as a set. Many years ago they decided not to order the names in the set, to avoid giving one of the ten the prestige of being *the* most wanted criminal. The names will be of different lengths, but since the set is so small, we will not waste a significant

Figure 4.16, Part 1   A program for counting the lowercase vowels in a set of char

```
PROGRAM CountVowels (input, output);

{ This program counts the vowels in an InputSet. The count is in a
set, not a string, so each different vowel counts only once. }

TYPE
  ElementType = char;
  SetType     = SET of ElementType;

{ Note: The definition ARRAY[1..MaxSize] OF ElementType could have
been used, with the appropriate procedure and function definitions. }

VAR
  AnyVowels   : SetType;
  InputSet    : SetType;
  Letter      : ElementType;
  VowelCount  : integer;
  VowelSet    : SetType;
  WasAdded    : boolean;

PROCEDURE NewSet (VAR SetName : SetType);

{ Procedure defined in fig. 4.3. }

PROCEDURE AddElement (SetElement      : ElementType;
                      VAR SetName     : SetType;
                      VAR AddedToSet  : boolean);

{ Procedure defined in fig. 4.3. }

FUNCTION IsElement (SetElement : ElementType;
                    SetName    : SetType) : boolean;

{ Function defined in fig. 4.4. }

FUNCTION Size (SetName : SetType) : integer;

{ Function defined in fig. 4.5. }

PROCEDURE Intersect (SetA, SetB : SetType;
                     VAR SetC    : SetType);

{ Procedure defined in fig. 4.6. }
```

Figure 4.16, Part 2   A program for counting the lowercase vowels in a set of char

```
PROCEDURE PrintLetterSet (SetName : SetType);

  VAR
    Index : ElementType;

  BEGIN
    write ('The input set is');
    FOR Index := 'a' TO 'z' DO
      IF IsElement (Index, SetName) THEN write (Index : 2);
    writeln
  END; { PrintLetterSet }

{ Main program. }

BEGIN

  { Define the VowelSet. }

  NewSet (VowelSet);
  AddElement ('a', VowelSet, WasAdded);
  AddElement ('e', VowelSet, WasAdded);
  AddElement ('i', VowelSet, WasAdded);
  AddElement ('o', VowelSet, WasAdded);
  AddElement ('u', VowelSet, WasAdded);

  { Read the InputSet. }

  NewSet (InputSet);
  REPEAT
    read (Letter);
    AddElement (Letter, InputSet, WasAdded)
  UNTIL eoln;

  PrintLetterSet (InputSet);

  { Form the intersection. }

  Intersect (InputSet, VowelSet, AnyVowels);

  { Determine the size of the intersection. }

  VowelCount := Size (AnyVowels);
  writeln ('The input set contains ', VowelCount : 1,
           ' distinct vowels.')
END. { CountVowels }
```

Figure 4.17, Part 1   Procedure to replace a set element

```
TYPE
  ElementType = UserSelectedType;
  SetType     = SET OF ElementType;

VAR
  IsntInSet : boolean;
  SetA      : SetType;
  SetB      : SetType;

PROCEDURE AddElement (SetElement      : ElementType;
                      VAR SetName     : SetType;
                      VAR AddedToSet  : boolean);

{ Procedure defined in fig. 4.3. }

PROCEDURE DeleteElement (SetElement          : ElementType;
                         VAR SetName         : SetType;
                         VAR DeletedFromSet  : boolean);

{ Procedure defined in fig. 4.4. }

FUNCTION IsElement (SetElement : ElementType;
                    SetName    : SetType) : boolean;

{ Function defined in fig. 4.4. }
```

amount of storage by assuming that the names are all the same length, say twenty-five characters. Whenever one of the people named on the list is caught or dies, then that name is replaced by a new name. This is an updating problem: find the name to be changed, and replace it.

We solve this problem by using a general replacement procedure (fig. 4.17). This procedure assumes that each data element requires the same amount of space, so that there is no difficulty in that regard. This procedure performs three major operations, defined by the function IsElement and the procedures DeleteElement and AddElement. Since these are performed in sequence, the complexity of Replace is the maximum of the complexity of these. Table 4.2 shows the computation.

The procedure Replace can now be used for any set element replacement problem. All that is required is the proper definition of the element type. For the "ten most wanted" list problem, the element type (in Pascal) is a PACKED ARRAY of twenty-five characters and the ARRAY implementation *must* be used.

To traverse a set we have introduced the function GetAnother. While this performs the basic traversal from one end of a set to the other, there are two variations we shall discuss briefly, leaving their implementations as exercises.

Figure 4.17, Part 2   Procedure to replace a set element

```
{ Main procedure. }

PROCEDURE Replace (OldSetElement : ElementType;
                   NewSetElement : ElementType;
                   VAR SetName   : SetType;
                   VAR NotInSet  : boolean);

{ This procedure locates OldSetElement in SetName and replaces it by
NewSetElement. If OldSetElement is not in the set, NotInSet is set
to true and SetName is not changed. }

  VAR
    DeletedFromSet : boolean;
    AddedToSet     : boolean;

  BEGIN
    IF IsElement (OldSetElement, SetName) THEN
      BEGIN
        DeleteElement (OldSetElement, SetName, DeletedFromSet);
        AddElement (NewSetElement, SetName, AddedToSet);
        NotInSet := false

        { Assert: DeletedFromSet is true because of the IF
        statement; AddedToSet is true. }

      END
    ELSE

      { Assert: OldSetElement is not in SetName. }

    NotInSet := true
  END; { Replace }
```

Table 4.2.   Complexity of Replace

	SET Implementation	ARRAY Implementation
IsElement	$O(1)$	$O(n)$
DeleteElement	$O(1)$	$O(n)$
AddElement	$O(1)$	$O(n)$
Overall	$O(1)$	$O(n)$

First, analogous to GetAnother is the function GetPrevious, which returns the element immediately before the given one in the set. Its implementations exactly parallel those of GetAnother.

Second, we must consider the starting point for a traversal. GetAnother requires that at each step we specify the element currently under scrutiny, as the starting point for locating the next one. It does not say where we began the traversal. Ordinarily, we think of a traversal as starting at one end of the set and going to the other. But in some circumstances it is better to begin one traversal where the previous one ended. Suppose, for example, that we are scanning text, looking for the first occurrence of "computer" following an occurrence of "digital." Our first scan locates an occurrence of "digital." We do not then want to begin at the beginning to locate "computer," since this might locate an occurrence *before* the word "digital," which is not what was specified. We must begin the search for "computer" at the occurrence of "digital."

Beginning a traversal at some point other than one end of the set causes only one problem: in searching to the other end of the set, we never examine the portion before the starting point. This may or may not be important. If it is, we want to do a **wraparound** or **circular traversal,** continuing at the beginning of the set after we have examined its end. We can accomplish this simply by starting over at the beginning once we have reached the end. If the set is represented by an ARRAY, this simply means resetting the search index to 1:

```
FOR I := K + 1 TO N DO
   { whatever must be done to SetName[I] }
```

followed by

```
FOR I := 1 TO K DO
   { whatever must be done to SetName[I] }
```

By using the MOD† function, we can accomplish this circular traversal in a single construct:

```
I := K + 1;
REPEAT
   { whatever must be done to SetName[I] };
   I := (I + 1) MOD N
UNTIL I = K + 1;
```

Suppose we wish to merge two sets of elements. The result is, of course, the union of the two sets. Thus, merge is simple to accomplish using a SET representation. However, an ARRAY implementation requires quite a bit of work,

---

†Recall that m MOD n is defined to be the remainder (between 0 and $n - 1$) obtained upon dividing m by n.

because of the need to eliminate duplicate elements. If the sets were sorted into the same order, the problem would not be so great, as we shall see in chapter 11. However, for unsorted sets (that is, sets as a mathematician defines them) the simplest way to accomplish this is to take one set as the basis of the union, then check each element of the other set against every element in the first one to see if it is already included. Thus, for an ARRAY implementation, set union or merger is an $O(n^2)$ operation. We leave writing this in Pascal as an exercise.

4.5 Multisets

One very useful extension of the set concept is the idea of a **multiset,** which is a "set" in which duplicate elements are allowed. There are many applications of this concept. For example, the collection of examination grades in a course is generally a multiset: we cannot insist that each student have a distinct grade. The same is true of any collection of test data. Generally several tests will produce the same results. Thus we must allow the processing of multisets, or sets with duplicate elements.

Since the SET type of Pascal does not allow for multiple occurrences of an element, we cannot use the Pascal SET type to implement multisets. Our implementation, therefore, will be as ARRAYs. We observe that the ARRAY implementation for an ordinary set will also work for multisets, with some slight changes. These changes have an effect on the efficiency of various operations.

(We might try to sneak around the prohibition on multiple elements in a SET by considering a SET whose elements are themselves SETs. Then we could place one copy of each multiple element in a different (SET) element of the large SET. However, this is not permitted, since the element type for a Pascal SET must be an ordinal type.)

Operations on multisets may or may not be easier than the corresponding operations on sets. On the one hand, since multisets can have multiple elements, we do not need to check for duplicates and eliminate them when we add an element. Thus, in the ARRAY implementation adding elements to a multiset is more efficient than adding elements to a set. On the other hand, whenever we delete an element, we will not generally know how many times that element occurs in the multiset. In some situations we may be satisfied with deleting just one occurrence of the element. In this situation, element deletion will be the same for both sets and multisets implemented as ARRAYs. However, in other situations we may want all occurrences of the element deleted. This may increase the complexity of deleting an element, since we must check for multiple occurrences. These modifications to the ARRAY implementation will be left as exercises.

Let us consider merging multisets. If the multisets are unordered, we can simply append the second one to the end of the first one (fig. 4.18). Note that standard Pascal requires a separate MultisetMerge procedure for each different combination of maximal set sizes. Some extended Pascals allow dynamic allocation of array sizes by passing the size to the procedure, thus allowing the use of a single procedure for all different set merges. Other languages such as Modula-2 also permit dynamic allocation of array sizes.

Figure 4.18   Multiset merge

```
CONST
  MaxSize = UserSelectedSize; { Maximum size. }

TYPE
  ElementType = UserSelectedType;
  SetType     = RECORD
                  SetItself : ARRAY[1..MaxSize] OF ElementType;
                  SetSize   : 0..MaxSize
                END;

FUNCTION Size (SetName : SetType) : integer;

{ Function defined in fig. 4.11. }

PROCEDURE MultisetMerge (MultiSetA, MultiSetB : SetType;
                         VAR MultiSetC        : SetType);

{ SetType is a predefined RECORD type, with an ARRAY large enough to
hold each of the three multisets, and subscripted 1..MaxSize. The
procedure merges arrays MultiSetA and MultiSetB into array MultiSetC
by copying the elements of MultiSetB into MultiSetC after copying
the elements of MultiSetA. }

VAR
  Index : 1..MaxSize;
  SizeA : 0..MaxSize;
  SizeB : 0..MaxSize;

BEGIN

  { Assert: MultiSetA, MultiSetB, and MultiSetC have been defined,
  but MultiSetA and MultiSetB may be empty. }

  SizeA := Size (MultiSetA);
  SizeB := Size (MultiSetB);
  FOR Index := 1 TO SizeA DO
    MultiSetC.SetItself[Index] := MultiSetA.SetItself[Index];
  FOR Index := 1 TO SizeB DO
    MultiSetC.SetItself[Index + SizeA] := MultiSetB.SetItself[Index];
  MultiSetC.SetSize := SizeA + SizeB
END; { MultisetMerge }
```

Let us examine this procedure briefly. We are assuming that the implementation for multisets parallels that for sets represented as ARRAYs. Thus we assume that the ARRAY containing the multiset is one field of a RECORD, with the size of the array in the other field of the RECORD, and that Size retrieves that value. Note that the size, as we use it here, is *not* the number of distinct elements in the multiset but, rather, the total number of element occurrences. Thus the size of $\{a, a, b\}$ is three, not two.

While it is important that MultiSetA and MultiSetB be defined, this procedure does not require that they be nonempty for correct operation. If either multiset is empty, the corresponding FOR loop will be skipped, and if both are empty, MultiSetC.SetSize will be set to 0, as is appropriate.

This procedure is of complexity $O(m + n)$, where SizeA $= O(m)$ and SizeB $= O(n)$, since the loops are not nested but are executed sequentially. This is the same as $O(\max(m,n))$, since the larger set will dominate the time required for developing the merged set. (Think about what happens if $m = 20$ and $n = 1{,}000{,}000$.)

For many applications of multisets, the concept of **order** is important. For example, the order in which words occur in a text, or in which letters occur in a word, is significant. Similarly, the order in which events occur plays an important role in many data processing applications. Seismic data for oil well drilling, for example, are ordered by the positions at which the data are taken. A bank needs to maintain a record of deposits and withdrawals on each account, ordered by the time received. Note that none of these applications requires sorting to establish the ordering of the multiset. Nor are we able to use the ordering to shorten search and traversal times. Yet we do not have the freedom to disregard totally the given order of the words or numbers.

Summary

This chapter has covered two straightforward representations of sets, both in the SET datatype of Pascal and in ARRAYs. We have also examined multisets as a data structure of high utility. For each of these structures, we have considered the operations to be done on them and provided algorithms for many of them.

The chapter has also continued the systematic use of abstract data types (ADTs). It may have occurred to you, particularly as we discussed the SET implementation of sets, that use of the abstract data type can involve a bit of inefficiency. After all, if we can find the intersection simply by computing SetA * SetB, why build a procedure Intersect (SetA, SetB) just to implement that one line of code? The abstract data type is indeed a two-edged sword. The *dull* edge is the possible inefficiency that is introduced, both in terms of extra space to store the procedure and function codes and in terms of extra time to call and execute them. With the speed of operation and the large amount of storage that are available today, even on microcomputers, these inefficiencies matter little. The *sharp* edge of the ADT sword is that we can separate the system implementation details from the application. The application programmer does not need to worry about how the set operations are implemented, any more than he or she worries about how boolean expressions are evaluated, how addition is done, or how reals are represented. The ADT allows the application programmer to focus completely on what the operations do, rather than on how this is accomplished. In effect, an ADT provides a sound extension of the base language, available for use by any programmer.

Vocabulary

bit map
circular traversal
complement
difference
empty set
intersection
multiset
order
relative complement

sentinel
set
subset
symmetric difference
union
universal set
Venn diagram
von Neumann computer
wraparound traversal

Reference

Cooper, Doug. *Standard Pascal User Reference Manual.* W. W. Norton & Co., New York, 1983.

Problems

4.1. Given a universe of the integers from 1 to 15 and the sets $A = \{2, 4, 6, 8, 10\}$, $B = \{1, 3, 5, 7\}$, and $C = \{3, 6, 7, 14\}$, find:

    A. $A \cup B$
    B. $A \cap B$
    C. $(A \cup B) \cap C$
    D. $A \triangle C$
    E. $B - C$
    F. $C - B$
    G. $(A \cup B) - C$
    H. $(A \cap B) \triangle C$
    I. $\overline{A}$
    J. $\overline{(A - C)} \triangle B$
    K. $C \triangle B$
    L. $B \cap \overline{C}$

4.2. Use Venn diagrams to verify your answers to the previous problem.

4.3. Given the sets $A = \{1, 5, 83, 62, 14, 3, 11, 4\}$ and $B = \{2, 4, 26, 84, 62, 5, 3\}$, and the universe 1..84, find and draw Venn diagrams for $A \cup B$, $A \cap B$, $A \triangle B$, $A - B$, $B - A$, $\overline{A}$, and $\overline{B}$.

4.4. Show that for any sets A and B, the union can be defined in terms of the intersection and the complement, and the intersection can be defined in terms of the union and the complement.

4.5. List the eight subsets of $\{14, \text{orange}, \text{Karen}\}$.

4.6. How does your Pascal translator implement sets? Are the set operations such as union and intersection $O(1)$? What about the operation IN?

4.7. What are the values of FirstCode and LastCode in each of these situations:
Universe of letters, EBCDIC code;
Universe of digits, EBCDIC code;
Universe of letters, ASCII code;
Universe of digits, ASCII code.
(See appendix A.)

4.8. We have discussed using FOR Index := FirstElement TO LastElement to traverse a SET. How would you traverse a SET in reverse order? In particular, what loop construct would you use to search the alphabetical characters from "z" to "A"?

4.9. Look in *ACM Computing Surveys, Communications of the ACM,* and *IEEE Computer Magazine* for articles that deal with non–von Neumann computers. (Hint: Look for articles which reference John Backus's article "Can Programming Be Liberated from the von Neumann Style? A Functional Style and Its Algebra of Programs," in *Communications of the ACM,* Vol. 21, No. 8, Aug. 1978.)

4.10. For each of the following constructs indicate whether you should use a set or a multiset to implement it. Which ones must be ordered?
    A. The list of examination scores for this course
    B. The Associated Press top ten college football teams
    C. The *Sporting News* all-American hockey team
    D. The *New York Times* best-seller list
    E. The presidential candidates who ran in the 1984 New Hampshire Democratic primary
    F. Temperature readings at noon for Bullhead City, Arizona, during the month of May
    G. The figures in this book
    H. The IQs of the faculty
    I. The stores where you can purchase your two favorite kinds of cheese
    J. The teams the New York Mets will play during the month of August

4.11. Write a single Pascal conditional statement which prints out the word "Eureka" if the character variable "Initial" is an uppercase letter.

4.12. Although mathematicians do not permit duplicate elements in a set, it is possible to define a set implementation that does permit duplicates using an ARRAY as the base type. How would such an implementation differ from the multiset implementation? What would be its advantages and disadvantages compared to the ARRAY implementation of sets that we have given? Would the complexities of any of the operations change, and if so, how?

Programs

4.1. Implement the set operations union, difference, symmetric difference, and complement for sets stored as SETs. Use the sets of problem 4.3 to check your procedures.

4.2. Implement the set operations union, difference, symmetric difference, and complement for sets stored as ARRAYs. Use the sets of problem 4.3 to check your procedures.

4.3. For both SET and ARRAY implementations of sets, write a GetAnother function that generates an error message, rather than the first element of the set, in the event that the input element is the last set element. What change does this require in the ADT definition?

4.4. Investigate the time required for various set operations using both the SET and the ARRAY implementations. For this, use 100 sets of each of several different sizes, say with 1, 10, 100, and 1000 elements.

4.5. Implement and test the FindVowels program, from the skeleton in fig. 4.13, using both the SET and the ARRAY implementations of sets. If your system permits you to gather timing data on the runs, experiment with sets of various sizes to compare the complexities of the two implementations.

4.6. Implement FindVowels directly using Pascal SETs, without regard to the ADTs. Compare the run time of this implementation with that using ADTs and SETs.

4.7. Revise FindVowels and CountVowels to work with text containing both upper- and lowercase letters.

4.8. Write a program to count the number of prime numbers in a set of integers in the range 1..200, using the set operations of this chapter. Run this program using both the SET implementation and the ARRAY implementation. If your version of Pascal does not allow a SET this large, do this exercise using the largest SET of integers that you can implement.

4.9. Write an ADT definition for GetPrevious which returns the element preceding the current one in the set. Implement this for a set stored as an ARRAY. Write a simple driver program, and use it to test your procedure.

4.10. One way to compact a string of alphabetic data is to remove all blanks and punctuation. Write a procedure that will do this for a string of at most fifty characters. Test your procedure with a simple driver routine.

4.11. Another way to compact alphabetic data is to remove any vowel that does not begin a word and reduce all double letters to single ones. Write and test a procedure for doing this. Does it matter which of these operations is done first?

4.12. Write a program that merges two sets (not ordered) of reals which are represented as

```
ARRAY[1..30] OF real
```

and places the result in a third array. Discuss all assumptions.

4.13. Rewrite the Pascal code fragment below using a sentinel and counter to eliminate the read (N) statement. Which method is preferred? Why?

```
Sum := 0;
read (N);
FOR I := 1 TO N DO
  BEGIN
    read (X);
    Sum := Sum + X
  END;
writeln ('Average is ', Sum/N);
```

4.14. Modify the ADTs for sets to serve for multisets. Implement these ADTs using an ARRAY as the base type for the multiset.

5

Sets: Linked List Representation

Introduction

While the representation of sets by arrays has much to recommend it, including ease of processing, it has its flaws. First, as we have mentioned, many programming languages require that the components of an array be all of the same type—for example, all integer or all character. Yet there are many practical situations that call for mixed data types, such as a name, an identification number, and a salary. Second, updating an ordered array may require a relatively large amount of data movement. Thus we ask whether we can store sets in ways that will allow for mixed data types and efficient updating, and if so, what price we will have to pay for this.

We have already used a RECORD as a device to store an array of data. Clearly, we could use a RECORD with several data fields that are ARRAYs—one the name array, a second the identification number array, the third the salary array, and so forth. Thus we have a convenient means of handling the problem of mixed data types: give each its own ARRAY within a RECORD.

In this chapter we study a different use of RECORDs. If we want to keep a set sorted in some order, such as alphabetical order, and the set is dynamic, in the sense that there are many additions and deletions, storing the set as an ARRAY forces us to do much work. Every time we add an element, we must move several other elements out of the way; and every time we delete an element, we must either close up the resulting gap or mark it so that we know it is a gap. In general, storing a dynamic set as an ARRAY forces us to spend quite a bit of time shuffling data back and forth. In what follows we shall see that the RECORD data structure provides us with a method for avoiding lengthy updates. The method, called ''linked lists,'' avoids the data movement problem entirely, by using a chain passing through all the data cells. When we add or delete an element, we simply change the chain linking the elements.

Figure 5.1   Fruits, linked in input order

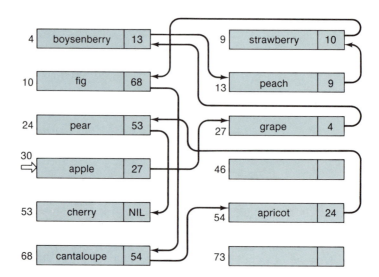

5.1 Sets with scattered storage: linked lists

In sequentially stored sets, we know that we will find the element following a given one in the next storage location and the element preceding it in the preceding storage location. This is very efficient for sequential location of the set elements, but causes difficulties in updating, because of the need to move data around to make room for new data or to close the gap left by the removal of old data. In this section we explore another idea, one that leads us quickly from one set element to the next and at the same time does not require all the work for updating that sequential storage does.

The idea is not only to scatter the elements of a set throughout a section of storage, using whatever storage is conveniently available, but also to connect the set elements together explicitly, by including with each a **pointer** that identifies the storage location or **address** of the next element. This structure is called a **linked list.**

Suppose that the data items are the names of ten fruits, which arrive as input in this order: apple, grape, boysenberry, peach, strawberry, fig, cantaloupe, apricot, pear, and cherry. Suppose that they are stored in the indicated locations:

apple	30	fig	10
apricot	54	grape	27
boysenberry	4	peach	13
cantaloupe	68	pear	24
cherry	53	strawberry	9

Figure 5.2   Fruits, linked in sorted order

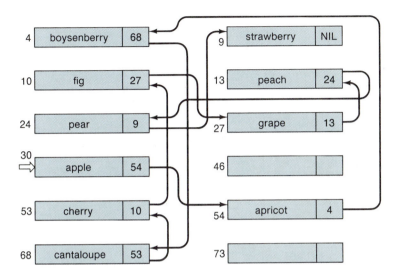

Figure 5.3   Fruits, linked in storage order

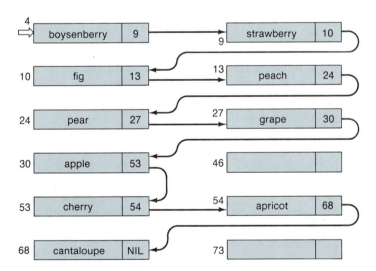

We can form a linked list simply by pointing from one to another. Here are three ways of doing that. Figure 5.1 shows the linkage that would result using the order in which the words were given. Note that each cell contains both a word and the address of the next word in the list. The last cell in the list contains a special **null address** or **null pointer,** symbolized by **NIL,** since there is nothing to which to point. Figure 5.2 shows another linkage, which follows the sorted order of the list. Finally, figure 5.3 shows the linkage reflecting the storage order.

Figure 5.4   Adding "plum," input order linking

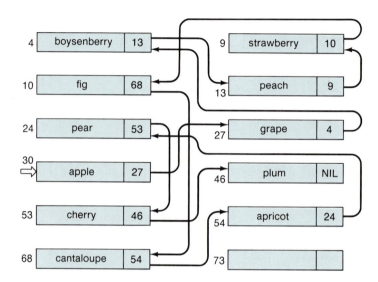

A linked list is a very flexible and common data structure. It is particularly useful in situations involving dynamic data, with frequent additions and deletions. Items are added or deleted simply by changing the values of the pointers linking the list. However, searching now takes longer since a linked list must be traversed linearly, because the elements are not stored sequentially.

Suppose we want to add the word "plum" to the list and we have determined somehow that it will be stored in location 46. If the list is linked in input order, we simply replace the null pointer for "cherry" by a pointer to the new cell (fig. 5.4). The pointer for plum is set to NIL.

If the list is linked in sorted order, then we must first locate the position of "plum" on the list. However, we do not need to move any data. Since we see that "plum" belongs between "pear" and "strawberry," we simply change the pointer of "pear" to point to "plum," and make "plum" point to "strawberry" (fig. 5.5).

In either situation, aside from the effort of searching for the correct location in a sorted list, the amount of work involved in adding an element is constant and is independent of the size of the list. Thus, adding a new element to a linked list, once we have determined its location, is an $O(1)$ operation.

Deletion is equally simple. Suppose that we wish to delete the word "apple" from the list linked in storage order. "Grape" currently points to "apple," and "apple" points to "cherry." Simply make "grape" point to "cherry" (fig. 5.6). Note that "apple" still points to "cherry," but that there is nothing pointing to "apple." Effectively, the word has been removed from the list. If we wish, we can be a bit neater, by detaching "apple" completely from the list and adding it to another linked list, a list of available memory. In either case, the amount of work involved following a search for the word is independent of the size of the set—another $O(1)$ operation.

Figure 5.5   Adding "plum," sorted linking

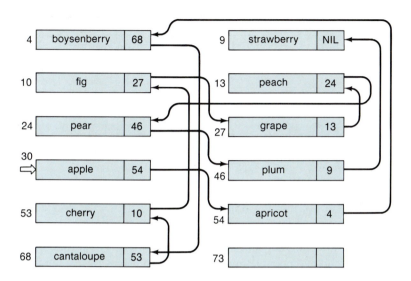

Figure 5.6   Deleting "apple," storage linking

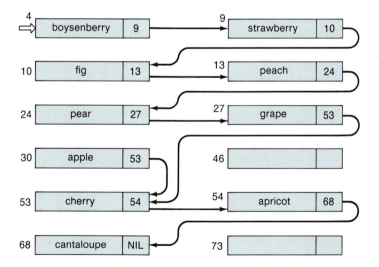

Figure 5.7   **Continuing the search**

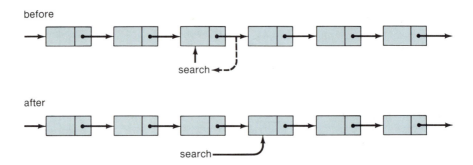

5.2 Searching and changing a linked list

The heart of the linked list concept is that we have pointers that tie together the cells of the list, directing our movements within the list. We presume that the search process follows a pointer through the list and leaves the pointer pointing at the desired cell once it is found. But what happens if the cell is not in the list? In a sorted list we would recognize this as soon as we had seen a cell beyond the desired one. We would be pointing to the location where the desired cell should be, if it were there. But in an unsorted list we would search the entire list and come to the end without finding the cell.

When searching a list we must keep at least two pointer systems active. One is the set of pointers that join cells in the list, together with the pointer that indicates which cell starts the list. These pointers must remain as they are, so that we do not change the list structure, or possibly lose cells in the list. We shall refer to these as the **list pointers.** The other is the pointer that we actually use for the search. This pointer initially takes the value of the pointer to the head of the list and then successively assumes the values of the other list pointers as it works its way down the list. This pointer we shall call the **search pointer.**

With this in mind, suppose that we have been searching for a cell and the search pointer is now pointing at a cell somewhere in the middle of a list. We can easily find the next cell, by picking up the list pointer associated with our present cell and using that to continue (fig. 5.7). We know we have come to the end of the list when the next pointer we pick up is the null pointer, NIL. That is, when the search pointer starts out by pointing to the first cell (or head of the list) and eventually becomes NIL, we have traversed the entire list.

Let us examine in some detail the surroundings of our pointer, which is somewhere in the middle of the list. (We must later consider what happens when the pointer is at one end or the other of the list.) First, we recognize that the search pointer may not be pointing exactly where we want it to point. Suppose that we are searching the fruit list, given in alphabetical order. If we are looking for "pear" and find it, the pointer will indeed point to "pear." But if we are searching for the last cell in the list containing a fruit beginning with "g," we will not recognize this until we find the first fruit beyond that one. That is, the pointer will really be one position beyond the fruit we want.

Another problem may arise. Suppose that we are pointing at "pear" and that we want to delete this fruit from the list. In theory, we just change the pointer in the previous element (which now points at "pear") to point to the fruit following "pear." But this means that somehow we must remember what the previous fruit in the list was.

Similarly, when we want to add a cell to a list, we may want to add it before the cell that the search pointer indicates, and hence need to know the previous cell.

There are three common ways to solve this problem. One is to keep a trailer pointer, following the search pointer but always one cell behind it. While this is sometimes very useful, it means keeping an extra pointer system current, an added complication. A second method is to keep a "reverse" pointer in each cell, pointing back to its predecessor. This also has the disadvantage of maintaining an extra pointer system. The other common method is to "look ahead." That is, rather than ask questions about the current cell, ask them about the next cell, the one that follows the current cell in the list.

Each of these methods requires some special handling for the head of the list. When the search pointer is pointing at the head of the list, there is no cell for a trailer or reverse pointer to indicate. Using the technique of asking about the next cell does not have this problem, but does have the problem that the head of the list is not the "next" cell for any cell. Thus a separate question must be asked.

5.3 An ADT for linked lists

Now that we have explored the concept of a linked list, let us construct an ADT for this data type. We shall need the usual operations: create a new list, search a list for a cell which holds a given element, add a cell to an existing list, and delete a cell from an existing list. We may also wish to compute the length or size of a linked list.

With this in mind, we present an abstract data type for lists. Note that for the linked list implementation, ListName, ListPointer, and SearchPointer are interpreted as pointers to the list, with ListName always pointing to the first item on the list.

In the following definitions the term "Value" may refer to many different value fields. For example, it might refer to all the record except the pointer fields. It may also refer to a single field in a cell, such as a social security number or a ZIP code. As usual, each operation returns an error if any variable is undefined, or any needed value is missing.

NewList (ListName)—sets ListName to an empty list.

Search (ListName, Value, SearchPointer)—sets SearchPointer to the location of the first cell of ListName which contains Value.

BuildListAtFront (ListName)—builds a list by repeatedly appending cells at the front of the list ListName.

BuildListAtBack (ListName)—builds a list by repeatedly appending cells at the back of the list ListName.

InsertCellBeforePointer (ListName, ListPointer, Value)—gets a cell from cell storage and places Value in it before inserting the cell in the list before the cell currently indicated by ListPointer.

InsertCellAfterPointer (ListName, ListPointer, Value)—gets a cell from cell storage and places Value in it before inserting the cell in the list after the cell currently indicated by ListPointer.

DeleteCellAtPointer (ListName, ListPointer)—deletes the cell of ListName to which ListPointer currently points. ListName still represents a list (which may be empty). ListPointer still points to the cell to which it originally pointed. Note that this cell has been deleted from ListName.

DeleteCellFollowingPointer (ListName, ListPointer)—deletes the cell of ListName following the one to which ListPointer currently points. If ListPointer points to the last cell in ListName, no deletion occurs. ListName still represents a list (which may be empty). ListPointer still points to the cell. Note that this cell has been deleted from ListName.

FreeList (ListName)—returns all cells of ListName to cell storage.

Size (ListName)—counts the number of cells in the list ListName.

While this ADT is developed with linked lists in mind, it serves equally well for lists implemented as arrays. We may consider an array as a special kind of list where the pointers are implicit in the subscripts. A list with one "Next" field can be implemented as a one-dimensional array, where the predecessor and successor to a given cell are adjacent to it in storage. While we normally think of $A[1]$ as the first cell and $A[n]$ as the last cell of an array of n elements, we could just as easily consider $A[n]$ as the first cell and $A[1]$ as the last cell.

There are two unfortunate points in dealing with linked lists. One is that searching a linked list is an $O(n)$ process. We can search a sorted, sequentially stored list using a **binary search** in $O(\lg n)$ time. This depends on two things: the items are sorted into order, and the location of the next item to be examined can be calculated directly. However, even if the cells in a linked list contain items that are sorted into order, we cannot calculate the search addresses as we could for the $O(\lg n)$ search. What, for example, is the search address of the middle item in the list? We have no way to compute it other than tracing down the list. Thus, for a linked list, we are forced to use a **linear search** to find an item. (See problem 5.5.)

The other unfortunate point about a linked list is that we must store the addresses explicitly. This may require additional storage; but it may not, if there is sufficient room in a computer word to accommodate both the data and the next address.

5.4 Pascal implementation of linked lists

The idea behind linked lists is fairly simple, but implementing this idea in a programming language requires a bit of work and lots of care. Some languages, such as FORTRAN, do not have facilities for linked lists. For such languages we must "fake" a linked list through the use of arrays or some other mechanism. Pascal, fortunately, does provide a pointer mechanism and procedures to create and destroy cells, which are necessary for this kind of data structure. Here is a simple way to use it.

The syntax of the Pascal pointer structure revolves around the symbol **caret,** that is used to denote a pointer. The easiest way to remember the syntax is to observe that this symbol combines with a variable name in a logical way. Suppose that the variable name is "Cell." Then "^Cell" is a *pointer to Cell,* while "Cell^" would be *Cell points to...* . In the first of these, Cell holds data and something is pointing to it; in the second, Cell is the name of the pointer, which is pointing to some data location.

Pointers in Pascal can be used in several ways, the simplest being to use them in conjunction with records. In figure 5.8, Fruit is a record type having two fields. One field is called "Goodie" and is of the type FruitNameType. This is the **data field** of the record. The other field is called "Next" and is of type FruitPointer. We see also that the type FruitPointer is a pointer to Fruit (note the syntax). Thus Next is a **pointer field,** pointing to another record of the type Fruit. We have defined one variable, Grocery, which is a FruitPointer, that is, a pointer to a record of type Fruit. Note that we have not directly defined any cells!

Figure 5.8   First implementation of fruit

```
CONST
  MaxSize = 12; { Maximum size }

TYPE
  FruitNameType = ARRAY[1..MaxSize] OF char;
  FruitPointer  = ^Fruit;
  Fruit         = RECORD
                    Goodie : FruitNameType;
                    Next   : FruitPointer
                  END;

VAR
  Grocery : FruitPointer;
```

Figure 5.9   Second implementation of fruit

```
CONST
  MaxSize = 12; { Maximum size }

TYPE
  FruitNameType = ARRAY[1..MaxSize] OF char;
  Fruit         = RECORD
                    Goodie : FruitNameType;
                    Next   : ^Fruit
                  END;

VAR
  Grocery : ^Fruit;
```

Alternatively, we can implement fruit without explicitly defining the FruitPointer type (fig. 5.9). The choice between these two methods is largely a matter of taste.* The main advantage of the method of figure 5.8 (which we shall use) is that it enables us to define many pointers to Fruit without including the symbol "^" in each definition (that is, it is easier to read).

It is important to be clear on the distinction among Grocery, Grocery^, Grocery^.Goodie, and Grocery^.Next. Figure 5.10 shows this distinction. In the figure, the highlighted portion corresponds to the name in quotes. From the diagram we see that both Grocery and Grocery^.Next are pointers, Grocery^.Goodie is a data field, and Grocery^ refers to the entire record.

---

*Some Pascal implementations, such as Turbo Pascal, may not be able to handle the second definition.

Figure 5.10   The parts of a pointer-record system

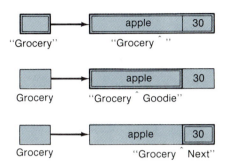

Figure 5.11   Allocation of a new cell of type Grocery

Grocery

The first process in building a list is to get it started. In Pascal, this is accomplished by the **new** procedure, which allocates a new storage cell of the type pointer value. Note that this does not assign any values into the cell pointed to by the pointer, but simply assigns storage space and makes the pointer point to it. For example, the instruction

        new (Grocery)

allocates storage for a new record of type Fruit and makes Grocery point to the new record. We may think of this as shown in figure 5.11.

The procedure "new" has a counterpart, **dispose,** which is used to release space whenever we are through with a record. The instruction

        dispose (Grocery)

deletes the storage pointed to by the Grocery pointer. Note that, just as "new" does not assign any data value, "dispose" does not delete any value: it simply returns Grocery^ to a storage pool so that we can no longer find and use it. Further, the value of the pointer variable Grocery no longer serves any purpose.

Figure 5.12   Pascal implementation of NewList and FreeList

```
TYPE
  ListPointer = ^List;
  List        = UserSelectedType;

VAR
  ListName : ListPointer;
```

Table 5.1   Basic list operations

ADT	Pascal
NewList (ListName)	ListName := NIL;
FreeList (ListName)	dispose (ListName);

"Dispose" must be used carefully, for if we "dispose" of a cell in the middle of a list, then there may be no way to reach the cells that follow it. Pointers which refer to storage no longer in use (disposed of) are called **dangling references.** When all pointers to a piece of storage are destroyed before the storage is disposed of, that storage is called **garbage.** The process of recovering such storage for further use is called **garbage collection.**

Two of the basic operations defined in the ADT, NewList and FreeList, correspond to standard procedures in Pascal. We must first declare the appropriate types and variables (fig. 5.12) before we define the operations (Table 5.1).

We can build a list by adding elements either at the front, **head** of the list, or at the back, **tail.** We illustrate both methods. It is a good idea with either method to seal the end of the list with a NIL pointer. Adding data at the head of the list is easiest (see fig. 5.13). The procedure GetString is used instead of a simple read statement "read (Grocery^.Goodie)" since not all implementations of Pascal can read strings.

Figure 5.13   Building a list at the head

```
PROCEDURE GetString (VAR Item : FruitNameType);

{ Reads an item into the record. }

   VAR
     I : 1..MaxSize;

   BEGIN
     FOR I := 1 TO MaxSize DO read (Item[I]);
     readln
   END; { GetString }

PROCEDURE BuildListAtFront (VAR Grocery : FruitPointer);

{ Initialize the list, sealing the end and placing the first
datum. }

   VAR
     FruitPtr : FruitPointer;

   BEGIN

     { Assert: There is a global datatype defined in fig. 5.8. }

     new (Grocery);
     Grocery^.Next := NIL;

     { Assert: There is at least one item to be entered. }

     GetString (Grocery^.Goodie);

     { Now, continue reading data into the head of the list. }

     WHILE NOT eof DO
       BEGIN
         new (FruitPtr);
         GetString (FruitPtr^.Goodie);
         FruitPtr^.Next := Grocery;
         Grocery := FruitPtr
       END
   END; { BuildListAtFront }
```

Figure 5.14   The first datum ("apple") in a list

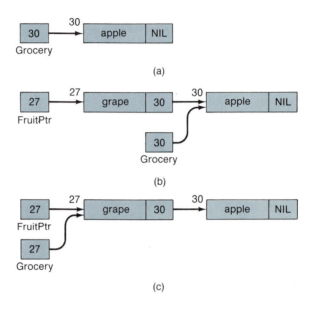

(a)

(b)

(c)

Figure 5.15   Three more data entered at the head of the list

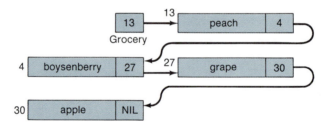

The first instruction in the loop of BuildListAtFront creates a new record, with FruitPtr pointing to it. The next two instructions establish the two fields of this record (fig. 5.14), by getting a new datum and by setting the Next field to point to the previous record.

The final instruction in the loop resets Grocery to point to the latest record created. If we are not at the end of the input, then the WHILE loop is executed until the end of the input is found. Each cycle through the loop creates a new pointer (FruitPtr); assigns its data field, Goodie, the input value; sets its pointer field, Next, to point at the record that Grocery indicates; and resets Grocery to point to the new record. Figure 5.15 shows the first three cycles of this, loading the values "grape," "boysenberry," and "peach." Note that the linked list formed by BuildListAtFront is the reverse of the list shown in figure 5.1.

Figure 5.16   Building a list at the tail

```
PROCEDURE BuildListAtBack (VAR Grocery : FruitPointer);

{ Initialize the list, placing the first datum and
initializing a tail pointer. }

   VAR
      FruitPtr : FruitPointer;
      Tail     : FruitPointer;

   BEGIN

      { Assert: There is at least one item to be entered. }

      new (Grocery);
      GetString (Grocery^.Goodie); { GetString from fig. 5.13. }
      Tail := Grocery;

      { Now, continue reading data into the tail of the list. }

      WHILE NOT eof DO
        BEGIN
           new (FruitPtr);
           Tail^.Next := FruitPtr;
           GetString (FruitPtr^.Goodie);
           Tail := FruitPtr
        END;

      { Seal the end of the list. }

      Tail^.Next := NIL
   END; { BuildListAtBack }
```

Because the pointers in a list point from the head of the list toward the tail, it is important that we keep track of the head, by keeping a pointer to it. This makes loading data into the tail of a list a little more cumbersome, since we need another, separate pointer to indicate the tail. The code for this is given in figure 5.16, where we assume that all variables have been properly declared in a containing block. Note that in this code, a pointer "Tail" is initialized to the same value as Grocery, and then moves along through the list as data are added. Thus Grocery continues to point to the head of the list. Once all data have been entered, the list is sealed with a NIL pointer (fig. 5.17).

After a list has been built, many operations depend on traversing the list to locate a particular datum. Figure 5.18 is the code for this. We call the pointer that traverses the list "Trace."

Figure 5.17   Loading data at the tail of the list

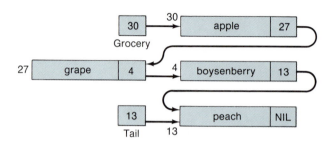

Figure 5.18   Code for traversing a list in search of a value

```
PROCEDURE Search (Grocery    : FruitPointer;
                  GoodFruit  : FruitNameType;
                  VAR Trace  : FruitPointer);

{ Initialize "Trace" to the head of the list, and search
the list for the value of the variable "GoodFruit." }

{ Assert: The list Grocery is not empty, and GoodFruit
is in the list. }

  BEGIN
    Trace := Grocery;
    WHILE Trace^.Goodie <> GoodFruit DO
      Trace := Trace^.Next;

    { Upon exiting the loop, "Trace" points to the record
    containing the value of "GoodFruit." }

END; { Search }
```

Now that we can locate a given element within a linked list, we can discuss inserting and deleting elements from the list. We consider insertion first.

We may wish to insert an element into a list immediately before the element that we have found in traversal, or immediately following it. For the latter, create a cell for new data and insert it in the list (fig. 5.19).

Figure 5.20 shows an example of this, with "apple," "boysenberry," and "grape" in the list, and "fig" inserted after "boysenberry." The bracketed numbers correspond to the steps indicated in the procedure of figure 5.19.

One way to insert an element before the located one is to keep a second pointer trailing along one record behind the trace pointer, and then make the insertion

Figure 5.19   Insertion after a located element

```
PROCEDURE InsertCellAfterPtr (Grocery  : FruitPointer;
                              Trace    : FruitPointer;
                              NewFruit : FruitNameType);

{ Code to insert an element, NewFruit, after the one
indicated by Trace. }

  VAR
    FruitPtr : FruitPointer;

  BEGIN

    { Assert: Trace is not NIL. }

    new (FruitPtr);                        { Step 1 }
    FruitPtr^.Goodie := NewFruit;          { Step 2 }
    FruitPtr^.Next := Trace^.Next;         { Step 3 }
    Trace^.Next := FruitPtr                { Step 4 }
  END; { InsertCellAfterPtr }
```

Figure 5.20   Inserting "fig"

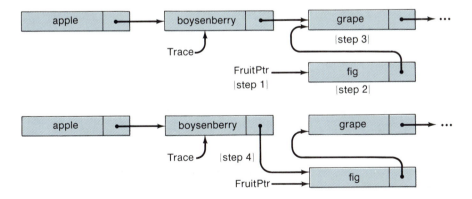

after the trailing pointer. In some situations this may be the easiest thing to do (see program 5.7). A compact way is to move the located data out of the way and insert the new data where it was (fig. 5.21).

The second of these instructions is one we have not previously met. Recall that FruitPtr^ indicates an entire record —the one to which FruitPtr is pointing. Hence this instruction assigns to this record the contents of the record Trace^ to which Trace points. With this one instruction we can copy both the data and the

Figure 5.21   Insertion before a located element

```
PROCEDURE InsertCellBeforePtr (Grocery  : FruitPointer;
                               Trace    : FruitPointer;
                               NewFruit : FruitNameType);

{ Code to insert new data, NewFruit, into a list before the element
indicated by Trace. }

  VAR
     FruitPtr : FruitPointer;

  BEGIN

     { Assert: Trace is not NIL. }

     new (FruitPtr);                { Step 1 }
     FruitPtr^ := Trace^;           { Step 2 }
     Trace^.Goodie := NewFruit;     { Step 3 }
     Trace^.Next := FruitPtr        { Step 4 }
  END; { InsertCellBeforePtr }
```

Figure 5.22   Insertion of "New Fruit" before "Goodie$_2$"

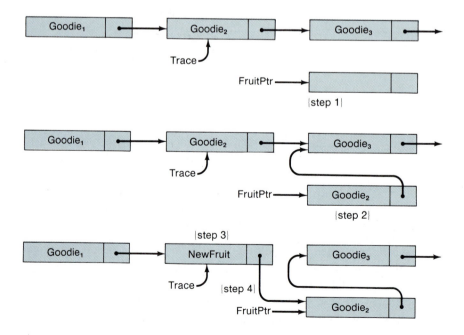

Figure 5.23   Deletion at the pointer

```
PROCEDURE DeleteCellAtPtr (Grocery : FruitPointer;
                          Trace   : FruitPointer);

{ Deletion of the located element. }

  VAR
    Auxiliary : FruitPointer;

  BEGIN

    { Assert: "Trace" and "Trace^.Next" are not NIL. }

    Auxiliary := Trace^.Next;
    Trace^ := Trace^.Next^;
    dispose (Auxiliary)
  END; { DeleteCellAtPtr }
```

Figure 5.24   Deletion at "Trace" (deletes "boysenberry")

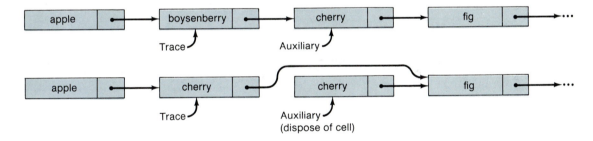

pointer fields, along with anything else in the record. The operation of this code is shown in figure 5.22, with the steps of the procedure marked. Note that step 2 copies the entire record Trace^ into FruitPtr^.

The element deleted from a list is generally either the one we have located or the one immediately following it. Figures 5.23 and 5.24 give the code and a "before and after" diagram for the first type of deletion.

To interpret this procedure correctly, we read the right-hand side of the second assignment statement from left to right. Using the pointer Trace, find the record to which it points (Trace^). Then find the pointer field in that record (Trace^.Next) and finally locate the record to which that points (Trace^.Next^). This record then replaces the record to which Trace currently points (Trace^). Deletion following the pointer is equally simple (figs. 5.25 and 5.26).

Figure 5.25   Deletion following the pointer

```
PROCEDURE DeleteCellFollowingPtr (Grocery : FruitPointer;
                                  Trace   : FruitPointer);

{ Deletion of the element following the located one. }

   VAR
     Auxiliary : FruitPointer;

   BEGIN

     { Assert: "Trace" and "Trace^.Next" are not NIL. }

     Auxiliary := Trace^.Next;
     Trace^.Next := Trace^.Next^.Next;
     dispose (Auxiliary)
   END; { DeleteCellFollowingPtr }
```

Figure 5.26   Deletion following "Trace" (deletes "cherry")

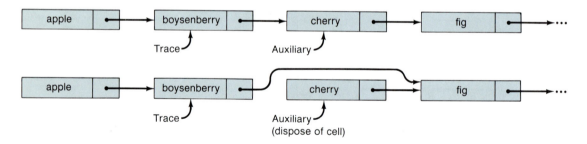

Interpretation of this procedure is done in the same manner. Once we have the record Trace^.Next^, we identify its pointer (Trace^.Next^.Next). This value is then substituted for the pointer Trace^.Next in the record Trace^.

Although we have discussed linked lists assuming a single pointer field forming the linkage, we can have multiple pointer fields in a record. Often this is very useful. For example, in a **doubly linked list** there is a second pointer field that points backward through the list. This enables us to traverse the list in both the forward and backward directions, which facilitates searching and deletion in a list (see fig. 5.27).

With a singly linked list we have two ways of initiating a search for an element. Either we start each time at the head of the list, or we start from wherever we are in the list. The first method can be very inefficient if most of the time we are looking for elements in the sequence in which they occur in the list: it would

Figure 5.27   A doubly linked list

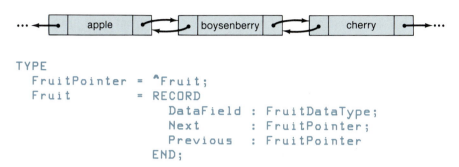

```
TYPE
   FruitPointer  =  ^Fruit;
   Fruit         =  RECORD
                       DataField  :  FruitDataType;
                       Next       :  FruitPointer;
                       Previous   :  FruitPointer
                    END;
```

Table 5.2   Comparison of list search movements

Element Number	Method 1	Method 2	Method 3
1	0	26	48
10	9	35	30
24	23	49	2
25	24	0	0
26	25	1	1
40	39	15	29
50	49	25	49

be much more efficient to go from where we are on to the next element. But the second method can also be inefficient. If the element we want occurs before the present element in the list, then this procedure forces us to examine the remainder of the list unsuccessfully, then continue the search from the head of the list.

With a doubly linked list we can search in both directions from wherever we are. The procedure for this is quite simple. Initiate both a forward and a backward search pointer wherever we are, with one pointer tracing the forward links through the list and the other pointer tracing the backward links. Then alternately move first the forward pointer, then the backward pointer. Implementation of this is left as an exercise.

Here is an example to show what happens. Suppose that we have a list of fifty elements and that we are currently examining the twenty-fifth element in the list. We shall count the number of pointer movements to locate various elements by each of the three methods. Let Method 1 be singly linked, starting the search at the head of the list. Let Method 2 be singly linked, starting the search at the present element. And let Method 3 be doubly linked, with the search pointers alternating from the present position. Table 5.2 gives the movement count for locating various elements in the list.

We see from table 5.2 that none of these methods is universally quick. Method 1 works well if we expect the next element to be near the head of the list. Method 2 works effectively if we expect the next element to be just ahead of the present one. And Method 3 is the best one to use if we expect the next element to be near the present one, but either before or behind it. Overall, each is an $O(n)$ search process. With randomly distributed searches there is no reason to expect one method to be significantly better than the others.

Multiple links are also useful in other situations. Suppose, for example, that we have a personnel file and that we would like to keep it sorted both by employee number and by name. This can be done by maintaining two pointer fields in each record, one of which links the list in alphabetical order of the names, with the other linking it in employee number order (fig 5.28). (See program 5.14.)

Finally, it is useful at times to replace the NIL pointer at the end of a list with a pointer back to the head of the list. This creates a **circular list,** which has the advantage that any traversal begun in the middle of the list automatically continues from the front of the list if the desired element has not been found by the time the end of the list is reached. It has the disadvantage that we must remember the starting point of the traversal (with a pointer). Then if the desired element is not in the list, the search can stop when we return to the starting point. (See figure 5.29.)

5.5 Sets as linked lists

Obviously, there is much flexibility in the way we approach linked list representations. Thus, when we implement the abstract data type "set" as a linked list there are many choices. We present here one implementation. You may prefer a slightly different one. For this implementation we assume this TYPE definition:

```
TYPE
   ElementType = UserSelectedType;
   SetType     = ^SetElement;
   SetElement  = RECORD
                    SetMember   : ElementType;
                    NextElement : SetType
                 END;
```

Creating a set is simply a matter of initializing a set to the empty set (fig. 5.30). This is clearly an $O(1)$ operation, independent of the ultimate set size.

Figure 5.28   Employee list with two links

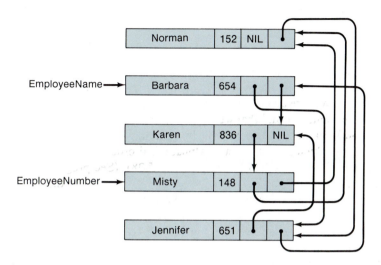

```
TYPE
  EmployeePointer = ^Employee;
  Employee        = RECORD
                        EmployeeName   : EmployeeNameType;
                        EmployeeNumber : EmployeeNumberType;
                        NextName       : EmployeePointer;
                        NextNumber     : EmployeePointer
                    END;
```

Figure 5.29   Circular list

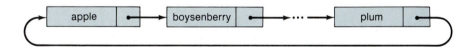

Figure 5.30   Creating a new set as a linked list

```
PROCEDURE NewSet (VAR SetName : SetType);

{ This procedure initializes a set. }

  BEGIN
    SetName := NIL
  END; { NewSet }
```

Figure 5.31   The function IsEmpty for a linked list set

```
FUNCTION IsEmpty (SetName : SetType) : boolean;

{ This function determines if the set is empty. }

  BEGIN
    IsEmpty := SetName = NIL
  END; { IsEmpty }
```

It is also an $O(1)$ task to determine if a set is empty (fig. 5.31).

As usual with set implementations, we must be able to determine if an element is present before adding or deleting it. For a linked list implementation this is an $O(n)$ task since we have no way of knowing where the next element is without following the pointers (fig. 5.32).

Adding a new element to the set is itself an $O(1)$ process. However, the entire procedure for doing this is $O(n)$ since we must check to make sure the element is not already present (fig. 5.33).

Similarly, element deletion is $O(1)$, but the procedure is $O(n)$ since we must first locate the element (fig. 5.34).

The procedure GetAnother is supposed to return the element following the given one in the set list. This means that we must first find the given element in the list if it is there, and also decide what to do if it is not there. Hence this is also an $O(n)$ procedure (fig 5.35).

Figure 5.32   The function IsElement for a linked list set

```
FUNCTION IsElement (GivenElement : ElementType;
                    SetName       : SetType) : boolean;

{ The function determines if GivenElement is an
element of SetName. }

  VAR
    InSet      : boolean;
    SetBuilder : SetType;

  BEGIN
    InSet := false;
    SetBuilder := SetName;
    WHILE (SetBuilder <> NIL) AND (NOT InSet) DO
      BEGIN
        InSet := SetBuilder^.SetMember = GivenElement;
        SetBuilder := SetBuilder^.NextElement
      END;
    IsElement := InSet
  END; { IsElement }
```

Figure 5.33   Building a set as a linked list

```
PROCEDURE AddElement (GivenElement    : ElementType;
                      VAR SetName     : SetType;
                      VAR AddedToSet  : boolean);

  VAR
    SetBuilder : SetType;

  BEGIN
    IF NOT IsElement (GivenElement, SetName) THEN
      BEGIN
        new (SetBuilder);
        SetBuilder^.NextElement := SetName;
        SetName := SetBuilder
      END;
    AddedToSet := true
  END; { AddElement }
```

Figure 5.34   DeleteElement for a linked list set

```
PROCEDURE DeleteElement (GivenElement      : ElementType;
                         VAR SetName       : SetType;
                         VAR DeletedFromSet : boolean);

{ This procedure deletes the given element from the set. }

  VAR
    Present  : SetType;
    Previous : SetType;

  BEGIN
    IF IsElement (GivenElement, SetName) THEN
      BEGIN
        IF SetName^.SetMember = GivenElement THEN
          BEGIN
            Present := SetName;
            SetName := SetName^.NextElement;
            dispose (Present)
          END
        ELSE
          BEGIN
            Present := Setname;
            WHILE (Present^.SetMember <> GivenElement) DO
              BEGIN
                Previous := Present;
                Present := Present^.NextElement
              END;
            Previous^.NextElement := Present^.NextElement;
            dispose (Present)
          END;
        DeletedFromSet := true
      END
    ELSE
      BEGIN
        DeletedFromSet := false;
        writeln ('Error: Given element is not in the set.')
      END

  { Assert: FailedToDelete is false if and only if GivenElement
  was in SetName. }

  END; { DeleteElement }
```

Figure 5.35   GetAnother for a linked list set

```
FUNCTION GetAnother (GivenElement : ElementType;
                     SetName       : SetType) : ElementType;

{ This function returns the element following the given one in the
set. }

  VAR
    SetBuilder : SetType;

  BEGIN
    IF (NOT IsElement (GivenElement, SetName)) OR
       (SetName = NIL) THEN
      BEGIN
        writeln
          ('Error: Element is not in the set or the set is empty.');
        writeln ('No value is assigned to Function GetAnother.')
      END
    ELSE
      BEGIN

        { Assert: SetName <> NIL. }

        SetBuilder := SetName;
        WHILE (SetBuilder^.SetMember <> GivenElement) DO
          SetBuilder := SetBuilder^.NextElement;
        IF (SetBuilder^.NextElement <> NIL) THEN
          GetAnother := SetBuilder^.NextElement^.SetMember
        ELSE

          { Assert: GivenElement is the last element in SetName. }

          GetAnother := SetName^.SetMember
      END
END; { GetAnother }
```

Figure 5.36   Size for a linked list set

```
FUNCTION Size (SetName : SetType) : integer;

{ This function determines the size of the set. }

  VAR
    Count       : integer;
    SetBuilder  : SetType;

  BEGIN
    Count := 0;
    SetBuilder := SetName;
    WHILE SetBuilder <> NIL DO
      BEGIN
        Count := Count + 1;
        SetBuilder := SetBuilder^.NextElement
      END;
    Size := Count
  END; { Size }
```

Table 5.3   Complexities of basic linked list set operations

NewSet	$O(1)$
IsEmpty	$O(1)$
IsElement	$O(n)$
AddElement	$O(n)$
DeleteElement	$O(n)$
GetAnother	$O(n)$
Size	$O(n)$

Finally, the function Size involves tracing the entire set list to count it, another $O(n)$ operation (fig. 5.36).

As we might expect, the complexities of these implementations are directly related to the way in which we can manipulate the lists and locate elements within them. Table 5.3 summarizes these complexities.

5.6 Multisets

Implementation of multisets with linked lists presents many of the same problems and opportunities that implementation with arrays does. Reviewing the above procedures, we see that NewSet, IsEmpty, IsElement, and Size remain the same.

Figure 5.37   The multiset to sorted set development diagram

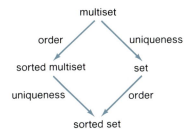

AddElement becomes the simpler $O(1)$ operation since we do not need to check for the prior presence of the element to be added. DeleteElement may remain the same, but if we wish to delete all occurrences of the element more work will be involved. Either way, it is still an $O(n)$ process, for a single sweep through the set suffices to remove all copies of the specified element.

GetAnother remains the same for multisets as for sets. However, we must recognize that for a multiset GetAnother will retrieve the element following the *first* occurrence of the specified element that it finds. Since there may be more than one occurrence of the specified element, it is important to know where this procedure starts. If GetAnother is written to start from the beginning of the multiset each time, then as long as the multiset does not change it will always retrieve the same next element. But if it starts from wherever it is, then GetAnother will generally retrieve a different next element every time it is called—namely, all the next elements following occurrences of the specified one.

In a sense, multisets form a data type that is simpler than the one for sets. This is because we do not need to worry about duplication of elements. Another possible approach to defining data structures and types is to begin with multisets, and then specialize the definitions by adding conditions of uniqueness (to get sets) or order (to get sorted multisets and sets) (fig. 5.37).

Summary

In this chapter we have discussed one of the more flexible types of data structures, the linked list. The purpose of this and other more sophisticated data structures is to provide us with a data model that more closely matches reality, and that is easier and quicker to manipulate.

Vocabulary

address	linear search
binary search	linked list
caret	list pointer
circular list	new
dangling reference	NIL
data field	null address
dispose	null pointer
doubly linked list	pointer
garbage	pointer field
garbage collection	search pointer
head	tail

Problems

5.1. Redraw the links in fig. 5.2 so that the figure represents reverse alphabetical order.

5.2. Assume that cell 73 contains "kumquat." Show the effect on figs. 5.1, 5.2, and 5.3 after linking in this new cell in the appropriate given order.

5.3. Given the TYPE and VAR declarations in fig. 5.8, give the type of the following expressions:

      A. Grocery
      B. Grocery^
      C. Grocery^.Goodie
      D. Grocery^.Goodie[7]
      E. Grocery^.Next
      F. Grocery^.Next^

5.4. Given the data types in fig. 5.27 and the declaration

    `VAR Munch : Fruit;`

what values do Munch.Previous^.Next^ and Munch.Next^.Previous^ have?

5.5. Suppose that you have a second pointer system available in a sorted linked list. Devise a way to use this to make search time significantly less than $O(n)$.

Programs

5.1. Using the global data types described in fig. 5.8, write a procedure which will print out the "Goodie" fields given a pointer to the head of the list.

5.2. Write a boolean function named "IsThere." The function header is

```
FUNCTION IsThere (Basket : FruitPointer;
                  Sample : FruitNameType) : boolean;
```

The function returns the value "true" if and only if the fruit "Sample" is the "Goodie" field of one of the elements of the list Basket. (See fig. 5.8.)

5.3. Write a procedure LexInsert which inserts a fruit into its proper place in a lexicographically ordered list of fruit pointed to by the pointer variable FruitSalad.

5.4. Using the global data types described in fig. 5.8, write a procedure Order which rearranges the list elements of the list pointed to by the variable Head into lexicographic order.

5.5. Implement FindVowels and CountVowels using the linked list definition of sets given in section 5.5.

5.6. Write a procedure which reverses the links in any linked list given a pointer to its head (which might be empty). For example, the list

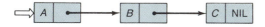

becomes

You should only manipulate pointers. No information should be moved. (Hint: You can do it with three local pointer variables.)

5.7. Write code to search a list for a value using a Trace pointer and a Trailer pointer that follows it by one record, and then to insert a new datum into the list before the record indicated by the Trace pointer.

5.8. Write a program which produces a cross-reference listing of reserved words in Pascal programs. The cross-reference listing should contain all reserved words which occurred and the line number from the input file for each occurrence (not counting blank or comment lines). For the function GetAnother in fig. 5.35 the output of your program should be:

reserved word	line number
FUNCTION	1
VAR	3
BEGIN	5, 8, 14
IF	6, 18
NOT	6
OR	6
NIL	7, 18
THEN	7, 18
END	12, 22, 23
ELSE	13, 20
WHILE	16
DO	16

5.9. Write a program which reads in sets of nonblank characters and represents them internally as linked lists. Remember, you are implementing sets, not multisets! For example:

Input Data   Sets

HOLYCOW

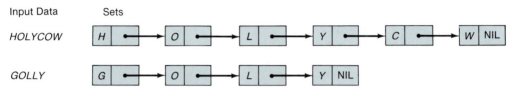

GOLLY

5.10. Extend the previous program by implementing the set operations of union and intersection. For example, union forms this list:

Intersection forms this list:

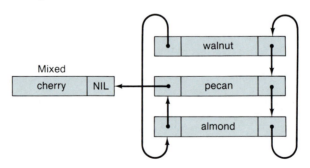

5.11. Redo programs 5.9 and 5.10 implementing sets as circular lists.

5.12. Write a procedure that alternately searches backward and forward in a doubly linked list to find a desired element.

5.13. Assume you are given the data types in fig. 5.27 and a doubly linked list of fruits pointed to by the variable Mixed which is of type FruitPointer. Suppose that for some reason, one pointer is faulty. For example, the "Previous" pointer for "pecan" erroneously points to "cherry." Write a procedure which can correct one destroyed pointer, wherever it occurs.

Example:

Your procedure should cause the "Previous" pointer in "pecan" to point to the "walnut" cell. Note that due to redundant links it is always possible to repair one faulty link.

5.14. Write procedures for inserting and deleting records in an employee file that has one pointer system keeping it linked in employee number order and a second pointer system keeping it linked in alphabetical order.

5.15. Consider the following representation of polynomials using linked lists:

$$x^6 - 3x^2 + 42:$$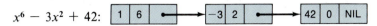

Write a procedure which will build such a representation from input data in the form:

$$
\begin{aligned}
&1,6 \\
-&3,2 \\
&42,0
\end{aligned}
$$

and display the polynomial on two lines as:

	6				2			
x		$-$	3	x		$+$	4	2

5.16. Write a procedure which will take two polynomials as described in program 5.15 and add them.

5.17. Write a procedure which will take two polynomials as described in program 5.15 and compute their product.

5.18. Instead of using *new* and *dispose* to manage data for the polynomial problems (programs 5.15–5.17) manage the free cells with a list of available storage. You should supply two new procedures, NewNew and NewDispose. The procedure NewNew(*p*) removes a cell from the front of the list of available storage and makes *p* point to the cell. The procedure NewDispose(*p*) takes the cell pointed to by *p* and appends it to the front of the available space list.

Example:

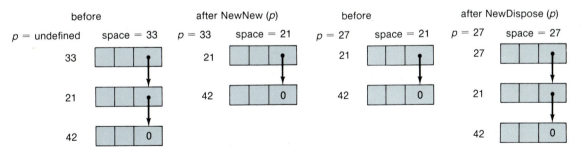

5.19. Show how you would implement the list structures used in the examples in section 5.4 in BASIC or FORTRAN. What are the BASIC and FORTRAN analogues of pointers?

6

Stacks and Queues

Introduction

For many applications, the sequence in which data are received is important, even though the data may not be ordered in any other way. The two most important forms of **precedence ordering** are the stack and the queue. These concepts relate to the order in which data items are processed.

6.1 Stacks

A **stack** follows a "last in, first out" (**LIFO**) discipline: the last item placed in the stack is the first one to be processed. This is the type of "processing" undergone by a stack of cafeteria plates or by the discard pile in a solitaire game. Very roughly, it is the type of "processing" met in loading and unloading a crowded elevator car. In computing, stacks arise in the processing of arithmetic or other expressions by a compiler or interpreter.

Here is an example. Suppose that we want to process the assignment statement $D := A * (B + C)$, where all the values involved are integers. We cannot do the computation until we know the values of A, B, and C. We cannot do the multiplication until we know the value of $B + C$. In other words, a reasonable sequence of operations is

fetch C

fetch B

compute $B + C$

hold the result temporarily, calling it $T1$

fetch A

compute $A * T1$ and hold the result temporarily in $T2$

assign the result in $T2$ to D

Now suppose that we represent this expression in this form

$$:= D * A + B C$$

Observe that by reading this form of the expression from right to left we have the calculation laid out properly. We just hold any variable values that come along, or perform any operations and hold their values:

fetch and hold C

fetch and hold B

add the last two items that we have, and hold the result

fetch and hold A

multiply the last two items we have, and hold the result

fetch and hold D

assign the value of the second item held to the first item

In this calculation we have essentially used a stack, since we hold items as they are fetched or calculated and then use the most recently held items first. The problem of deriving the second expression, called **prefix notation,** from the first, called **infix notation,** is solved by a technique called "tree traversal," which will be discussed in chapter 10.

Stacks are also important in the processing of procedure and function calls. Suppose that we have a main program *P* that calls a procedure *A*. Suppose that *A* in turn calls procedure *B*, which calls function *C*, which calls procedure *D*. Generally, these calls are not the last instructions in their respective program units. That is, once we have finished with procedure *A* we must still return to the main program to complete its work; after finishing procedure *B* we must return to complete procedure *A;* and so forth. This is a typical LIFO operational discipline: we have suspended operations in *P, A, B,* and *C, in that order,* to call on procedure *D*. It is important that when we resume operations in these outer program units, we do so in the order *C, B, A,* and *P*. That is, the last program unit suspended must be the first one resumed.

Procedure and function calls are in effect shifts from one set of instructions to another. If we are to resume the first (calling) set of instructions properly, then information must be saved. Let us consider the call of procedure *B* from procedure *A*. The following information must be saved:

The location in *A* to which we must return once *B* is finished.

The values in *A* that are to be used as actual parameters in *B*, or pointers to these values.

If *B* were a function, a pointer to the location in *A* where the function value is required.

Space for the local variables of *B*.

All this information is placed in a structure called a **stack frame** when *B* is called. This stack frame is placed on the stack, where it resides until *B* is finished. Observe that it contains all the data necessary for running *B*, together with the reference point that tells at what instruction to resume the operation of *A*.

6.2 Queues

A **queue** follows a "first in, first out" (**FIFO**) discipline: the first job in line is the one to be processed next. Queues occur whenever a number of jobs are waiting to be processed. We are familiar with them as lines at the post office or the grocery checkout counter. The same type of line occurs when several jobs are waiting to be processed by a computer.

A queue is used whenever it is important to preserve order among the data items. Suppose, for example, we have six data items that arrive in the order *A, B, C, D, E, F*. If we use a queue to organize the processing, then we handle these items in the given order. In contrast, if we use a stack to handle the items, then they may get out of order. Suppose that it takes a long time to process *A* and that, while we are doing that, *B, C,* and *D* arrive. Using a stack, we would process *D* next. Perhaps that takes a moderate amount of time, during which *E* arrives. Then *E* is handled next; but if *E* takes only a little time to process, we may also begin processing *C* before *F* arrives. Thus the order in which these items would be handled by a stack might be *A, D, E, C, F, B*—quite different from the original order.

Just as a stack frame is useful for maintaining information about processes or data that are in a stack, a **queue frame** serves a similar function for a queue.

6.3 Abstract data types for stacks and queues

Stacks and queues can be implemented in several different ways, but however they are implemented, we want them to have the same properties as far as the user is concerned. Thus we begin by defining abstract data types that will embody these properties.

For each of these data structures, we must be able to create a new one, tell whether an existing one is full or empty, and add and delete elements. In addition, we will want to examine an element in the stack or queue without necessarily removing it. Finally, we may also wish to determine the number of elements in the structure.

For each of these structures, only the element at one end of the structure is considered accessible at any time, namely the element at the top of the stack or the front of the queue. The remaining elements are considered inaccessible. For example, suppose that we have a six element stack. Then the first element placed on the stack is at the bottom, the second one is next to the bottom, and so forth. To get at the third element from the top (which was the fourth one placed on the stack), we must first remove the top or most recently placed element, and the element below that. Only then will the third element be at the top of the stack, and accessible. We see that the size of the stack changes as elements are added or removed for processing, but note that the first element placed is always in a fixed position until it is removed (fig. 6.1).

To understand the operations, we must note the two **boundary conditions** that apply. One is that the structure (stack or queue) may be empty. Obviously, in this case we cannot delete an element from the structure. The other boundary condition is that the structure is full—there is no more memory space available to hold new stack or queue elements. In this situation we cannot insert additional elements into the structure. Any operations we do must take these conditions into account. This is done by means of two boolean functions, **empty** and **full,** which check for these conditions.

We first give the abstract data type for a stack. Elements are added to, or removed from, a stack only at one end, the **top.** The operations we need for a stack are these:

Create (Stack)—makes a new (empty) Stack and returns the properly initialized Stack.

Figure 6.1   Stack operation

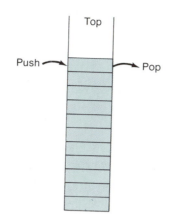

Empty (Stack)—returns "true" if the Stack is empty, "false" otherwise.

Full (Stack)—returns "true" if the Stack is full, "false" otherwise. (This function is a concession to the realities of a finite memory. In the abstract, a stack should never become full.)

Push (Element, Stack)—inserts Element into the Stack as a new top element, with the previous top element becoming the next-to-top or second stack element.

Pop (Stack)—removes and returns the current top element in the Stack, making the former next-to-top element the new top one. If the Stack contained only one element prior to the operation, the Stack becomes empty.

Peek (Stack)—returns the value of the current top element in the Stack but does not remove it.

Size (Stack)—returns the number of elements in the Stack.

For a queue, the list of operations is similar. However, we note that for this type of structure, we add elements at one end, the **rear,** and remove them from the other, the **front.** Thus both ends of a queue change (fig. 6.2). Here are the queue operations:

Create (Queue)—makes a new (empty) Queue and returns the properly initialized Queue.

Empty (Queue)—returns "true" if the Queue is empty, "false" otherwise.

Full (Queue)—returns "true" if the queue is full, "false" otherwise. (This function is a concession to the realities of a finite memory. In the abstract, a queue should never become full.)

Figure 6.2   Queue operation

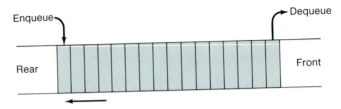

Enqueue (Element, Queue)—inserts Element into the Queue as a new rear element, with the previous last element becoming next-to-rear.

Dequeue (Queue)—removes and returns the current front element of the Queue, making the former second element the new front one.

Peek (Queue)—returns the value of the current front element in the Queue but does not remove it.

Size (Queue)—returns the number of elements in the Queue.

6.4 Stacks as arrays

Implementation of a stack (or a queue) requires two types of things: organized space for the data, and an access discipline that only allows the user to utilize the top of the stack (or the front and rear of the queue). We have studied two space organizations for sets: arrays and linked lists. Each of these space organizations is suitable for holding the data of a stack or queue.

We first consider implementing the stack as a Pascal ARRAY. For this implementation, we use a RECORD type similar to what we used for sets (fig. 6.3). Recall that use of a RECORD is necessary to enable us to have an arbitrary ElementType. However, be aware that stacks implemented in this way cannot contain a mixture of element types. Creation of a stack is straightforward (fig. 6.4). We can easily recognize the two boundary conditions: the stack is empty if StackName.Top = 0, and it is full if StackName.Top = StackSize. Hence the required functions are defined in figure 6.5.

Of the remaining operations we wish to define, **pop** and **peek** must know if the stack is empty and **push** must know if it is full. **Size** does not need to know either condition. Figure 6.6 has these four procedures. In practice, the error messages we have included in the Push, Pop, and Peek operations should be replaced by some operational code that alerts the user and allows the choice of some other operation. As the code now stands, a message will be displayed, but an *undetermined value* (garbage) will be returned, and program operation will continue unabated.

Figure 6.3　　The ARRAY stack, embedded in a RECORD

```
CONST
  StackSize = UserSuppliedSize; { Maximum possible stack size. }

TYPE
  ElementType = UserSuppliedType;
  StackType   = RECORD
                  Top        : 0..StackSize;
                  StackArray : ARRAY[1..StackSize] OF ElementType
                END;
```

Figure 6.4　　Stack creation

```
PROCEDURE Create (VAR StackName : StackType);

{ This assumes prior declaration of StackType. }

  BEGIN
    StackName.Top := 0
  END; { Create }
```

Figure 6.5　　"Empty" and "Full" functions for a stack

```
FUNCTION Empty (StackName : StackType) : boolean;

{ StackName.Top is the location of the top element on the stack. }

  BEGIN
    Empty := StackName.Top = 0
  END; { Empty }

FUNCTION Full (StackName : StackType) : boolean;

{ StackName.Top is the location of the top element on the stack. }

  BEGIN
    Full := StackName.Top = StackSize
  END; { Full }
```

Figure 6.6   The basic stack operations

```
PROCEDURE Push (StackIn       : ElementType;
                VAR StackName : StackType);

{ Note that this procedure has the effect of increasing the stack
size. }

  BEGIN
    IF NOT Full (StackName) THEN
      WITH StackName DO
        BEGIN
          Top := Top + 1;
          StackArray[Top] := StackIn
        END
    ELSE
      writeln ('Error on pushing: stack full.')
  END; { Push }

FUNCTION Pop (VAR StackName : StackType) : ElementType;

{ Note that this function has the effect of reducing the stack
size. }

  BEGIN
    IF NOT Empty (StackName) THEN
      WITH StackName DO
        BEGIN
          Pop := StackArray[Top];
          Top := Top - 1
        END
    ELSE
      writeln ('Error on popping: stack empty.')
  END; { Pop }

FUNCTION Peek (StackName : StackType) : ElementType;

  BEGIN
    IF NOT Empty (StackName) THEN
      Peek := StackName.StackArray[StackName.Top]
    ELSE
      writeln ('Error on peeking: stack empty.')
  END; { Peek }

FUNCTION Size (StackName : StackType): integer;

  BEGIN
    Size := StackName.Top
  END; { Size }
```

Figure 6.7   The possible effect of queue migration

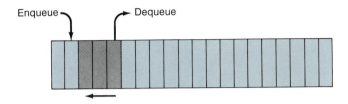

Figure 6.8   A circular queue

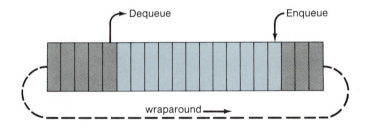

Both Push and Pop have the effect of changing the value of Size. This is an important effect to note, for if we compute the value of Size and then perform either Push or Pop, the computed value will be wrong.

6.5 Queues as arrays

Enqueue, adding elements at one end (the rear) of a queue and **dequeue,** deleting them from the other end (the front) introduces two programming problems. First, we must keep track of both ends of a queue; second, the queue tends to migrate through storage as it is processed. The latter can be a serious problem, as uncontrolled queue migration resulting from faulty programming can destroy other data.

Implementation of the functions and operations for a queue is similar to implementation for a stack. One variation that is important for maximum storage utilization is to use a **circular queue.** Since a queue implemented in an array tends to migrate through storage as elements are added and deleted, it is possible to come very rapidly to the end of the allotted storage space and have very few data left in the queue (fig. 6.7).

If the front and rear locations in a queue are computed modulo the allotted storage size, then the queue can wrap around in a circle, recycling the portion of the space that has already been used and vacated (fig. 6.8).

Figure 6.9   The ARRAY queue, embedded in a RECORD

```
CONST
  QueueSize = UserSuppliedSize; { Maximum possible queue size. }

TYPE
  ElementType = UserSuppliedType;
  QueueType   = RECORD
                  Front      : 1..QueueSize;
                  Rear       : 1..QueueSize;
                  QueueArray : ARRAY[1..QueueSize] OF ElementType
                END;
```

While computation of the front and rear locations by modular arithmetic is simple, the computation of the Empty and Full functions is now a little tricky. Since we will use the Rear pointer to store but never retrieve an element, we set Rear to point to the next available location. Then the empty and full conditions are both indicated by Front = Rear MOD AvailableSpace. There are two possible ways to distinguish between the conditions.

One way is to keep track of whether we are emptying or filling the queue. When we check for the empty or full condition and find that Front = Rear, then if the last operation removed an element from the queue, it must be empty, while if the last operation added an element to the queue, it must be full.

Here is an example. Suppose that we have space for five elements in the queue, with the locations numbered from 0 through 4. Initially, Front and Rear both have the value 1: the queue is empty. Suppose that we add three elements: 17, 3, 59. Now Front = 1 (since we have removed none) and Rear = 4. Add two more elements, filling the queue. Now Rear = 1, the same value as Front. Next, remove two elements, 17 and 3. This does not change the value of Rear, but now Front = 3 and there is space available in the queue. Finally, add two new elements, 43 and 10 (in locations 1 and 2). Now Front = Rear = 3, once again indicating a full queue.

A different way is never to allow the queue to become completely full. If we maintain one open space, then the empty condition will be indicated by Front = Rear while the full condition will be indicated by Rear trailing Front by one location, or (Front − Rear) MOD AvailableSpace = 1. You might try the preceding example using this method of queue management and a queue of size six, so that you can hold five elements at a time.

Either way of distinquishing between these conditions is satisfactory. Once one way or the other has been chosen, implementation of a circular queue is easy. The basic functions and operations for a circular queue are given in figure 6.10. It is assumed that QueueSize and ElementType are specified by the calling program, and that QueueType is defined in figure 6.9.

Figure 6.10, Part 1   The basic circular queue operations

```
PROCEDURE Create (VAR QueueName: QueueType);

{ This assumes prior declaration of QueueType. }

  BEGIN
    QueueName.Front := 1;
    QueueName.Rear := 1
  END; { Create }

FUNCTION Empty (QueueName : QueueType) : boolean;

  BEGIN
    Empty := QueueName.Front = QueueName.Rear
  END; { Empty }

FUNCTION Full (QueueName : QueueType) : boolean;

  BEGIN
    WITH QueueName DO
      Full := (Rear + 1) MOD QueueSize = Front
  END; { Full }

PROCEDURE Enqueue (Queuein       : ElementType;
                   VAR QueueName : QueueType);

{ Note that this procedure has the effect of
increasing the queue size. }

  BEGIN
    IF NOT Full (QueueName) THEN
      WITH QueueName DO
        BEGIN
          QueueArray[Rear] := QueueIn;
          Rear := (Rear MOD QueueSize) + 1
        END
    ELSE
      writeln ('Error on enqueue: queue full.')
  END; { Enqueue }
```

Figure 6.10, Part 2   The basic circular queue operations

```
FUNCTION Dequeue (VAR QueueName : QueueType) : ElementType;

{ Note that this function has the effect of reducing the queue
size. }

  BEGIN
    IF NOT Empty (QueueName) THEN
      WITH QueueName DO
        BEGIN
          Dequeue := QueueArray[Front];
          Front := (Front MOD QueueSize) + 1
        END
    ELSE
      writeln ('Error on dequeue: queue empty.')
  END; { Dequeue }

FUNCTION Peek (QueueName : QueueType) : ElementType;

  BEGIN
    IF NOT Empty (QueueName) THEN
      Peek := QueueName.QueueArray[QueueName.Front]
    ELSE
      writeln ('Error on peeking: queue empty.')
  END; { Peek }

FUNCTION Size (QueueName : QueueType) : integer;

  BEGIN
    WITH QueueName DO
      Size := (Rear - Front) MOD QueueSize
  END; { Size }
```

Stacks and queues are both extremely useful for many problems, but in some situations the fact that operations are limited to the ends of the structure means that these types of structures are not appropriate. When they can be used, they are very efficient. In effect, at any given time the entire stack or queue, except for the end elements, is invisible and plays no part in operations. Hence all operations on stacks and queues are independent of the structure size; that is, they are $O(1)$ processes.

6.6 Stacks as linked lists

In sections 6.4 and 6.5 we discussed the implementation of stacks and queues in sequential storage. These particular structures are in fact more easily implemented as linked lists. Because of the dynamic growth and shrinkage of stacks and queues, a linked list implementation is in many ways most natural.

Consider first the stack, recalling that data are added to and removed from the stack at just one end, and that the other end just "drifts off" into limbo until we have deleted enough data to work our way back down to it. A linked list with a single pointer to the head behaves in exactly this way. We already have the algorithms for adding or deleting an element at the head of the list; and if the list is a stack, these are basically the only data manipulation algorithms that we need.

The two boolean functions that are associated with stacks, Empty and Full, are implemented in different ways. Suppose that we think of Grocery as a stack. When the Grocery list is empty, if we try to read data from it we will cause a run time error. To avoid this we can initialize Grocery by

```
Grocery := NIL.
```

Then we can check for an empty stack by asking

```
IF Grocery = NIL THEN ...
```

Since we have not limited the size of a stack by embedding it in a fixed array, the size is limited only by the available storage. Hence a "stack full" condition occurs as a run time error whenever all of memory is in use. To avoid premature occurrence of this condition it is important to use the *dispose* operator whenever an element has been popped from the stack, thus freeing that space for further use. Here are the four basic stack operations, realized with a linked list structure (fig. 6.11).

The stack data structure as we have defined it in this section requires that we count the cells in the list every time we need to know the size of the list. An alternative to this procedure would be to include a size field in the stack definition and keep it updated whenever we pushed or popped an element. One way to do this would be to add a new special header for every stack:

```
StackHeader = RECORD
                 Head : StackPtr;
                 Size : integer
              END;
```

Figure 6.11, Part 1   The basic stack operations

{ *These procedures assume the following global TYPE definitions.* }

```
TYPE                              character.
   ElementType  = UserSuppliedType;
   StackPtr     = ^StackElement;
   StackElement = RECORD
                     Element : ElementType;
                     Next    : StackPtr
                  END;

PROCEDURE Create (VAR Stack : StackPtr);
```

{ *This assumes prior declaration of StackPtr.* }

```
   BEGIN
      Stack := NIL
   END; { Create }

FUNCTION Empty (Stack : StackPtr) : boolean;

   BEGIN
      Empty := Stack = NIL
   END; { Empty }

FUNCTION Full (Stack : StackPtr) : boolean;
```

{ *Note: This is a theoretical implementation that assumes that a linked list stack can never be full.* }

```
   BEGIN
      Full := false
   END; { Full }


PROCEDURE Push (StackIn   : ElementType;
                VAR Stack : StackPtr);
```

{ *Note that this function has the effect of increasing the stack size.* }

```
   VAR
      Temp : StackPtr;
```

Figure 6.11, Part 2   The basic stack operations

```
BEGIN
  IF NOT Full (Stack) THEN
    BEGIN
      new (Temp);
      Temp^.Element := StackIn;
      Temp^.Next := Stack;
      Stack := Temp
    END
  ELSE
    writeln ('Error on pushing: stack full.')
END; { Push }

FUNCTION Pop (VAR Stack : StackPtr) : ElementType;

{ Note that this function has the effect of reducing
the stack size. }

  VAR
    Temp : StackPtr;

  BEGIN
    IF NOT Empty (Stack) THEN
      BEGIN
        Temp := Stack;
        Pop := Temp^.Element;
        Stack := Temp^.Next;
        dispose (Temp)
      END
    ELSE
      writeln ('Error on popping: stack empty.')
  END; { Pop }

FUNCTION Peek (Stack : StackPtr) : ElementType;

  BEGIN
    IF NOT Empty (Stack) THEN
      Peek := Stack^.Element
    ELSE
      writeln ('Error on peeking: stack empty.')
  END; { Peek }
```

Figure 6.11, Part 3   The basic stack operations

```
FUNCTION Size (Stack : StackPtr) : integer;

  VAR
    Count : integer;
    Temp  : StackPtr;

  BEGIN
    Count := 0;
    Temp := Stack;
    WHILE Temp <> NIL DO
      BEGIN
        Count := Count + 1;
        Temp := Temp^.Next
      END;
    Size := Count
  END; { Size }
```

This addition would, of course, require modification of the various operations, particularly entailing an additional step every time we call Push or Pop. If the size of the stack is frequently used in some application, then this type of definition would be appropriate. However, if the size is only of rare interest, then it is more efficient to compute it only whenever we need it.

6.7 Queues as linked lists

Consider next the queue, where data are added at one end and deleted at the other. We have discussed an algorithm for adding data at the tail of a list, and it is simple to delete data from the head of a list. Thus we have also a natural implementation for a queue. Note that the list pointers in a queue are oriented from the front (deletion point) to the rear (addition point).

As with the stack, a "queue full" condition will occur only when all available memory has been used, and will result in a run time error. The "queue empty" condition will be indicated by the fact that the front pointer is NIL. Thus it is easy to test for the "queue empty" condition. The queue operations and functions for linked lists are given in figure 6.12.

Figure 6.12, Part 1   The basic queue operations

```
{ These procedures assume the following global TYPE
definitions. }

TYPE
  ElementType   = UserSuppliedType;
  QueuePtr      = ^QueueElement;
  QueueElement  = RECORD
                      Element : ElementType;
                      Next    : QueuePtr
                  END;
  QueueType     = RECORD
                      Front : QueuePtr;
                      Rear  : QueuePtr
                  END;

PROCEDURE Create (VAR Queue : QueueType);

  BEGIN
    Queue.Front := NIL;
    Queue.Rear  := NIL
  END; { Create }

FUNCTION Empty (Queue : QueueType) : boolean;

  BEGIN
    Empty := Queue.Front = NIL
  END; { Empty }

FUNCTION Full (Queue : QueueType) : boolean;

{ Note: This is a theoretical implementation that
assumes that a linked list queue can never be full. }

  BEGIN
    Full := false
  END; { Full }
```

Figure 6.12, Part 2   The basic queue operations

```
PROCEDURE Enqueue (QueueIn   : Elementtype;
                   VAR Queue : QueueType);

{ Note that this procedure has the effect of
increasing the queue size. }

  VAR
    Temp : QueuePtr;

  BEGIN
    IF NOT Full (Queue) THEN
      BEGIN
        new (Temp);
        Temp^.Element := QueueIn;
        Temp^.Next := NIL;
        IF Queue.Rear <> NIL THEN
          Queue.Rear^.Next := Temp;
        Queue.Rear := Temp;
        IF Queue.Front = NIL THEN
          Queue.Front := Temp
      END
    ELSE
      writeln ('Error on enqueue: queue full.')
  END; { Enqueue }

FUNCTION Dequeue (VAR Queue : QueueType) : ElementType;

{ Note that this function has the effect of reducing
the queue size. }

  VAR
    Temp : QueuePtr;

  BEGIN
    IF NOT Empty (Queue) THEN
      BEGIN
        Temp := Queue.Front;
        Dequeue := Temp^.Element;
        Queue.Front := Temp^.Next;
        dispose (Temp)
      END
    ELSE
      writeln ('Error on dequeue: queue empty.')
  END; { Dequeue }
```

Figure 6.12, Part 3   The basic queue operations

```
FUNCTION Peek (Queue : QueueType) : ElementType;

  BEGIN
    IF NOT Empty (Queue) THEN
      Peek := Queue.Front^.Element
    ELSE
      writeln ('Error on peek: queue empty.')
  END; { Peek }

FUNCTION Size (Queue : QueueType) : integer;

  VAR
    Count : integer;
    Temp  : QueuePtr;

  BEGIN
    Count := 0;
    IF NOT Empty (Queue) THEN
      WITH Queue DO
        BEGIN
          Temp := Front;
          WHILE Temp <> NIL DO
            BEGIN
              Count := Count + 1;
              Temp := Temp^.Next
            END
        END;
    Size := Count
  END; { Size }
```

As with a stack, we could alternatively include a size field in the definition of QueueType and update it whenever Enqueue and Dequeue are called. This would eliminate the need to count the queue cells every time we need to know the size.

One advantage of using linked lists for stacks and queues resides in their dynamic nature. We need allocate only sufficient storage to serve our purposes at any moment and can easily release the storage back to a general pool when it is not needed, by use of the *dispose* operator. Furthermore, the problem of the migrating queue is automatically solved. Linked list implementations, such as that in Pascal, continually allocate new storage from the "free" pool of storage that is not presently in use. Thus there is no way for a queue to migrate into the space occupied by some other data structure.

The boundary conditions, of stack or queue being empty or full, must be considered in any operations. We have seen that for both stacks and queues the empty condition can be checked by testing for a NIL pointer. There is no problem if the stack or queue has been properly initialized.

However, with linked storage, a stack or queue full condition will happen when memory is full, and the system automatically flags that as a run time error. If we have been careful to dispose of storage as we have popped elements from the stack or queue, then there is little that can be done by the programmer. The processing must halt until more memory becomes available upon the completion of some other process. If, however, we have been careless and not always disposed of unneeded storage, we may be able to continue operating by "garbage collecting," or locating and freeing storage that is no longer in use.

Summary

In this chapter we have examined stacks and queues as particular data structures of high utility. Two different types of implementations have been given—as arrays, and as linked lists. For each of these structures, we have considered the operations to be done on them and provided algorithms for many of them. We have observed that the linked list implementation provides great flexibility as the structures expand and contract during the course of use.

Vocabulary

boundary condition	pop
circular queue	precedence ordering
dequeue	prefix notation
empty	push
enqueue	queue
FIFO	queue frame
front	rear
full	size
infix notation	stack
LIFO	stack frame
peek	top

Problems

6.1. Think of some examples in everyday life where queues and stacks are encountered. Is a grocery store line a queue or a stack? What about the doctor's office when you do not have an appointment and (as usual) the doctor is running late?

6.2. Given that four animals will arrive in the order rabbit, monkey, cow, then pig, we can use a stack to scramble the order. For example, push rabbit, push monkey, pop, push cow, pop, push pig, pop, pop causes the animals to leave the stack in the order monkey, cow, pig, rabbit. However, the order pig, rabbit, cow, monkey is not possible to arrange. Why is this so? Which of the twenty-four possible permutations of the animals are possible to obtain using a stack? What is the answer if you use a queue rather than a stack?

6.3. Assume you are given a fixed number of memory locations, say 100, and have the constraint that this is all the memory available for a program's stack storage. Show how two stacks could be implemented so that overflow would occur only when the sum of the sizes of the stacks exceeded 100 locations. In other words, if Stack1 requires 82 memory locations, then there is no overflow as long as Stack2 requires 18 or fewer locations, and vice versa. Does your solution generalize to three or more stacks?

6.4. Discuss how stacks can be used to model the execution of recursive procedures and functions.

6.5. Read about coroutines. How can stacks be used to model coroutine calls and resumes?

6.6. Stacks are so important to computing that several manufacturers have designed machines with stack-based architecture, or with stacks as important components of the architecture. Read about the architecture of the PDP-11, the Motorola 68000, and the Burroughs computers.

6.7. Explain (with an example) the statement made in the text that a queue implemented in an array tends to migrate through storage as elements are added and deleted.

6.8. Evaluate the following integer expressions:

```
100 MOD 15
 23 MOD 12
100 MOD 23
100 - (100 DIV 23) * 23
 24 MOD (-3)
```

6.9. Set up a queue as a doubly linked list. How does this facilitate adding elements to the queue and deleting them from it?

6.10. Write a single Pascal assignment statement which assigns the boolean value "true" to the boolean variable IsSeventeen if the integer variable Number is a multiple of 17 and the value "false" otherwise.

Programs

6.1. Write a program which prints out all the possible permutations of the integers 1, 2, 3, and 4 using a stack. Some possible permutations are 4321 and 3421, while the permutations 4123 and 4312 are not possible. (Extra credit: Read about Catalan numbers and relate them to this problem.)

6.2. Write a program to test your solution to Problem 6.3.

7

Hash Coding

Introduction

Once we have stored large numbers of data within a computer there are two principal classes of operations to be performed on these data, regardless of the specific type stored. One class consists of the operations associated with maintenance and updating of the data. Whatever the data are, we need to include operations for adding or deleting data, and for modifying or correcting stored data. The amount of updating and maintenance required depends heavily on the specific data: some data stores need continual updating, while others are essentially fixed, except when occasional errors found while using the data are corrected.

The other main class of operations are those associated with search and retrieval of the data for computation or some other purpose. Again, the details of search and retrieval operations depend heavily upon the data. We might consider this group of operations as more fundamental, for some of the update operations, such as "change Joe Smith's address to . . . ," depend initially on a search to locate the proper datum.

Linked lists introduced in chapter 5 are one means of easing the updating problem. Data can be introduced to, or removed from, an ordered linked list without shuffling the data that are already there. Furthermore, since data stored in a linked list can be located anywhere within the computer memory, there is relatively little impact on other data in memory. While a linked list eases the updating problem, it does not permit a rapid search for data. The only way to find a particular datum is to trace down the list by following the list pointers. In this chapter we examine hash coding: a way of using sequential memory without any pointers, that scatters the data throughout storage in a manner unlikely to produce a need to move data as we update, but that permits us to locate any specific datum rapidly. Hash coding is not a perfect data storage method either, as it has its own costs and inefficiencies. First and foremost, it is impossible to retrieve hash coded data in some specific order, say alphabetically, without an immense amount of work. Second, hash coding methods may require as much as 20 to 30 percent excess memory capacity for efficient operation.

7.1 Sets with scattered storage: hash coding

A linked list structure solves the data movement problem for updating, but it does not solve the problem of locating data in storage. In fact, because the data are not well organized in memory but are scattered about in the order in which memory cells become available, the search for a datum is always linear. If we build a list of several hundred or thousand items, a search for any one of them will be costly.

There are two solutions to this costly search. One is to keep the linked lists reasonably short. This by itself does not help us much. We would need to have a rather large directory to know where each list starts. Then this directory may be either a sorted, sequentially stored list with update problems or a linked list with search problems. The other solution is to scatter data around memory but in a way that enables us to remember roughly where any single item is stored.

In this chapter we discuss one method of storing sets that allows us to access any datum almost immediately and that at the same time does not require much data movement. As we shall see, this method, **hashing,** has the advantage that the costs of storing, locating, and updating data are essentially constant and are not dependent on the size of the set. It has the disadvantage that we are unable to deal efficiently with ordered sets using this type of scheme.

The idea is to scatter the data widely throughout storage. Suppose, for example, that we have 1024 memory locations available and only twenty data items to store. Obviously there is enough space available. We can spread the data around in memory, with plenty of space available in between for new items. The only problem is remembering where we stored everything so that we don't need to do a sequential search of the entire memory.

The key to success is to use the data item itself as a solution to its location in memory. Somehow, from the datum itself we compute the memory location. This is called **hash coding.** Here is an example, using 10 data items and 100 words of memory.

Suppose that the data items are the words "apple," "apricot," "boysenberry," "cantaloupe," "cherry," "fig," "grape," "peach," "pear," and "strawberry" that we used for the linked list examples. Assume that the memory locations are numbered from 0 through 99. Let us compute the memory locations by assigning numerical values to the letters of each word, adding up the numbers, and taking the remainder upon division by 100. Suppose that we use the ASCII codes for the letters. Thus "a" has the value 97, "b" has the value 98, and so on through "z," which has the value 122. (One advantage of doing this is that we can use

Figure 7.1   Hashing function "FindMemory"

```
{ This function assumes that WordType is defined as a
PACKED ARRAY[1..12] OF char. }

FUNCTION FindMemory (Word : WordType) : integer;

  VAR
    Index    : 1..12;
    Location : integer;

  BEGIN
    Location := 0;
    FOR Index := 1 TO 12 DO

      { Assert: Word has no embedded blanks between
      letters and a blank terminates any word shorter
      than twelve letters. }

      IF Word[Index] <> ' ' THEN
        Location := Location + ord (Word[Index]);
  FindMemory := Location MOD 100
END; { FindMemory }
```

the **ord** function in Pascal to compute these values directly.) Thus "apple" would have the value $(97 + 112 + 112 + 108 + 101)$ MOD 100, or 30. Here is what we find:

apple	30	fig	10
apricot	54	grape	27
boysenberry	4	peach	13
cantaloupe	68	pear	24
cherry	53	strawberry	9

The function FindMemory computes the address for each word entered, by the method we have defined (fig. 7.1). We see that this function assigns a different storage location to each of these words. Such a function is called a **hash function.** It is a mapping from a data value called a **key** to a storage area called the **address space.** In our example, the key is the fruit name and the address space consists of locations 0, . . . , 99. This mapping is also called a **key to address transformation.**

There are many different hash functions, or ways to calculate the storage locations. We can, for example, convert the data to numerical equivalents by straight substitution of the ASCII values for characters ("apple" becomes 97112112108101), then square the number and take two of the middle digits. Or we can convert the data to numerical values and use those as input to a random number generator. No method of computing the addresses is perfect, but most methods work reasonably well for typical data mixes. Of course, if we know that our data will contain many items that cluster together under a given hashing method because of a common characteristic, then we should choose a different method that will spread them out more.

Here is an example. Suppose that a catalog order store serves a neighborhood and that its customers come to the store to pick up their orders. If the store has a large number of customers, then at any one time there are likely to be many customer orders awaiting pickup. The store's problem is to organize these orders so that they can be located and given to customers efficiently. A great amount of updating of the stock is required, since new orders arrive and old orders are picked up daily. Hence sequential storage (perhaps by customer name) is not a good method.

A bright clerk in the store suggests that every customer should have a number that is easily remembered and that the orders should be stored by number. She reasons that if enough different numbers are used, then even if a few customers have the same number there will only be a few orders to search whenever a customer comes by, and at the same time it will be easy to deposit incoming orders in the correct bin. The customers have two easily remembered numbers: their ZIP codes, and their phone numbers. ZIP codes would not be good to use, simply because most of the store's customers would have one of perhaps two or three ZIP codes: each of the very few storage bins would have many orders in it, and searching for an order would take a long time.

The telephone number offers a better choice, but even here proper choice is important. The store does not need to use the entire phone number. That would give every customer (family) a distinct and separate bin but would probably require several thousand bins. The prefix, such as 233– or 692–, would provide a thousand different numbers. This is probably more bins than the store needs or can efficiently handle, but there is a more serious problem, the same problem that rules out using the ZIP codes. Because the phone number prefix indicates the local exchange, most of the store's customers have one of a small number of prefixes. Out of the thousand bins, perhaps ten or fifteen would be crowded, and the rest would remain empty.

The clerk suggests using the last two digits of the telephone number. This provides 100 bins, a reasonable number to handle. While there will be several people with the same last two digits, whose orders will be stored in the same bin, there is no reason to believe that any specific pair of digits is more common *as the last two digits of the phone number* than any other pair. Hence the clerk expects that the bins would be used about equally. The store may have several

Figure 7.2   Fruits added using linear probing

4: boysenberry   46: plum
9: strawberry   53: cherry
10: fig   54: apricot
                             55: nectarine
13: peach
                             68: cantaloupe
24: pear
27: grape   86: watermelon
30: apple

thousand customers. But if experience indicates that at any one time the average number of orders that have arrived but not been picked up is 350, then the store could expect that each one of the bins would normally contain 3 or 4 orders to be claimed. It should be easy to find the right one.

The advantage of hash coding is that we compute the location of each datum in a fixed amount of time: the time necessary to do the computation is independent of the size of the set. ("What's your phone number?") Thus, to store a datum is an $O(1)$ process and to determine if a datum is already there is also an $O(1)$ process: compute the address where it should be, and check. The disadvantages are (1) this can use quite a bit of memory, (2) it is very difficult to produce a sorted list from hash coded data, since the data are not stored in any conventional order, and (3) a good hash function may be hard to define.

Clearly, there is another flaw in this method. Suppose that we have only 100 storage locations, as in the fruit example. Then certainly by the time we store the 101st word, and probably some time before, we are going to try to store a word on top of one already there. For example, we could add "plum" (46) and "watermelon" (86) to the list; but "nectarine" (53) would interfere with "cherry." When two or more data should be stored in the same location, we have a **collision** that must be resolved. There are several ways to do this. The simplest, and least effective, is **linear probing** or **linear open addressing**: just increment the address (wrapping around to 0 after 99) until we find an open slot for the new word. In our example, we would put "nectarine" in location 55, since location 54 is also already occupied (fig. 7.2).

Collision resolution is one of the more difficult aspects of hash coding, and a number of rather sophisticated algorithms have been proposed to solve the problem. The linear probing scheme is, as we have mentioned, one of the least effective of these. Other schemes that we shall discuss later in this chapter include **rehashing, quadratic probing,** and **chaining** or **bucketing.**

Let's look at linear probing, to see why it is poor. Since the idea behind hashing is to spread the data apart to minimize the likelihood of interference, a good hash function will distribute the data uniformly throughout the available storage. If we use linear probing when collisions occur, the uniformity of distribution is lost.

For example, we placed "cherry" in location 53 and "apricot" in location 54. So far, so good. There has been no collision. But now we come upon "nectarine" and find that it too should be in location 53, which is already occupied. With linear probing, we try to place it in location 54, which is also occupied, and end up placing it in location 55. Now we have a block of three storage cells occupied. Any other names that hash into locations 53, 54, or 55 will result in another collision. We have formed a **cluster** of three cells. We might argue that wherever we place "nectarine" there is the possibility of a collision. True, but consider cell 56. Now it becomes the target for any word that hashes into 53, 54, 55, or 56. If we had put "nectarine" elsewhere, the only word that could wind up in cell 56 (at this stage) is one that hashes directly there.

The clustering effect of linear probing is cumulative. By using linear probing to determine storage location, we have made it four times as likely that a word will end up in cell 56. Now any word hashing into one of the four locations, 53, 54, 55, or 56, may end up in cell 56 rather than just those words that hash directly into the cell. But the next step is that words hashing into *five* different cells, 53, 54, 55, 56, or 57, will wind up in cell 57, and so forth. As more and more data are stored, these chains just become longer and longer. The result is, first, that some cells will become heavily used and, second, that when we look for a word in storage, as the storage fills up we will need to examine longer and longer chains of cells to locate the word.

We can, in fact, calculate the average number of cells we must search. Statisticians call this average the **expected value**, since it is the number of cells we would expect to search on the average. We define the **load factor,** α, to be the fraction of storage that has been used. For example, once we have stored the fifteen fruit names we have mentioned, our load factor is $\alpha = 15/100 = 0.15$.

When we have another fruit name to consider, our search for it may be successful (we find it in memory) or unsuccessful (we do not find it). If we consider the process, we see that we should expect different search lengths depending on whether we are successful. For simplicity we assume that a given cluster of cells contains only words that hash into the initial location. (If there is a mixture of words hashing to different locations, the analysis is similar but more tedious.) If the word is present, the search will be successful and we will find it somewhere within the cluster, certainly by the time we have examined the entire cluster. But if the word is not present, the search will be unsuccessful. We will only know this when we have searched the entire cluster plus one more cell—the empty cell that tells us we have come to the end of the cluster. Thus we conclude that a successful search will almost always take less time than an unsuccessful one. Only when the cluster contains just one word, the desired one, or is empty will the search time be the same. A complete analysis of linear probing as a method of resolving collisions shows that the expected number of probes, or cells to examine, is approximately

$$S_{\text{LP}} = 0.5\left(1 + \frac{1}{(1 - \alpha)}\right)$$

Figure 7.3   Probe length curves for linear probing

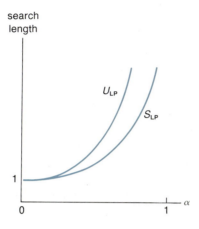

for a successful search, and

$$U_{LP} = 0.5\left(1 + \frac{1}{(1 - \alpha)^2}\right)$$

for an unsuccessful search.

For example, suppose that the allotted storage is half full. Then the load factor is 0.5, and these formulas tell us that we can expect a successful search to take (on the average) 1.5 probes and an unsuccessful search to take 2.5 probes. If the item we want is really there, then it should be either the first item we examine, or the second. Only rarely will we need to examine more than two items. The reason the unsuccessful search takes longer is that we must look at all possibilities—and then take one more look to be sure we are at the end of the chain.

The derivation of these formulas is beyond the scope of this book and is given in Knuth (1973). The important thing to notice is that the load factor appears in the denominator, so that the number of probes becomes arbitrarily large as the load factor approaches 1 (fig. 7.3). Nevertheless, linear probing is so simple that it is quite widely used when the load factor can be kept small. Here is the point: no matter how large the set is, the search time is constant, independent of set size. And if we keep the storage load factor down to a reasonable value, like 0.5, the search time is quite short (1.5 probes for a successful search, 2.5 probes for an unsuccessful one).

The problem of clustering that we see in linear probing is further complicated by the clusters themselves. As they grow, the space between them decreases. This increases the likelihood that clusters will grow together, forming **superclusters.** Nor is the problem alleviated by placing the additional input data two cells away, or five cells away: the difficulty is due to the linearity, not the adjacency of the cells.

Table 7.1	Sample key values
4686	4424
0615	4784
6603	0920
9603	1057
4772	2235

Table 7.2	Addresses computed by modulus
06	04
15	04
03	00
03	17
12	15

7.2 Hash functions

We have mentioned that there are different methods of selecting a hash function. In this section we discuss several of them. Recall that the objective of a hash function is to map the data, through their key values, to an address space so that they are uniformly distributed and there are a minimal number of collisions.

First, we restrict our attention to numerical keys, since the computer addresses that we will use are numerical. As we mentioned in section 7.1, alphabetical keys are handled by converting them to numerical keys in some way and then dealing with the numerical keys. For purposes of illustration, we shall assume the key values given in table 7.1, and that we are hashing into a space with twenty possible addresses, numbered 0 through 19.

One very simple way to convert key values to addresses is to reduce them modulo the size of the address space. For example, this would be reduction modulo 20, yielding the addresses of table 7.2.

The results of this (or any) method of address computation depend heavily on the key values. We see that for this particular set of values, there are three pairs of values that hash into the same locations and that two of these (03 and 04) will run together to form a supercluster.

Another method of computing the address is the **mid-square** method. For this method, the key value is squared, and the required number of digits are taken from the middle of the squared value and reduced modulo the address space size if necessary. For our example, 4686 squares to 21,958,596. The middle two digits are 58, yielding an address of 18. The complete results are given in table 7.3. With this particular data set, the resulting addresses are more poorly distributed than those obtained by direct modulus computation. This is not always the case.

Table 7.3	Addresses computed by mid-square
18	11
18	06
19	06
17	17
11	15

Table 7.4	Addresses computed by folding
12	08
01	11
09	09
19	07
19	17

A third method of computing the address is by **folding.** There are a number of variants of this, but the main idea is to break the key up into pieces of the size needed, add them together, and then reduce the result modulo the address space size. For example, since we need two digits, we would break each key into two digit groups and add them. Thus 4686 would become 46 + 86. This produces 132, which reduces to 12 modulo 20. The complete results are shown in table 7.4.

Folding produces better addresses—for this particular key set but not necessarily in general. One variation of folding is to reverse the digits of some of the folds, just as though the numerals were written on paper and actually folded over. Thus, for 4686, we might fold and reverse the top half, producing 64 + 86, which yields an address of 10; or we might fold and reverse the bottom half, producing 46 + 68, or an address of 14. The overall results for these variants are similar.

These methods are simple, but they tend to be susceptible to patterns in the key values. For example, if the keys tend to be largely even numbers, then reduction modulo 20 would produce largely even addresses, leaving the odd address cells unused. Hence, before using one of these methods, we should examine the key values carefully for patterns and perhaps try some sample values.

One method that is widely used, with good results, is to employ a **random number generator.** This is a function specifically designed to produce all the possible storage address values, with no discernible pattern of occurrence. The most common random number generators are the **linear congruential generators,** which have the form

address $= (c_1 \cdot$ key $+ c_2)$ modulo address space size.

If the constants c_1 and c_2 are properly chosen, and the key values are uniformly distributed (not clustered about a few values), the address distribution is very good. Using m to denote the available memory (address space) size, there are three general rules for choosing the constants:

$c_1 - 1$ should be a multiple of p for each prime factor p of m;

$c_1 - 1$ should be a multiple of 4 if m is a multiple of 4;

c_2 and m should have no factors in common other than 1.

For example, if the available memory size is 512, then $c_1 - 1$ should be an even number (by the first rule), and in particular a multiple of 4 (by the second rule). Rule 3 will be satisfied by any c_2 that is an odd number.

Another example: If the available memory size is 234, then $c_1 - 1$ should be a multiple of 2, 3, and 13, the prime factors of 234. That is, $c_1 - 1$ should be a multiple of 78. The second rule does not apply since m is not a multiple of 4. Thus $c_1 - 1$ should be one of 0, 78, or 156, the only multiples of 78 that are less than the memory size. Next we choose any c_2 that has no factors in common with 234, so that the third rule applies. In this example, c_2 could be 5, 7, 11, or any one of several other values.

These three rules are not arbitrary, but have their basis in the branch of mathematics known as **number theory.** Their whole purpose is to provide a set of constants for the linear congruential generator that will produce a sequence of numbers (addresses) containing all possible values. If other constants are chosen, violating one or more of these rules, the generated numbers will start to repeat before all possible values are produced. For example, if we choose $c_1 = 1$ (that is, $c_1 - 1 = 0$), $c_2 = 5$, and begin with 0, then the generator produces 0, 5, 10, ... , 230, 1, 6, 11, ... , 231, 2, ... , gradually running through all the numbers from 0 to 233. But if we choose $c_1 = 1$ and $c_2 = 4$, then the generator produces only even numbers: 0, 4, 8, ... , 232, 2, 6, ... , 230, 0, ... We obtain even poorer results if we choose $c_1 = 2$ and $c_2 = 5$, with only about 12 percent of the possible address values generated: 0, 5, 15, 35, 75, 155, 315, 167, 105, 215, 201, 173, 117, 5, ...

7.3 Collision resolution

In our discussion of collisions we stated that the critical factor was not that data items were stored adjacent to one another but, rather, the linearity of collision resolution, which forced all colliding data items to follow the same path through storage. The other collision resolution methods we have mentioned are all attempts to remove the linearity factor, and hence to reduce the formation of clusters. In this section we investigate these other collision resolution methods.

Figure 7.4   Collisions in linear hashing

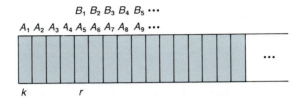

The rehashing method relies on using a second, different hash function in case the first causes a collision. For example, we might choose mid-square as the first method and folding as the second method. Or we might use two linear congruential generators with different constant values. If the second hashing is properly done, this also reduces cluster formation. Usually, the second hashing is done directly from the address computed by the first hashing rather than starting over from the original key.

In **quadratic hashing,** the next location is determined by a quadratic incrementing function rather than by a linear one. Thus, rather than add the same constant value to the address each time we encounter a collision, we increment the address by values that increase quadratically. That is, the size of the increment increases as the square of the number of probes needed for finding an open address. As the following example shows, this greatly reduces the likelihood of repeated collisions.

Consider two data, A_1 and B_1, and suppose that we decide to use the simplest linear probing, increasing the location by one each time. Suppose that the data $A_2, A_3, \ldots$ all hash into the same location, k, as A_1. Then, using linear probing, these data will be placed in cells $k, k + 1, k + 2, k + 3$, and so on. Now suppose that the data $B_2, B_3, \ldots$ all hash into the same location, r, as B_1. If r is slightly larger than k, eventually one of the A data will hash into the B_1 location. For example, if $r = k + 4$, then A_5 will hash into that location. From then on, the A and B data will hash into the same locations. Figure 7.4 shows that when the A cluster grows into the space that the B cluster would normally occupy, a supercluster containing both A and B items will result. This leads to lengthy searches, either to locate an A or a B item, or to find space to insert one.

Now suppose that instead of using the linear increments 1, 2, 3, 4, ... (from the original location) to resolve collisions, we use the quadratic increments 1, 4, 9, 16, ... Then the A data will fall into locations $k, k + 1, k + 4, k + 9,$ $k + 16$, and so forth. If the B data hash into location $r = k + 4$, then with the same quadratic increments their successive locations are $k + 5, k + 8, k + 13,$ $k + 20$, and so forth. Note that except for the first location, $k + 4$, the two series of storage addresses differ. Thus there is much less chance of two data hashing to the same address. Similarly, if a C series starts at location $k + 1$, successive locations would be $k + 2, k + 5, k + 10, k + 17$, and so on. Only when the

Figure 7.5   Reduction of collisions in quadratic hashing

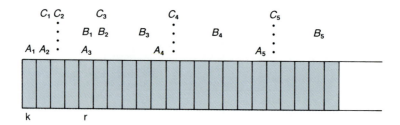

Figure 7.6   Fruit names hashed into buckets

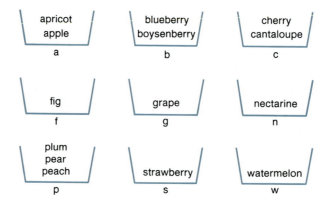

different data series start at the same location is there significant interference between them (see fig. 7.5). It can be shown that the expected number of probes using this method is essentially the same as it is in the chaining method, which we discuss next.

The simplest method of avoiding collisions is to form a **chain** or **bucket** for each hash address, providing storage locations that are not included in the hash table. This is, in fact, what the catalog sales store we mentioned in section 7.1 is doing. A customer's order is hashed into a bucket by the last two digits of the customer's telephone number. When the customer calls for the order, a linear search is made through the appropriate bucket. Note that the items within any one bucket are generally not sorted into any particular order.

Let us look again at our fruit example. Suppose that we were to use our 100 storage locations to set up twenty-five buckets, each holding four names. We could then use the simple hash algorithm of assigning a name to a bucket by its first letter, placing all "y" and "z" fruits in the last bucket (fig. 7.6).

Figure 7.7   Collision resolution by chaining for fruit names, with linked list buckets

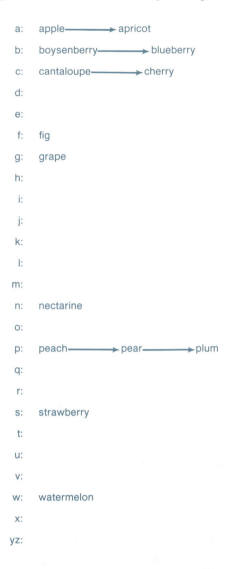

With our given list of fruits, we would have at most three names in a bucket. Since the buckets do not interfere with each other, we have no collision problem until one of the buckets overflows. For the proper choice of bucket sizes, this is very unlikely. One way to avoid any decision on bucket size is to implement each bucket as a linked list. We could, for example, decide to use the first twenty-five storage locations as header locations for our buckets and use the other seventy-five locations as needed to store the remaining data items in each bucket. Assuming that we could place both the data item and the pointer in the same cell, the storage picture might look like figure 7.7.

Figure 7.8   Probe length curves for chaining or bucketing

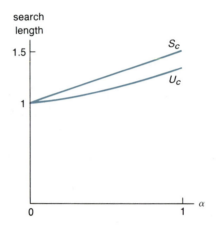

Chaining as a collision resolution method has great merit. In fact, the expected number of probes for the chaining method is approximately

$$S_C = 1 + \alpha/2$$

for a successful search, and

$$U_C = e^{-\alpha} + \alpha$$

for an unsuccessful search. Observe that in these expressions the load factor is in the numerator, so that the expected number of probes is always less than 1.5. (See fig. 7.8.)

Conflict resolution complicates the search and retrieval process to some extent, but these are still $O(1)$ processes, and if memory utilization is kept relatively low, say less than about 70 percent, then the constants involved in computing the processing time are still relatively small.

7.4 Implementation of basic set operations

We now turn to implementing the basic set operations for a hashed representation of sets. Recall that the ADT for sets specifies seven of these:

NewSet (SetName),

AddElement (SetElement, SetName, AddedToSet),

DeleteElement (SetElement, SetName, DeletedFromSet),

IsEmpty (SetName),

IsElement (SetElement, SetName),

GetAnother (SetElement, SetName),

Size (SetName).

In addition, we shall implement Intersect (SetA, SetB, SetC) as typical of the mathematical operations on sets.

For this implementation, we must assume some hashing technique. We shall assume that SetType is ARRAY[1..MaxSize] OF ElementType. Thus Hash is a function that maps from ElementType to an address space that we shall call HashArea. For our present purposes it is not important to specify Hash exactly. However, we shall assume that linear probing is used to resolve collisions. (Other collision resolution techniques can be used if we wish.)

We also assume that there is a specific value, Null, of type ElementType, that indicates the absence of any element. In addition we need another specific value, Marked, to indicate a deleted element. Here is the reason for that. Suppose that two elements, say A and B, hash into the same location, with A being the first element there. Then B is placed elsewhere. If we use, for example, linear probing, then in searching for B we check the first location, find A, and go on to the next, finding B. Now suppose that A is deleted. How do we find B? When we delete A, we could check the next location to see if the datum there should be moved to the location where A was; but we would not know (without considerable work) whether B originally hashed to its present location or was moved there because of the presence of A. Hence we would not know whether B should be moved back to A's location. But if we leave B where it is, then we find the empty location (where A was) and are forced to conclude, erroneously, that B is not in the set. The value "Marked" informs us that something (A) was in that location but has been removed. Thus we know that even though B is not there, we should check further because it might have been placed elsewhere due to a collision.

The plan is to initialize HashArea to Null, and then check against that and Marked to find if any element is stored in a given location. A simple hash function and the procedure NewSet are given in figure 7.9.

To complete the implementation we must provide procedures and functions corresponding to the operations specified in the set ADT. This is done in figures 7.10 through 7.15. The function IsElement determines whether a given element is in a given hashed set (fig. 7.10). Adding an element to a set is not completely straightforward, since we must handle collision resolution and detect an error condition when the set is full (fig. 7.11). In deleting an element, we must first verify that it is in the set. The procedure returns an error message if it is not (fig. 7.12). IsEmpty determines whether the set is empty or not (fig. 7.13). We must also be able to determine the size of a hashed set (fig. 7.14). Finally, we must be able to fetch another element from a hashed set when we have processed a given one (fig. 7.15).

Figure 7.9   A simple hash function and NewSet

```
TYPE
  ElementType = UserSuppliedType;
  SetType     = ARRAY[1..MaxSize] OF ElementType;

FUNCTION Hash (SetElement : ElementType;
               SetName     : SetType) : integer;

{ This is a very simple hash function. A different
one can be used as long as the procedure call is the
same. }

  BEGIN
    Hash := (SetElement MOD MaxSize) + 1
  END; { Hash }

PROCEDURE NewSet (VAR SetName : SetType);

{ Procedure to create a new set. }

  VAR
    Location : 1..MaxSize;

  BEGIN
    FOR Location := 1 TO MaxSize DO
      SetName[Location] := Null
  END; { NewSet }
```

Figure 7.10   Determining whether an element is in a set

```
FUNCTION IsElement (SetElement : ElementType;
                    SetName    : SetType) : boolean;

{ Returns true if SetElement is in SetName, false otherwise. }

  VAR
    FirstLocation : 1..MaxSize;
    Location      : 1..MaxSize;

  BEGIN
    FirstLocation := Hash (SetElement, SetName);
    IF SetName[FirstLocation] = SetElement THEN
      IsElement := true
    ELSE
      BEGIN
        Location := FirstLocation;
        REPEAT
          Location := (Location MOD MaxSize) + 1
        UNTIL (SetName[Location] = SetElement) OR { Found It }
              (SetName[Location] = Null) OR       { Not Present }
              (Location = FirstLocation);         { Exhausted Set }
        IsElement := SetName[Location] = SetElement
      END
  END; { IsElement }
```

Figure 7.11, Part 1   Adding an element to a hashed set

```
PROCEDURE AddElement (SetElement      : ElementType;
                      VAR SetName      : SetType;
                      VAR AddedToSet : boolean);

{ Procedure to add an element to a set. Hash is a predefined
function returning a potential location. This procedure also uses an
internal function IsNotFull to determine whether the set has a Null
or Marked element. Elements can be added only if there is at least
one Null or Marked location. }

  VAR
    Location : 1..MaxSize;

  FUNCTION IsNotFull (SetName : SetType) : boolean;

  { Returns true if the set has at least one Null element, false
  otherwise. }

    VAR
      IsNotYetFull : boolean;
      Location      : 1..MaxSize;

    BEGIN
      Location := 1;
      IsNotYetFull := (SetName[Location] = Null) OR
                      (SetName[Location] = Marked);
      WHILE (NOT IsNotYetFull) AND (Location < MaxSize) DO
        BEGIN
          Location := Location + 1;
          IsNotYetFull := (SetName[Location] = Null) OR
                          (SetName[Location] = Marked)
        END;
      IsNotFull := IsNotYetFull
    END; { IsNotFull }

  BEGIN
    AddedToSet := IsNotFull (SetName);
    IF AddedToSet THEN
      BEGIN
        Location := Hash (SetElement, SetName);
        IF IsElement (SetElement, SetName) THEN
          writeln ('Can''t add: ', SetElement, ' is already in set.')
        ELSE

          { SetElement is not in the set so add it. }
```

Figure 7.11, Part 2   Adding an element to a hashed set

```
        BEGIN
          WHILE (SetName[Location] <> Null) AND
                (SetName[Location] <> Marked) DO
            Location := (Location MOD MaxSize) + 1;
          SetName[Location] := SetElement
        END
    END
  ELSE
    writeln ('Error: Set is full. ', SetElement, ' not added.')
END; { AddElement }
```

Figure 7.12   Deletion of an element from a hashed set

```
PROCEDURE DeleteElement (SetElement       : ElementType;
                         VAR SetName       : SetType;
                         VAR DeletedFromSet : boolean);

{ Procedure to delete an element from a set. }

  VAR
    FirstLocation : 1..MaxSize;
    Location      : 1..MaxSize;

  BEGIN
    Location := Hash (SetElement, SetName);
    FirstLocation := Location;
    IF (SetName[FirstLocation] <> SetElement) AND
       (SetName[FirstLocation] <> Null) THEN
      REPEAT
        Location := (Location MOD MaxSize) + 1
      UNTIL (SetName[Location] = SetElement) OR { Found it }
            (SetName[Location] = Null) OR        { Not there }
            (Location = FirstLocation);          { Exhausted set }

    { If we found it, then delete it. }

    DeletedFromSet := IsElement (SetElement, SetName);
    IF SetName[Location] = SetElement THEN
      SetName[Location] := Marked
    ELSE
      writeln ('Error: ', SetElement, ' is not in the set.')
  END; { DeleteElement }
```

Figure 7.13   Determining whether a hashed set is empty

```
FUNCTION IsEmpty (SetName : SetType) : boolean;

{ Returns true if SetName is empty, false otherwise. }

  VAR
    EmptySoFar : boolean;
    Location   : 1..MaxSize;

  BEGIN
    Location := 1;
    EmptySoFar := (SetName[Location] = Null) OR
                  (SetName[Location] = Marked);
    WHILE EmptySoFar AND (Location < MaxSize) DO
      BEGIN
        Location := Location + 1;
        EmptySoFar := (SetName[Location] = Null) OR
                      (Setname[Location] = Marked)
      END;
    IsEmpty := EmptySoFar
  END; { IsEmpty }
```

Figure 7.14   The size of a hashed set

```
FUNCTION Size (SetName : SetType) : integer;

{ Returns the number of elements in SetName. }

  VAR
    Count    : 0..MaxSize;
    Location : 1..MaxSize;

  BEGIN
    Count := 0;
    FOR Location := 1 TO MaxSize DO
      IF (SetName[Location] <> Null) AND
         (SetName[Location] <> Marked) THEN
        Count := Count + 1;
    Size := Count
  END; { Size }
```

Figure 7.15   GetAnother for a hashed set

```
FUNCTION GetAnother (SetElement : ElementType;
                     SetName    : SetType) : ElementType;

{ Returns the next element in SetName. If SetElement
is not in the set, it returns the "first" element
it finds. If the set is a singleton, it returns
SetElement. }

  VAR
    FirstLocation : 1..MaxSize;
    Location      : 1..MaxSize;

  BEGIN
    IF IsEmpty (SetName) THEN writeln ('Error: Set is empty.')
    ELSE
      BEGIN
        IF IsElement (SetElement, SetName) THEN
          BEGIN
            IF Size (SetName) = 1 THEN GetAnother := SetElement
            ELSE

              { Assert: SetName has at least two elements, one of
              which is SetElement. }

              BEGIN
                Location := Hash (SetElement, SetName);
                FirstLocation := Location;

                { Locate SetElement. }

                WHILE SetName[Location] <> SetElement DO
                  Location := (Location MOD MaxSize) + 1;

                { Now find the successor of SetElement and
                return it. }

                REPEAT
                  Location := (Location MOD MaxSize) + 1
                UNTIL (SetName[Location] <> Null) AND
                      (SetName[Location] <> Marked);
                GetAnother := SetName[Location]
              END
          END
        ELSE writeln('Error: ',SetElement,' is not in the set.')
      END
  END; { GetAnother }
```

Figure 7.16   Set intersection, hashed sets

```
PROCEDURE Intersect (SetA, SetB : SetType;
                        VAR SetC    : SetType);

{ SetC is the intersection of SetA and SetB. }

   VAR
      Location    : 1..MaxSize;
      SetElement  : ElementType;
      WasAdded    : boolean;

   BEGIN
      NewSet (SetC);
      FOR Location := 1 TO MaxSize DO
         BEGIN
            SetElement := SetA[Location];
            IF (SetElement <> Null) AND (SetElement <> Marked) THEN
               IF IsElement (SetElement, SetB) THEN
                  AddElement (SetElement, SetC, WasAdded)
         END
   END; { Intersect }
```

The complexity analysis of these operations is interesting, since the best and worst cases differ. First, we see that NewSet and Size both involve examination of the entire address space set aside for the set. Hence these operations are $O(1)$—they are independent of the size of the set. Here, in particular, is a situation where to think of $O(1)$ as a short time is very wrong, since the *entire* address space must be examined. Nevertheless, the time to do this is independent of the size of the set being examined or initiated.

For all the other operations, in the best case we find the desired element or space immediately, independently of the set size. Hence, best case performance is $O(1)$. However, in the worst case, performance is $O(n)$. For example, it is possible (but highly unlikely) that each element to be added hashes to the first location already occupied by a set element and that all set elements are sequentially located. Then we must search the entire set to find a place for the new element. However, we observed that if we use chaining rather than linear probing to resolve collisions, then we can expect a search to examine at most 1.5 locations on the average, independent of set size. Hence the average case performance for hashing with chaining is also $O(1)$.

Now we consider Intersect (SetA, SetB, SetC). We shall use the operations we have just defined. Note that since Hash takes both an element and a set as arguments, each of the three sets involved will have its own space within storage. Our procedure is to scan the space of SetA, locating each element in it. We then check whether this element is in SetB and, if it is, add it to SetC. The procedure is given in figure 7.16. While this procedure loops through the entire space of

SetA, this loop is $O(1)$, since it is independent of the size of SetA. Again, $O(1)$ is a constant, but not short, time. Thus the overall complexity of Intersect is the maximum of the complexities of IsElement and AddElement. We have already seen that these are $O(1)$ in the best case and $O(n)$ in the worst case.

Because linear probing can seriously degrade performance when the load factor is high, we need to be more precise about the time complexity of these operations. Let us examine the best and worst cases for each of the eight operations we have defined. We shall see that in all of these operations, the worst case involves traversing the entire hash space. Thus for this finer analysis we distinguish between $O(1)$, when we do a very small number of operations, and $O(\text{MaxSize})$, when we need to examine the entire space. Observe that the actual set size is usually less than MaxSize.

NewSet: Each potential element must be initialized, and there are MaxSize of them. Hence in both the best and the worst cases the time complexity is $O(\text{MaxSize})$.

IsElement: The best case occurs when we find the element on the first probe. This has time complexity $O(1)$. But in the worst case (for example, when all elements hash to the same location), we would need to search all MaxSize elements and either find it as the last one or not find it at all. For this, the complexity is $O(\text{MaxSize})$.

AddElement: In the best case, IsNotFull immediately finds a Null location, and we hash directly into an unoccupied location where we can place SetElement. Since each of these is $O(1)$, the best case is $O(1)$. In the worst case, IsNotFull searches the entire hash space and finds a Null on the last try (or finds that there is none). If in this situation all elements hashed to the same location, we might then need to probe all MaxSize locations to find the unoccupied cell. The time complexity in the worst case is thus $O(\text{MaxSize})$.

DeleteElement: Deletion itself is one simple step, but we must first find the element. In the best case, we find it on the first try, so the complexity is $O(1)$. But in the worst case, we may have the entire hash space almost filled with other elements or markers, and only find SetElement on the last probe. Hence the worst case complexity is $O(\text{MaxSize})$.

IsEmpty: This operation depends on finding an element in the set. Thus in the best case we find an element immediately and can conclude that the set is not empty in $O(1)$ time. In the worst case, we would have to search through nearly MaxSize marked (deleted) elements before determining, on the last one, whether the set still contained an unmarked element. Hence the worst case time is $O(\text{MaxSize})$.

Size: Size involves a simple loop examining each location of the hash space. Hence, in both the best and worst cases, the time complexity is $O(\text{MaxSize})$.

Table 7.5	Time complexity for hashed operations	
	Best	**Worst**
NewSet	O (MaxSize)	O (MaxSize)
IsElement	O (1)	O (MaxSize)
AddElement	O (1)	O (MaxSize)
DeleteElement	O (1)	O (MaxSize)
IsEmpty	O (1)	O (MaxSize)
Size	O (MaxSize)	O (MaxSize)
GetAnother	O (1)	O (MaxSize)
Intersect	O (MaxSize)	O (MaxSize^2)

GetAnother: Both the best and the worst cases occur when we have two adjacent elements in the hash space. In the best case, we start at the first of these, and immediately find the other, in $O(1)$ time. In the worst case, these are the only two elements in the set, and we start at the second one. Then we must traverse the entire hash space, wrapping around through its beginning location, to find the other element. The time is $O(\text{MaxSize})$.

Intersect: We begin with an outer loop through the entire hash space, so the best we can expect is $O(\text{MaxSize})$. But this loop contains within it a call to IsElement, so the overall complexity is the product of $O(\text{MaxSize})$ and the complexity of IsElement. Hence the best case is $O(\text{MaxSize})$ and the worst case is $O(\text{MaxSize}^2)$.

This discussion is summarized in table 7.5.

Summary

In this chapter we have discussed the use of a hash coded structure as a more flexible data model. As an example, we have implemented a set as a hashed structure.

Vocabulary

address space	key to address transformation
bucket	linear congruential generator
bucketing	linear open addressing
chain	linear probing
chaining	load factor
cluster	mid-square
collision	number theory
expected value	ord
folding	quadratic hashing
hash coding	quadratic probing
hash function	random number generator
hashing	rehashing
key	supercluster

Reference

Knuth, Donald E. *The Art of Computer Programming*. 3 Vol., Addison-Wesley, Reading, Mass., 1973.

Problems

7.1. Suppose you are given the following data:

24   63   91   42   26   18   33   78   92   11

and the hash function $h(x) = x$ mod 10. Show the memory layout (locations 0–9) after placing these data into memory. Use linear probing to resolve any collisions.

7.2. We defined the function IsNotFull for use in AddElement, but in some of the other set procedures and functions, such as DeleteElement, we ignored this function and checked fullness by a return to the initial value found. Why did we not use IsNotFull in these situations?

7.3. Discuss implementations with hash coded sets for union, difference, complement, and symmetric difference. Determine the best and worst case time complexity for each operation that you have defined.

7.4. Define the basic set functions for hash coded sets, using chaining to resolve collisions.

Programs

7.1. Write a procedure which will "scatter" Pascal's reserved identifiers into 100 table locations using linear probing. Write a boolean function IsReserved which returns "true" if and only if its argument is a Pascal reserved word.

7.2. Redo program 7.1 using chaining instead of linear probing.

7.3. Generate 1000 random integers, and using the hash function $h(x) = x$ mod 1000 insert them into a hash table of size 1000 using linear probing. Use these data to verify the formulas given in the text,

$$S_{LP} = (0.5)\left(1 + \frac{1}{(1 - \alpha)}\right),$$

$$U_{LP} = (0.5)\left(1 + \frac{1}{(1 - \alpha)^2}\right),$$

where α is the load factor.

7.4. Look up quadratic probing in the library. Redo program 7.3 using quadratic probing. How do the results compare?

7.5. Redo program 7.3 using chaining to resolve collisions. Verify the formulas

$$S_C = 1 + \alpha/2, \qquad U_C = e^{-\alpha} + \alpha.$$

8

Tables and Other Complex Structures

Introduction

Our discussion up to this point has focused on linear structures—those structures that are used to represent simple sets of objects. In this chapter we extend the concepts and operations to higher dimensional structures. These structures include tables and arrays, lists with sublists, and more complex record forms. These are the first data structures sufficiently rich to provide a wealth of major applications, including most business records, database systems, numerical and other scientific applications, and pictorial data.

8.1 The ADTs for tables and arrays

We begin with a word on terminology. The basic data structure in this chapter is the ***n*-dimensional table.** The elements of the table may be considered to have two components: a data **entry,** and a **position** or **location** in the table. We place no restriction on the data entry. It can be as simple as a digit or a character, or a highly complex entity. The position is an *n*-dimensional vector whose components are chosen from appropriate finite coordinate sets. Thus $\langle 7, 13 \rangle$ identifies a position in the seventh row and thirteenth column of a two-dimensional table, while $\langle$January, 14, Albany$\rangle$ identifies a position in the "January" row (presumably from the set of months), "14" column (days of the month), and "Albany" layer (state capitals) in some three-dimensional table.

Whenever the entries in a table are **homogeneous,** that is, all of the same type, we refer to the table as an **array.** (Strictly speaking, the Pascal ARRAY is one-dimensional. Even the two-dimensional ARRAY[1..M, 1..N] OF DataType is really defined as ARRAY[1..M] OF ARRAY[1..N] OF DataType. We take the more reasonable view that an array can have any finite number of dimensions.) If, in addition, a set of "algebraic" operations can be performed on the entries of an array or homogeneous table, we call the array a **matrix.** Most frequently the entries in a matrix are numbers, and we wish to perform standard arithmetic operations on them.

We wish to develop an ADT for tables. Since there are no restrictions on table entries, the ADT will be fairly simple, covering the basic functions of storing and retrieving data entries. We begin by observing that each data entry may be quite complex, with several properties or **attributes.** These attributes are divided into two classes, those that correspond to the position coordinates, often called the **keys,** and those that do not correspond to coordinates but are embedded with the data entry itself. For example, suppose that we wish to develop a table of the grades that students in a school get in various courses during one term. Here are three possible ways to do that.

If we are primarily interested in individual students, we might develop a one-dimensional table with the student name as the key attribute. The other attributes, which would form part of each data entry, might include student identification number, course number, and homework and test grades in each course. Note that since a student normally takes more than one course per semester, each entry would contain data for *all* the courses that an individual student was taking.

If, however, we are primarily interested in the courses, we might develop a one-dimensional table with the course number as the key attribute. Now all the other attributes, including the student name, would be part of the data entry. In this situation, each entry would contain data for *all* students taking a given course.

A third way to organize these data is to form a two-dimensional table with both student name and course number as key attributes. Now the data entry would contain all the other data except these two items. An individual entry would be much simpler—just the record of one student in one course.

The designation of key attributes relates strongly to the manner in which we wish to use the table. Suppose that we wish to recover the record of one student. In the first and third organizations this would be relatively simple, since we have the student name as a **coordinate** into the table. But in the second arrangement we have no direct way to locate the student. We would have to retrieve the record for each course and then search that to determine if that was a course the given student took.

Why not make all attributes keys? To do so would greatly complicate the process of organizing the data, since this would include organizing the data according to many "key" attributes that are very unlikely to be used in a search process. For example, we probably would not want to know the records of all students whose first name was Susan or who lived on Maple Avenue; but a student record may very well contain both the first name and the address of the student. If we are never (well, hardly ever) going to search on a given attribute, there is no point in making it a key and adding it into the coordinate system.

With this discussion, we are ready to define the operations for the abstract data type, table.

CreateTable (TableName, KeyValues)—creates a table called TableName, whose coordinates are the KeyValues. Entries in the table are initialized to a "missing" value. CreateTable returns an error if TableName designates an existing table.

DeleteTable (TableName)—deletes the table called TableName. It returns an error if no such table exists.

IsEmpty (TableName)—returns "true" if the table TableName is empty, "false" if it is not empty. It returns an error if the table does not exist.

AddEntry (TableName, EntryValue)—creates a table entry for EntryValue. Note that this extracts the key values from EntryValue. It returns an error if not all key values are defined or if the table does not exist.

FindEntry (TableName, KeyValues)—given one or more key values, returns *all* table entries corresponding to those keys, together with their full key values. It returns an error if there is no such entry or if the table does not exist.

DeleteEntry (TableName, KeyValues)—given one or more key values, deletes *all* table entries corresponding to those keys. It returns an error if there is no such entry or if the table does not exist.

We make several observations on this ADT. First, there are three levels of "missing" involved. At the top level, the table itself is missing (does not exist). The various operations all return an error in this case (except CreateTable). At the second level, the table is defined, but a specific entry within the table is missing. Again, the appropriate operations return an error in this case. Finally, while a data entry as a whole may be defined, certain parts of it may not be. For example, a student record may be missing a telephone number or the grade in a particular course. This level of "missing" is not handled by the given ADT but must be handled by the ADT for the individual data entry.

Second, there must also be an ADT for the individual data entries. All that the present ADT does is to define how the entries are added to or deleted from a table, and how a search is done. Nothing is said about the structure of the individual data entries (other than the key versus non-key attribute distinction), or about operations on the individual entries.

Third, because of the potential complexity and variety of the individual data entries, no "update" operation has been included. This is handled by retrieving the desired entry, modifying it outside the table (according to its ADT), and then entering the altered value into the table. This is accomplished by the sequence FindEntry, DeleteEntry, modify the entry, and AddEntry.

Fourth, the FindEntry and DeleteEntry operations are defined to function on partial sets of key values, locating all entries that match those values which have been defined.

Fifth, this is a very general ADT and leaves several questions unresolved, which must be settled for specific table uses. For example, nothing has been said about the duplicate key problem: What should be done if we try to make an entry into a position that already contains data? In some situations we wish to add to the existing data, in others we may wish to overwrite the existing data, and in still others we may wish to signal an error.

Similarly, the only matching that this ADT allows is an exact match. Frequently we wish to allow range or approximate matches also. For example, "Find all senators whose annual income from speaking engagements exceeds $50,000." If these or other types of operations are desired, the ADT must be extended to handle them.

We turn now to the ADT for the array data structure. Since we have defined an array to be a table with homogeneous data entries, we find that the ADT for a general table is precisely what we want for an array as well. That is, we can use the operations in the table ADT without any change. The only two ways in which the homogeneity of an array has any influence come in the implementation. First, it is now necessary to check that the entries added to an array are indeed homogeneous; second, the homogeneity may permit more efficient implementation of some of the operations than would be possible in a general table.

8.2 Implementation of tables

Many programming languages, including Pascal, do not directly allow the implementation of a table data structure. While the operations we have defined seem simple enough, we have noted that in specific instances additional operations might also be wanted. The potential variety of these operations implies that a truly general table implementation will be complex. Then too, the inhomogeneity of the entries within the table and the potential variety of these entries make it difficult to define a general table structure efficiently. As we shall see later, even those languages and programming systems that include a table data structure frequently limit the table entries to a few commonly used types.

However, if a table has a simple enough structure, it is possible to implement an appropriate data structure in Pascal. The structure that is used for this is an ARRAY of RECORDs. Note that since this is an array, the entries are homogeneous. Any inhomogeneities in the table must be hidden within the record structure.

Suppose, for example, that we wish to create a table that contains the student records for a particular course. For each student we will certainly want to record the name, the grades on homework assignments, and the grades on tests. This gives us a base RECORD type to use in the table:

```
TYPE
  StudentInfo = RECORD
                StudentName : ARRAY[1..30] OF char;
                Homework    : ARRAY[1..15] OF integer;
                Test        : ARRAY[1..3] OF 0..100
              END;
```

Note that in the definition we have assumed at most fifteen homework assignments, three tests, and numerical grades on all assignments and tests. We could, of course, change these assumptions. We may also want to include other information, such as the course number, the student's telephone number, and perhaps a field for the instructor's comments. We could then declare a table by

```
VAR
  Class : ARRAY[1..ClassSize] OF StudentInfo;
```

where ClassSize is a defined integer constant.

While this gives us an implementation of a table, it is not fully satisfactory. For example, we might like to use the student name as a key into the table; but this structure does not permit that, since the array indices are numerical.

In this example we have defined a one-dimensional array whose entries are student records. Despite the deficiencies of this implementation, it has enough generality that the implementation of a table as an array of records can be used in many applications.

8.3 Two-dimensional tables and arrays

The array of records, as we have discussed it, enables us to implement a table with one key per record. When we have more than one key, the same method can be extended in the form of a two- or three-dimensional array of records. This type of organization frequently provides better access to the data and matches our intuitive image of the data organization more closely.

Table 8.1   University rankings

University Factors:	#Students 1	Cost 2	Chem Rank 5	Astro Rank 3	Overall
Cal Tech	1765	$13,034	2	1	334
Cornell	17146	$13,005	8	6	287
Harvard	16037	$13,800	1	4	328
MIT	8935	$14,400	5	7	300
Stanford	12341	$13,851	4	NA	233
UC, Berkeley	30010	$8,237	3	3	323
UC, San Diego	n/l	n/l	10	NA	202
Chicago	7833	$12,902	6	NA	226
Illinois	34632	$7,128	9	14	262
Wisconsin	43075	$6,420	7	5	299
	1	−1	49	30	
	−1	−1	43	25	
	−1	−1	50	27	
	0	−1	46	24	
	0	−1	47	0	
	−1	0	48	28	
	−1	−1	41	0	
	1	0	45	0	
	−1	1	42	17	
	−1	1	44	26	

The basic development of two-dimensional tables and arrays is straightforward. Just as we identify the cells in a one-dimensional array by a single subscript on a variable name (for example, Grade[13]), so also we identify the cells in a two-dimensional table or array by an ordered pair of subscripts. However, the inhomogeneity that is specified in our definition of a table still causes difficulties in many implementations. Consider, for example, table 8.1, which presents data about ten of the country's leading universities.

This two-dimensional table was, in fact, developed using the **spreadsheet** program Lotus 1-2-3, and it illustrates the type of inhomogeneities that are common in tables. Within the table, "NA" denotes "not applicable" and is interpreted by Lotus 1-2-3 as a zero value; in contrast, "n/l" denotes "not listed" and is interpreted as a numerical value larger than any listed. To discuss the table, we present first figure 8.1, which shows the regions in the table.

We observe that the general layout of the table is by rows and columns. But the regions specified in figure 8.1 do not follow the row and column layout exactly. Region *A* contains the row and column headings that define the table for the user. These headings are unnecessary for the computer. We note that they are all characters. Region *B* contains numerical factors that are used in the calculations defined within the table. The values are provided by the user and can be changed at will. Regions *C, F, G,* and *I* are all blank. (Note also that there could be blank lines within regions *A* and *B*.)

Figure 8.1   Regions in table 8.1

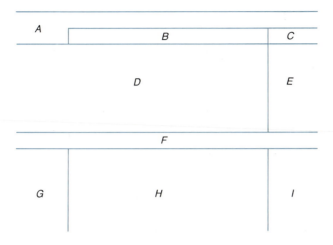

Region *D* contains the data that have been entered into the table, and region *E* contains values that have been calculated from these data. Region *H,* finally, contains some intermediate results that were used in obtaining the values in region *E.* In the first column of *H,* the value is −1 if #Students exceeds 13,000, +1 if it is less than 8000, and 0 otherwise. The second column is similarly defined, with the breakpoints at $13,000 and $7500. Note that in both columns "n/l" counts as a large value. This is needed instead of "NA" so that the corresponding value is −1 rather than +1. Since fifty schools are considered in the chemistry ranking, the value in the third column is 51 − Chem Rank. Thus the leading university has value 50 in this column, the second has value 49, and so forth. Similarly, in the fourth column the value is 31 − Astro Rank, or 0 if the entry is "NA." The overall score is obtained by multiplying each intermediate value by the corresponding factor and adding. For example, the score for Cal Tech is

$$1 \cdot 1 + 2 \cdot (-1) + 5 \cdot 49 + 3 \cdot 30 = 334.$$

We also observe that while the data are largely numerical except for the university names, three of the columns contain a mixture of numerical and alphabetical characters. In addition, we observe that the rows in the bottom half of the table are different from the rows in the main portion of the table.

(The data in the #Students and Cost columns are taken from Peterson's *Competitive Colleges,* 4th ed. The entry "n/l" indicates that there was no listing for the university in this source. The Chem Rank and Astro Rank data represent the 1984 Gourman Report rankings of these universities in chemistry and astronomy, respectively. Again, an entry "NA" indicates that the university was not among those listed in the rankings.)

All these differences in the data can be handled simply and automatically with Lotus 1-2-3 or any of the other spreadsheet programs, such as VisiCalc or CalcStar. In addition, these programs automatically handle the exceptional non-numeric data in calculations involving the numerical columns.

If we attempt to define this table in Pascal, we find that, because of the variations in the data entries, a simple definition is virtually impossible. However, let us try.

First, let us observe that regions D and E are the heart of the table. All the other data displayed in the table can be hidden. This observation allows us to concentrate our efforts on one major data type: the record defining a row in D and E. The basic record definition is

```
TYPE
   UniversityRank = RECORD
                    UniversityName : ARRAY[1..13]
                                        OF char;
                    NoStudents     : 0..50000;
                    Cost           : 0..20000;
                    ChemRank       : 0..50;
                    AstroRank      : 0..30;
                    Overall        : integer
                    END;

VAR
   Factor     : ARRAY[1..4] OF integer;
   University : ARRAY[1..20] OF UniversityRank;
```

With this definition, the column headings that appear in the displayed table are absorbed into the type definition. That is, we have chosen field names that are essentially the same as the column headings, and the headings themselves will never explicitly appear as data. (They can, of course, be displayed in the output to the user.) By the choice of ranges for the values and subscripts, we have allowed some room for expansion of the table. The factors are given as a separate array, and all the intermediate calculation results now become hidden in the programs that process the data and produce the values in region E.

The only problem remaining with this implementation is handling the exceptional non-numeric values for some of the data. Here are two ways of doing this, both of which involve some additional processing. One way is to define some absurd numerical values arbitrarily and rely on the programs to interpret these correctly. For example, we might substitute 0 for each of the non-numeric values in region D. Quite clearly, something would seem to be wrong if the number of students at a school were 0 or the cost were 0, and we could easily interpret a 0 in the ranking columns as indicating an unranked school. The danger is that the "absurd" values may not be absurd. (Deep Springs College, for example, lists its costs as $0.)

Figure 8.2   Pseudocode for intermediate calculations

```
IF (NoStudents >= 13000) OR
   (StudentExceptionCode) THEN
  StudentInterm := -1
ELSE
  IF NoStudents < 8000 THEN
    StudentInterm := 1
  ELSE
    StudentInterm := 0;

IF (Cost >= 13000) OR (CostExceptionCode) THEN
  CostInterm := -1
ELSE
  IF Cost < 7500 THEN
    CostInterm := 1
  ELSE
    CostInterm := 0;

IF ChemExceptionCode THEN
  ChemInterm := 0
ELSE
  ChemInterm := 51 - ChemRank;

IF AstroExceptionCode THEN
  AstroInterm := 0
ELSE
  AstroInterm := 31 - AstroRank;
```

The other way of handling exceptional values in Pascal is through the **variant record.** We will discuss this concept thoroughly in section 8.4. For now, suffice it to say that the variant record concept permits us to combine two or more possible definitions for the record fields into one record type definition. We then rely on the program to determine which definition applies. In the present example, the variant that we want would define alphabetic data, say ARRAY[1..3] OF char, as alternatives for the fields NoStudents, Cost, ChemRank, and AstroRank.

Figure 8.2 presents Pascal-like **pseudocode** that defines the intermediate value computations. To use these code fragments in a program, we must tie the variable names to the data structure and put the exception handling mechanisms in place.

Our implementation in Pascal has resulted in a data structure that is an ARRAY[1..20] OF UniversityRank, permitting us as many as twenty universities in the table. How are these to be arranged? That is, what is to be meant by University[7]? We could arbitrarily assign numbers to the various schools. But if we observe the given table, we find that each university has a ranking in chemistry and that, in fact, these are supposedly the top ten universities in that field. Thus, if we could guarantee that every university in the table stands among the top twenty in chemistry, we could use the chemistry ranking as the array subscript. University[7] would be the seventh ranked university in chemistry, the University of Wisconsin. But if, for example, the thirteenth ranked university were missing, and the twenty-fourth ranked were included, then the line for University[13] would be blank, and there would be no line in the table for University[24].

This implementation of the table is a one-dimensional array. Implementation as a two-dimensional array is possible but presents some problems. The basic definition is not the problem. We simply define an enumerated type "Header," whose possible values are the column headings we want, and then use a value from this ordered set as our second coordinate of the array:

```
TYPE
    Header = (UniversityName, NoStudents, Cost,
              ChemRank, AstroRank, Ranking);

VAR
    University : ARRAY[1..20, Header] OF SchoolRecord;
```

The problem arises because the array implementation forces a uniform definition of SchoolRecord, when we want alphabetic values in some positions, numerical values in others, and possibly exceptional values in still others. The variant record can be used to define the possible value types; but this is a weak definition, since we will have lost control of the specific type in each location. That is, there would no longer be any way to guarantee, for example, that UniversityName would really be an alphabetic array.

Thus our ability to define general two-dimensional tables in Pascal is distinctly limited. We note that in most spreadsheet programs the problem of variant fields does not arise, since the programs have the ability to define value types for individual positions or blocks of positions. However, spreadsheets are generally limited to two-dimensional tables and have difficulty representing higher dimensional tables. Fortunately, there is not much need for such tables.

Another two-dimensional table that finds use in business is the **decision table** (fig. 8.3). This type of table is divided horizontally into two sections, the **condition section** and the **action section,** and vertically into two sections, the **heading section** and the **rule section.** Each rule consists of a specific combination of conditions and elicits a specific set of actions. In our example, the rule conditions are specified by *"Y"* or *"N"* (representing yes and no), and the actions to be taken by *"X."*

In this example, the two input values to be considered are the quantity received and the quantity sold. The first line of the table tells us that if the quantity received is less than zero (presumably an error or a stop condition), then Decision Rule 5 applies. The Action portion of the table tells us that the only action under

Figure 8.3   A simple decision table

Inventory Report	Decision Rule				
Condition:	1	2	3	4	5
Quantity rec'd < 0	N	N	N	N	Y
Quantity rec'd = 0	Y	Y	N	N	N
Quantity rec'd > 0	N	N	Y	Y	N
Quantity sold > 0	N	Y	N	Y	—
Action:					
Avail = Initial	X	X			
Avail = Initial + Rec'd			X	X	
Final = Avail	X		X		
Final = Avail − Sold		X		X	
Enter line in report	X	X	X	X	
Get next record	X	X	X	X	
Stop					X

Rule 5 is to stop. The second and third lines of the Condition portion tell us what to do in the event that the quantity received is either zero or greater than that. The fourth line of the Condition portion tells us that the particular action depends on whether any have been sold. Putting these together, we see, for example, that Rule 2 applies if we have received no new inventory but have sold some. The action under these circumstances has four components: the available inventory is what we started with; the final inventory is that quantity less the amount sold; we enter a line item in our report; we get the next record.

In scientific and technical work, the two-dimensional array arises repeatedly in the form of a numerical matrix. Most frequently it is associated with the solution of a system of linear equations that may represent an optimization problem of some kind. For these arrays, the computational rules of **linear algebra** or **matrix algebra** apply. For programming, these rules could be formalized as an abstract data type that would include automatic checking for conformance to the rules—but we leave that as an exercise.

8.4 Variant records

We begin with a caution. As mentioned earlier, the term "record" has been used historically to denote a component of a file—that is, a block of related data within a file that will be treated as a single logical unit. The Pascal RECORD falls within this concept of a single logical unit, but is a very specific instance of the concept, that may or may not be associated with a file. We shall distinguish between these two meanings by writing "record" for the general construct and "RECORD" for its Pascal implementation. Formally, a **record** is a single group of logically related data.

The Pascal RECORDs we have used up to now have been simple and straightforward. We may regard a RECORD as an n-tuple, where n is the number of fields. Although these fields are often simple structures, we have alluded to the possibility of more complex RECORD forms. Recall that in the Biography example of chapter 3 the third definition given was a RECORD, one of whose fields was itself a RECORD (fig. 3.4).

We can iterate this kind of complexity for RECORDs, since each field in a RECORD can be arbitrarily defined. While it is possible to devise complex structures in this manner, we make two observations. First, the complexity is limited because of the hierarchical nature of these definitions. We can define subfields of a given field to several depth levels, but if we diagram the structure developed, we find that nowhere do two fields have the same identical subfield (although they may have subfields with identical data values). The farther we go, the more new subfields we must define.

Second, people simply do not organize data in exceedingly fine and complex detail, probably because such an organization quickly grows beyond our ability to understand and control it. We allow unlimited subdivision of fields because we cannot set an arbitrary limit that is guaranteed to be sufficient and reasonable, and also because much of the theory and many of the algorithms become simpler if we do not need to account for limitations. But in practice, it is rare to find data organizations that go deeper than three or four levels.

Since people do not generally organize deep structures of data, the interesting extension of the record type lies not in this replication of structure in depth. It lies, rather, in the idea of being able to view the data within the record in several different ways.

Consider, for example, the stock of a small hardware store. This may include such items as screwdrivers, hammers, power saws, lawn mowers, bolts and nuts, screening, paint, and so forth. In the store's records, certain data associated with these items will have a common form. For instance, each item will have a name, a part number in the store's inventory, a quantity count, a unit cost, and a unit selling price. However, there are also obvious differences in the descriptions of these items. We would want to describe a lawn mower by whether it is a rotary or reel mower; whether it is gas, electric, or hand powered; the width of the cut; and so forth. Such descriptions hardly fit a screwdriver or wire screening. Quite possibly we will also need to take into account the codes various manufacturers use in assigning their own part numbers to their products (fig. 8.4).

One way to handle this is to allow separate fields for each of the common descriptors and one large string field to hold all the unique descriptors. This is simple but difficult to use efficiently. In particular, it makes updating records inefficient since we must always handle many fields that have no relevance to a particular datum. A better way is to define a record structure that allows for variants or different field arrangements within the record.

Figure 8.4   Variations on a hardware stock record

Column headers: name, stock no., quantity, cost, price

name	stock no.	quantity	cost	price					
bolt					MID	head	length	diam	thread
hammer					MID	style	weight		
mower					MID	form	power	width	
paint					MID	kind	base	use	size	paint color	color code
screen					MID	material	mesh	screen color	

MID = Manufacturer's ID

The concept of a **variant record part** allows us to overlay on storage several different record definitions, choosing the one that is appropriate for representation of a particular set of data, based on the data in the record. By using appropriate field identifiers, we are able to determine automatically which variant of the record we are using.

Consider our hardware store record. By using variant record parts, we can define different fields for each type of stock, using in each record the variant that fits the stock being described. Pascal provides an implementation of this idea based on the CASE statement. A simplified version (not containing all stock types) of the hardware record might then appear as in figure 8.5.

Each of the variants given in this RECORD definition corresponds to one of the possible record types shown in figure 8.4. Note that the first five fields are fixed and are the same regardless of which variant is chosen to complete the RECORD. The problem with this, from the standpoint of good programming practices, is that adding a new type of item to the stock, or modifying the specifications of an existing item, requires changing the source code that defines PartRecord and recompiling the program. This is a weakness of Pascal that is avoided in some other languages.

The use of a variant record part allows us to address directly the various characteristics of the items in stock. This makes it simple to enter, change, or retrieve data using these characteristics. We could, for example, easily determine the QuantityOnHand of Chinese red oil-based enamel, gallon size, since each characteristic is directly addressable.

In Pascal, the following rules apply in using variant record parts.

First, a record definition may contain at most one variant part, and it must be the last part of the record. Note, however, that the variant part may have variant parts nested within it.

Figure 8.5   Hardware stock record, with variant

```
TYPE
  Item         = (Bolt, Hammer, Mower, Paint, Screening);
  BoltIDType   = { Manufacturer's ID specification };
  HammerIDType = { Manufacturer's ID specification };
  MowerIDType  = { Manufacturer's ID specification };
  PaintIDType  = { Manufacturer's ID specification };
  ScreenIDType = { Manufacturer's ID specification };
  HammerStyle  = (Claw, BallPeen, Tack, Sledge);
  HeadType     = (Hex, Square);
  MaterialType = (Aluminum, Brass, Nylon);
  PaintKind    = (Enamel, Flat, Varnish, Stain);
  ScreenColor  = (Silver, Black, Gray, Brass, White);
  PartRecord   = RECORD
                   ItemName       : Item;
                   ItemID         : PACKED ARRAY[1..10] OF char;
                   QuantityOnHand : integer;
                   UnitCost       : real;
                   UnitPrice      : real;
                   CASE WhichType : Item OF
                     Bolt      : (BoltID   : BoltIDType;
                                  Head     : HeadType;
                                  Length   : real;
                                  Diameter : real;
                                  Thread   : integer);
                     Hammer    : (HammerID : HammerIDType;
                                  Style    : HammerStyle;
                                  Weight   : integer);
                     Mower     : (MowerID  : MowerIDType;
                                  Form     : (Rotary, Reel);
                                  Power    : (Gas, Electric, Hand);
                                  CutWidth : 12..36);
                     Paint     : (PaintID  : PaintIDType;
                                  Kind     : PaintKind;
                                  Base     : (Oil, Acrylic, Latex);
                                  Use      : (Interior, Exterior);
                                  Size     : (Pint, Quart, Gallon);
                                  PColor   : PACKED ARRAY[1..15]
                                                  OF char;
                                  ColorCode : integer);
                     Screening : (ScreenID : ScreenIDType;
                                  Material : MaterialType;
                                  Mesh     : integer;
                                  SColor   : ScreenColor)
                 END; { PartRecord }
```

Second, all the field identifiers used must be unique. (This is good practice, even if it weren't required.)

Third, the variant part is denoted by a CASE statement which has a slightly different form from the usual CASE statement. The case determiner (in our example, Bolt, Hammer, Mower, Paint, Screening) may or may not occur as a separate field value in the record. It is permissible to have several different cases with the same definition, as in the usual CASE statement. For example, we could have a case

```
Bolt, Screw : ...
```

Note that the fields for each case are given in a parenthesized list. An empty list, (), is permissible. Finally, note that there is no END for the CASE statement, the END for the RECORD serving that purpose.

Fourth, it is not required that all variants be of the same length. Sufficient storage will be allocated to hold the longest defined variant.

Finally, it is an error to try to access a field that is not within the variant part actually in use. Thus, if we were to refer to the Diameter of a Paint, an error would occur. (Be warned that many Pascal implementations do not check for variant errors at run time.)

8.5 Sequential storage of arrays and tables

We organize data into an array because the array matches some significant characteristics of the data. Each row of the array may represent related data that should be kept together, such as the grades of one particular student. Similarly, each column of the array may represent data of the same type, such as a specific type of expenditure in a ledger. Because of these data relationships, the integrity of the rows and columns of an array is important to the user in building and manipulating the array.

A fundamental principle of data abstraction is that the user should be able to handle the data as he or she sees fit, without concern about how the computer is actually manipulating the data. Thus the abstract data type should correspond very closely to the user's view of the world: how the data are organized and handled. And the user should be able to handle the data at that abstract level. Pascal was developed before computer scientists had come to grips fully with the concept of data abstraction. Thus, while Pascal incorporates many sound concepts related to modern programming practice, unfortunately data abstraction as it is now understood is not one of them.

But someone must take on the task of assuring that the implementation of an abstract data type accurately mirrors the abstraction. This person has the task, for example, of making sure that the entries in a table are stored in an organized way and that the routines that process these entries match the storage structure, so that they are always operating on the correct data elements. Furthermore, this person has an obligation to make sure that the implementation is reasonably efficient. Thus we move now from the clean world of abstraction into the "nitty-gritty" of detailed storage implementation.

Let us assume that we are concerned with storing an array, each entry requiring exactly one unit of storage. Generalization to tables with inhomogeneous data is possible, but more complicated because the amount of storage required for different entries within the table may vary widely. We shall begin with a two-dimensional array and generalize to a three-dimensional array in section 8.6. From that, the mechanism for handling n-dimensional arrays will be clear.

Since the integrity of the rows and columns of an array is important to the user, it is natural to consider an implementation that preserves as much of this integrity as possible. This is a sequential storage implementation. (In section 8.8 we shall consider a list storage implementation.) Pascal and other higher level languages maintain row and column integrity automatically. It is instructive, however, to examine how this is done, since the same types of techniques can be applied to maintaining integrity in other data structures, such as higher dimensional, triangular, or hexagonal arrays.

It is a fact of standard computer system architecture that the memory cells are addressed linearly, as though the entire memory were one long sequential list. We must thus find a way to map a two-dimensional array into this storage so as to maintain the row and column integrity. Two things are clear. First, there is no way in which we can store the array that keeps each row intact in storage *and* each column also intact: something has to give. Second, no matter how we store the array, if we have a sound algorithm for storing it, then we can usually develop a sound algorithm for retrieving each row or each column.

Throughout our discussion we shall assume a standard set of array indices, each running from 1 through some positive integer. In general, it is only necessary that the array indices are consecutive elements from some well-ordered set, taken in increasing order. Thus we could use the letters e, f, g, h, i, j, in that order, as values of an array index, or the names of the months in order. Pascal allows such indexing, although some other languages such as FORTRAN and BASIC do not.

The common methods of storing a two-dimensional array are by row or by column. If we store an array by row, each row of the array is located in contiguous storage and easily accessible. This is called storage in **row major order.** From the programming standpoint, each column is just as easily accessible, although physically the column is dispersed in memory. With storage by column, in **column major order,** each column is located in a block of memory and the rows are broken up. Consider, for example, the array in figure 8.6. Storing this array by row results in the memory distribution

$$a_{11} \quad a_{12} \quad a_{21} \quad a_{22} \quad a_{31} \quad a_{32} \quad a_{41} \quad a_{42}$$

Figure 8.6   A small two-dimensional array

$$a_{11} \qquad a_{12}$$

$$a_{21} \qquad a_{22}$$

$$a_{31} \qquad a_{32}$$

$$a_{41} \qquad a_{42}$$

while storing it by column results in

$$a_{11} \quad a_{21} \quad a_{31} \quad a_{41} \quad a_{12} \quad a_{22} \quad a_{32} \quad a_{42}$$

In both cases, it is easy to recover a specific array entry if its subscripts are known.

Let us develop a formula for row major storage of a two-dimensional array, using the above example as our guide. First, we suppose that a_{11} is stored at some known memory address, b. Then we have the storage assignment of figure 8.7 for the array.

Note that each row contains two entries and that the first row is in locations $b + 0$ and $b + 1$, the second row in locations $b + 2 + 0$ and $b + 2 + 1$, and the third in locations $b + 4 + 0$ and $b + 4 + 1$. This generalizes to an $m \times n$ array, for which the first j elements of the ith row will be in locations

$$b + n(i - 1), \quad b + n(i - 1) + 1, \quad \dots, \quad b + n(i - 1) + j - 1.$$

Thus, for an $m \times n$ array A sequentially stored by rows, with the first entry in location b, the entry a_{ij} is stored at location

$$b + n(i - 1) + (j - 1).$$

In our example, since $m = 4$ and $n = 2$ we find a_{32} in location $b + 2(3 - 1) + (2 - 1)$, or in location $b + 5$.

The elements in the ith row are found by fixing the value of i and incrementing j from 1 to n; and the elements in the jth column are found by holding the value of j constant and incrementing i from 1 to m. Basically, the formula states that the location of a_{ij} is found by skipping $i - 1$ complete rows of n entries each and going $j - 1$ locations beyond the first entry in its row.

A similar formula holds for a two-dimensional array stored in column major order. In this case, the entry a_{ij} is located at

$$b + m(j - 1) + (i - 1).$$

Verification of this is left as an exercise.

Figure 8.7   Row-ordered array storage

Address	Content
b	a_{11}
$b + 1$	a_{12}
$b + 2$	a_{21}
$b + 3$	a_{22}
$b + 4$	a_{31}
$b + 5$	a_{32}
$b + 6$	a_{41}
$b + 7$	a_{42}

Suppose now that we have an array A in memory. We face the problem of manipulating this data structure. Observe first that it is quite easy to access the entry a_{ij} in this array. In a higher level language, such as Pascal, the user simply writes A[I,J], and lets the compiler worry about locating the entry, according to its formulas. Thus updating an array is quite simple.

Adding or deleting entries in an array, however, leads to some problems. Suppose that A is an $m \times n$ array, stored by rows. What if we wish to add a new row or column to the array? This is not an uncommon problem in practice. Perhaps an application program using an array has been in use for some time, and the user decides that it would be useful to include another column of information within the array. For example, if our array represents student grades on tests, we might decide to add another test grade. Or perhaps the program is only being tested when we discover that we have inadvertently omitted two rows from the array. Spreadsheets, such as Lotus 1-2-3, are very convenient in this respect, for the spreadsheet system itself provides the facility for adding or deleting rows and columns, automatically adjusting the rest of the array. If we are using the facilities of a higher level language such as Pascal to manage the arrays, there is again little difficulty, as we simply change the array declaration and recompile the program. But if we are writing our own array management routines, then changes must probably be made within each management routine.

Adding a new row in row major order is not very difficult. We determine where the row should begin and move everything beyond there up *by n locations, the number of entries in a row.* This is essentially the same problem as adding a new entry in a sorted sequential list. (Note that the sorting here is implicit, by row number, then column number.) The formula for locating entries within the array remains the same, since the new block of storage represents an entire row.

Adding a new column, however, is somewhat more difficult since the column elements are not located in a single block in storage. For example, if we wish to add a new second column to the array in figure 8.6, making the old second column the new third one, this (or the equivalent) is required:

Figure 8.8   Adding a new column to a row-stored array

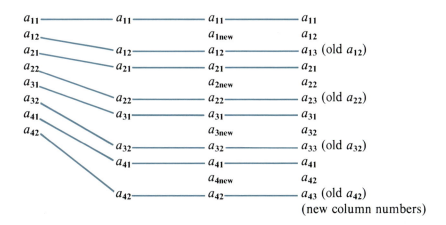

(new column numbers)

1. move entry a_{42} down four places and rename a_{42} as a_{43};

2. move entries a_{32} and a_{41} down three places and rename a_{32} as a_{33};

3. move entries a_{22} and a_{31} down two places and rename a_{22} as a_{23};

4. move entries a_{12} and a_{21} down one place and rename a_{12} as a_{13};

5. enter the new elements as a_{12}, a_{22}, a_{32}, and a_{42} (fig. 8.8).

Note that this process changes the formula for locating the entries, since the size of each row increases by one. An alternative procedure is to recopy the old array into new locations, leaving space for the added column.

As a practical matter, unless the user chooses to write his or her own access formulas, array access is handled automatically by the language compiler or interpreter. Many programming languages require that the user specify the array size at compile time. This reserves a block of storage of size mn (for an $m \times n$ array). If not all of this storage is used initially, then array growth can take place within this block, without the necessity of changing access formulas. Array growth beyond these limits is not permitted.

However, if the language implementation allows dynamically defined arrays, whose sizes are not known until run time, then the processor must allow for possible changes of size. Note that this is the situation for many spreadsheet programs, such as Lotus 1-2-3, which allow the user to insert rows or columns into the spreadsheet table as needed.

Because of the implied relationships among the entries in a row or in a column, rarely will we wish to sort all the elements of a table or an array into some particular order. However, frequently we need to have the rows or the columns or both arranged in some order. Thus, if each row contains data related to a specific

Figure 8.9   Table form for mailing list

FName MI LName   Street   City   State   ZIP   Phone

date, then it is reasonable to have the rows sorted into chronological order. If each column then represents the data associated with some identifiable entity and these entities are ordered in some way, it is also reasonable to have the columns so ordered. For example, an apartment manager may want the entry Money[Month, Apt] to be the amount of rent that has been paid on a particular apartment (Apt) in a particular month (Month). It is reasonable then for the manager to want the array rows in calendar order and the columns in the order of the apartment numbers.

Sorting a table is thus basically a linear sort (see chapter 11), performed for each dimension that should be in sorted order. The only problem is to remember, if we are sorting the rows, to move all the entries in a row whenever we decide to reorder the rows. Since the sorting is usually done on the basis of the elements in a given column (to sort by rows), an auxiliary table can be helpful in the process. This auxiliary table contains the key column of elements and the row number for each of the keys. Sorting this $m \times 2$ table is quickly done, and we can then read from it the order in which the rows of the original table should be placed. Here is an example.

Suppose that our table contains the information necessary to form a mailing list, with each row containing the data for a particular individual. These data have been entered in a specific order (first name, middle initial, last name, street address, city, state, ZIP code, telephone number) for each individual, but no attempt has been made to keep the list of individuals in any order (fig. 8.9). For our example $m = 10$ and $n = 8$.

We now wish to alphabetize this 10×8 table by last name. Suppose that the names were entered in the order

Gaiki, French, Boling, Brooks, Morris, Thomas, Schmelzkopf, Silvestri, Crissler, Toder.

From the given data we can form a 10×2 table consisting of the last names (LName) and index numbers giving the order in which they were entered (fig. 8.10).
Now sort this list alphabetically, remembering to move the entire row each time (fig. 8.11).

Note that the effort to sort this table is independent of the number of elements in the rows of the original table. Each row could have contained several thousand elements without affecting the sorting time, since we have actually sorted

Figure 8.10   Mailing list names

1	Gaiki
2	French
3	Boling
4	Brooks
5	Morris
6	Thomas
7	Schmelzkopf
8	Silvestri
9	Crissler
10	Toder

Figure 8.11   Mailing list names, sorted

3	Boling
4	Brooks
9	Crissler
2	French
1	Gaiki
5	Morris
7	Schmelzkopf
8	Silvestri
6	Thomas
10	Toder

only the auxiliary table, with just two elements per row. We can now form the new, sorted table of names and addresses by taking, in order, the 3rd, 4th, 9th, 2nd, . . . , 10th rows of the original table (fig. 8.12).

The entire process is: form the auxiliary table, sort the auxiliary table, form the new table using the sorted auxiliary table as a guide. Because of the diversity of data in a table such as the one we are considering, a Pascal RECORD is an appropriate data structure for one row of the table. Thus the entire table can be represented as an ARRAY of RECORDs. To form the auxiliary table, we need only create a new table of the same form, with but two fields per record. One of the fields is the index of the original record in its array; the other is the data from the key field to be sorted. We leave this task as a programming exercise.

The procedure of figure 8.13 implements the sorting of this auxiliary array. The procedure used here is a recursive binary insertion sort; any other sort could have been chosen. Because we have implemented each row of the table as a record, we can move an entire row simply by moving one record. For a discussion of recursion please see chapter 9. Insertion sorts are explained in chapter 11.

Figure 8.12   The sorted mailing list

FName	MI	LName	Street	City	State	ZIP	Phone
George	C	Boling	.				
Jim	M	Brooks		.			
Bob	T	Crissler		.			
Sidney	C	French			.		
Ronlon	T	Gaiki				.	
Ben	K	Morris				.	
Herman	W	Schmelzkopf					.
Leonard	S	Silvestri					.
Ben	R	Thomas					.
Dave	W	Toder					.

Figure 8.13, Part 1   Procedure for sorting a table by rows

```
CONST
   RowSize    = UserSuppliedNumberOfRows;
   ColumnSize = UserSuppliedNumberOfColumns;

TYPE
   RowRange    = 1..RowSize;
   ColumnRange = 1..ColumnSize;
   ElementType = RECORD
                   Index : RowRange;
                   Name  : PACKED ARRAY[ColumnRange] OF char
                 END;
   ArrayType   = ARRAY[RowRange] OF ElementType;

VAR
   I,J    : integer;
   Matrix : ArrayType;

PROCEDURE BinaryInsert (Element      : ElementType;
                        VAR SortedSet : ArrayType;
                        VAR SetSize   : integer);

{ A procedure to produce a sorted set by binary insertion. }

{ Procedure found in Figure 11.4 }
```

Figure 8.13, Part 2   Procedure for sorting a table by rows

```
PROCEDURE AuxiliaryTableSort (Size        : integer;
                              VAR Matrix : ArrayType);

   VAR
      I            : RowRange;
      SortedSize : integer;

   BEGIN
      FOR I := 1 TO Size DO
         Matrix[I].Index := I;
      SortedSize := 0;
      FOR I := 1 TO Size DO
         BinaryInsert (Matrix[I], Matrix, SortedSize)
   END; [ AuxiliaryTableSort }
```

Finally, to determine the order of the rows in the sorted table, we need only examine the index field of the auxiliary table records. This, too, we leave as a programming exercise.

Combining or merging two tables is most often done when the tables agree in one of their dimensions. That is, the tables involved will have either the same number of rows or the same number of columns. For example, suppose that each row of one table contains examination grades for a student and that each row of another table contains essay grades for the same student. We may then decide to merge the two tables, so that we have all the grades for each student in a single table. In this case, the two tables would agree on rows but have different columns.

Figure 8.14   Merging two tables of grades

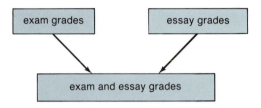

We would merge them into a single table with the same row structure, but with a column for each column in the two initial tables (fig. 8.14).

In a variation of this, we may have kept the grade tables separate for students in two or three sections of a course and then decided to merge these tables into one to obtain overall course statistics. In this situation, all the columns would agree across the tables, and we would merge the tables into a new one with more rows but the same number of columns.

We may, in fact, view the addition of a single row or column to a table as a merging of an $m \times n$ table with a $1 \times n$ table or an $m \times 1$ table, respectively. Merging in general involves the same difficulties as we found for the single row or column case.

Assuming that the tables in question are stored by row, merging a second table of size $k \times n$ with the first one of size $m \times n$ as additional rows creates no problem. The same storage function is used, with only the difference that the row index now runs from 1 to $m + k$ rather than from 1 to m. However, if the second table has dimensions $m \times k$ and we are merging it in as additional columns, then the storage function must be changed by replacing the value n by the value $n + k$: a_{ij} in row major order is now located at

$$b + (n + k)(i - 1) + (j - 1).$$

There are occasions when it is desirable to reshape a table, array, or matrix. The most common of these occurs in mathematical processing, when it may be necessary to use the transpose of a matrix. If A is an $m \times n$ matrix, then its **transpose** is the $n \times m$ matrix B, defined by $b_{ij} = a_{ji}$ for all i and j. One way to achieve this reshaping is simply to read the A matrix into a new location by rows, storing it by columns, as in the procedure of figure 8.15. Doing this requires storage for both matrices (at least temporarily), but allows us to use the built-in access calculations to reach each entry. If storage is a problem, we have two alternatives. We might use one temporary location to exchange the matrix elements:

```
Temp := A[I, J];
A[I, J] := A[J, I];
A[J, I] := Temp;
```

Figure 8.15   Procedure to transpose a matrix

```
PROCEDURE Transpose (A : MatrixType;
                     VAR B : TransMatrixType);

{ Note: If MatrixType is ARRAY[1..M,1..N] OF type,
then TransMatrixType is ARRAY[1..N,1..M] OF type. We
assume that the matrix types and their sizes are
given in global definitions. }
  VAR
    I : 1..M;
    J : 1..N;

  BEGIN
    FOR I := 1 TO M DO
      FOR J := 1 TO N DO
        B[J, I] := A[I, J]
  END; { Transpose }
```

We leave it as an exercise to determine what the FOR loop ranges should be for this solution.

The other alternative is to keep just one matrix, but to use the built-in access functions when regarding it as one matrix, say *A,* and create our own access functions for use when regarding it as the transpose, *B.* Thus the built-in functions might access the matrix by rows and the user-defined functions by columns. This is rarely done in higher level languages, since the transpose can be easily accessed by a double FOR loop, with the outer loop running through the columns and the inner loop running through the rows.

Far less common is the need to change both the row and column size of the matrix in other ways, although this can be done. We observe, for example, that a 4 × 6 matrix requires 24 storage cells. So also does a 2 × 12 matrix and an 8 × 3 matrix, among others. Thus once we have the 24 cells allocated we could regard them as containing an $m \times n$ matrix for any m and n such that $mn = 24$, without relocating the data within the area. All that is needed is to define new access functions for each view of the matrix. Note that a 6 × 4 matrix obtained in this manner is *not* the transpose of the original 4 × 6 matrix that was stored in the space.

Finally, we come to the concept of "marrying" data structures, or combining two data structures of different types. Tables are frequently involved in this type of hybrid structure. For example, we might have a set of tables. One example would be the tables of grades for each course in a department. As we have seen, a table is a natural structure for the grades within a single class. (Class grade books are laid out in this way.) If we want to consider all the courses within a department, we could easily model these as a set of course grade tables. Then

Figure 8.16   Two-level access for departmental grades

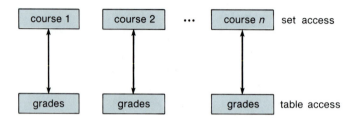

within each course we would have access to the grades through the table structure and for the department as a whole we would access the courses through the set structure.

In this type of situation the key idea is that we have two distinct levels of access to the data, hence we can invoke the operations from two distinct data types. For our example, the ADT for sets would apply whenever we are working with the data for several courses within a department, and the ADT for tables would apply as we focus our attention on the grades within any one course (fig. 8.16).

Similarly, the idea of a table of entries, each of which is another data structure, is important. Typically, we might have a table of records. In a grade book, for example, the basic table might be students by semester, with each entry in the table being a record of that student's activity during a particular semester. This record might include numerical and letter grades in each course, along with the semester and overall grade point average, and the student's rank in his or her class. In this situation, we use the regularity of the table structure to locate individual records and then the flexibility of the record to store the specific data in the most appropriate manner.

8.6 Three-dimensional arrays

Recall that the storage function for an $m \times n$ array, stored in row major order, is

$$b + n(i - 1) + j - 1$$

and that a similar function holds if the array is stored by columns. These storage functions extend readily to three or more dimensions. For example, one storage function for an $h \times m \times n$ array is

$$b + mn(i - 1) + n(j - 1) + k - 1,$$

where $\langle i, j, k \rangle$ represents the position within the array. The only difficulty is that the number of possible storage functions grows rapidly. For a two-dimensional array we have storage by row, then column, or by column, then row.

If we call the third dimension the "plane," then for a three-dimensional array we have six possibilities:

plane,	row,	column
plane,	column,	row
row,	plane,	column
row,	column,	plane
column,	plane,	row
column,	row,	plane

In general, an n-dimensional array has $n!$ possible storage functions.

The way in which we treat multidimensional data is flexible and open to individual preference. For example, we may choose to think of an array as the representation $\langle$ row, column, data $\rangle$. But we may also choose to think of it using the representation $\langle$ position, data $\rangle$, where "position" in turn has the structure $\langle$ row, column $\rangle$. The correspondence between these two representations is in fact one of the memory mappings we have defined,

$$\langle \text{position, data} \rangle \approx \langle \langle \text{row, column} \rangle , \text{data} \rangle \approx \langle \text{row, column, data} \rangle .$$

8.7 Special array shapes

While the rectangular array is a very appropriate data structure for many problems, to insist that data that can be arranged in such an array *must* be so arranged is as restrictive as insisting that all buildings must be rectangular. Many situations arise in which another arrangement of the data is possible and perhaps advantageous. For example, data relating to the loading of cargo on the floor of a building or the deck of a ship would fit naturally into an array that has the same shape as the floor or the deck. Requiring the data to be in a rectangular array may mean introducing some zero values that correspond to points lying outside the natural structure. In some situations, forcing the data into a "normal" rectangular array may result in an array 80 percent or more of whose data are zeros. There are also natural situations involving arrays that are quite clearly not rectangular, such as the array of cells in a honeycomb (see section 1.8) or the array of seeds in the head of a sunflower. In these situations, a data structure reflecting the hexagonal arrangement of the honeycomb or the spirals in the sunflower might be more appropriate.

Thus, in this section, we shall examine a few of the more common special array shapes. In some situations these alternative shapes provide substantial savings in storage or processing time. In other situations it may turn out that the rectangular array is best: the benefit in considering the alternative lies in the fresh insight it gives about a class of problems, leading possibly to innovative ways of handling the rectangular array.

Many situations arise in which the natural data structure is an array, but the array contains very few data. Frequently the arrays are matrices—two-dimensional numerical arrays on which we wish to do some calculations. Here are three typical examples.

Finite element methods in engineering are based on approximating a curved surface such as an airfoil or a ship's hull, or a three-dimensional body such as a large reservoir by data taken at hundreds or thousands of points arranged in an array on the surface or in the solid. The behavior of the physical object under stress or temperature change, for example, is approximated by equations showing the interaction of one point on the model with its neighbors. Thus we may have several hundred variables representing different points in the model, but the equations relating these variables may each contain only four to eight values. Potentially we have an $n \times n$ matrix, with n very large, each row and column of which contains fewer than ten nonzero elements.

Linear programming is a technique for modeling complex systems based on the solution of a system of linear equations within specified constraints. Large linear programming problems that are encountered in modeling complex industrial processes may involve several thousand equations in tens of thousands of variables, with each equation involving only a small number of these variables. Again, we have a conceptual matrix of several million entries, only a few thousand of which are nonzero.

Information retrieval systems are often based on **key words** that describe the content of the documents within the system. The match between key words and documents is represented in a **document-term matrix,** which is used to search for documents containing a particular combination of key words. This matrix may conceptually contain a million or more rows (the documents) and ten to fifteen thousand columns (the key words). Yet each document is represented by ten to twenty key terms: most entries in the matrix are blank.

In each of these situations, the matrix contains a large number of zero or blank entries. Such matrices are called **sparse.** There is no precise criterion for when a matrix is sparse. Certainly a matrix with fewer than 1 percent of its entries filled is sparse, and a matrix with fewer than 10 percent of its entries filled is probably also sparse. But a matrix with, say, 25 percent of its entries filled may or may not be considered sparse, depending on the application. One reasonable guideline is that an $n \times n$ matrix is sparse if the number of nonzero or nonblank entries is $O(n)$. This implies that the average number of significant entries per row or column of the matrix is constant and does not depend on the size of the matrix.

In this type of situation it borders on gross negligence to consider using the full matrix. Not only does the full matrix involve massive amounts of storage, but also we must spend much time processing zeros or null data. Some other form of representation for the matrix should be used.

The linked list representation which we study in the next section is one candidate for use in these situations. This representation involves one set of links for each row and another for each column of the matrix. The representation is, in fact, ideal for situations that do not call for mathematical manipulation of the matrices. Thus we would consider this representation as a reasonable candidate for modeling the document-term matrix.

Figure 8.17   Matrix addition, sequentially stored matrix

```
CONST
  MaxColumnSize = UserSuppliedMaxCol;
  MaxRowSize    = UserSuppliedMaxRow;

TYPE
  ElementType = UserSuppliedArithmeticType;
  MatrixType  : ARRAY[1..MaxRowSize, 1..MaxColumnSize]
                  OF ElementType =

PROCEDURE MatrixAdd (M, N  : integer;
                     A, B  : MatrixType;
                     VAR C : MatrixType);

  VAR
    I : 1..MaxRowSize;
    J : 1..MaxColumnSize;

  BEGIN

  { Assert: 1 <= M <= MaxRowSize;
  1 <= N <= MaxColumnSize. }

    FOR I := 1 TO M DO
      FOR J := 1 TO N DO
        C[I, J] := A[I, J] + B[I, J]
  END; { MatrixAdd }
```

The linked list representation can also be used in mathematical situations where matrix algebra is to be applied, but its use in these cases is more difficult. Consider, for example, the simplest of these operations, adding two matrices together. By the rules of matrix algebra, the two matrices must be of the same size, $m \times n$, and addition is performed by adding the elements in corresponding positions. That is, $C = A + B$ if and only if, for each i and j, $c_{ij} = a_{ij} + b_{ij}$. With a sequentially stored matrix, this procedure is a "one-liner" (fig. 8.17).

With a linked list representation of the matrices, for each entry in A we must determine whether we have a corresponding entry in the other array, B, and conversely. The entry in C may then be the entry in A, the one in B, or the sum of them, depending on the situation. Similar, but more complex, difficulties arise when the mathematical processing to be done is more complicated. We shall examine these procedures in the next section.

Fortunately, there are alternatives other than full sequential storage or linked list storage for representing a sparse matrix. Some of these alternatives are easier to use mathematically and even provide conceptually sound representations of the physical problem associated with the matrix.

Figure 8.18   A band matrix

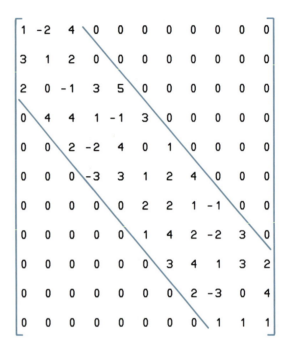

Some physical problems can be represented nicely by a **band matrix.** In such a matrix, all nonzero values are concentrated in a relatively narrow band about the main diagonal (fig. 8.18). This type of matrix is frequently appropriate in situations involving a large number of data elements, where each data element interacts with only a very small number of others. Such a situation produces a double savings. First, a large amount of storage is saved by not storing the triangular blocks of zeros. Second, the amount of work required to process the matrix is reduced significantly. For example, the technique called **Gaussian elimination** for solving the linear equations represented by a matrix is an $O(n^3)$ technique. For a band matrix with **bandwidth** β, the corresponding technique is $O(n\beta^2)$. Since n may be of the order of magnitude 1000 and β of the order of magnitude 10, the savings can be impressive.

If a band matrix is appropriate, we can easily define a storage function that permits storage of only the narrow band containing nonzero values (and possibly a very small number of zero values). Suppose, for example, that we have an $n \times n$ matrix, V, and all of the nonzero values lie within a band of width $2k + 1$ centered about the main diagonal. Thus, for row i, only the columns $j = i - k, i - k + 1, \ldots, i - 1, i, i + 1, \ldots, i + k - 1, i + k$ contain data. Consider the storage function

$$b + 2k(i - 1) + (j - 1).$$

Figure 8.19   The storage for a band matrix

$$\begin{bmatrix} 0 & 0 & 1 & -2 & 4 \\ 0 & 3 & 1 & 2 & 0 \\ 2 & 0 & -1 & 3 & 5 \\ 4 & 4 & 1 & -1 & 3 \\ 2 & -2 & 4 & 0 & 1 \\ -3 & 3 & 1 & 2 & 4 \\ 0 & 2 & 2 & 1 & -1 \\ 1 & 4 & 2 & -2 & 3 \\ 3 & 4 & 1 & 3 & 2 \\ 2 & -3 & 0 & 4 & 0 \\ 1 & 1 & 1 & 0 & 0 \end{bmatrix}$$

With this function, v_{11} is located at address b. In row i, j takes on values from $i - k$ to $i + k$. Hence the storage locations for this row are from

$$b + 2k(i - 1) + (i - k - 1) \quad \text{to} \quad b + 2k(i - 1) + (i + k - 1)$$

or from

$$b + (2k + 1)i - 3k - 1 \quad \text{to} \quad b + (2k + 1)i - k - 1.$$

The first storage location for row $i + 1$ (for $V[i + 1, i + 1 - k]$) is thus

$$b + (2k + 1)(i + 1) - 3k - 1 = b + (2k + 1)i - k,$$

the first location beyond the storage for row i. Hence this storage function achieves the row-by-row storage of the band within V that contains nonzero values, without storing any values outside this band. In effect, we have stored the matrix as an $n \times (2k + 1)$ matrix, including a small number of wasted cells at each end of the matrix (fig. 8.19). The sum of two such matrices (of the same bandwidth) is given by the procedure in figure 8.20.

Figure 8.20   Matrix addition, band matrices

```
CONST
  N = UserSuppliedSize;
  K = UserSuppliedBandwidth;

TYPE
  BandType = ARRAY[1..N, -K..K] OF real;

PROCEDURE BandAdd (MatrixA, MatrixB : BandType;
                   BandWidth        : integer;
                   VAR MatrixC      : BandType);

{ A procedure to add two matrices of size N X N, with
nonzero elements within a band of width 2 * BandWidth
+ 1 centered about the diagonal. }

  VAR
    I : 1..N;
    J : -K..K;

  BEGIN
    FOR I := 1 TO N DO
      FOR J := -BandWidth TO BandWidth DO
        MatrixC[I, J] := MatrixA[I, J] + MatrixB[I, J]
  END; { BandAdd }
```

Another form of matrix that is sometimes useful is a **triangular matrix.** Suppose that we have a **symmetric matrix,** that is, an $n \times n$ matrix A for which $a_{ji} = a_{ij}$ for all i and j (fig. 8.21). Such a matrix obviously uses nearly twice the storage that is needed, since each off-diagonal entry occurs twice. Hence we could save storage by using either a **lower triangular matrix** or an **upper triangular matrix** (fig. 8.22).

Let us derive the storage function for a lower triangular matrix. Because successive rows in such a matrix are increasingly long, the function is a little more complex. Row 1 contains only one entry, stored in location b. Row 2 contains two entries, stored in locations $b + 1$ and $b + 2$. The three entries of row 3 are then stored in locations $b + 3$, $b + 4$, and $b + 5$. Continuing in this manner, we see that successive rows begin in locations

$$b, \quad b + 1, \quad b + 3, \quad b + 6, \quad b + 10, \quad b + 15, \quad ... ,$$

and end in locations

$$b, \quad b + 2, \quad b + 5, \quad b + 9, \quad b + 14, \quad ... .$$

Figure 8.21   A symmetric matrix

$$\begin{bmatrix} 3 & -1 & 2 & 2 & 0 & 3 & 4 \\ -1 & 0 & 5 & 2 & -4 & 2 & 3 \\ 2 & 5 & 1 & 3 & -3 & 2 & 1 \\ 2 & 2 & 3 & -1 & 2 & 4 & 5 \\ 0 & -4 & -3 & 2 & 4 & 5 & -5 \\ 3 & 2 & 2 & 4 & 5 & 1 & 1 \\ 4 & 3 & 1 & 5 & -5 & 1 & 3 \end{bmatrix}$$

Figure 8.22   Triangular matrices

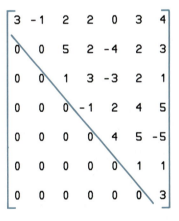

The beginning numbers (0, 1, 3, 6, 10, 15, ...) are the **triangular numbers,** given by the general formula $n(n - 1)/2$. The ending numbers are each 1 less than one of the triangular numbers. This leads to the storage formula for the location of a_{ij},

$$b + i(i - 1)/2 + (j - 1).$$

In this formula the first two summands give the beginning of the ith row, while the last summand gives the distance from the beginning of the row to the jth element.

Figure 8.23 **A row (or column) of a triangular matrix**

$$\begin{bmatrix} 3 & & & & & & \\ -1 & 0 & & & & & \\ 2 & -5 & -1 & & & & \\ 2 & 2 & 3 & -1 & & & \\ 0 & -4 & -3 & 2 & 4 & & \\ 3 & 2 & 2 & 4 & 5 & 1 & \\ 4 & 3 & 1 & 5 & -5 & 1 & 3 \end{bmatrix}$$

Figure 8.24 **Combined storage for triangular matrices**

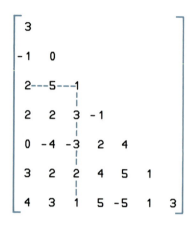

$$C = \begin{bmatrix} b_{11} & a_{11} & a_{12} & a_{13} & a_{14} \\ b_{21} & b_{22} & a_{22} & a_{23} & a_{24} \\ b_{31} & b_{32} & b_{33} & a_{33} & a_{34} \\ b_{41} & b_{42} & b_{43} & b_{44} & a_{44} \end{bmatrix}$$

While this saves some storage, it makes many mathematical calculations a little more complicated. The location of the element $A[i,j]$ is given by $\mathrm{loc}(A[\max(i,j), \min(i,j)])$. The entire i^{th} row (or column) is now found by tracing the row out to the diagonal entry and then following the column downward (fig. 8.23).

We can combine the storage of upper and lower triangular matrices of the same size in the simple scheme for figure 8.24. With this storage scheme, the A and B matrices are recovered by the relations

$$a_{ij} = c_{p,q+1} \quad \text{and} \quad b_{ij} = c_{qp},$$

where

$$p = \min(i,j) \quad \text{and} \quad q = \max(i,j).$$

Figure 8.25   Neighbors in a hexagonal array

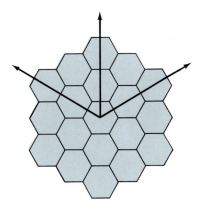

Figure 8.26   Coordinates for a hexagonal array

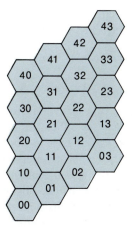

Finally, we take a brief look at **hexagonal arrays,** which are useful in studying honeycombs or in playing the game "hex." The IBM "data cell" mass storage device is also arranged as a hexagonal array. In the usual array, each entry has neighbors in two directions, by row or by column. In a hexagonal array, however, each entry has neighbors in three directions (fig. 8.25).

We might think that because there are neighbors in three directions, three coordinates should be used to identify each entry. However, a little experimentation shows that this method of identification leads to inconsistencies. Instead, we require only two coordinates (fig. 8.26). Notice that in one direction (upward) the first coordinate increases normally while the second remains constant, and in

Figure 8.27   Coordinate view of hexagonal array

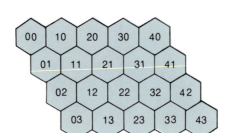

the second direction (upward to the right) the first coordinate remains fixed while the second increases. In the third direction (upward to the left) the first coordinate increases and the second one decreases, so that the sum of the coordinates remains constant.

We now observe that in an ordinary array, the sum of the coordinates along one set of diagonals is also constant. For example, for the entries a_{41}, a_{32}, a_{23}, and a_{14}, the sum of the coordinates is 5. Thus we may view the hexagonal array as a distorted rectangular array (fig. 8.27) and use the same storage functions that we have used for arrays.

8.8 Two-dimensional lists

With simple sets we have found that sequential storage, while relatively compact and in many ways accessible, causes difficulties in the updating of the sets. We have now seen that similar difficulties arise in storing tables sequentially. In addition, we have found that with the normal methods of storing two-dimensional tables we will have either each row stored contiguously or each column, but not both. With simple sets, we turned to a linked list structure to alleviate some of the updating problems, and found that this type of structure had its own advantages and disadvantages. We turn now to the storage of a two-dimensional table as a doubly linked list, with one link representing the row structure and the other representing the column structure. Conceptually, this puts the rows and columns on an equal footing. In addition, this type of storage has some distinct advantages when we have large tables that contain very small numbers of data.

Recall that in dealing with simple sets stored as linked lists we introduced a second set of pointers to facilitate traversal of the set in both directions. With a two-dimensional table, we most readily make use of the second pointer set to implement the second direction in the table. Rather than use a third and fourth pointer system to achieve traversal in the opposite directions, we make the two pointer systems circular, so that each row pointer points from the last column to the first one, and similarly for each column pointer (fig. 8.28).

Figure 8.28   Linked list representation of a table

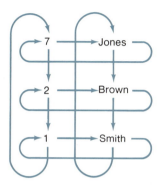

This double pointer system gives us great freedom in traversing an array or table. By following the pointers we may move from one location within the array to any other, often in a number of different ways. Because of this great flexibility, and the fact that the rows and columns each have particular significance, it is important to keep track of where we are within the table or array. There are basically two ways of doing this. One way is to keep track of which row or column we are accessing at any given time. If we are working entirely within a single row or column at any one time, this is easy to do. But if we are mixing row and column movements, this may be time consuming. For example, suppose that we have accessed an element in one position and move to the next element in its row. This element is obviously in some column, but it may be difficult to determine which column.

The other way of keeping track of our location is to store with each datum its coordinates in the table. Thus, for position $\langle i,j \rangle$ within the table, we have a record consisting of the values of i and j, together with whatever data we have stored at that location and the two pointers. Obviously this requires more storage than we need for each position in a sequentially stored table. But if not all table positions contain data, then the total storage required may be less using pointers. For example, suppose that each datum requires 3 bytes of storage, each i or j value requires 1 byte, and each pointer requires 1 byte. Conventional storage of an $m \times n$ table would then require $3mn$ bytes, but if only k of the data locations actually contain data, then linked list storage of the table would require $7k$ bytes of memory—$3k$ bytes for the data, $2k$ bytes for the subscript values, and $2k$ bytes for the pointers. In this case, linked list representation requires less storage than conventional representation if $k < 3mn/7$ or if the table is less than 42 percent full.

Figure 8.29   A disconnected linked list array

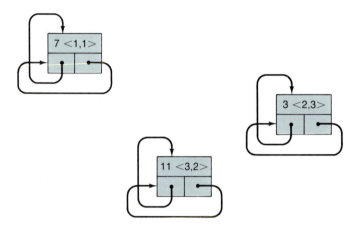

There is one basic flaw with this system, namely, that the entire data structure might be disconnected. Consider, for example, the array in figure 8.29. Note that there is no connection between any two of the three nonzero elements.

One way to correct this flaw is to introduce a new row and a new column into the array. These locations will be "illegal" for storing data, but will provide the "headers" necessary to locate each row and column (fig. 8.30).

Linked list storage of a table or array is of most benefit in situations that call for a high flexibility of access in a dynamic environment. Thus, whenever there are a large number of updates, including additions and deletions as well as data changes, this storage method should be considered. Remember, however, that there are disadvantages. If the table is relatively full, linked list storage requires more space and may require greater access time. And if storage space is extremely limited, then more compact storage of the table can be achieved by eliminating the link pointers, even though this will generally mean longer access times.

Let us return now to the problem of matrix arithmetic using linked list matrices. As we mentioned in the previous section, matrix operations with linked list matrices involve verifying that we have corresponding elements in the two matrices we are adding or multiplying. Without the headers this can be quite difficult, since there is no easy way to access a specific location in such a matrix. For example, suppose that we want to add matrices A and B, and we are looking at an element in position $A[3, 7]$. To locate element $B[3, 7]$—or to find that there is no such element—in the absence of the headers, we would need to use the pointers to work our way through the B matrix until we have reached or passed that location. However, the headers give us access to a single row or column at a time, enabling us to perform addition and multiplication efficiently.

Figure 8.30   A thread through a linked list array with row and column headers

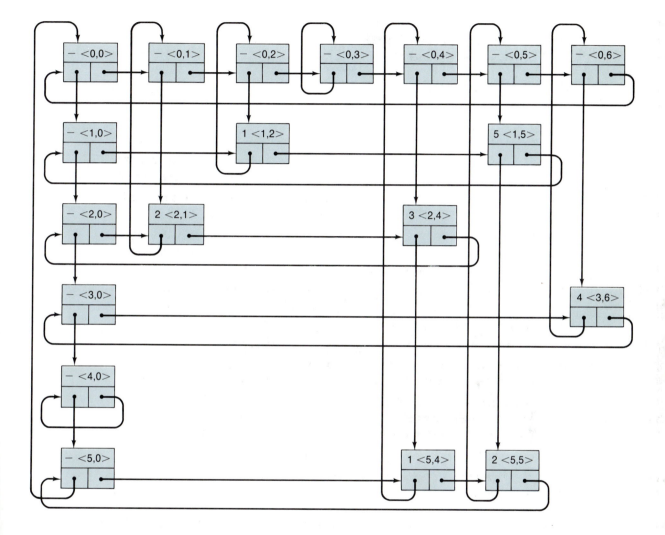

To determine the entry in position [I, J] in the matrix product $A \times B$, we multiply entries in row I of A by corresponding entries in column J of B and add the products. Clearly, the only products that add to the result are those for which both the A entry and the B entry are nonzero. Here is a function that computes a single term of the product (fig. 8.31). While the data type is given as real, the routine is easily adapted to integer matrices.

This function returns the value of the product term at location [I, J]. It should be called by a procedure that uses RowA and ColumnB, the row and column pointers, to place this term in position in the product matrix. We leave this procedure as an exercise.

Figure 8.31, Part 1   Product term formation, linked list matrices

```
{ We assume that the matrices have row and column headers. }

CONST
  MaxRowSize     = UserSuppliedMaximumRowSize;
  MaxColumnSize = UserSuppliedMaximumColumnSize;

TYPE
  ArrayPointer = ^ArrayElement;
  ArrayElement = RECORD
                   Data        : real;
                   Row         : 0..MaxRowSize;
                   Column      : 0..MaxColumnSize;
                   NextRow     : ArrayPointer;
                   NextColumn  : ArrayPointer
                 END;

FUNCTION ProductTerm (RowA    : ArrayPointer;
                      ColumnB : ArrayPointer) : real;

  VAR
    RowTrace    : ArrayPointer;
    ColumnTrace : ArrayPointer;
    Term        : real;

  BEGIN

    { We assume that the matrices A and B have data, and are of the
    correct size, that is, that the number of columns of A is the
    same as the number of rows of B. }

    Term := 0.0;

    { The first entries are not in the headers, so position pointers
    at the first datum in the row and column. }

    RowTrace := RowA^.NextRow;
    ColumnTrace := ColumnB^.NextColumn;

    { Terminate when one of the trace pointers comes back to a
    header. }

    WHILE (RowTrace <> RowA) AND (ColumnTrace <> ColumnB) DO
      IF RowTrace^.Row = ColumnTrace^.Column THEN
```

Figure 8.31, Part 2   Product term formation, linked list matrices

```
    BEGIN
      Term := Term + RowTrace^.Data * ColumnTrace^.Data;
      RowTrace := RowTrace^.NextRow;
      ColumnTrace := ColumnTrace^.NextColumn
    END
  ELSE
    IF RowTrace^.Row < ColumnTrace^.Column THEN
      RowTrace := RowTrace^.NextRow
    ELSE
      ColumnTrace := ColumnTrace^.NextColumn;
  ProductTerm := Term
END; { ProductTerm }
```

Addition of two linked list matrices may be thought of as a two step process. First, we add the elements in corresponding rows of the matrices as though these rows were independent circular vectors, but carrying along the correct column numbers. Then we make a pass "across" the resulting set of vectors, linking up elements in the same columns. The addition function is similar to the product term function, except that we do not accumulate an overall sum, and we can ignore only those column locations for which there is no entry in either of the input matrices. We leave this procedure also as an exercise.

8.9 Two-way lists

The pointer system for a linked list allows us great flexibility in the size of the list and in adding and deleting entries, but it has the rather serious drawback that it is unidirectional: the pointer always points forward, to the next element in the list. This makes it difficult to back up to an earlier entry in the list. We first introduced another pointer system when we needed a way to retrace our steps through a data structure (see chapter 5). A single pointer system allows us to proceed forward through a linked list, but leaves us with few options for locating data that precede our current position in the list.

One option is to keep a fixed pointer to the head of the list (which we should undoubtedly keep in any case) and just start afresh whenever we wish to see data we have already passed. If the data are actually in the list, this causes little problem. However, if the data are missing, then we must either keep track of where we were in the list when we restarted the search, or search the entire list. It should be clear that this can be done, but that it is neither elegant nor efficient.

Figure 8.32   Circular list

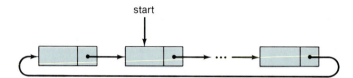

Figure 8.33   Two-way list

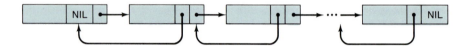

In many applications, the datum that we want is "near" the one that we are presently scanning. Hence we would like to be able to move forward or backward within a list a short distance to locate the item. Obviously, our brute force method of simply starting over is inefficient in this respect: we may need to search a large number of items in the list to find one that is only two or three positions back from the current position.

An alternative to the restart procedure is the circular list. Such a list has a single pointer system, but rather than "ground" the pointer system by setting the last pointer to NIL, we make the last pointer point back to the list beginning. A circular pointer system solves the problem of having access to each datum in the list without needing to decide each time whether we should continue to search forward in the list or restart from the beginning.

The circular list, however, has two associated problems. First, it is even more inefficient than the "restart from the beginning" method in locating a datum just recently passed. Second, we need a special pointer or marker to indicate where we were when a search process started. Without this, if a desired datum were not in the list, we would circle forever around the list looking for it (fig. 8.32).

A second system of pointers within a data structure allows us much more flexibility in moving about within the structure. The simplest such system is the two-way list, already discussed in chapter 5. This type of list has a second pointer system that runs counter to the main pointer system. Thus, from any point in the list, we can move forward or backward with equal facility (fig. 8.33).

A two-way list can be implemented either in the normal way, with NIL pointers at each end, or circularly. In either case, we can search for a datum by alternating pointer movements: first advance the forward pointer and check that datum. If it is not the desired one, then advance the backward pointer and check

Figure 8.34   A quick-search list

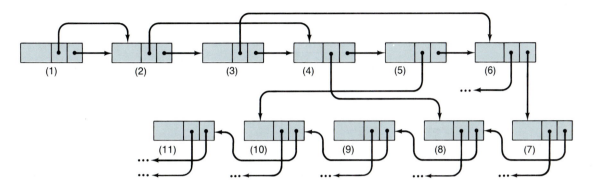

that datum. If the list is implemented with NIL pointers at each end, we will know that a datum is not in the list when both pointers have reached NIL. If the implementation is circular, then the fact that a datum is missing will be indicated when both pointers point to the same location.

Here is a different application of a second link system. Let us consider a simple linked list. Such a list can be sorted or unsorted. If we wish to print out the list frequently in sorted order, then there is an advantage to keeping the list sorted. However, because of the linked nature of the list, we cannot take advantage of the sorting to reduce search time: we must search the list linearly. Now suppose that we add a second forward-pointing link system but arrange these pointers to advance us more rapidly through the list. How can we do this, and what advantage would this system have?

If we think of a sorted sequential list, binary search works rapidly because we can quickly bypass half the list, then half the chosen half, and so forth. Thus, if we could arrange things so that the second pointer system bypasses half the linked list, we might significantly reduce the search time. But bypassing half the list implies that we know how long the list is, and one of the reasons for using a linked list in the first place is that we can keep the length indefinite. Let us try a related approach: using the second pointer to advance to a list element twice as far down the list as the present one. The effect is shown in figure 8.34.

It is not immediately clear that this approach helps, but let us consider a specific instance. Suppose that we want to find the 76th datum in the list. We have a pointer from cell 38 to cell 76, and one from cell 19 to cell 38. Since 19 is an odd number, we cannot divide by 2. At this point our system relies on the pointer from cell 18 to cell 19. Working back this way, we see that we can access cell 76 by the sequence 1, 2, 4, 8, 9, 18, 19, 38, 76. This is certainly much quicker than advancing one cell at a time through the list!

Figure 8.35   A quick-search tree list, redrawn

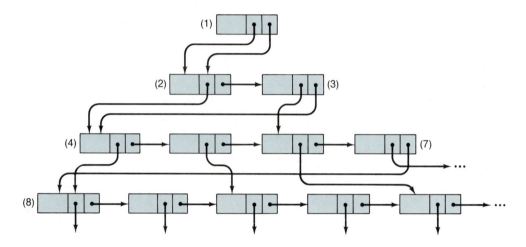

To see why this works and how well it works, let us redraw the list (fig. 8.35). When we draw the list in this way, it is clear that while one pointer system is the usual linear linkage through the list, the other basically imposes a tree-like structure on the list. In chapter 10 we shall show that searching a binary tree is an $O(\lg n)$ operation. Thus we would expect that access to cell n in this list is essentially an $O(\lg n)$ operation. Because of this resemblance to a binary tree (see chapter 10), we call this structure a **tree list.**

Being able to access a cell this quickly depends on two things: knowing which cell we want and knowing which path to take. Clearly there are quite a few paths to a given cell, such as the 76th one in the list. Here is the algorithm for reaching a given cell.

1. Begin with the binary representation for the cell number. Start the pointer at cell 1 in the list.

2. Discard the leading bit in the representation. If we have discarded the entire number, quit. Otherwise, go to step 3.

3. If the pointer is at cell k, move the pointer to cell $2k$ (down a level in the tree list).

4. If the leading bit is 1 and the pointer is at cell k', move the pointer to cell $k' + 1$ (to the right).

5. Go to step 2.

Observe that at each step we move down a level in the tree list, and sometimes we also shift to the right one cell. For example, here is how we reach cell 76. First, we need its binary representation, 1001100. We set the pointer to cell 1 and discard the leading bit, leaving 001100. We next (step 3) set the pointer to cell 2, and since the leading bit is 0, we leave the pointer there, returning to step 2. Discard the next bit, leaving 01100. Move the pointer to cell 4, leaving it there. The next iteration of step 2 removes one more bit, leaving 1100. Move the pointer to cell 8, and since the leading bit is 1, move it next to cell 9. Using step 2, discard the leading bit, leaving 100. Again, move the pointer to double the cell number, cell 18, and since the leading bit is 1, move it on to cell 19. Repeating, discard the leading bit, leaving 00. Move the pointer to cell 38; discard the leading bit (leaving 0); move the pointer to cell 76; discard the leading bit (leaving nothing). Since we have exhausted the binary representation, we stop. We are at the correct cell. Figure 8.36 shows a Pascal implementation of this algorithm. Notice that we use two pointers, one pointing to the next cell in the list and the other pointing to the cell with double the cell number.

The proof that this is an $O(\lg n)$ algorithm is simple. There is one cycle through the process for each bit in the binary representation of the number. But the number of bits needed in this representation is $\lceil \lg n \rceil$.

This same addressing scheme works well when the list is sorted and we are searching for a particular data value but do not know where it is in the list. However, we cannot get the $O(\lg n)$ search time that is possible with a sequential, sorted list. Consider the example in figure 8.37, where we have included the data values along with the cell numbers and the pointers. Note that the cell numbers identify the position within the list and not the address within storage. Thus cell number 5 is the fifth one in the list—but may be anywhere in storage.

Suppose that we want to locate the datum "RRK." To progress rapidly through this structure, we try doubling the cell number whenever we need to advance. Thus we compare RRK with the data in cells 1, 2, 4, and 8, finding that it is larger than any of these. Then we find that it is smaller than the datum in cell 16, which indicates that the value is located in the fourth row of the tree, if it is there at all. We can then search across this row until we find it, but this is not very efficient.

Consider this. If we were to search the list linearly, then in the worst case the datum we want would be at the end of the list. We would need to perform n comparisons for a list of length n. Using the tree list, the worst case occurs when the datum we want is in the last full row in the tree list. Assume that the row is complete. We need $\lg n$ comparisons to reach that row, but the row itself contains roughly half the elements in the list. If we were to search that row linearly, we need approximately $\lg n + n/2$ comparisons in the worst case. This is better than n comparisons but is still an $O(n)$ process. Note that we cannot perform a binary search directly on this last row, since it is a linked, rather than a sequential, list.

Figure 8.36, Part 1   Program for rapid list traversal

```pascal
PROGRAM TreeList (input, output);

{ A program to compute the search path to a specified
location in a tree list. }

TYPE
  BinPointer = ^BinList;
  BinList    = RECORD
                   Bit     : 0..1;
                   NextBit : BinPointer
               END;

VAR
  AddOne     : BinPointer;
  Direction  : BinPointer;
  Location   : integer;
  NextCell   : integer;

PROCEDURE DisplayDown (VAR CellName : integer);

  BEGIN
    write ('Start at cell ', CellName : 3, ' and take the ');
    writeln ('down path to cell ', CellName * 2 : 3, '.');
    CellName := 2 * CellName
  END; { DisplayDown }

PROCEDURE DisplaySibling (VAR CellName : integer);

  BEGIN
    write ('From cell ', CellName : 3);
    writeln (' go to cell ', CellName + 1 : 3, '.');
    CellName := CellName + 1
  END; { DisplaySibling }

BEGIN
  write ('What location do you wish? ');
  readln (Location);
  writeln ('Determining the path to ', Location : 3, '.');
  IF Location >= 1 THEN

     { Get the binary expansion of Location. }

    BEGIN
      Direction := NIL;
      WHILE Location >= 1 DO
```

Figure 8.36, Part 2   Program for rapid list traversal

```
BEGIN
  new (AddOne);
  AddOne^.Bit := Location MOD 2;
  Location := Location DIV 2;
  AddOne^.NextBit := Direction;
  Direction := AddOne
END;

{ Now determine and display the path. }

NextCell := 1;                              { Step 1 }
writeln ('Starting at Cell 1');
IF Direction^.NextBit <> NIL THEN
  BEGIN
    Direction := Direction^.NextBit;    { Step 2 }
    REPEAT
      DisplayDown (NextCell);           { Step 3 }
      IF Direction^.Bit = 1 THEN        { Step 4 }
        DisplaySibling (NextCell);
      Direction := Direction^.NextBit   { Step 2a }
    UNTIL Direction = NIL               { Step 2b }
  END
END;
writeln ('We have reached the desired cell.')
END. { TreeList }
```

Figure 8.37   A loaded tree list

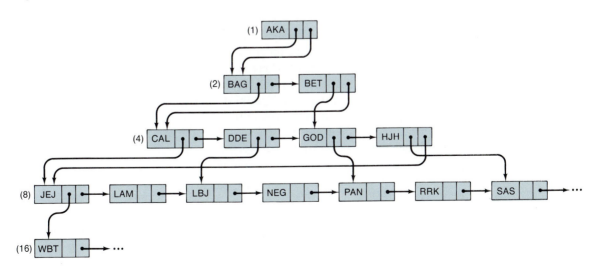

We would like to determine quickly whether the datum we want is in the right or left half of its row, then in the right or left half of that half, and so forth. In other words, if we could come up with a search method that would cut the last row in half each time, we would have a better method.

Let's resume our example, searching for "RRK." We have decided that it is in the fourth row of the tree list. Observe that the two halves of this row are distinguished at the second row of the structure: we can reach the left half from cell 2 and the right half from cell 3. Since we already know that the correct position is in the fourth row, we now follow the path from cell 2, through cells 3 and 6, to cell 12, in the correct row. We find that the datum there precedes RRK, so that the correct location is in the right half of the row. We split this half in the same way: follow the path from cell 6 through cell 7 to cell 14. Since that datum follows RRK, we know that cell 13 is the correct location if RRK is in the list.

This process involves two types of list pointer tracing: with and without comparisons. Comparisons along the way are avoided since we know that the desired datum, RRK, is in the bottom row. Here is the full sequence:

Trace with compare: 1, 2, 4, 8, 16 (too far);

Trace without compare: (from 2), 3, 6, 12;

Compare 12 (not far enough);

Trace without compare: (from 6), 7, 14;

Compare 14 (too far);

Trace without compare: (from 12), 13;

Compare 13 (success!).

In general, the first trace sequence involves (roughly) $\lg n$ pointers. The second, since we start at the second row of the tree list, involves $\lg n - 1$ pointers; the third involves $\lg n - 2$ pointers, and so forth. In the first sequence, we have $\lg n$ comparisons, but in each other sequence we have only one comparison.

How many sequences are there in the worst case? If the last row is the kth one, we need one sequence to reach the first element in the row (cell 2^k), another to divide the bottom row in half, a third to divide it into fourths, and so forth. Basically, we need $\lg n$ sequences to find the correct cell in this row and each sequence requires one comparison. Counting the comparisons, we find that we need roughly $2\lg n$ comparisons at worst to locate a given datum, such as RRK. The number of pointer movements is roughly

$$\lg n + (\lg n - 1) + (\lg n - 2) + \ldots + (\lg n - \lg n),$$

a number of the order $\lg^2 n$. The whole process is $O(\lg^2 n + 2\lg n)$, which is equivalent to $O(\lg^2 n)$. The number of comparisons is $O(\lg n)$, just as it is for a sequential sorted list; but it costs more to find which elements to compare.

Figure 8.38   Inverted file links

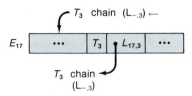

8.10 Multipointer lists

As we permit a more general use of pointers and more pointer systems to be associated with a given data structure, we open many possibilities for treating lists in a flexible manner. This general type of list, with multiple sets of pointers linking data within the list, is known as a **multilist** or **plex.** The examples we have discussed all exhibit a large degree of regularity, but there is no reason to require this regularity of a general multilist system. Of course, each individual pointer system will have a purpose; but these purposes may not coordinate well with one another.

One major use of a plex is to maintain a list in several sorted orders at once. We may wish to have a personnel file sorted by name, by address, and by employee number, for example. Rather than keep three separate copies of the list, it is probably cheaper and more efficient to keep one copy of the list with three separate pointer systems (or six, if we want double linking for each sort sequence).

Multiple pointer systems may also be useful with an inverted file system. Recall that a linked list is one method of relating all file entries that have the same field value. Such a representation must involve a separate linked list for each entry in the file index. Because of the relatively large number of entries in the index and the fact that a given file entry will relate to only a few index terms, it is not practical to have a separate field in the datum for each index term. A better way is to pair the link explicitly with the index term in each file entry. For example, if file entry E_{17} contains index term T_3, then the representation for this term should be $\langle T_3, L_{17,3} \rangle$, where $L_{17,3}$ is the link from entry E_{17} to the next entry containing term T_3 (fig. 8.38). A search for entries containing term T_3 follows the link system $L_{\_,3}$. One of these links points to entry E_{17}. Knowing that this entry contains term T_3, we can search the entry for the pair $\langle T_3, L_{17,3} \rangle$, recovering the pointer $L_{17,3}$ to locate the next entry containing T_3.

In plexes, data structure maintenance becomes a difficult problem. The simplest maintenance problem occurs in adding a file entry to an inverted file system. Normally there is no sorting within each of the index term lists. Hence a new item can simply be added at the head (or the tail) of the list for each of its index terms.

In situations when the lists are sorted, addition of a new element requires somewhat more care, since each sorting sequence must be maintained. The simplest way to do this is the most obvious: work with each list in turn, linking the new element into it in its correct sorted position.

Deletion of an element is a trickier proposition, but not difficult to handle if we are careful. The chief problem arises when we decide to remove the element from one of its lists without affecting its membership on other lists. In this case, we must take care to keep the element, removing only its linkages into the one list. The exception to this comes when the element is removed from its final list, so that we do want to delete it from the file.

8.11 LISP-like lists

We now discuss a list structure that is very important for the field of artificial intelligence. Rather early in the history of modern computing, people recognized that much of the work to be done involves the manipulation of lists of objects rather than direct computation applied to the objects themselves. Languages such as FORTRAN and BASIC have a primary orientation toward algebraic computations on numerical objects and are not particularly well suited for list manipulation. As a result, several programming languages were designed that focused primarily on list manipulation. Of these, the language called **LISP,** has survived and become a dominant basis for much work in artificial intelligence. Thus we look briefly at lists as they are defined in LISP and at some of the basic operations that can be done on them.

An **atom** is a string of nonblank characters. It is important to note that certain characters, particularly "(" and ")", are not allowed in the string. Normally, we think of atoms as being words, identifiers, and numerals, although they are not limited to this range.

A **list** (in the LISP sense) is defined in this way:

1. The symbol () is a list, the **empty list** or **null list.**

2. If A is an atom or a list, then (A) is a list.

3. If A and B are atoms or lists, then $(A\ B)$ is a list.

4. Lists are formed only by finitely many applications of rules 1–3.

Here are some typical lists:

(book)

(data structures and algorithms)

((data structures) and algorithms)

((Time) (flies) (like (an arrow)))

(())

The first of these lists has one atom in it. The second has four elements, which are all atoms, while the third has three elements—a list and two atoms. The three elements of the fourth list are all lists, one of which has two elements itself. The final example is a list with one element, which happens to be the empty list.

The key operations that are done on a LISP list involve the extraction of elements from the list, the addition of elements to the list, and the manipulation of elements in the list. The operations are CAR, CDR, SETQ, APPEND, LIST, CONS, REVERSE, SUBST, LAST, and LENGTH. While these may be written slightly differently in different dialects of LISP, we shall follow the conventions of MACLISP. The reader is referred to Winston and Horn (1984) for more details and limitations. In general, each operation is presented as a list, consisting of the operation name followed by its arguments.

CAR returns the first element in the list. For example,

```
(CAR '(data structures and algorithms))
```

returns **data**, while

```
(CAR '((data structures) and algorithms))
```

returns **(data structures)**.

CDR returns a list containing all except the first element. For example,

```
(CDR '((Time) (flies) (like (an arrow))))
```

returns **((flies) (like (an arrow)))**.

The single quotation mark that appears in the above expressions is necessary to direct the evaluation of a list. Consider the list

```
(CAR (CDR (sum 3.14 -5))).
```

Here we have a list of two elements, the first an operation, and the second a list whose first element is also an operation. Should we perform both operations, and if so, in what order? If we perform the operation CAR first, it takes the list (CDR (sum 3.14 −5)) as its argument and returns the first element of this list, which is CDR. But then CDR has no list upon which to operate. If we perform CDR first, its argument list is (sum 3.14 −5), so it returns (3.14 −5). Hence we are left with the expression (CAR (3.14 −5)). The operation CAR can now return the element 3.14. But perhaps we want to do only the CAR operation, to find out whether the next element is CDR. The single quote is used to indicate the end of the evaluation, which is then done from the inside out. Thus

```
(CAR (CDR '(sum 3.14 -5)))
```

returns the element 3.14, while

```
(CAR '(CDR (sum 3.14 -5)))
```

returns CDR.

The operation SETQ takes two arguments, setting the value of the first to be the second. Thus

```
(SETQ Title '((data structures) and algorithms))
```

would give the symbolic atom Title the value

```
((data structures) and algorithms).
```

APPEND, LIST, and CONS all construct lists and thus perform functions opposite those of CAR and CDR. APPEND creates a list from the elements of the lists that are its arguments. Thus

```
(APPEND Title Title)
```

returns

```
((data structures) and algorithms
(data structures) and algorithms).
```

LIST makes a list out of its arguments (not the *elements* of its arguments). Thus

```
(LIST Title Title)
```

returns

```
(((data structures) and algorithms)
((data structures) and algorithms)).
```

In this example, APPEND creates a six element list, while LIST creates a two element list. LIST takes any finite number, *n,* of arguments and returns an *n*-element list whose elements are the arguments.

CONS is the basic list constructor, which adds a new first element to a list:

```
(CONS 'fundamental '((data structures) and
algorithms))
```

returns

```
(fundamental (data structures) and algorithms).
```

The operation REVERSE reverses the order of these elements:

```
(REVERSE '((data structures) and algorithms))
```

returns

```
(algorithms and (data structures)).
```

SUBST is the substitution operator, taking three operands. These are the new element, the element for which it is substituted, and the list in which the substitution is to be done:

```
(SUBST 'information 'data '((data structures)
and algorithms))
```

returns

```
((information structures) and algorithms).
```

LAST returns a list containing only the last top level element on its argument list:

```
(LAST '((data structures) and algorithms))
```

returns `(algorithms)`. Note that CAR and LAST are not quite symmetric: CAR returns an element, while LAST returns a list.

Finally, the operation LENGTH returns the number of elements in a list:

```
(LENGTH '((data structures) and algorithms))
```

returns `3`, the number of elements.

LISP also has other operations, including standard arithmetic, which we shall not discuss.

Now that we have seen the types of operations that LISP allows, let us create an abstract data type reflecting these. We shall call this abstract type **LispList.** Our principal convention will be the use of parentheses to enclose a list.

Create (LispList)—returns () as the value of LispList. It returns an error if LispList already exists.

Car (LispList)—returns the first element of LispList. It returns an error if LispList is undefined or the empty list.

Cdr (LispList)—if LispList $= (A \ B \ ... \ Z)$, it returns the list $(B \ ... \ Z)$. It returns an error if LispList is undefined or the empty list.

Set (LispList1, LispList2)—assigns to LispList1 the value of LispList2. It returns an error if LispList2 is undefined.

Append (LispList1, LispList2)—if LispList1 $= (A \ ... \ M)$ and LispList2 $= (N \ ... \ Z)$, it returns $(A \ ... \ M \ N \ ... \ Z)$. It returns an error if either LispList1 or LispList2 is undefined.

List (LispList1, ... , LispList$n$)—returns the list (LispList1 ... LispList$n$). It returns an error if any of the LispList1, ... , LispList$n$ are undefined.

Cons (Element, LispList)—If LispList $= (A \ ... \ Z)$, it returns the list (Element $A \ ... \ Z$). It returns an error if LispList is undefined.

Reverse (LispList)—if LispList $= (A \ ... \ Z)$, returns the list $(Z \ ... \ A)$. It returns an error if LispList is undefined.

Subst (Element1, Element2, LispList)—returns a list obtained from LispList by replacing each occurrence of Element2 as an element of LispList by Element1. It returns an error if LispList is undefined.

Last (LispList)—if LispList $= (A \ ... \ Z)$, returns (Z).

Length (LispList)—returns an integer whose value is the number of elements in LispList. It returns an error if LispList is undefined.

With this ADT, we should be able to begin to construct a LISP emulator in any language that we choose. If this is properly done, then the user need not be aware of the choice of languages, for the results obtained by applying the emulator to a list will be the same as if we had used a genuine LISP program.

As an example of implementing this ADT, let us do a partial implementation of Car in Pascal. We take as the data structure implementation an ARRAY of characters. This implementation assumes that the first element in the list is an atom; it will *not* work correctly if the first element is itself a list (fig. 8.39).

Figure 8.39   Partial Pascal implementation of LISP 'Car'

```
CONST
  ElementLength = UserSuppliedMaxElementLength;
  ListLength    = UserSuppliedMaxListLength;

TYPE
  ElementType  = ARRAY[1..ElementLength] OF char;
  LispListType = ARRAY[1..ListLength] OF char;

{ We assume that Error is an error-handling routine. }

PROCEDURE Car (LispList    : LispListType;
               VAR Element : ElementType);

  VAR
    I : 1..ListLength;

  BEGIN

    { We assume that Error is an error-handling routine. }

    IF LispList[1] <> '(' THEN Error
    ELSE
      BEGIN

        { Clear Element to spaces. }

        FOR I := 1 TO ElementLength DO
          Element[I] := ' ';

        { Fill Element with the first atom in the list. }

        I := 2;
        WHILE (LispList[I] <> ' ') AND
              (LispList[I] <> ')') DO
          BEGIN
            Element[I - 1] := LispList[I];
            I := I + 1
          END
      END
  END; { Car }
```

Summary

In this chapter we have introduced the concept of a table as an *n*-dimensional structure and have examined some of the operations we might want to carry out on tables. We have gone from the abstraction to the highly concrete in discussing ways in which a table can be represented. Considering arrays and matrices as special cases of tables, we have also examined the use of special types of arrays and matrices, either to match closely a sparsity of data or to mirror accurately the application which is modeled by the array. In the course of our discussion, we have also examined the concept of a variant record, as used in Pascal. Finally, we have examined some variations on list structures, including plexes and LISP-like lists.

Vocabulary

action section
array
atom
attribute
band matrix
bandwidth
column major order
condition section
coordinate
decision table
document-term matrix
empty list
entry
finite element method
Gaussian elimination
heading section
hexagonal array
homogeneous entries
information retrieval
key
key word
linear algebra
linear programming
LISP
LispList

list
location
lower triangular matrix
matrix
matrix algebra
multilist
n-dimensional table
null list
plex
position
pseudocode
record
row major order
rule section
sparse matrix
spreadsheet
symmetric matrix
transpose
tree list
triangular matrix
triangular number
upper triangular matrix
variant record
variant record part

References

Gourman, Jack. *The Gourman Report: A ratings of undergraduate programs in American and International Universities,* 4th revised edition, 1983–84. National Education Standards, Los Angeles, Calif.

Peterson's Competitive Colleges, 4th ed. Karen C. Hegener, ed., Peterson's Guides, Princeton, NJ.

Winston, Patrick Henry, and Horn, Berthold Klaus Paul. *LISP,* 2nd ed. Addison-Wesley, Reading, Mass., 1984.

Problems

8.1. Locate a manual or detailed description for one of the spreadsheet programs. Identify the operations that correspond to our primary data structure operations (create, insert, delete, search, ...). Identify five different operations that the particular spreadsheet program allows on the data structure beyond the basic ones.

8.2. Show that for an $m \times n$ table A stored by columns whose first entry is stored at location b, the entry a_{ij} is located at

$$b + m(j - 1) + i - 1.$$

8.3. The storage formulas for tables are based on having tables of type ARRAY[1..M, 1..N] OF ElementType. Develop the corresponding formulas for tables of type ARRAY[Q..R, S..T] OF ElementType,
    a. for storage by rows,
    b. for storage by columns.

8.4. Suppose that we were to store an array by diagonals. For example, the table of fig. 8.6 would be stored in the order

a_{11} a_{21} a_{12} a_{31} a_{22} a_{41} a_{32} a_{42}.

Devise a general method for recovering row i from an $m \times n$ array stored in this manner.

8.5. Suppose that we were to store an array in a spiral manner. For example, a 3×3 array would be stored as

a_{11} a_{12} a_{13} a_{23} a_{33} a_{32} a_{31} a_{21} a_{22}.

Devise a general method for recovering column j from an $m \times n$ array stored in this manner.

8.6. Determine whether your compiler stores arrays by row, by column, or in some other order.

8.7. Suppose that you are using a 12 × 31 array named Values, where each row represents the data for a month, that the rows are given in calendar order, and that you are using the month names as the values of the first array index. How would you implement the calculation to locate a particular value in the array, for example, Values[August, 6]? Note: Pascal implements this automatically, but we are asking how you would do it if it were needed.

8.8. Write the storage function for an $n \times n$ upper triangular matrix.

8.9. Using the tree list structure given in the text, show that the number of cells visited to reach cell n is at most $2[\lg n]$. Can you find a better bound? What is the minimum number of cells visited?

Programs

8.1. Fig. 8.15 presented matrix transposition using separate storage for the matrix and its transpose. It was suggested that an $m \times n$ matrix can be transposed within its own space by using a temporary storage location. Modify fig. 8.15 so that this second method of transposition works correctly.

8.2. Write a procedure that accepts an $m \times n$ matrix of integers, stored by columns, and allows the user to expand the matrix by entering either a new row or a new column. Your procedure should take as input m, n, and an indicator for row or column expansion. Then, at the appropriate time, the procedure should accept the entries for the new row or column. Write the procedure so that it prints out both the original and revised matrices and their sizes. To keep the matrix an easily manageable size, assume that both m and n are at most 20.

8.3. Write a procedure that generates the auxiliary table needed for the sorting procedure shown in fig. 8.13.

8.4. Write a procedure that uses the sorted auxiliary table generated by the procedure in fig. 8.13 to properly copy the original table into a new, sorted table.

8.5. Write a procedure for searching a two-dimensional matrix of reals to locate a given real value, such as the largest or smallest value. The procedure should return either the first location at which the value is found or a report that it does not occur within the matrix.

Matrix multiplication is defined by $C = A \times B$ if and only if A is an $m \times p$ matrix, B is a $p \times n$ matrix, and C is an $m \times n$ matrix with

$$c[i,j] = \sum_{h=1}^{p} a[i,h]b[h,j]$$

for each $i = 1, \dots, m$ and $j = 1, \dots, n$.

8.6. Write a procedure for multiplying two matrices that are sequentially stored by rows.

8.7. Write a procedure for storing a real datum in a matrix represented by a double circularly linked structure. The procedure should accept as input each real datum together with its proper location, move the access pointer from wherever it currently is to the new location, and write the datum into the matrix. Note that the proposed location may be a new one or one presently occupied by a datum (which will be replaced).

8.8. Write a procedure for multiplying two matrices stored as doubly linked lists.

8.9. Write a procedure for multiplying two $n \times n$ matrices of bandwidth k.

8.10. Write a procedure for multiplying two $n \times n$ lower triangular matrices.

8.11. Write a procedure to form the product of two matrices in linked list format, using the ProductTerm function defined in the text.

8.12. Write a procedure to compute the vector sum of two vectors given as circularly linked lists.

8.13. The problem with the partial implementation of Car in Pascal (fig. 8.39) is that it will not properly handle lists whose first element is itself a list. For example:

given   the procedure returns

((data) structures)   **(data**
((data structures) and algorithms)   **(data**

Extend this partial impementation so that it correctly returns the Car of any list presented to it. (Be careful: The first element may be a list whose first element is a list whose first element is a list whose... .)

Projects

8.1. Using the procedure of program 8.12, write a procedure to add two matrices given in linked list format. This requires very careful tracing of the two pointer systems. One way to avoid a mix-up is to handle only the row pointers during the addition and make a separate pass over the array afterward to install the correct column pointers.

8.2. Write an ADT for linear algebra, including matrix addition and multiplication, and matrix transpose.

8.3. Complete the implementation of the LispList ADT in Pascal.

9

Iteration and Recursion in Algorithms and Data Structures

Introduction

Solution of a particular problem frequently requires repeated application of an algorithm. Such is the case, for example, in trying to find a root of a polynomial equation. With some specific choice of initial value we apply an algorithm to find an approximate root and then repeat the process, using the approximate root as a new initial value. If the initial value is properly chosen, the approximate roots will converge to an actual root and we can terminate the repetitive process as soon as our approximate root is "close enough" by some criterion.

At times it is also helpful to use a repetitive technique to define a data structure. For example, we can define an n-dimensional array as an array of $(n - 1)$-dimensional arrays. Or we can define a tree as constructed from smaller trees. This technique may seem circular, but actually spirals in toward a conclusion because we are moving to smaller and simpler structures. Ultimately, we arrive at a simple structure that can be directly defined.

This chapter focuses on such repetitive techniques. In particular, we shall examine "iterative" techniques, which move directly from an initial point toward some end, and "recursive" techniques, which keep the initial point fixed but modify the end so that it is easier to reach.

Figure 9.1   Iteration

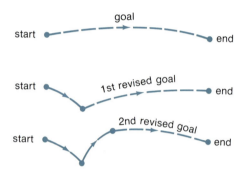

9.1 Iteration and recursion

Suppose that we are playing a game and that at some point we decide what is finally necessary to win the game. How do we then achieve that final necessity? To be more concrete, suppose that we are playing a board game, such as chess, checkers, or hex. How do we make a sequence of moves that will take us from our present position to a winning position?

One way to do this is to determine what moves are possible from our present position, decide on a "good" move, and make it. We hope this move will bring us closer to the winning position. Generally it leaves us with the same question: how do we make a sequence of moves to win?

Another strategy to use in playing the game is to consider the winning position carefully. Perhaps we can find a different position from which we can easily reach the winning position in one move. We hope it will be easier to find a way to reach the new position from our present one than it was to reach the winning one. Generally, however, we are left with the same question: how do we make a sequence of moves to win?

The first strategy is called **iteration.** Iteration may be defined as a strategy of repeated application of an algorithm or definition in which each application beyond the first directly uses the result of the previous applications to advance toward the desired result (fig. 9.1).

The second strategy is called **recursion.** Recursion may be defined as a strategy of repeated application of an algorithm or definition in which the first application builds a subgoal from which we can reach the desired goal, and in general the ith application builds a subgoal from which we can reach the $(i - 1)$st subgoal, provided that the $(i - 1)$st application of the algorithm or definition is successful in allowing us to reach the $(i - 2)$nd subgoal (fig. 9.2).

Figure 9.2   Recursion

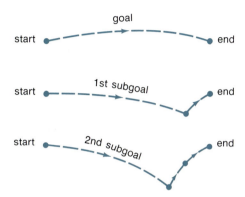

Here are examples of an iterative and a recursive algorithm to achieve the same goal. We know that for any positive integer *n, n* factorial, *n!*, is defined to be the product of the integers from 1 to *n*,

$$n! = 1 \cdot 2 \cdot 3 \cdot \ldots \cdot n.$$

Because we can only multiply two numbers together at one time, we cannot directly compute this value. However, we know that

$$1! = 1,$$
$$2! = 2 \cdot 1!,$$
$$3! = 3 \cdot 2!,$$

and so forth. Thus we have an iterative algorithm for computing *n!*, namely, compute 1!, 2!, 3!, ... until we reach *n!* (fig. 9.3).

The iteration in this algorithm is embodied in the step

```
Factorial := Factorial * I
```

where the current value of Factorial is used to compute a new value of Factorial. In this algorithm and the one shown as figure 9.4, a validity check is made on the input data ($N \geq 0$), and an error message issued in case of bad data. Observe that even if the input value is bad we still return a value, so that the function always produces an integer output. However, the error value is chosen to be a value that would never be returned for valid input.

Figure 9.3   Iterative algorithm for factorial

```
FUNCTION IterativeFactorial (N : integer) : integer;

{ Computes N! iteratively. }

  VAR
    Factorial : integer;
    I         : integer;

  BEGIN
    IF N >= 0 THEN
      BEGIN
        Factorial := 1;
        FOR I := 2 TO N DO
          Factorial := Factorial * I
      END
    ELSE

      { Error message for N < 0. }

      BEGIN
        writeln ('Factorial is undefined for negative integers.');
        writeln ('The value -1 is returned.');
        Factorial := -1
      END;
    IterativeFactorial := Factorial
  END; { IterativeFactorial }
```

The same function, $n!$, can be computed recursively. We observe that $n! = n(n-1)!$, so that if we knew the value of $(n-1)!$ we could then compute the value of $n!$. Similarly, $(n-1)! = (n-1)(n-2)!$, so that knowing the value of $(n-2)!$ allows us to compute $(n-1)!$ and hence to compute $n!$. Working our way back, we ultimately find that we need the value of $1!$, which is defined to be 1 (fig. 9.4). The recursion in this algorithm is embodied in the statement

```
RecursiveFactorial := N * RecursiveFactorial (N - 1)
```

since the current value cannot be determined until the preceding value, RecursiveFactorial $(N-1)$, is known.

Later in this chapter we shall discuss the merits of iterative versus recursive algorithms and when to use each kind. For now, we note that RecursiveFactorial requires much more storage than IterativeFactorial, since we must set aside space for each of the intermediate values, $(n-1)!$, $(n-2)!$, ... , until we have figured out $1!$ and can then fill in these intermediate values.

Figure 9.4   Recursive algorithm for factorial

```
FUNCTION RecursiveFactorial (N : integer) : integer;

{ Computes N! recursively. }
  BEGIN
    IF N > 1 THEN
      RecursiveFactorial := N * RecursiveFactorial (N - 1)
    ELSE
      IF N IN [0, 1] THEN RecursiveFactorial := 1
      ELSE

        { Error message for N < 0. }

        BEGIN
          writeln
            ('Factorial is undefined for nonpositive integers.');
          writeln ('The value -1 is returned.');
          RecursiveFactorial := -1
        END
  END; { RecursiveFactorial }
```

Here are examples of iterative and recursive definitions of a data structure. We shall use for our examples a string of characters. An iterative definition is:

A null character is a string. If S is a string and c is a single character, then cS is a string. The only strings are those formed by these rules.

Observe that this definition, like an iterative algorithm, begins with the simplest structure and constructs more complex structures from it, in this case by concatenating a new character onto the front of the string.

A recursive definition proceeds by breaking down a complex structure into simpler ones:

A structure S is a string if either S is a null string or S consists of a single character followed by a string.

To use this definition we must first check to see if S is the null string. If not, we determine if S begins with a character. If it does, we strip the first character off, leaving a remainder S'; then we must apply the definition to determine if S' is a string. We are only able to answer the question if we are unable to carry out the stripping process at any point (so that we do not have a string), or if we strip away every character and are left with the null string (so that we have a string).

Both iterative and recursive definitions have their uses, which we shall discuss later in this chapter. From this example, we may observe that an iterative definition seems natural if we wish to construct a particular structure, while a recursive definition is perhaps more natural if we wish to analyze a structure to determine its type.

9.2 Iterative algorithms

Iteration in an algorithm is characterized by a loop structure that repeats some action until an ending criterion is satisfied. Thus many algorithms involve iteration. We tend to classify an algorithm as iterative if the iteration is a major portion of the algorithm rather than just some minor housekeeping operation.

One iterative algorithm that we have discussed is the substring matching algorithm, IsSubstring, of chapter 3. This algorithm can be described by the rule pattern

1. Start the pattern search at position 1 in the string.

2. While the pattern is unmatched and we are not at the end of the string, advance the pattern one position and iterate (return to step 1).

3. Quit when the pattern is matched or we are at the end of the string.

Because the loops in an iterative algorithm are explicit and visible, complexity analysis for this type of algorithm is usually straightforward. We have merely to count the number of times we go through the major loop and the amount of effort involved each time. However, even this must be carefully done. In a mergesort, for example, each iteration may involve more work than the previous one, since we are handling successively larger sets.

One characteristic of iterative algorithms is that they tend to make immediate use of generated data. Thus they do not require large amounts of space to hold data values until they are used. We can see this in an algorithm for generating **Fibonacci numbers.** The Fibonacci numbers are defined by the function

$$f(0) = 1,$$
$$f(1) = 1,$$
$$f(n) = f(n-1) + f(n-2) \text{ for } n > 1.$$

This generates a series of numbers 1, 1, 2, 3, 5, 8, 13, 21, ...

From this definition, we see that in general the value of a Fibonacci number is the sum of the values of the two preceding ones. An iterative algorithm to generate Fibonacci numbers thus only needs to retain the two preceding values (fig. 9.5). This algorithm could easily have been written to store the values in an array and avoid the data switching. But that requires more storage and also requires a limit on the value of N, so that we can define the array.

Figure 9.5   Iterative algorithm for Fibonacci numbers

```
FUNCTION IterativeFibonacci (N : integer) : integer;

{ A function to generate the Nth Fibonacci number. }

   VAR
      Fa, Fb, Fc : integer;
      I          : integer;

   BEGIN

      { Assert: N >= 0. }

      Fc := 1;
      IF N > 1 THEN
         BEGIN
            Fa := 1;
            Fb := 1;
            FOR I := 2 TO N DO
               BEGIN
                  Fc := Fa + Fb;
                  Fa := Fb;
                  Fb := Fc
               END
         END;
      IterativeFibonacci := Fc
   END; { IterativeFibonacci }
```

One flaw that mars some iterative algorithms is that they may involve an excessive amount of work. This is particularly true when the algorithm involves a search for the answer. Suppose, for example, that we wish to determine whether the number 149,283,406,497 can be written as the product of at most five prime numbers. An iterative technique would be to examine all prime numbers less than or equal to the given number, then all pairs of primes, all triples of primes, and so forth, until we had either found a suitable product or exhausted all the possibilities. "Exhausted" is the correct word: this involves an immense amount of work!

9.3 Recursive algorithms

Recursive algorithms are at once both wonderful and terrible. They are wonderful because they often reveal very succinctly the nature of the problem to be solved. They are terrible because they frequently involve large amounts of storage to hold intermediate results.

Figure 9.6   Recursive algorithm for Fibonacci numbers

```
FUNCTION RecursiveFibonacci (N : integer) : integer;

{ A function to generate the Nth Fibonacci number. }

  BEGIN

    { Assert: N >= 0. }

    IF N <= 1 THEN
       RecursiveFibonacci := 1
    ELSE
       RecursiveFibonacci := RecursiveFibonacci (N - 1) +
                               RecursiveFibonacci (N - 2)
  END; { RecursiveFibonacci }
```

Let us begin with a recursive algorithm for Fibonacci numbers that derives from the same definition we used in section 9.2. The idea is to work backward from the desired result, determining exactly which intermediate problems must be solved. Once we get back to a starting point, then we can proceed forward, generating and using the intermediate results as we go. For example, suppose that we want to calculate $f(5)$. The thinking is this:

$f(5) = f(4) + f(3)$. Therefore postpone finding $f(5)$ until we have found $f(4)$ and $f(3)$.

$f(4) = f(3) + f(2)$. Therefore postpone finding $f(4)$ until we have found $f(3)$ and $f(2)$.

$f(3) = f(2) + f(1)$. Therefore postpone finding $f(3)$ until we have found $f(2)$ and $f(1)$.

$f(2) = f(1) + f(0)$. Therefore postpone finding $f(2)$ until we have found $f(1)$ and $f(0)$.

At this point we have stacked up four unsolved problems: $f(5)$, $f(4)$, $f(3)$, and $f(2)$, some of which are needed more than once. Fortunately, the definition immediately gives us $f(1)$ and $f(0)$. Hence we can reverse our direction and calculate $f(2)$. Having that, we then calculate $f(3)$, followed by $f(4)$ and $f(5)$. Figure 9.6 is the algorithm for this.

Figure 9.7   Subgoal sequence for Fibonacci numbers

```
 push RF(5) (onto the stack)
 push RF(4)
 push RF(3)
 push RF(2)
*compute RF(1)
 compute RF(0)
*pop and compute RF(2) (from *RF(1) and RF(0))
 hold *RF(2), while we compute RF(1)
*pop and compute RF(3) (from *RF(2) and RF(1))
 hold *RF(3), while we push RF(2)
@compute RF(1)
 compute RF(0)
@pop and compute RF(2) (from @RF(1) and RF(0))
*pop and compute RF(4) (from *RF(3) and @RF(2))
 hold *RF(4), while we push RF(3)
 push RF(2)
#compute RF(1)
 compute RF(0)
#pop and compute RF(2) (from #RF(1) and RF(0))
 hold #RF(2), while we compute RF(1)
#pop and compute RF(3) (from #RF(2) and RF(1))
*finally, pop and compute RF(5), (from *RF(4) and #RF(3))
```

The algorithm shown as figure 9.6 directly captures the definition of Fibonacci numbers. While it does not seem to involve any storage at all, except for the final result, the recursive statement in the ELSE clause actually hides a rather large stack of unsolved subproblems during execution. This is especially true since the intermediate results will be used several times, but there is nothing in the algorithm that remembers them once calculated. For N = 5, the sequence of pushing and popping on the subproblem stack is shown in figure 9.7.

Another way to view this computation is as a tree of subgoals (fig. 9.8). In this tree the symbols "*," "#," and "@" correspond to the labels of the lines in figure 9.7.

We see that to compute $F(n)$ this way we need a stack of depth $n - 1$ plus storage for three intermediate results at a time. Thus the amount of storage for this recursive algorithm is $O(n)$, contrasting with the $O(1)$ storage required by the iterative algorithm. Note also that computing $RF(5)$ involves computing $RF(4)$ once, $RF(3)$ twice, $RF(2)$ three times, $RF(1)$ five times, and $RF(0)$ three times. Recall that the iterative approach computes each of these values only once.

Figure 9.8   Subgoal tree for Fibonacci numbers

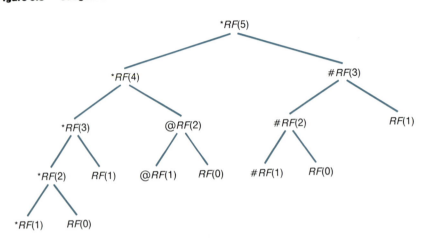

A recursive approach can also be used to determine whether 149,283,406,497 can be written as a product of five or fewer primes. The idea is to note partial solutions and use them. For the given number, it is easy to determine that 3 is a factor. Hence we write the number as 3 · 49,761,135,499. The original question can be answered positively if and only if we can write the larger factor as a product of at most four primes. Thus we stack the original problem and recursively try to solve this new subproblem. For this problem this approach is more reasonable than the iterative approach.

Tree traversal algorithms found in chapter 10 also are good examples of recursive algorithms. These algorithms, which are used for examining all vertices of a tree, are usually defined by stating the order in which subtrees are visited, with the stipulation that the subtrees themselves are visited "in the same way," that is, by recursively applying the traversal algorithm to the subtrees.

There we will see the calling of a procedure from within itself that is characteristic of recursive algorithms. In contrast, an iterative algorithm does not call itself but operates on different data within one use of the algorithm until the problem is solved.

We can define a general schema for recursive algorithms. These algorithms involve reducing the calculation to some base case that can be easily handled. There are four parts to the schema:

1. Calculate the base case, if applicable.

2. Otherwise, calculate the split into one or more subcases.

3. Apply (recursively) the algorithm to each of the subcases.

4. Fit the subcases back together to form the solution.

Figure 9.9   Fibstring extension rules

$$\alpha\, a \longrightarrow \alpha\, aa$$
$$\alpha\, a \longrightarrow \alpha\, ab$$
$$\alpha\, b \longrightarrow \alpha\, ba$$

Figure 9.10   Fibstring examples

aaaaaaaaa

aaab

ababa

abaabaaabaaba

babaaba

baabab

9.4 Data structure definition

An **iterative definition** for a data structure begins with a simple case and allows us to construct successively more complex examples of the structure. This type of process, also called an **inductive definition,** is not goal directed and hence is not especially suitable for determining whether a given structure is of a certain data type. However, it is useful whenever we wish to generate examples of a data type for study.

For example, let us consider the set of rules for generating a class of data structures that we shall call "Fibstrings." A **Fibstring** is a string of "*a*" and "*b*" whose generation rules are given in figure 9.9.

1. A string consisting of a single "*a*" or "*b*" is a Fibstring.

2. Any Fibstring may be extended to a new Fibstring depending on the rightmost character according to the rules:
   if the character is "*a*," extend the string by either "*a*" or "*b*,"
   if the character is "*b*," extend the string by "*a*."

Following these rules, we can easily generate examples of Fibstrings (fig. 9.10).

A **recursive definition** of a data structure follows a pattern closely related to that of recursive algorithms. In fact, the relationship is close enough that often the definition forms the basis of a recursive algorithm to determine whether a structure is of a given type. In general, a recursive data structure definition contains a base case for which the structure is exactly defined, together with recursive rules for breaking down a given structure until the base case is revealed.

For example, here is the recursive definition of a string found in section 9.1:

1. If S is empty, it is a string.
2. Otherwise, if $S = cS'$, where c is a character, then it is a string if and only if S' is a string.
3. These are the only strings.

Contrast this with the iterative definition of a string:

1. If S is empty, it is a string.
2. Otherwise, if c is a character and S' is a string, then $S = cS'$ is a string.
3. These are the only strings.

These two definitions show the close relationship between iteration and recursion. The connotation differs between the definitions. The iterative definition is **synthetic,** telling us that we construct a new string, S, from an old one, S', by adding a character to the front of S'. The recursive definition is **analytic,** telling us that we determine if a structure, S, is a string by seeing if it consists of a character followed by a structure that we can identify as a string. Since we are more frequently in the situation of **parsing** or decomposing a structure to determine its data type than of synthesizing a structure of a given type, recursive data type definitions are often more useful than iterative ones.

We will also see recursive data type definitions in defining trees. The heart of the definition is the concept that a structure is a tree if it consists of a number of trees joined together at a common root.

9.5 Recursion and complexity

Determining the complexity of a recursive algorithm is a reasonably difficult task. For iterative algorithms, the loops are generally visible, and it is only a matter of carefully counting the number of times through each loop and the amount of work within each loop.

For a recursive algorithm, the situation is more complex since the looping structure is hidden in the recursive calls to the algorithm. The complexity is generally determined by finding a **recurrence relation** that holds for the process and solving that for the complexity.

Suppose that we examine the recursive algorithm for computing a Fibonacci number. The recurrence relation is generated by assuming that the algorithm takes time $T(n)$ for input n. We see that the computation for input n consists of the computations for inputs $n - 1$ and $n - 2$, plus an addition step. Hence we can conclude that

$$T(n) = T(n - 1) + T(n - 2) + C,$$

where C represents the time necessary to do the addition.

There are several methods for solving recurrence relations to achieve an explicit expression for $T(n)$. We can, for example, try substituting the recurrence for $T(n - 1)$ and $T(n - 2)$. This yields

$$
\begin{aligned}
T(n) &= T(n - 1) + T(n - 2) + C \\
&= (T(n - 2) + T(n - 3) + C) + (T(n - 3) + T(n - 4) + C) + C \\
&= T(n - 2) + 2T(n - 3) + T(n - 4) + 3C.
\end{aligned}
$$

Try another round of substitution:

$$
\begin{aligned}
T(n) &= (T(n - 3) + T(n - 4) + C) + 2(T(n - 4) + T(n - 5) + C) \\
&\quad + (T(n - 5) + T(n - 6) + C) + 3C \\
&= T(n - 3) + 3T(n - 4) + 3T(n - 5) + T(n - 6) + 7C.
\end{aligned}
$$

Another round of substitution produces

$$
\begin{aligned}
T(n) &= T(n - 4) + 4T(n - 5) + 6T(n - 6) + 4T(n - 7) \\
&\quad + T(n - 8) + 15C.
\end{aligned}
$$

We recognize the coefficients of the T terms as binomial coefficients and the coefficient of the C term as $2^k - 1$ where k is the number of substitutions. This is illusory, for eventually the terms become $T(1)$ and $T(0)$, which do not generate further addition operations.

To conduct this line of reasoning properly, we must see what happens when the substitutions terminate. We know that $f(1)$ and $f(0)$ are directly generated. Let us assume that the values are preset and do not count in our time calculation. Thus $T(1)$ and $T(0)$ are both zero. Then to find $T(2)$ takes time C, just one addition. For $T(3)$ we find that

$$T(3) = T(2) + T(1) + C = C + 0 + C = 2C.$$

That is, calculating $T(3)$ requires calculating $T(2)$, plus one more addition.

Similarly, $T(4)$ requires calculating $T(3)$ and $T(2)$, plus one more addition. The total is $2C + C + C = 4C$. Let us continue for a few more:

$$T(5) = T(4) + T(3) + C = 4C + 2C + C = 7C,$$
$$T(6) = T(5) + T(4) + C = 7C + 4C + C = 12C,$$
$$T(7) = T(6) + T(5) + C = 12C + 7C + C = 20C,$$
$$T(8) = T(7) + T(6) + C = 20C + 12C + C = 33C.$$

This series, $0C$, $0C$, $1C$, $2C$, $4C$, $7C$, $12C$, $20C$, $33C$, ... , appears to be growing at a slower rate than 2^n. In fact, the coefficients are each one less than the corresponding Fibonacci number (1, 1, 2, 3, 5, 8, 13, 21, 34, ...). Hence we conclude that the time required to calculate the nth Fibonacci number by this recursive method is proportional to the size of the number. Other methods of generating the Fibonacci numbers show that this is $O(1.62^n)$ (see Korfhage 1967, pp. 3–6).

While many recurrence relations can be quite difficult to solve, two of the most common kinds, linear and geometric, are easily solved. The results are of sufficient use that it pays to remember them.

A **linear recurrence** has the form

$$T(1) = C,$$
$$T(n) = T(n - 1) + D, \quad n > 1,$$

for some constants C and D. This type of recurrence appears when we are linearly decreasing the number of data being handled. It says that to process an algorithm for $N = n$, we process it for $N = n - 1$ and then do a fixed amount of extra work.

If we experiment with this recurrence, we find the following sequence:

$$T(1) = C,$$
$$T(2) = T(1) + D = C + D,$$
$$T(3) = T(2) + D = C + 2D,$$
$$T(4) = T(3) + D = C + 3D,$$
$$T(5) = T(4) + D = C + 4D.$$

...

We see immediately that $T(n) = C + (n - 1)D$. This solution can be checked by substituting it into the recurrence relation.

The simplest **geometric recurrence** is

$$T(1) = C,$$
$$T(n) = 2T(n/2) + D, \quad n > 1.$$

This occurs whenever we split a set of size n into two sets of size $n/2$ and process both of them. Thus this recurrence is typical of the better sorting techniques. In chapter 11 we will see that these techniques are $O(n \lg n)$.

Recall that we are seeking an upper bound on the complexity. Thus any function $f(n)$ for which $f(n) \geq T(n)$ for all sufficiently large n will do. If we try $f(n) = an \lg n$, for any constant a, we see that we are off to a bad start, for $f(1) = 0$ while $T(1) = C$. However, any function of the form $f(n) = an \lg n + b$ will satisfy $f(1) \geq T(1)$ provided that $b \geq C$. So let us assume that a function of this form will provide an upper bound for all $k < n$,

$$T(k) \leq ak \lg k + b,$$

and try to extend this result to $k = n$. Here is the calculation:

$$
\begin{aligned}
T(n) &= 2T(n/2) + D \leq 2f(n/2) + D \\
&= 2a(n/2) \lg (n/2) + 2b + D \\
&= an \lg (n/2) + 2b + D \\
&= an \lg n - an + 2b + D \\
&= an \lg n + b + (b + D - an) \\
&= f(n) + (b + D - an).
\end{aligned}
$$

We will have $T(n) \leq f(n)$ if $b + D - an \leq 0$. This is true for any positive n when $a \geq b + D$.

To summarize, we need $b \geq C$ and $a \geq b + D$. Choose $b = C$ and $a = C + D$ to satisfy these inequalities. We then have for all values of n,

$$T(n) \leq (C + D)n \lg n + C,$$

or $T(n)$ is $O(n \lg n)$.

Summary

The concepts of iteration and recursion are closely related. Each presents a method for solving a problem by defining and attacking subproblems in a systematic way. In iteration, we keep the goal fixed and seek to redefine the starting point for the solution into a series of points nearer and nearer the goal. In recursion, we keep the starting point fixed and seek to find a series of subgoals extending back from the goal toward the starting point.

Both iteration and recursion are important methods for algorithm definition and for data structure definition, as they share the common theme of replacing a given problem by a series of problems that are easier to solve.

We have also touched briefly on the subject of recurrence relations, whose solution is necessary to obtain complexity estimates for recursive procedures.

Vocabulary

analytic definition
Fibonacci numbers
Fibstring
geometric recurrence
inductive definition
iteration
iterative definition

linear recurrence
parsing
recurrence relation
recursion
recursive definition
synthetic definition

Reference

Korfhage, Robert R. *Logic and Algorithms*, John Wiley & Sons, New York, 1967.

Problems

9.1. Solve the more general linear recurrence

$$T(1) = C,$$
$$T(N) = AT(N - 1) + D, \quad N > 1,$$

for arbitrary positive constants A, C, and D.

9.2. How many times is $F(2)$ computed when a recursive algorithm is used to compute $F(n)$, the nth Fibonacci number? (Assume $n > 2$.) How many times is $F(2)$ computed when the iterative algorithm is used? Which is the better method for computing a Fibonacci number, and why?

Programs

9.1. Write an iterative FUNCTION to compute the sum of the first N elements of a vector of reals. Write a recursive FUNCTION for the same computation. Discuss the relative merits of these two solutions to the problem of finding the sum.

Projects

9.1. In chess, a queen can attack any piece that is in its row or column, or that is aligned diagonally with it. The "Eight Queens" problem is to place eight queens on a chessboard so that none of the queens can attack any other one. Devise a recursive algorithm to solve this problem. See figure 9.11.

9.2. In chess, a knight's move consists of moving two squares in one direction (along its row or column) and then one square at right angles to the first portion of the move. A "Knight's Tour" is a movement of a knight over a chessboard so that it lands on each square exactly once and returns to its original square. Devise a recursive algorithm to generate a knight's tour from an arbitrary starting position. See figure 9.11.

Figure 9.11   Queen and knight moves

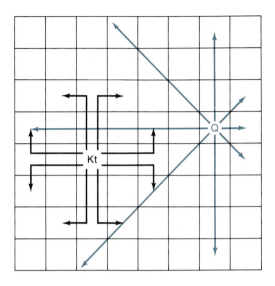

9.3. The rules for symbolic differentiation are generally stated recursively. For example,

$$\frac{d(fg)}{dx} = f\frac{dg}{dx} + g\frac{df}{dx}$$

where f and g are functions of x. Write a program to do symbolic differentiation.

9.4. Consider the simple BNF grammar for arithmetic expressions

$$<\text{expression}> ::= <\text{real}> | <\text{expression}> + <\text{expression}> |$$
$$<\text{expression}> - <\text{expression}> |$$
$$<\text{expression}> * <\text{expression}> |$$
$$<\text{expression}> / <\text{expression}> |$$
$$(<\text{expression}>)$$

Write a recursive recognizer for arithmetic expressions based on this grammar. The output should show, for each operator, its two operands.

Example expressions:
   3.14
   2.715 + 3.14
   ((2.79) − 3.26) * (9.015)

10

Trees

Introduction

One of the most important and widely used data structures is the tree—a
hierarchical arrangement of data wherein each datum (except one) has
exactly one "parent" and each datum may have zero or more "children."
This type of structure is used for family trees, corporate organization charts,
sentence parsing, library indexing systems, and a host of other applications.
In this chapter we examine tree structures. Our concentration is primarily on
binary trees, with a maximum of two children per datum, since this type is
particularly easy to implement and can be used to represent an arbitrary
tree. We study representations of these trees and methods of traversing,
searching, and reorganizing them. We close the chapter with a section on
"B-trees," a type of tree that is particularly useful for organizing massive
amounts of data, such as we might find on a disk.

10.1 Trees

The concept of a tree originates in the branch of mathematics called **graph theory.** Graph theorists have a number of definitions of "tree," all of which can be proven equivalent to one another. For our purposes, however, these definitions are generally inadequate in two major ways. First, most tree definitions are somewhat difficult to check. That is, it requires some effort to determine whether a given data structure is in fact a tree and to use the properties of a tree in operations on that structure. For that reason, we shall pick one definition that is particularly well suited to computing. Second, the trees graph theorists study are bare and unoriented. In computing, we want trees to hold data, and generally we want to have both an up-down and a left-right orientation to the tree. Thus, even if the traditional definitions of "tree" were suitable, we would need to supplement the definitions with extra information.

We shall define "tree" recursively. That is, we shall define "tree" in terms of itself. Roughly, a tree will be defined as a set of smaller trees, related in a particular way. This type of definition has two advantages. First, it leads to an algorithm for determining whether a structure is a tree by checking smaller and smaller structures. This algorithm converges to an answer, simply because the structures eventually reduce to structures containing only one element. Second, we shall see that this recursive definition matches well with a large number of processes that essentially operate by breaking a tree into smaller trees and then applying the process to each of the smaller trees.

Here is the definition. The empty set is a **tree,** called the **empty tree.** Let R be a singleton set containing only one element. A finite structure,

$$T = < R, T_1, T_2, \ldots, T_n>,$$

is a tree if (1) $n = 0$ (a single node tree) or (2) $n > 0$ and $T_1, T_2, \ldots, T_n$ are non-empty, disjoint trees. The singleton R is called the **root** of the tree T, and the trees $T_1, \ldots, T_n$ are called **subtrees** of T. A **node** of T is either R or a root of some subtree.

Suppose that T is a non-empty tree. Then it has a root R and subtrees T_1, $T_2, \ldots, T_n$, for some $n \geq 0$. If $n > 0$, then each subtree T_i has a root, R_i. We say that R_i is a **child** of the root R and that R is the **parent** of R_i. Note that while a given node may have many children, it has at most one parent. (Which node has no parent?) For given nodes A and D in a tree, we say that A is an **ancestor** of D and that D is **descendant** of A if there is a chain $A = N_1, \ldots, N_k = D$ such that, for each $i = 1, \ldots, k - 1$, N_i is the parent of N_{i+1}.

The parent–child relation is the only relation directly allowed in a tree. From this relation, however, we may develop others, such as the ancestor–descendant relation. Another useful relation is the **sibling** relation: two nodes are siblings if and only if they have the same parent.

Figure 10.1   The basic tree types

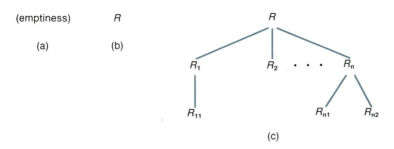

Figure 10.2   Two data structures

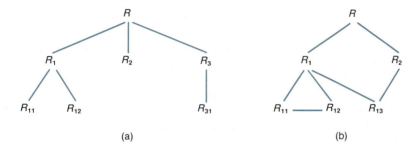

Graphically, we depict the relationship between a node and one of its children by a line joining points or circles representing the two nodes. When the nodes are labeled we often substitute the label for the point or circle (fig. 10.1). Note that in a general tree (fig. 10.1c) each of the nodes R_1, R_2, ... , R_n is a child of the primary root, R, and also the root of its own subtree.

Let us examine the structures in figure 10.2, to determine whether these are trees. In figure 10.2a, we have marked one node "R." We take this to be the root of what may be a tree. By the definition, since R is not isolated, each node directly related to it is a child and should be the root of its own subtree. These child nodes are R_1, R_2, and R_3. R_1 is not isolated, but also has two children, R_{11} and R_{12}. Thus R_1 is potentially a root of a subtree. R_2, however, is isolated. Hence it is the root of a subtree consisting only of itself. R_3 has one child, R_{31}. Hence R_3 is also potentially the root of a subtree. Turning now to the "subtree" at R_1, we find both R_{11} and R_{12} to be isolated. Hence each of them is the root of a one-node tree. Since each of these is a tree, we conclude that R_1 is indeed the root of a subtree. Similarly, R_{31} is the root of a one-node tree, and hence R_3 is the root of a subtree. Thus we have dissected the structure, identifying each subtree and the corresponding roots.

Figure 10.3   The tree with R_3 as root

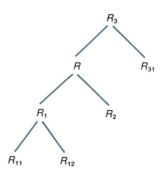

This type of analysis is typical of a recursive definition. We had to postpone any decision on whether the entire figure was a tree until we had made decisions on the various subtrees. For two of these subtrees, we again had to postpone a decision until we had analyzed their subtrees.

Applying the terminology we have defined to figure 10.2a, R is the parent of R_1, R_2, and R_3. The node R_1 is the parent of R_{11} and R_{12}, and both R and R_1 are ancestors of R_{12}. Similarly, R_{31} is a descendant of R. There is a **chain** from R to each node in the tree.

The structure we have defined has more properties than the "tree" of graph theorists. In the first place, there are implicit top to bottom and left to right orderings, which have no counterparts in graph theory. In the second place, while we have fixed R as the root, in a graph-theoretic tree any node could be the root. A graph theorist could, for example, consider R_3 as the root. We would draw the resulting tree by picking the tree up by its new root and letting it hang (fig. 10.3). (In graph theory a **rooted tree** is a tree that has a specific designated root; it still does not have either of the implied orderings.)

Now consider figure 10.2b. Here R has two directly related nodes, R_1 and R_2. These are potential roots of their own subtrees. However, if we look at the descendants of R_1, we find two difficulties. First, the line between R_{11} and R_{12} indicates a relationship between these, which is not permitted in a tree. Hence, on this basis alone, the structure is not a tree. But in addition, we find that R_{13} is related to both R_1 and R_2, as shown by the lines in figure 10.2b. This violates the condition that the "subtrees" for R_1 and R_2 be disjoint and unrelated. Hence, for this reason also, the structure is not a tree.

The number of children of a node in a tree is called its **branching factor.** The branching factor for a tree is the maximum of the branching factors of its nodes. The nodes of a tree are divided into three classes: the root, the **leaves** or **terminal nodes** (nodes with branching factor zero), and the **interior nodes** (all others). The **length** of a chain in a tree is one less than the number of nodes (including the end points) in that chain; that is, it is the number of edges included in the chain. A **branch** in a tree is a chain from the root to a leaf. The **height** of a tree is the length of a longest branch.

Figure 10.4   Binary tree

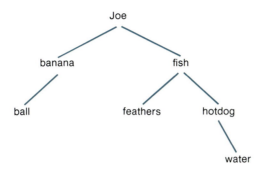

Looking again at figure 10.2*a*, the branching factor is 3 for R, 2 for R_1, 1 for R_3, and 0 for all other nodes. The leaves are R_{11}, R_{12}, R_2, and R_{31}; the interior nodes are R_1 and R_3. The branches are (R, R_1, R_{11}), (R, R_1, R_{12}), (R, R_2), and (R, R_3, R_{31}). The tree has height 2.

We have mentioned both an up-down and a left-right orientation in trees for data structures. These orientations are implicit in the discussion we have presented. For the up-down orientation, we think of the root of a tree as the base, or **level** 0, its direct descendants as level 1, their direct descendants as level 2, and so forth. By convention, computer scientists usually draw trees "upside down," with the root at the top. The left-right orientation, when it is important, is given by the numbering of the children, as in $R_1, R_2, ... , R_n$.

The nodes at various levels in the tree of figure 10.2*a* are

level 0: R,

level 1: R_1, R_2, R_3,

level 2: R_{11}, R_{12}, R_{31}.

10.2 Binary trees

We now face a minor dilemma. On the one hand, we do not want to restrict the branching factor of a tree, since rather large branching factors may fit the data very well. For example, we should not restrict (in a data structure) the number of children a parent can have or the number of supervisors a manager might have reporting to him or her. On the other hand, allowing complete flexibility of the branching factors can lead to inefficient implementations of tree structures in storage. Fortunately, there is a way out of this dilemma.

A **binary tree** is a tree with branching factor of at most two. That is, each node in the tree has at most two children (fig. 10.4). It may seem that binary trees are restrictive, but a slight change of viewpoint allows us to represent any tree by a binary tree. Hence the restriction is not as serious as it might seem.

Figure 10.5   Representation of a tree by a binary tree

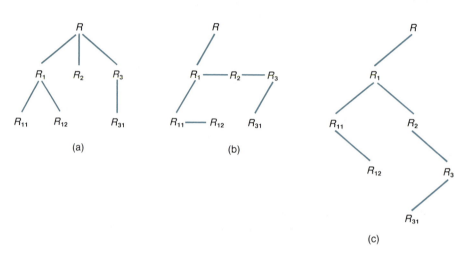

(a)   (b)

(c)

Here is the representation. Rather than think of the relationships within a tree as being "parent–child," we think of them as being "parent–oldest child," and "sibling–next younger sibling." This changes the tree linkages for the tree in figure 10.5a to those shown in figure 10.5b, resulting in a binary tree representation of the same data. The binary tree is redrawn more conventionally in figure 10.5c. (By convention, the "oldest child" is the leftmost node.)

We shall concentrate our efforts on binary trees for most of the rest of this chapter. Hence "tree" will be understood to mean "binary tree" unless otherwise specified. We observe that in a (binary) tree the terms **left child** and **right child** of a given node are unambiguous.

For the abstract data type, binary tree, we postulate the following operations and functions. In this development, we identify a non-empty binary tree with its root.

> **Create** (BinTree)—creates an empty binary tree, BinTree. It returns an error if BinTree is already defined.
>
> **IsEmpty** (BinTree)—a boolean function returning "true" if BinTree is empty, "false" otherwise. It returns an error if BinTree is undefined.
>
> **MakeTree** (BinTree1, Item, BinTree2)—makes a binary tree whose root contains the datum Item, with left child BinTree1 and right child BinTree2. It returns an error if either BinTree1 or BinTree2 is undefined.
>
> **Root** (BinTree)—a function returning the root node of BinTree. It returns an error if BinTree is undefined.

Datum (Node, BinTree)—a function, returning the datum stored at Node of BinTree. It returns an error if BinTree is undefined or if Node is not in BinTree.

LeftChild (Node, BinTree)—a function returning the left child of Node in BinTree. It returns Empty if Node has no left child in BinTree and an error if BinTree is undefined or if Node is not in BinTree.

RightChild (Node, BinTree)—a function returning the right child of Node in BinTree. It returns Empty if Node has no right child in BinTree and an error if BinTree is undefined or if Node is not in BinTree.

Parent (Node, BinTree)—a function returning the parent of Node in BinTree. It returns Empty if Node is the root of BinTree and an error if BinTree is undefined or if Node is not in BinTree.

InTree (Datum, BinTree)—a boolean function returning "true" if Datum is in BinTree and "false" otherwise. It returns an error if BinTree is undefined.

Location (Datum, BinTree)—a function returning the location of Datum in BinTree. It returns an error if BinTree is undefined.

FullNode (Node, BinTree)—a boolean function returning "true" if Node is in BinTree and Node has two defined children, "false" if Node is in BinTree and Node has fewer than two defined children. It returns an error if either BinTree is not defined or Node is not in BinTree.

IsLeaf (Node, BinTree)—a boolean function returning "true" if Node is a leaf of BinTree, "false" otherwise. It returns an error if either BinTree is not defined, or Node is not in BinTree.

Graft (Node, BinTree, Bush, Direction)—grafts the binary tree Bush onto BinTree by creating an edge with Node as one endpoint and the root of Bush as the other endpoint. The root of Bush becomes the left or right child of Node according to the parameter Direction. Graft returns an error if any of the parameters is not defined, or if Node is not in BinTree, or Node already has a left or right child, according to Direction.

Prune (Node, BinTree, Bush)—removes the subtree of BinTree rooted at Node, including Node. The removed subtree becomes Bush. Prune returns an error if BinTree is undefined or if Node is not in BinTree.

Expand (Node, BinTree, Bush)—replaces Node by Bush by identifying the root of Bush with Node in BinTree. It returns an error if any of the parameters is not defined, or if Node is not a leaf of BinTree.

Clip (Node, BinTree)—removes the subtree of BinTree rooted at Node, leaving Node as a leaf in BinTree. It returns an error if BinTree is undefined or if Node is not in BinTree.

Figure 10.6   A (left) balanced binary tree

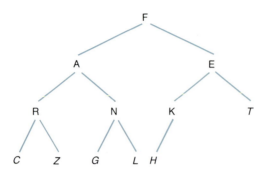

Figure 10.7   Linked representation of a binary tree

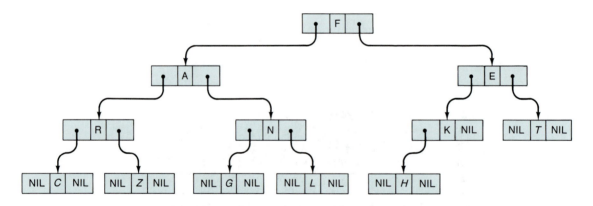

Implementation of this ADT for a binary tree is similar to the other implementations we have done and is left as an exercise. Note that the implementation will depend on the storage representation chosen for the tree and its nodes.

A binary tree is **balanced** if (1) all leaves lie on the same level, l, or two adjacent levels, $l - 1$ and l, and (2) there are no missing nodes at level $l - 1$. If in addition the nodes at level l occupy the leftmost positions the tree is called **left balanced** (fig. 10.6).

The fact that each node of a binary tree may have two children leads to some complications in storage of the tree. We cannot organize the tree in storage so that both children are adjacent to their parent for all nodes in the tree. One way to store a tree is to organize the storage according to some fixed method of traversing the tree. This will be discussed in the next section. Another method is to store the tree as a linked representation, with two pointers (LeftChild and RightChild) at each node (fig. 10.7).

Figure 10.8   Numbering a left balanced tree

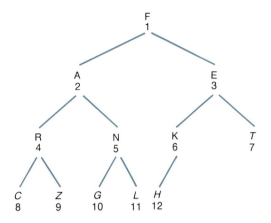

Figure 10.9   Storing a left balanced tree

F	A	E	R	N	K	T	C	Z	G	L	H
1	2	3	4	5	6	7	8	9	10	11	12

This linked representation is deficient in that there is no way to determine the parent of a given node. This deficiency can be removed by adding a third pointer to facilitate retracing the tree. Three methods of doing this (pointer to root, pointer to parent, pointer to sibling) are explored in the exercises.

If a binary tree is left balanced, then a simple sequential storage scheme works well. Suppose that we number the nodes of the tree sequentially, beginning at the root and progressing from left to right through each level (fig. 10.8). The tree may now be stored in consecutive locations, according to the numbering (fig. 10.9). Note that the children of the node at location i are at locations $2i$ and $2i + 1$, and the parent of the node at location i is at location i DIV 2. Thus it is easy to locate both the parent and any children of a given node. (This is the same storage implementation that we will see in chapter 11 for tournament sorts and heaps.) Observe that in this tree node 6 has only one child, node 12. The next node added will be node 13—the other child of node 6.

10.3 Tree traversal

Traversing a tree is more complex than traversing a set because of the multiple ways in which we may progress. We think of the traversal in relationship to the root of the tree, as one stable reference point. There are four common methods of tree traversal—level order, inorder, preorder, and postorder.

Figure 10.10   Level order traversal of a binary tree

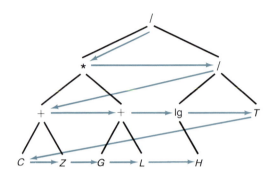

For **level order traversal** we begin at the root, then traverse the first level from left to right, then the second level from left to right, and so forth (fig. 10.10). We have already met this traversal. A linear scan of the balanced tree stored in figure 10.9 is a level order traversal of the tree.

A procedure for level order traversal is not easy to describe in the abstract, since this traversal disregards the structure of the tree. That is, the parent–child connection is ignored. For example, the fourth node retrieved, "+," is the "niece" of the third node, "/," but the fifth node, the other "+," is the "brother" of the fourth node. Then later on, the twelfth node, "*H*," is the "second cousin" of the eleventh node, "*L*." If we use the storage suggested for a left balanced tree, the procedure for level order traversal is very simple (fig. 10.11).

Inorder traversal corresponds to the manner in which we usually write algebraic statements. The rule is that we traverse first the left subtree, then the root, then the right subtree (fig. 10.12). Note that this procedure, figure 10.13, is recursive—it calls itself to handle the subtrees. The same is true for preorder and postorder traversals, which follow.

Observe that inorder traversal of the binary tree picks up the operators and operands of the expression

$$((C + Z) * (G + L)) / (\lg H / T)$$

in the order in which they occur in the expression.

Preorder traversal visits the root before anything else and then traverses the children from left to right (figs. 10.14 and 10.15). The order in which the nodes of our sample tree are picked up is

$$/ * + C Z + G L / \lg H T.$$

Figure 10.11   Level order traversal procedure

```
CONST
  MaxSize = UserSuppliedMaximumSize;

TYPE
  ElementType = UserSuppliedType;
  BinaryTree  = ARRAY[1..MaxSize] OF ElementType;

PROCEDURE Visit (Node : ElementType);

  BEGIN
    writeln (Node)
  END; { Visit }

PROCEDURE LevelOrder (BinTree : BinaryTree;
                      Size    : integer);

{ Level order traversal. Size is the number of nodes
in the binary tree. }

  VAR
    I : integer;

  BEGIN
    FOR I := 1 TO Size DO
      Visit (BinTree[I])
  END; { LevelOrder }
```

Figure 10.12   Inorder traversal of a binary tree

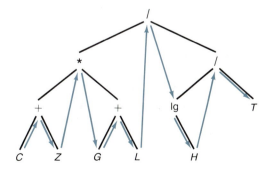

Figure 10.13   Inorder traversal procedure

```
TYPE
  ElementType = UserSuppliedTypes;
  NodePointer = ^Node;
  Node        = RECORD
                    LeftChild  : NodePointer;
                    Value      : ElementType;
                    RightChild : NodePointer
                END;

PROCEDURE Visit (Value : ElementType);
  BEGIN
    writeln (Value)
  END; { Visit }

PROCEDURE InOrder (Node : NodePointer);

  BEGIN
    IF Node^.LeftChild <> NIL THEN
      InOrder (Node^.LeftChild);
    Visit (Node^.Value);
    IF Node^.RightChild <> NIL THEN
      InOrder (Node^.RightChild)
  END; { InOrder }
```

Figure 10.14   Preorder traversal of a binary tree

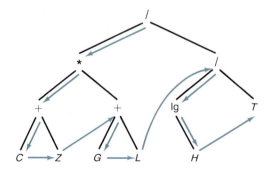

Figure 10.15   Preorder traversal procedure

```
TYPE
  ElementType  = UserSuppliedType;
  NodePointer  = ^Node;
  Node         = RECORD
                   LeftChild  : NodePointer;
                   Value      : ElementType;
                   RightChild : NodePointer
                 END;

PROCEDURE Visit (Value : ElementType);
  BEGIN
    writeln (Value)
  END; { Visit }

PROCEDURE PreOrder (Node : NodePointer);

  BEGIN
    Visit (Node^.Value);
    IF Node^.LeftChild <> NIL THEN
      PreOrder (Node^.LeftChild);
      IF Node^.RightChild <> NIL THEN
      PreOrder (Node^.RightChild)
  END; { PreOrder }
```

While this may seem strange, observe that if we read this from left to right, each operator is encountered before its operands. Similarly, reading from right to left we see each operand before the operation that applies to it. This suggests that a right-to-left scan would result in our having the data available when we come to doing each operation, a property that does not hold for inorder traversal. This scan permits us to compute some part of the result every time we encounter an operator, stacking the results of the computation until they are needed:

T	H	$\lg H$	$\lg H / T$	L	G	$G + L$	Z	C
	T	T		$\lg H / T$	L	$\lg H / T$	$G + L$	Z
				$\lg H / T$			$\lg H / T$	$G + L$
								$\lg H / T$

$C + Z$	$(C + Z) * (G + L)$	$((C + Z) * (G + L)) / (\lg H / T)$
$G + L$	$\lg H / T$	
$\lg H / T$		

Figure 10.16   Postorder traversal of a binary tree

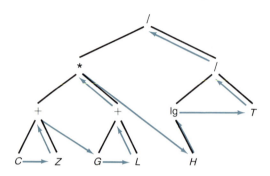

Similarly, **postorder traversal** visits the node after traversing all the subtrees (fig. 10.16). For this traversal, the order of picking up the nodes in the sample tree is

$$C \, Z + G \, L + * \, H \lg T \, / \, /.$$

Reading this from left to right, we encounter each operand before its corresponding operator (fig. 10.17). This scan results in a stacking of partial computations similar to, but not identical with, the stacking given by preorder traversal:

C	Z	$C + Z$	G	L	$G + L$	$(C + Z) * (G + L)$
	C		$C + Z$	G	$C + Z$	
				$C + Z$		

H	$\lg H$	T
$(C + Z) * (G + L)$	$(C + Z) * (G + L)$	$\lg H$
		$(C + Z) * (G + L)$

$\lg H / T$	$((C + Z) * (G + L)) / (\lg H / T)$
$(C + Z) * (G + L)$	

Observe that level order, preorder, and postorder traversals are easily generalized to arbitrary (nonbinary) trees, but that inorder traversal is particular to binary trees. (Exactly when would we visit the root if we had three or more subtrees?)

Figure 10.17   Postorder traversal procedure

```
TYPE
  ElementType = UserSuppliedType;
  NodePointer = ^Node;
  Node        = RECORD
                  LeftChild  : NodePointer;
                  Value      : ElementType;
                  Rightchild : NodePointer
                END;

PROCEDURE Visit (Value : ElementType);
  BEGIN
    writeln (Value)
  END; { Visit }

PROCEDURE PostOrder (Node : NodePointer);

  BEGIN
    IF Node^.LeftChild <> NIL THEN
      PostOrder (Node^.LeftChild);
    IF Node^.RightChild <> NIL THEN
      PostOrder (Node^.RightChild);
    Visit (Node^.Value)
  END; { PostOrder }
```

10.4 Binary search trees

Our discussion thus far has said nothing about the distribution of data among the nodes of a binary tree. Indeed, this distribution is often dictated by the use of a particular tree. One use of a binary tree is to parse or decode a program statement. In this use the resulting **parse tree** reflects the structure of the statement (fig. 10.18). For such a tree there is no easy way to locate a specific data entry.

One common use of a binary tree requires that we know how to locate specific data entries. A **binary search tree** is a binary tree with its data *specifically organized for searching*. We conceive of a search as beginning at the root, then proceeding through the tree in an effort to locate the desired item. For this purpose, we generally assume that a datum is stored at each node. At each node, we compare the node datum with the desired item. If they match, we are through; otherwise we must search further. When there is no match we need to know whether to take the left branch or the right branch from that node.

In order to organize data for searching, we follow the convention that all data less than the datum at a given node are in its left subtree (if they are in the tree at all) and all data greater than the node datum are in the right subtree. Then our search algorithm is very simple (fig. 10.19).

Figure 10.18   Parse tree

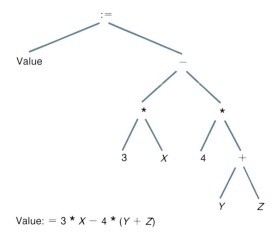

Value: = 3 * X − 4 * (Y + Z)

Figure 10.19   Algorithm for binary search

```
TYPE
   NodeElement = UserSuppliedType;
   NodePointer = ^Node;
   Node        = RECORD
                    LeftChild  : NodePointer;
                    Value      : NodeElement;
                    RightChild : NodePointer
                 END;

FUNCTION BinaryTreeSearch (Item : NodeElement;
                           Root : NodePointer) : NodePointer;

   BEGIN
      BinaryTreeSearch := NIL;
      IF Item > Root^.Value THEN
         BEGIN
            IF Root^.RightChild <> NIL THEN
               BinaryTreeSearch := BinaryTreeSearch (Item, Root^.RightChild)
         END
      ELSE
         IF Item < Root^.Value THEN
            BEGIN
               IfRoot^.LeftChild <> NIL THEN
                  BinaryTreeSearch := BinaryTreeSearch (Item, Root^.LeftChild)
            END
         ELSE
            BinaryTreeSearch := Root
   END; { BinaryTreeSearch }
```

Figure 10.20   A worst case binary search tree

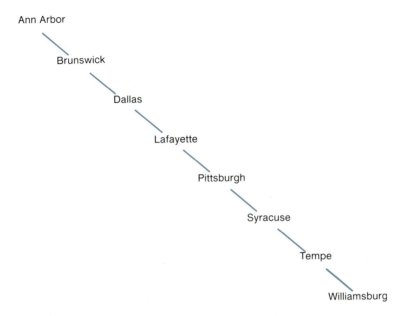

Using the algorithm shown in figure 10.19, we never take a wrong branch in our search through the tree. While we do not know initially whether the datum is actually in the tree, at each step we choose the only possible branch along which the datum could be. If we have not found it by the time we reach the end of the branch, then we know that it is not in the tree.

When a datum is not in the tree, we may merely wish to return that information or we may wish to add it to the tree. Since the algorithm BinaryTree-Search has located where the datum should be, if we want to add it to the tree we know exactly where to place it. If we do an inorder traversal of a binary search tree the nodes are visited in sorted order.

10.5 Tree balancing

How long does it take to travel from the root of a tree to one of the leaves? The answer obviously depends on the number of levels that must be passed. The worst case occurs when all entries in the tree are strung out along one long branch (fig. 10.20). In this case the search is a linear one, whose complexity is $O(n)$, for a set of size n.

What will be the best case? The best situation would be to have the longest branch of the tree as short as possible. Now suppose that the longest branch ends at level l and that at some previous level, perhaps $l - 1$, there is a missing node (fig. 10.21a). Clearly, by reorganizing the tree we could reduce the length of the longest branch (fig. 10.21b).

Figure 10.21   Shortening a long branch

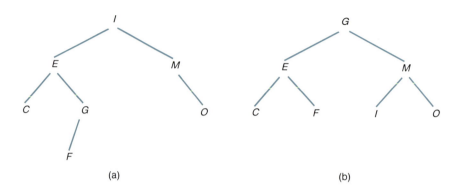

(a)   (b)

Table 10.1   Longest path in balanced binary tree

Number of Nodes in Tree	Length of Longest Path
1	0
2–3	1
4–7	2
8–15	3
16–31	4
32–63	5

Following this line of reasoning, the best binary search tree is a balanced one. For balanced trees, the length of the longest search path (number of nodes visited) is given in table 10.1. From studying the table, it is clear that the length of the longest path in a balanced binary tree with n nodes is $\lfloor \lg n \rfloor$. Since the binary search always traverses only one path, for a balanced tree it is an $O(\lg n)$ search. Thus there is a strong incentive to keep binary search trees balanced.

Unfortunately, tree balancing can involve quite a bit of work. Consider, for example, the tree of figure 10.22a. Adding "A" to this tree requires shifting the location of every element in the tree (fig. 10.22b).

The rebalancing is most easily accomplished by recognizing that inorder traversal picks up the entries in the tree in sorted order. Thus we could perform an inorder traversal, store the elements sequentially, and then use the addressing scheme that we suggested in section 10.2 for a balanced tree.

We have a small dilemma here. On the one hand, it is very easy to add a node to an arbitrary binary search tree: just find where the new datum belongs and add it. However, this mode of operation carries with it the danger that the tree may be tall and skinny, and hence that search of the tree may degrade to $O(n)$. On the other hand, we can keep the search time to $O(\lg n)$ by keeping the tree balanced—but that potentially involves a great deal of work.

Figure 10.22   Maximum work in rebalancing a tree

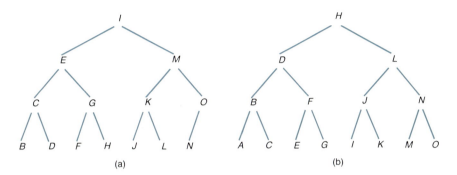

(a)   (b)

Figure 10.23   Sample AVL trees

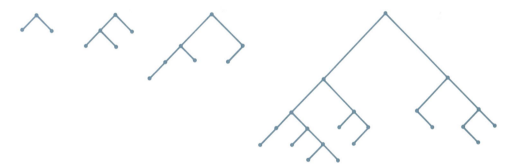

Is there some effective compromise? Yes, although it is not much used in practice. In 1962, Adel'son-Velskii and Landis developed a concept known as an **AVL tree** which has since been broadened to the concept of a **height-balanced tree.** The basic idea is to allow the binary tree to become slightly out of balance, but to maintain a strict control on the amount of imbalance. An AVL tree, for example, has the property that at each of its nodes, the height of the left subtree and the height of the right subtree differ by at most 1 (fig. 10.23). In other height-balanced trees, the allowable difference is greater, but still limited.

If we experiment with these trees, we see that they allow some latitude in the growth of a tree. It can be shown that rebalancing a height-balanced tree never involves the entire tree, except in the most trivial cases, but is instead a local operation, involving just a few nodes. Thus the work to rebalance a tree is kept small. At the same time, the effort required to search a height-balanced tree is still $O(\lg n)$, but with a larger constant than for a fully balanced tree. For example, if the time to search a fully balanced tree is $k \lg n$, then the time to search a corresponding AVL tree will be $1.5k \lg n$. For further information on height-balanced trees, see Foster (1973), Standish (1980), Tenenbaum and Augenstein (1981), or Wirth (1976).

Figure 10.24   A reserved word trie

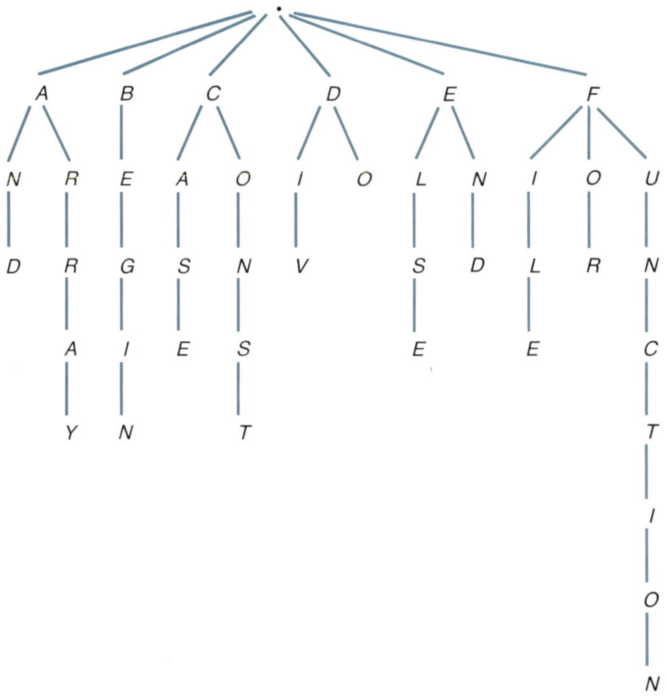

10.6 Tries

The binary search trees that we have defined have data at each node. Hence, in searching such a tree, we may follow a branch to its end, or halt part way down a branch, after having found the datum we want. Having data stored at each node tends to keep the tree relatively small. However, it also means that at each node we may need to compare the entire datum we have with that stored at the node.

Another method of organizing search trees involves the use of trees with greater branching factors, and with each edge labeled with the criterion under which it is to be taken. This type of tree is called a **trie.** While the term comes from the word "retrieve," it is usually pronounced "try" to distinquish it from "tree." A trie is often used in situations that call for the matching of a relatively small, fixed set of words. In this situation, each edge of the trie corresponds to a letter. The edges from the root to level 1 represent the first letter of a word, those from level 1 to level 2 represent the second letter, and so forth. Thus a path from the root into the trie corresponds to the spelling of a word. Here is an example.

The reserved words for Pascal include the following (among others):

AND	ARRAY	BEGIN	CASE
CONST	DIV	DO	ELSE
END	FILE	FOR	FUNCTION

Figure 10.25   A trie with termination symbols

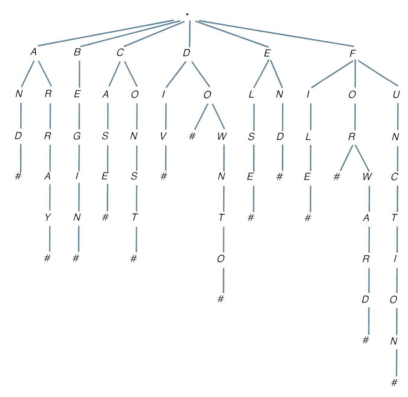

A trie to distinguish among these words is given in figure 10.24. Observe that the branching factor for this trie is six, one branch for each initial letter. Each of the words in the list corresponds to a distinct branch of the tree. Hence these branches can be traced by examining the words one letter at a time. Upon reaching the leaf, we know what word we have and can make an appropriate interpretation of it.

One slight difficulty exists with tries. We often have words that form the initial parts of other words. For example, both DO and DOWNTO are reserved words in Pascal, as are FOR and FORWARD. One way to resolve this is to agree that we can halt part way down a branch with a recognized word. The difficulty with this is deciding when to halt (for DO) and when not to (for DOW). A better way to handle this situation is to include some sort of termination symbol for each word. This solution is shown in figure 10.25, where "#" has been chosen as the termination symbol.

A trie has three principal advantages. First, since the matching at each stage is done on single characters, it can be done very quickly and simply. Second, a trie can easily be extended to include new words. Third, the amount of time required to search for a word is proportional to the length of the word. Since short words are used much more frequently than long words, this has the effect of providing a rapid search algorithm. These three traits combine to make a trie a good data structure for a spelling checker.

10.7 Huffman coding

We have discussed the balancing of binary trees, noting that if a binary tree is balanced, then traversal time from the root to a leaf is $O(\lg n)$, whereas for an arbitrary tree, traversal time may be $O(n)$, simply because in the worst case the tree can degenerate to a linear chain. Underlying this discussion has been the tacit assumption that all the search paths are equally likely or nearly so. However, situations arise in which this is not the case. For example, if we look at the frequencies of letters within a body of text, we find that not all letters occur equally often. In English, for example, the most frequent letters are "E," "T," "O," "A," "I," and "N"; and such letters as "Q," "X," and "J" occur much less often. Thus, if we were searching a tree to identify these letters, we would follow the paths to "E" and "T" much more frequently than the paths to "X" and "Q." Yet, if our tree is balanced and all the data are at the leaves of the tree, all these paths are of the same length. It is conceivable that by judiciously unbalancing the tree we could shorten the average search time, through the device of organizing short search paths for "E" and "T," and allowing longer search paths for "X" and "Q." This idea was exploited many years ago when Samuel F. B. Morse devised the Morse code: the codes for "e" and "t" consist of one character each, whereas the codes for "q" and "x" have four characters each.

In this section we explore a systematic way of arranging an unbalanced search tree that will take advantage of differing frequencies of occurrence of the data. The algorithm that we develop is known to provide the minimal average search path length over all trees having the given data stored at the leaves.

Suppose that we have the five fruits apple, cantaloupe, cherry, peach, and strawberry encoded at the leaves of a binary tree, as we might in the game of "Twenty Questions" (fig. 10.26). If these fruits occur with the frequencies 30, 72, 53, 13, and 9, respectively, then the average path length, weighted by frequency, will be

$$(3(30 + 72) + 2(53 + 13 + 9))/(30 + 72 + 53 + 13 + 9) = 2.576.$$

Suppose now that we think of this tree as representing binary encodings for the fruit names. If the left branch is "0" and the right branch is "1," then the code for apple is 000, the code for cantaloupe is 001, ... , and the code for strawberry is 11. The weighted average path length now becomes the weighted average code length. That is, if we were to encode a list of n of these fruits occurring in proportion to the given frequencies, then we would need an average of $2.576n$

Figure 10.26   Balanced binary tree for fruits

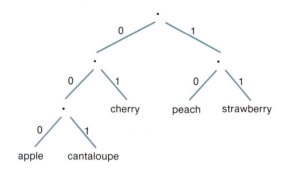

Table 10.2   Balanced fruit encoding

Fruit	Frequency	Count in 300	Code	Bits
apple	30	51	000	153
cantaloupe	72	122	001	366
cherry	53	90	01	180
peach	13	22	10	44
strawberry	9	15	11	30

bits for the encoding of each fruit. Suppose, for example, that we have a list of three hundred fruits occurring approximately in the given frequencies and that we wish to encode this list. Perhaps our first few fruits would be

cantaloupe, strawberry, apple, cantaloupe, peach.

Our encoding thus far would be 001, 11, 000, 001, 10. Table 10.2 shows the number of bits we can expect to use for the three hundred fruits. The total number of bits is 773, which is 2.577 times the number of fruits (300). (This differs from 2.576, the average path length, due to rounding the count to integer values.)

We can do better. Consider now the tree in figure 10.27. This tree is not balanced as the tree of figure 10.26 is, but if we calculate the weighted average path length, we find

$$(1 \cdot 72 + 2 \cdot 53 + 3 \cdot 30 + 4(13 + 9))/177 = 2.011.$$

Interpreting this again as an encoding for the fruits, we find cantaloupe represented by 1, cherry by 01, apple by 001, peach by 0001, and strawberry by 0000.

Figure 10.27   Weight-balanced tree for fruits

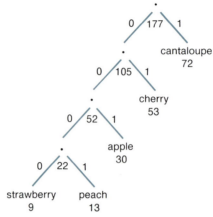

Table 10.3   Weight-balanced fruit encoding

Fruit	Frequency	Count in 300	Code	Bits
apple	30	51	001	153
cantaloupe	72	122	1	122
cherry	53	90	01	180
peach	13	22	0001	88
strawberry	9	15	0000	60

Observe that the most frequently occurring fruit (cantaloupe) has the shortest code and the least frequent fruit (strawberry) has the longest code. While these codes are of different lengths, the weighted average length, 2.011, is less than what we had with the balanced binary tree. It is, in fact, a minimal average length encoding for these fruits when they occur with the given frequencies. Table 10.3 shows the bit count for three hundred fruits. The total number of bits is 603, which is 2.010 times the number of fruits (300).

How can we build such a tree? Intuitively, it would seem best to place the most frequent words (fruits) nearest the root of the tree, so that they would be represented by the shortest codes. We can do this by building the tree from the least frequent words toward the most frequent. In our example, peach and strawberry have the lowest frequencies. They can be combined into a subtree of total weight (frequency) 22 (fig. 10.28a). Now, the two lowest weights are those for this subtree (22) and for apple (30). Combine these into the next subtree (fig. 10.28b). Continuing in this way, we arrive at the tree of figure 10.27.

Figure 10.28   Construction of the weight-balanced tree

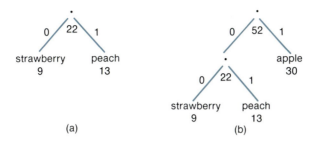

(a)   (b)

Figure 10.29   Construction of the meats tree

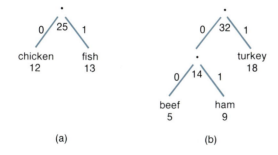

(a)   (b)

Here is another example. Suppose that we want to encode these words, with the given frequencies:

beef	5
chicken	12
fish	13
ham	9
turkey	18

First, we combine beef and ham into a subtree with total weight 14. Then, selecting chicken and fish as the two with the least weight, we combine those into a subtree with total weight 25 (fig. 10.29a). Now the least total weights belong to the beef-ham subtree and turkey. We combine these into a subtree (fig. 10.29b), and finally combine this with the other subtree, resulting in the final tree (fig. 10.30).

Figure 10.30   The final meats tree

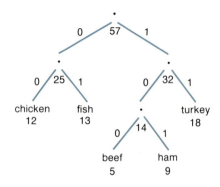

The resulting codes are

beef	100
chicken	00
fish	01
ham	101
turkey	11

The tree formed in this way is a **weight-balanced tree,** and the codes are called **Huffman codes.** In addition to having the minimum weighted average code length, they have another interesting property. Notice that no code is the initial fragment of any other one. This **unique prefix property** implies that a given string of bits will have only one decoding for a given set of codes. For example, the string

101100101110101101

can only be decoded as

ham, beef, ham, turkey, fish, fish, ham

using the meats coding. Of course, using the fruits coding, another interpretation will hold. The bad news is that this type of encoding is sensitive to transmission errors, with just one bad bit causing problems; the good news is that experiments show that it is self-correcting. For example, suppose that the fourth bit were mis-sent, resulting in the code string

101000101110101101.

The decoding for this would be

ham, chicken, fish, fish, turkey, fish, fish, ham.

The error has caused a mistake in the decoding: "beef, ham" has been decoded as "chicken, fish, fish." But within a few words the mistake has disappeared and the decoding is again correct.

Similarly, the loss or addition of a single bit does not affect the encoding for long. If the fourth bit were dropped rather than missent, the coding would be

10100101110101101.

This would decode to

ham, chicken, ham, turkey, fish, fish, ham.

Only one item has been affected.

One advantage we mentioned for tries is that the more frequent words tend to have shorter search paths. The Huffman code implements this advantage in a rigorous way. It can be shown without much difficulty that the minimum average binary code length for a given frequency distribution of words is achieved by the Huffman coding. That is, with a Huffman coding, the average code length is as small as possible. Hence this type of coding is very important in communications, where the number of data passing over the lines must be minimized. The fact that the code tends to be self-correcting means that it can be used directly in situations where there is not much line noise (errors). If quite a bit of noise is expected in transmission or if it is important to detect and correct any errors, then more sophisticated error-correcting codes can be used. Because these codes involve sending redundant information, a price is paid in the efficiency of transmission.

10.8 B-trees

Compared to accessing data within main memory, access to data on secondary storage, such as disk or tape, takes a very long time. Hence it is important for efficient use of a computer to make such access as fruitful as possible. If we need to locate a datum on disk, for example, we would like to do so with the fewest possible number of accesses. This implies that we should try to bring as many data as possible into main memory with each disk access and that we should try to organize the data on disk so that we can quickly locate the portion of secondary memory that holds the desired datum.

A tree is a good structure for locating data on disk. However, a binary tree is not really the best kind. Consider this. At each node in a binary tree we can choose one of two "halves." Recalling that twenty questions allow us to identify over a million different items, we see that we can locate any one byte on a twenty megabyte disk with twenty-five questions. However, each question might mean a separate disk access.

Suppose that we could decide among ten alternatives with each question rather than two. Then two questions would identify one hundred different items, six questions would identify one million, and only eight questions would be needed to identify each byte on a twenty megabyte disk. Clearly, the more alternatives we can identify with each question, the fewer questions, and hence the fewer potential disk accesses, we need.

This suggests that a good tree to use for locating data on secondary storage would be one with a high branching factor. One type of tree with this property is called a B-tree. A **B-tree of order m** is defined in this way:

1. each node other than the leaves and the root has between $\lceil m/2 \rceil$ and m children;

2. the root has at least two and at most m children;

3. all branches (to leaves) are the same length;

4. all leaves are empty, indicating a search failure.

In a B-tree of order m, the root and the internal nodes contain index keys that indicate which branch should be followed to locate a particular value. Since there are at most m children, there are at most $m - 1$ index keys.

We follow the same type of search pattern for a B-tree that we do for a binary tree. If we match a key, then the information for that key (or at least a pointer to it) can be found at that node. If the given key does not match any at the node, then its branch is found by determining whether it is larger or smaller than each of the keys in the node. If the key is not present in the B-tree, then ultimately we try to follow a branch that ends in an empty leaf.

A B-tree is constructed by beginning at the bottom level (nearest the leaves) and adding index keys successively to an internal node. When the number of index keys reaches m, the internal node is split in two (hence the $\lceil m/2 \rceil$) and another level of internal node is created. Here is an example.

Suppose that we wish to construct a B-tree of order 5 and that these data serve as index keys:

520, 760, 771, 589, 267, 799, 191, 302, 953, 580, 827, 479, 913, 161, 49, 947, 984, 936, 696, 358, 738, 512, 935, 198, 910, 728, 879, 991, 823, 200, 303, 664, 375, 690, 836.

Figure 10.31   First stage in a B-tree

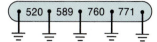

Figure 10.32   First split in the B-tree

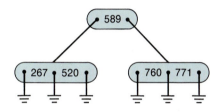

Figure 10.33   Second split in the B-tree

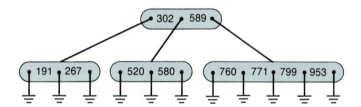

We may have up to four index keys in an internal node or the root, so the first root node contains the first four index keys in numerical order (fig. 10.31). In this figure we introduce the electrical ground symbol to denote an empty node. If we were to search this tree (with its one internal node), then we would be able to match any of the four given search keys, but any other key would lead to an empty leaf. For example, we would match the key 589, but the key 600 would lead to the third empty node. Similarly, the key 267 would lead to the first empty node.

Continuing the construction, the fifth value, 267, causes a split in the root node. A new root is created, containing the index key 589, with the remaining index keys split evenly between two internal nodes (fig. 10.32).

The next four values are added as index keys in the two internal nodes. Then the value 580 causes the left internal node to split, with the value 302 moving into the root node (fig. 10.33).

Figure 10.34   Location of keys 520 and 780

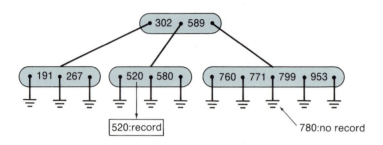

Figure 10.35   The B-tree with 22 index keys

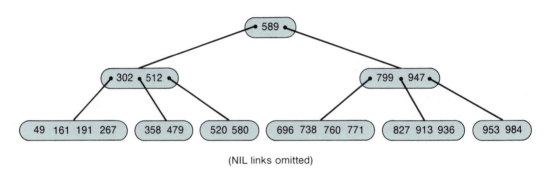

(NIL links omitted)

At this point, let us pause to examine the B-tree again. Nine different keys are represented. This means that the information associated with any of them is represented in the tree. For example, since 520 is in the second node at level 1, the information whose key is 520 either is directly in that node or can be found from a pointer in that node (fig. 10.34). Since the key 780 is not in the tree, searching for it will lead to an empty leaf.

This process continues. The next value to be inserted, 827, causes the right-most internal node to split, with 799 moving to the root. After a total of twenty-two index keys have been entered, the tree is that shown in figure 10.35. While a B-tree of any order can be defined, because of the way that the splitting is done, odd order B-trees are generally preferred.

To see how B-trees affect disk access, consider a B-tree of order 257 or $2^8 + 1$. To examine any one node we must be able to handle 256 index keys within main memory. This is well within the buffer capacity of large modern computers. Then just four disk accesses will allow us to identify $256^4 = 2^{32}$ locations on disk. This is larger than 2^{30}, which in turn is larger than 10^9—a value in the range of the number of bytes on the largest disks available today. Since a datum will almost always consist of more than one byte, a B-tree of this order is sufficient to allow us to access any specific datum on a disk in at most four attempts.

Perhaps on the theory that any good idea can be improved, a number of variants of B-trees have occurred in computing. The most important of these are the **B*-tree** and the **B+-tree.** The basic B-tree definition splits an internal node into two whenever it becomes full, thus assuring that these nodes are at least 1/2 full. The B*-tree employs a different splitting algorithm, which waits until two sibling nodes are full and then splits them into three. This assures that the internal nodes are at least 2/3 full. The advantages are better storage utilization and shorter search times, since the height of the resulting tree will generally be less.

The B+-tree is distinguished by the fact that all data reside at the leaves, whereas in an ordinary B-tree, data can occur at internal nodes. This permits sequential linking of the data in the leaves, providing additional search and access methods. The B+-tree is the basis of IBM's VSAM file access method. A thorough discussion of B-trees and their variations is given by Comer (1979).

Summary

Hierarchical organizations of information in human affairs arise so frequently that the tree is an essential data structure. In this chapter we have presented the principal facts and concepts that relate to trees as used in computer science. A clear understanding of binary trees in their various roles is important to searching and sorting work. B-trees, with their large branching factors, can significantly affect the storage and retrieval of information in disk files.

Vocabulary

ancestor	left balanced tree
AVL tree	left child
B-tree of order m	length
B*-tree	level
B+-tree	level order traversal
balanced tree	node
binary search tree	parent
binary tree	parse tree
branch	postorder traversal
branching factor	preorder traversal
chain	right child
child	root
descendant	rooted tree
empty tree	sibling
graph theory	subtree
height	terminal node
height-balanced tree	tree
Huffman code	trie
inorder traversal	unique prefix property
interior node	weight-balanced tree
leaf	

References

Adel'son-Velskii, G. M., & Landis, Y. M. An algorithm for the organization of information. *Dokl. Akad. Nauk SSSR,* **146,** 1962, 263–266. English translation in *Soviet Math. Dokl.,* **3,** 1962, 1259–1262.

Comer, Douglas. "The Ubiquitous B-Tree." *ACM Computing Surveys* **11,** 2 (June 1979): 121–137.

Foster, C. C. "A Generalization of AVL Trees." *Communications of the ACM* **16,** 8 (August 1973): 513–517.

Standish, Thomas A. *Data Structure Techniques.* Addison-Wesley, Reading, Mass., 1980.

Tenenbaum, Aaron M. and Augenstein, Moshe J. *Data Structures Using Pascal.* Prentice-Hall, Englewood Cliffs, N.J. 1981.

Wirth, Niklaus. *Algorithms + Data Structures = Programs.* Prentice-Hall, Englewood Cliffs, N.J. 1976.

Problems

10.1. Instead of thinking of the links in a tree as being from parent to children, we can think of the links as being to the eldest child, then from the eldest child to the next younger sibling (see fig. 10.5). Using these relationships, define an ADT for a general tree.

10.2. Show that the number of disk accesses for a B-tree of order m containing n keys is $O(\log_m n)$. From this one might argue that the time required to search a B-tree of order m is $O(\log_m n)$. Show, however, that it is more accurate to say that the search time is $O(\lg n)$. Hint: This is not just "constant fiddling," based on the fact that the two logarithms differ by a multiplicative constant. It is based instead on the fact that each internal node must be searched to locate the correct key after the node has been retrieved from secondary storage.

10.3. Do a level order, inorder, preorder, and postorder traversal of the trees in figures 10.21*a,* 10.21*b,* and 10.26.

Programs

For Programs 10.1 through 10.4, assume that the data structure for the binary tree is a record with one field for data and three fields for pointers to the parent node, left child, and right child.

10.1. Write a procedure for level order traversal of a binary tree, printing out each data element as it is encountered. Note in figure 10.11 the tree is stored as an array, not linked.

10.2. Complete the function for a binary search tree (fig. 10.19) to add a given node at the proper place in the binary search tree when it is not present. Further, instead of returning NIL as the value of the function it should now return a pointer to the new location.

10.3. Write a procedure to left balance an arbitrary binary tree.

10.4. Write a procedure to determine whether a given binary tree is an AVL tree.

10.5. Write a procedure to generate a trie for a list of up to ten words, each of no more than eight letters.

10.6. Write a procedure to generate a weight-balanced (Huffman) tree for a list of up to fifteen input data, given together with their frequencies.

Projects

10.1. Even if a binary tree is not balanced, we can store it sequentially as though it were a left balanced binary tree. The only requirement is that we have some way of recognizing the nodes that are empty. Assuming this sequential storage representation, provide an implementation for the ADT binary tree.

10.2. Assume that each node of a binary tree is represented as a record containing the data together with pointers to the parent, left child, and right child. Provide an implementation for the ADT binary tree.

10.3. Suppose that the node representation of a binary tree is as in project 10.2, except that only the eldest (leftmost) children have pointers to their parents. Instead of these pointers, all other children have pointers to their next-eldest sibling. Provide an implementation for the ADT binary tree.

10.4. Assume that each node of a binary tree is represented as a record containing the data together with pointers to the left and right children of the node and to the root of the tree. Provide an implementation for the ADT binary tree.

10.5. Implement the general tree ADT defined in problem 10.1.

10.6. Write an ADT for AVL trees by extending the given binary tree ADT. Then, using either the sequential or the linked list implementation (see projects 10.1, 10.2), implement a procedure to rebalance an AVL tree when a new node is added. Input to your procedure should be the tree with the new node added and some means of identifying the new node, such as a pointer to it.

10.7. Develop an ADT for B-trees, and give an implementation of this.

11

Basic Sorting Techniques

Introduction

The opportunities for increased efficiency in handling data become significant if we have the data sorted into some specific order rather than unordered as in the previous chapters. This is evident if we consider a data collection such as the dictionary or the telephone directory: to locate a word or name in either of these would be exceedingly difficult, were they not sorted into alphabetical order. In this chapter we consider methods of sorting sequentially stored data and the effect sorting has on operations on that data. Obviously, some work is involved in sorting the set; but if the set is reasonably stable, without excessive addition and deletion of elements, we often save enough effort on other operations to more than make up for the effort required to sort the set.

The distinguishing characteristic for the sets that we consider in this chapter is that they are generally sorted in **ascending** or **increasing order.** That is, for numerical data, we shall assume that the first element of the set is the smallest numerically, with each succeeding element larger than its predecessor. For alphabetic data, the first element of the set is the first one alphabetically, with each succeeding element following its predecessor in alphabetic or dictionary order. The assumption of ascending order is not significant. Exactly the same principles apply for sets in **descending** or **decreasing order.**

(In computing, special characters such as hyphens, apostrophes, or punctuation marks are ordered according to the EBCDIC or ASCII encoding that is used. Outside of computing, these characters are frequently handled inconsistently. See, for example, the beginning of the "D" section in the business pages of a large telephone directory. Probably there will be no consistency in the occurrence of spaces, hyphens, and other special symbols in the listings.)

This characteristic provides us with a common assertion that we shall see occurring in one form or another in each of our procedures, namely, that the procedure does not destroy any sorting that has taken place. While it is not necessary that a sorting procedure have this property, many of the simplest and most efficient ones do.

11.1 Insertion sorting

Creation of a sorted set can take place in two ways. We can sort the set as we create it, or we can create the set in an unordered manner and then worry about sorting it. We shall consider the former method first. Sorting a set while we create it can be done basically in two ways, insertion and placement. Placement sorting will be considered in section 11.2.

The concept of an **insertion sort** is simple: find where, among an already sorted set of elements, the new element should be; make room for it, and place it there. This is the type of sorting that people commonly do while rearranging a bridge hand. The player will look at each card and decide where it should be inserted among those already in order.

As an example, consider the set {t, i, f, v, o, l, u}, given in that order. Suppose that we want this set sorted in alphabetical order. An insertion sort is shown in figure 11.1, where the sorted elements are on the left and the unsorted on the right. The underlined character is the one being inserted.

The key difficulty here is making room for the new element. We cannot simply lift up the element that we find where the new one should be and place it at the end of the set: this would destroy the property that the set is sorted. Instead, we must move all elements above the new one to the right one space, to make room for the new one.

How do we find where the new one belongs? An obvious way is to start at one end of the set, say the front, and search until we find the proper location. If the set is in ascending order, this means traversing the set until we come upon an element that is larger than the new one. The new one should go just before that larger element. This is called a **linear insertion sort.**

The sad thing about this technique is that it is a sequential search, just like what we have used with an unordered set: we have made no use of the fact that the part of the set we already have is sorted. Consider, for example, the data set

{38, 37, 04, 47, 50, 90, 95, 76, 85, 22, 16, 87, 07, 30, 69, 12}.

If we apply a linear insertion sort to this set as we create it, we find the following process:

We simply place the first number, 38, in the set. There is nothing with which to compare it and nothing to move out of the way.

We compare the second number, 37, with the first number and find that the new number is smaller. Hence we move the first number to the right one position and add the second number to the set, resulting in {37, 38}. We have made one comparison and one move.

Comparing the third number, 04, with the leading number in the set, 37, we find that the new number is smaller. Hence it should be the leading number in the set. We move 38 one position and then 37, making room for 04. This combination of one comparison and two moves results in {04, 37, 38}.

Figure 11.1   Insertion sort example

$$\underline{t} \; i \, f \, v \, o \, l \, u$$

$$\underline{i} \, t \; f \, v \, o \, l \, u$$

$$\underline{f} \, i \, t \; v \, o \, l \, u$$

$$f \, i \, t \, \underline{v} \; o \, l \, u$$

$$f \, i \, \underline{o} \, t \, v \; l \, u$$

$$f \, i \, \underline{l} \, o \, t \, v \; u$$

$$f \, i \, l \, o \, t \, \underline{u} \, v$$

Table 11.1   Linear insertion

	Number of Comparisons	Number of Moves
38	0	0
37	1	1
04	1	2
47	3	0
50	4	0
90	5	0
95	6	0
76	6	2
85	7	2
22	2	8
16	2	9
87	10	2
07	2	11
30	5	9
69	10	5
12	3	13

We find that the fourth number, 47, is larger than 04, 37, and 38. Hence it goes at the end of the set, resulting in {04, 37, 38, 47}. This has required three comparisons, but we have not had to move any element to a new location.

When we carry out this process for the entire set, the numbers of comparisons and moves that occur are those given in table 11.1. We can make use of the information that the set is partially sorted by performing a **binary insertion sort.** The idea is to use a binary search rather than a sequential search to locate the position for inserting the next element into the set. Suppose that when we want to insert the new element into the set we already have k elements of the set properly sorted into ascending order. What can we say about element number $\lceil k/2 \rceil$ in the order, in the middle of the set? If k is odd this element is the middle one

Table 11.2	Binary insertion	
	Number of Comparisons	Number of Moves
38	0	0
37	1	1
04	1	2
47	2	0
50	3	0
90	3	0
95	3	0
76	3	2
85	3	2
22	3	8
16	3	9
87	3	2
07	4	11
30	4	9
69	4	5
12	4	13

in the set. If k is even, the element chosen is consistently the rightmost element in the first half of the set. Because the elements we have already placed in the set are sorted, if this middle element is larger than the new element, we know that the new element is in the first half of the set; if it is smaller, we know that the new element is in the second half of the set. *In either case,* we have eliminated one-half of the set with just one comparison. Now we can repeat the process on the other half of the set. Applying this technique to our example set, we find the values given in table 11.2.

In creating the sorted set, we have compared each new element to several of those already present. For linear insertion, the comparison began with the smallest element already present and proceeded through the set until we either came to the end or found a larger one. For binary insertion, we started the comparison at the middle each time, and then worked only in the smaller or larger half of the set. For example, to insert 85 into the set, we considered the sorted partial set

{04, 37, 38, 47, 50, 76, 90, 95}.

Splitting this in half, we compared 85 first with 47, the last element in the bottom half. (We could just as well have chosen to compare it with 50, the first element in the top half, just as long as we choose consistently.) Since 85 is larger, we use the top half of the set, split that, and compare 85 with 76. Once again, 85 is larger, so we use the top half, now {90, 95}, and compare 85 with 90. At this point we know where 85 belongs.

Comparing linear and binary insertion for even this small set, we can make four observations. First, there are no long comparison sequences for binary insertion. Second, the average number of comparisons is less for binary insertion than it is for linear insertion. Referring to the data in the two tables, we see sorting our sample set required an average of 4.1875 comparisons for each new element when we used linear insertion, but only an average of 2.75 comparisons when we used binary insertion. (This comparison is much more striking for very large sets.) Third, even though on the average there are fewer comparisons in a binary insertion than in a linear one, there are individual exceptions to that. For example, the binary insertion requires four comparisons to locate 07 properly (table 11.2), whereas the linear insertion requires only two comparisons. Fourth, we observe that for either method the number of data movements is the same.

What if the new element has the same value as the middle element in the set? Then we have two choices. If we really want a set, then the new element is already there and does not need to be added again. However, if we want a multiset, then we can place the new element either above or below the middle element, as suits us. In either case, we do not need to search further to find where it belongs.

The key to the savings in binary insertion is the fact that each cycle divides in half the number of elements among which the new element can be placed. With a set of 1024 elements, dividing the set in half just ten times will establish the proper place for the new element. We can determine this because $\lg(1024)$ = 10. The first division creates sets of half the original size (512 elements), the second creates sets of one-fourth the size (256 elements), the third creates sets of one-eighth the size (128 elements), and so forth, so that by the tenth division we have sets of size 1. On average, sequentially searching a set of this size to locate the place for the new element would involve 512 (that is, $n/2$) comparisons. Thus we have quite a savings.

Figure 11.2 shows the skeleton of a binary insertion sort procedure. We assume that ElementType has been defined in the main program and that SetType has been defined as ARRAY[1..MaxSize] OF ElementType, where MaxSize is larger than the value of SetSize.

BinaryInsert includes a procedure Search that is rather lengthy because we need to determine exactly where the new item should be inserted into the set. It is presented in figure 11.3, with figure 11.4 showing the full BinaryInsert procedure.

We call attention to two points about the Search procedure. First, a substantial portion of the work involves determining exactly where to place the new element. If we had only to confirm the presence or absence of the new element, the search code would be much shorter. Second, observe that in the parameter list for Search, FullSet is declared as a VAR parameter, even though we never alter its values. It is a common practice in Pascal to pass all ARRAY parameters as VAR because this saves both the time and space required to make a copy of the array if it were passed as a value (non-VAR) parameter.

Figure 11.2   Skeleton for binary insertion sort

```
CONST
  MaxSize = UserSuppliedMaximumSize;

TYPE
  ElementType = UserSuppliedType;
  SetType     = ARRAY[1..MaxSize] OF ElementType;

PROCEDURE BinaryInsert (Element        : ElementType;
                        VAR SortedSet  : SetType;
                        SetSize        : integer);

{ A procedure to produce a sorted set by binary insertion. }

  VAR
    GotIt : boolean;

  PROCEDURE Search;

  { Subprocedure to perform the search. }

  { Search by comparing the element to the middle element
  of the set, discarding half the set, and comparing again.
  Return Found/not Found, and location if Found. }

    BEGIN
    END; { Search }

  BEGIN

  { Search for the element in the set. }

    Search;
    IF NOT GotIt THEN

      { Assert: The element is not there. }

      { Move top part of set out of way, insert the new
      element, and adjust set size. }

      BEGIN
      END
  END; { BinaryInsert }
```

Figure 11.3, Part 1   Binary search procedure

```
CONST
  MaxSize = UserSuppliedMaximumSize;

TYPE
  ElementType = UserSuppliedType;
  SetType     = ARRAY[1..MaxSize] OF ElementType;

PROCEDURE Search (Low, High      : integer;
                  SearchElement : ElementType;
                  VAR FullSet    : SetType;
                  VAR Found      : boolean;
                  VAR Where      : integer);

{ Subprocedure to perform the search. }

{ Search by comparing the element to the middle element of the set,
discarding half the set, and comparing again. Return Found/not
Found, and location (Where) if Found. }

  VAR
    LookAt : 1..MaxSize;

  BEGIN

    { Assert: High >= Low }

    IF High > Low THEN
      BEGIN
        LookAt := (High + Low) DIV 2;

        { Assert: Low <= LookAt < High }

        IF SearchElement < FullSet[LookAt] THEN
          Search (Low, LookAt, SearchElement, FullSet, Found, Where)
        ELSE
          IF SearchElement > FullSet[LookAt] THEN
            IF LookAt > Low THEN
              Search (LookAt, High, SearchElement, FullSet, Found,
                      Where)
          ELSE

              { Assert: LookAt = Low }

              { Assert: High = Low + 1 }
```

Figure 11.3, Part 2   Binary search procedure

```
            IF SearchElement < FullSet[High] THEN
              BEGIN
                Found := false;
                Where := High
              END
            ELSE

              IF SearchElement = FullSet[High] THEN
                BEGIN
                  Found := true;
                  Where := High
                END
              ELSE

                { Assert: SearchElement > FullSet[High] }

                BEGIN
                  Found := false;
                  Where := High + 1
                END
        ELSE

          { Assert: SearchElement = FullSet[LookAt] }

          BEGIN
            Found := true;
            Where := LookAt
          END
    END
ELSE

  { Assert: High = Low }

  IF SearchElement = FullSet[Low] THEN
    BEGIN
      Found := true;
      Where := Low
    END
  ELSE

    { Assert: SearchElement has not been found. }
```

Figure 11.3, Part 3   Binary search procedure

```
      { In this case, set Where to the number of the element that
      should follow SearchElement in the array. }

      IF SearchElement < FullSet[Low] THEN
        BEGIN
          Found := false;
          Where := Low
        END
      ELSE

        { Assert: SearchElement > FullSet[Low] }

        BEGIN
          Found := false;
          Where := Low + 1
        END
END; { Search }
```

Figure 11.4, Part 1   Binary insertion sort

```
CONST
  MaxSize = UserSuppliedMaximumSize;

TYPE
  ElementType = UserSuppliedType;
  SetType     = ARRAY[1..MaxSize] OF ElementType;

PROCEDURE BinaryInsert (Element      : ElementType;
                        VAR SortedSet : SetType;
                        VAR SetSize   : integer);

{ A procedure to produce a sorted set by binary insertion. }

  VAR
    GotIt    : boolean;
    I        : 1..MaxSize;
    Location : integer;
```

Figure 11.4, Part 2   Binary insertion sort

```
PROCEDURE Search;

{ See fig. 11.3. }

{ Main procedure }

BEGIN
  IF SetSize = 0 THEN
    BEGIN

      { Assert: SortedSet is empty so add the element. }

      SortedSet[1] := Element;
      SetSize := SetSize + 1
    END
  ELSE
    BEGIN

      { Assert: SetSize < Top. }

      { Search for the element in the set. }

      Search (1, SetSize, Element, SortedSet, GotIt, Location);
      IF NOT GotIt THEN

        { Assert: The element is not there. }

        { Assert: SortedSet[1]..SortedSet[Location - 1] is sorted. }

        { Move top part of set out of way, insert new element, and
        adjust set size. }

        BEGIN
          FOR I := SetSize DOWNTO Location DO
            SortedSet[I + 1] := SortedSet[I];
          SortedSet[Location] := Element;
          SetSize := SetSize + 1
        END

        { Assert: SortedSet[1]..SortedSet[SetSize] is sorted. }

    END
END; { BinaryInsert }
```

As we expected, creating or building a sorted set requires more work than building an unsorted set. The effort of locating the position of each individual element is proportional to the logarithm of the set size. To see this, suppose that the number of comparisons to locate an element in a set of size 2^k is E, and suppose that we must now locate an element in a set of size 2^{k+1}, a set twice as large. The first probe into this set divides it into two sets of size 2^k, and we can immediately discard one of these two sets as not containing the given element. Thus in one step we have reduced our problem to one of finding the element in a set of size 2^k, which requires E comparisons. Hence the total number of comparisons to locate this element is $E+1$. Since one comparison is sufficient to locate an element in a set of size 1, a simple table shows that the effort is logarithmic as stated:

Set Size	Comparisons
1	1
2	2
4	3
8	4
16	5
32	6

Since we must do this for all n elements, the binary insertion sort requires $O(n \lg n)$ comparisons to locate the positions for all the elements to be inserted. However, we must also move elements out of the way whenever we insert a new element, and this process is an $O(n^2)$ one. When inserting the $(k+1)^{st}$ element, we can expect to move $k/2$ elements out of the way on the average. Thus the total number of element movements is $(1+2+...+n)/2 = n(n+1)/4$. This is $O(n^2)$. Note that in the worst case we would need to move each of the k elements out of the way, which is also an $O(n^2)$ process. In summary, for both the average and the worst case, binary insertion sort is an $O(n^2)$ process, since the data movements dominate over the data location effort.

In discussing the creation of a set by binary insertion, we have introduced a new method to traverse and search a set: binary splitting of the set. This traversal is always of order $\lg n$ for a set of n elements. The repeated splitting is the inverse of the operation of doubling. In asking how many times we need to split a set to get down to single-element pieces, we are asking what is the smallest power, k, of 2 such that 2^k is at least as large as n. That is, $k = \lceil \lg n \rceil$. Thus each time we use it, binary traversal is an order $\lg n$ process. The ability to use this type of process depends on having the set sorted, so that we know whether to look next in the right or left half, and sequentially stored, so that we know where to find the middle element of the set.

Figure 11.5   Placement sort example

```
t i f v o l u

        t

    i   t

  f i   t

  f i   t v

  f i  o t v

  f i l o t  v

  f i l o t u v
```

11.2 Placement sorting

The other method of sorting a set as we create it is a **placement sort.** This sort is useful if we know the size of the set being sorted and something about its elements, or at least an upper bound on the set size. In a computer, the placement sort frequently takes the form of a **bit map.**

Placement sorts may be used in special situations, when we know enough about each of the elements to decide immediately where it belongs without comparing it to other elements. The host or hostess at a dinner party generally thinks along these lines. Rather than picking some arbitrary seating arrangement for the guests and then rearranging it until the result is pleasing, he or she will consider each guest in turn and decide where the guest should sit. Figure 11.5 shows this process on our example set.

Suppose that we know that any set we encounter comes from a universal set of n elements. We can achieve a very compact representation of a set by allocating one bit to each element of the universal set, in a specified order. In the example we used for insertion sorts, the elements were positive integers, with the largest being 95. Suppose that our universal set consists of the integers $\{1, 2, . . . , 96\}$. We can allocate a string of ninety-six bits to represent this universal set, with the first bit representing "1," the second bit representing "2," and so forth. Then, as each element is added to the set, we simply make its bit in the representation to be "1" or "true." This method of creating a set requires a constant amount of work for each element—calculating its position. Hence it is an $O(n)$ set creation method. But it requires that we reserve a bit for each element of the universal set, whether or not that element is in the actual set being used, that we be able to manipulate the individual bits easily, and that we remember which bit represents each set element. Figure 11.6 is a procedure for creating a sorted set using this technique. We assume that BitArray has been defined as ARRAY[1..MaxSize] OF boolean. By defining Index and SetElement as subrange variables, we guarantee that the assertion will be checked automatically.

Figure 11.6   Bit map formation

```
CONST
  Marker  = 0;
  MaxSize = UserSuppliedSize;

TYPE
  BaseType    = 0..MaxSize;
  ElementType = 1..MaxSize;
  BitArray    = ARRAY[ElementType] OF boolean;

PROCEDURE GetElement (VAR NextElement : BaseType);

  BEGIN
    writeln ('Input the next element or the end of ',
             'set marker  ', Marker);
    readln (NextElement)
  END; { GetElement }

PROCEDURE BitSet (VAR NewSet : BitArray);

{ This procedure creates a bit map for a given set
of at most MaxSize integers. }

  VAR
    Index      : ElementType;
    SetElement : BaseType;

  BEGIN
    FOR Index := 1 TO MaxSize DO
    NewSet[Index] := false;

    { Procedure GetElement gets the next element
    of the set. }

    GetElement (SetElement);

    { Assert: 1 <= SetElement <= MaxSize }

    WHILE SetElement <> Marker DO
      BEGIN
        NewSet[SetElement] := true;
        GetElement (SetElement)
      END
  END; { BitSet }
```

Another placement sort is the **bin sort.** This requires fewer cells than does bit set formation, but each cell must hold a full data element rather than just a single bit. Hence the total storage required may be as much or more than that required by the bit set.

For a bin sort, we allocate a fixed number of bins and then place each set element in the appropriate bin. For example, let us consider the same set that we used earlier,

{38, 37, 04, 47, 50, 90, 95, 76, 85, 22, 16, 87, 07, 30, 69, 12},

and sort this into ten bins. The bins will be chosen to hold the numbers 00–09, 10–19, 20–29, and so forth. In our diagram of the result, the top of each bin is at the bottom of the picture:

04	16	22	38	47	50	69	76	85	90
07	12		37					87	95
			30						

Since we started with more than ten numbers and only ten bins, we could have asserted that at least one bin will hold more than one number. As we see, four bins hold two numbers, and one holds three. The numbers in these bins are not sorted into order, but there are only a few of them per bin, so it is easy to sort them correctly:

04	12	22	30	47	50	69	76	85	90
07	16		37					87	95
			38						

A full program for bin sorting is given in figure 11.7. This program contains user-defined constants BinSize, MaxValues, and NumberOfBins to specify the number of elements that can be held in a single bin, the maximum number of values to be used, and the number of available bins, respectively. The main program displays these numbers and initializes the bins to empty. It then reads in 100 values, places them into the appropriate bins, and sorts out the values within each bin. Finally, the program displays the results. The key procedures are InitializeBins, InsertInBin, and SortBin.

Figure 11.7, Part 1   Bin sorting

```
PROGRAM BinSort (input, output);

CONST
  BinSize      = UserSuppliedSize;
  MaxValues    = UserSuppliedValue;
  NumberOfBins = UserSuppliedNumber;

TYPE
  ElementType  = integer;
  Bin          = ARRAY[1..BinSize] OF ElementType;
  BinRange     = 1..NumberOfBins;
  BinArray     = ARRAY[BinRange] OF Bin;
  BinSizeRange = 0..BinSize;
  PointerToBin = ARRAY[BinRange] OF BinSizeRange;

VAR
  BinMarker : PointerToBin;
  BinPlace  : BinSizeRange;
  Bins      : BinArray;
  Count     : 0..MaxValues;
  Element   : ARRAY[1..MaxValues] OF ElementType;
  Index     : 1..MaxValues;

FUNCTION BinNumber (Key : ElementType) : BinRange;

{ This function determines in which bin a Key should be placed. The
computation is dependent on the number of bins. }

  BEGIN
    BinNumber := (Key DIV (100 DIV NumberOfBins)) + 1
  END; { BinNumber }

PROCEDURE InitializeBins (VAR BinPointer : PointerToBin);

{ This procedure initializes all the bin pointers to zero, which
empties all bins. }

  VAR
    Index : BinRange;

  BEGIN
    FOR Index := 1 TO NumberOfBins DO
      BinPointer[Index] := 0
  END; { InitializeBins }
```

Figure 11.7, Part 2   Bin sorting

```
PROCEDURE InsertInBin (Key             : ElementType;
                       VAR TheBin    : BinArray;
                       VAR BinPointer : PointerToBin);

{ This procedure places a Key in its appropriate bin and updates the
correct bin pointer to reflect the current size of the bin. }

   VAR
      SelectedBin : BinRange;

   BEGIN
      SelectedBin := BinNumber (Key);
      BinPointer[SelectedBin] := BinPointer[SelectedBin] + 1;
      TheBin[SelectedBin, BinPointer[SelectedBin]] := Key
   END; { InsertInBin }

PROCEDURE SortBin (VAR TheBin : Bin; BinSize : BinSizeRange);

{ A simple selection sort (see section 11.4) to sort out the
contents of the given bin. }

   VAR
      I          : BinSizeRange;
      J          : BinSizeRange;
      LowPlace   : BinSizeRange;
      Temporary  : ElementType;

   BEGIN
      FOR I := 1 TO BinSize - 1 DO
        BEGIN
          LowPlace := I;
          FOR J := I + 1 TO BinSize DO
            IF TheBin[LowPlace] > TheBin[J] THEN LowPlace := J;
          Temporary := TheBin[LowPlace];
          TheBin[LowPlace] := TheBin[I];
          TheBin[I] := Temporary
        END
   END; { SortBin }


PROCEDURE DisplayBin (VAR TheBins : BinArray;
                      BinPointer  : PointerToBin);

{ This procedure displays the bins. The idea is to display cross
sections of bins by asking if the element lies within the cross-
section layer (LineNumber) and either printing it out or displaying
an appropriate number of spaces. }
```

Figure 11.7, Part 3   Bin sorting

```
CONST
  FourSpaces = '    ';

VAR
  Index       : BinRange;
  LineNumber  : 1..BinSize;
  MaxBinSize  : 1..BinSize;

BEGIN

  { Display the header banner. }

  FOR Index := 1 TO NumberOfBins DO
    write (' Bin');
  writeln;
  FOR Index := 1 TO NumberOfBins DO
    write (Index : 4);
  writeln;
  FOR Index := 1 TO NumberOfBins DO
    write (' ---');
  writeln;

  { Determine the depth of the largest bin. }

  MaxBinSize := BinPointer[1];
  FOR Index := 2 TO NumberOfBins DO
    IF BinPointer[Index] > MaxBinSize THEN
      MaxBinSize := BinPointer[Index];

  { Display the bins. }

  FOR LineNumber := 1 TO MaxBinSize DO
    BEGIN
      FOR Index := 1 TO NumberOfBins DO
        BEGIN
          IF BinPointer[Index] >= LineNumber THEN
            write (TheBins[Index, LineNumber] : 4)
          ELSE
            write (FourSpaces)
        END;
      writeln
    END
END; { DisplayBin }
```

Figure 11.7, Part 4   Bin sorting

```
BEGIN { Main program }
  writeln ('Bin Size is ', BinSize : 3);
  writeln ('The Number of Bins is ', NumberOfBins : 3);
  writeln;
  InitializeBins (BinMarker);
  writeln;

  { Read and write 100 Key values, and insert them into the bins. }

  writeln ('Key Values' : 50);
  writeln;
  FOR Index := 1 TO 100 DO
    BEGIN
      read (Element[Index]);
      InsertInBin (Element[Index], Bins, BinMarker);
      write (Element[Index] : 4);
      IF Index MOD 20 = 0 THEN writeln
    END;

  { Display the bins. }

  writeln;
  writeln;
  DisplayBin (Bins, BinMarker);

  { Sort the bins and display them. }

  FOR Index := 1 TO NumberOfBins DO
    SortBin (Bins[Index], BinMarker[Index]);
  writeln;
  writeln;
  DisplayBin (Bins, BinMarker);

  { Display the sorted keys. }

  writeln;
  writeln ('Sorted Keys' : 50);
  writeln;
  Count := 0;
  FOR Index := 1 TO NumberOfBins DO
    BEGIN
      FOR BinPlace := 1 TO BinMarker[Index] DO
        BEGIN
          Count := Count + 1;
          write (Bins[Index, BinPlace] : 4);
          IF Count MOD 20 = 0 THEN writeln
        END
    END
END. { BinSort }
```

Figure 11.8 **Decision tree for sorting $\{A, B, C\}$**

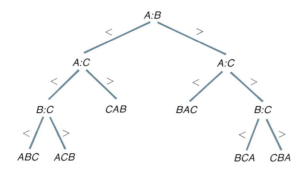

11.3 Lower bound on comparison sorting

Insertion and placement sorts are oriented toward the concept of sorting a set as we create it. We also have the option of creating the set in an unordered manner and then sorting it. This opens up the possibility of using other types of sorting techniques, which we now discuss. All the sorting techniques we discuss rely on a comparison of set elements, except the placement sorts.

We can show that any sort involving element comparison must be at least of order $n \lg n$. We observe first that a set of n elements can be arranged in $n! = n(n-1)(n-2) \ldots 2 \cdot 1$ possible orders. Any sorting process that involves comparison basically determines which of these $n!$ arrangements the set is in and replaces it by the sorted arrangement. If we consider a **decision tree** that shows the comparisons between pairs of elements, then each of the possible arrangements corresponds to the end of a path in the tree. For example, figure 11.8 shows such a tree for the set $\{A, B, C\}$.

Observe now that if we number the levels in this decision tree starting at zero, then the number of arrangements that can be represented at level i is 2^i. In our example, we can represent $8 = 2^3$ arrangements at the third, or bottom, level; but since we have only 6 arrangements to represent, some of these are represented at the second level. Similarly, for a set of four elements, $\{A, B, C, D\}$, there are $4! = 24$ possible arrangements. A four level decision tree is not enough, since it can only represent 2^4 arrangements. However, a five level tree can represent $2^5 = 32$ arrangements, more than enough to handle all the arrangements for a set of four elements.

To say this another way, if we have k arrangements to represent, we then need a tree with at least $\lceil \lg k \rceil$ levels. Hence, starting with a set of n elements for which we have $n!$ possible arrangements, we need a decision tree with at least $\lceil \lg n! \rceil$ levels.

To gain a feeling for the size of this number, we need to know something about the size of $n!$. The classical approximation for the factorial is Stirling's approximation,

$$n! \approx \sqrt{2\pi n}\ (n/e)^n.$$

Thus the logarithm of $n!$ is approximated by

$$\lg(\sqrt{2\pi n}\,(n/e)^n) = \lg\sqrt{2\pi} + \frac{1}{2}\lg n + n\lg n - n\lg e.$$

The third term, $n\lg n$, dominates this expression, establishing a **lower bound** for any sort involving comparisons.

We may also work from the definition

$$n! = n(n-1)(n-2)\ldots 2\cdot 1.$$

From this we see that

$$\lg(n!) = \lg(n) + \lg(n-1) + \lg(n-2) + \ldots + 1 + 0.$$

From this it is clear that $\lg(n!) < n\lg n$. These two results together show that

$$O(\lg n!) = O(n\lg n).$$

11.4 Selection sorting

Because of the lower bound on the complexity of any comparison sort, in one sense the binary insertion sort provides the best comparison we can expect, although the amount of data movement is still rather large. However, remember that two techniques of the same order may differ widely in actual processing time owing to differences in the constants, which relate to the amount of computation per cycle. One $O(n)$ process may require ten or one hundred times as much computation *per element* as another process which is also $O(n)$. Thus it is important to examine a number of different good sorting techniques. We shall see that the constants differ, and also that there are various other conditions that may make one technique or another preferable in a given situation. Remember that the creation of an unordered set in the computer is an $O(n)$ process which must be counted in any fine analysis of time to create a set to be sorted, but which gets lost in the coarser "big O" analysis of the overall time, because of the dominance of the sorting process itself.

A **selection sort** whereby we identify first the smallest element of a set, then the second smallest, and so forth, depends on having the entire set present. To use this idea we must enter the entire set and *then* sort it into order rather than sort the set while we are entering it. Figure 11.9 shows the same set as before, with a selection sort applied. We underline the element selected for the following line.

Figure 11.9   Selection sort example

$$t\ i\ \underline{f}\ v\ o\ l\ u$$

$$f\ \ t\ \underline{i}\ v\ o\ l\ u$$

$$f\ i\ \ t\ v\ o\ \underline{l}\ u$$

$$f\ i\ l\ \ t\ v\ \underline{o}\ u$$

$$f\ i\ l\ o\ \ \underline{t}\ v\ u$$

$$f\ i\ l\ o\ t\ \ v\ \underline{u}$$

$$f\ i\ l\ o\ t\ u\ \ \underline{v}$$

$$f\ i\ l\ o\ t\ u\ v$$

The concept behind a selection sort is straightforward. We select the smallest element of the given set and switch that with the first element. Then we set that aside and select the smallest element in the remainder of the set, switching that with the second element. This is continued until the entire set is sorted. Let's look at the example in figure 11.10. In each "select" operation, the smallest element is underlined; the bar indicates the portion of the set that has been sorted thus far.

From this example we make three observations. First, we may occasionally find an element in its proper place (see element 17 in fig. 11.10) so that no switch is necessary. Second, we do not need to go through the find and switch cycle for the last element in the set, since it will automatically be in the correct position after we have placed the next-to-the-last element. Third, because an increasing portion of the set is already in order, the number of comparisons that must be done decreases linearly with each find operation. To find the smallest element in a set of n elements, we must make $n - 1$ comparisons. To find the second smallest (after the switch), we make $n - 2$ comparisons. The total number of comparisons will be

$$(n - 1) + (n - 2) + (n - 3) + ... + 2 + 1 = n(n - 1)/2.$$

This is an "n^2" operation, which dominates the sorting process. It takes only n operations to form the unsorted set and at most n switches, since not every element must be switched. Hence this **straight selection sort** is an $O(n^2)$ operation. Figure 11.11 is a procedure for this.

Figure 11.10   Another selection sort example

find:	|	17	5	34	<u>2</u>	6	12	28	3	7	10	13	20	
switch:		2	| 5	34	17	6	12	28	3	7	10	13	20	
find:		2	| 5	34	17	6	12	28	<u>3</u>	7	10	13	20	
switch:		2	3	| 34	17	6	12	28	5	7	10	13	20	
find:		2	3	| 34	17	6	12	28	<u>5</u>	7	10	13	20	
switch:		2	3	5	| 17	6	12	28	34	7	10	13	20	
find:		2	3	5	| 17	<u>6</u>	12	28	34	7	10	13	20	
switch:		2	3	5	6	| 17	12	28	34	7	10	13	20	
find:		2	3	5	6	| 17	12	28	34	<u>7</u>	10	13	20	
switch:		2	3	5	6	7	| 12	28	34	17	10	13	20	
find:		2	3	5	6	7	| 12	28	34	17	<u>10</u>	13	20	
switch:		2	3	5	6	7	10	| 28	34	17	12	13	20	
find:		2	3	5	6	7	10	| 28	34	17	<u>12</u>	13	20	
switch:		2	3	5	6	7	10	12	| 34	17	28	13	20	
find:		2	3	5	6	7	10	12	| 34	17	28	<u>13</u>	20	
switch:		2	3	5	6	7	10	12	13	| 17	28	34	20	
find:		2	3	5	6	7	10	12	13	| <u>17</u>	28	34	20	
switch:		2	3	5	6	7	10	12	13	17	| 28	34	20	
find:		2	3	5	6	7	10	12	13	17	| 28	34	<u>20</u>	
switch:		2	3	5	6	7	10	12	13	17	20	| 34	28	
find:		2	3	5	6	7	10	12	13	17	20	| 34	<u>28</u>	
switch:		2	3	5	6	7	10	12	13	17	20	28	34	|

done!

Figure 11.11, Part 1   Straight selection sort

```
CONST
  MaxSize = UserSuppliedSize;

TYPE
  ElementType = UserSuppliedType;
  SetArray    = ARRAY[1..MaxSize] OF ElementType;

PROCEDURE StraightSelect (VAR SetName : SetArray;
                              Count     : integer);

{ A procedure for a straight selection sort of a set of at most
MaxSize elements. Count is the size of the set. }

  VAR
    I          : 1..MaxSize;
    J          : 1..MaxSize;
    Location   : 1..MaxSize;
    MinElement : ElementType;
```

Figure 11.11, Part 2   Straight selection sort

```
PROCEDURE SelectMin (VAR SetName : SetArray;
                         Front, Back : integer;
                         VAR Where   : integer);

{ This subprocedure finds the smallest element in the unsorted set
and returns its location. }

  VAR
    I        : 1..MaxSize;
    Minimum : ElementType;

  BEGIN
    Minimum := SetName[Front];
    Where := Front;
    FOR I := Front + 1 TO Back DO
      IF SetName[I] < Minimum THEN
        BEGIN
          Minimum := SetName[I];
          Where := I
        END
  END; { SelectMin }

{ Main procedure }

BEGIN

  { Assert: The input set has no repeated elements. }

  FOR I := 1 TO Count - 1 DO
    BEGIN

      { Invariant: The set is sorted through element I - 1. }

      SelectMin (SetName, I, Count, Location);
      IF (Location > I) AND (SetName[Location] < SetName[I]) THEN
        BEGIN
          MinElement := SetName[Location];
          SetName[Location] := SetName[I];
          SetName[I] := MinElement
        END
    END
END; { StraightSelect }
```

Figure 11.12   Tournament sort, first round

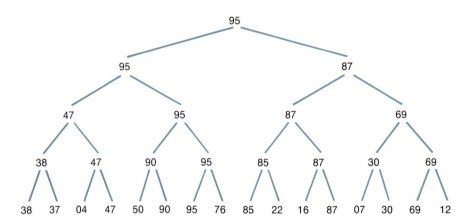

Since this straight selection sort is an n^2 process, for large sets it is less efficient than other types of sorts. However, it is simple to implement and works well for small sets. For example, a straight selection sort works well for the short lists that result from the first step of bin sorting.

A very common form of selection sort is the **tournament sort,** also known as the **tree selection sort.** The first name derives from the appearance of this technique in selecting the winner of a tournament. Suppose that we consider again the set

{38, 37, 04, 47, 50, 90, 95, 76, 85, 22, 16, 87, 07, 30, 69, 12},

and determine the highest number, the second highest, and so forth. In other words, suppose that we sort this set in descending order. The idea behind a tournament sort is to think of these numbers as scores, pair them off, and promote the higher of each pair of values. Then we repeat the process until a winner emerges. For example, from 38 and 37, we promote 38; from 04 and 47, we promote 47; and so forth. Then, in the second round, 38 and 47 are compared, with 47 promoted. The whole scheme for finding the "winner" is shown in figure 11.12. We see that 95 has appeared as the winner. We now remove 95 from the set to be sorted and promote the second place score. If we follow 95 back down through the tournament, we see that it was originally compared with 76. Hence 76 is promoted one level and compared with 90. Since 90 is larger, it is then promoted farther (fig. 11.13).

Figure 11.13   Tournament sort, second round

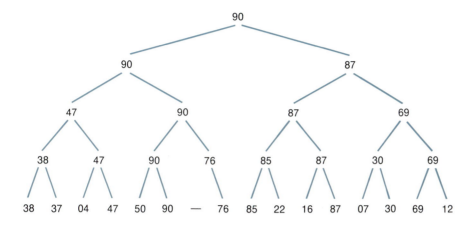

Figure 11.14   Tournament sort, third round

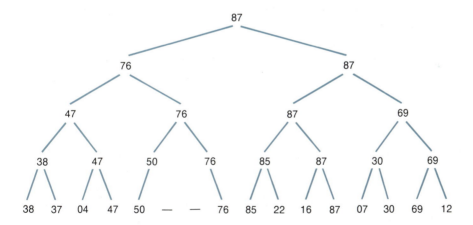

Let's carry out one more round. Remove 90, and promote its comparison score, 50 (fig. 11.14). It is clear that if we continue this process, eventually every number will be promoted to the top and the set will be sorted in descending order, 95, 90, 87, 85, 69, 50, ... , 07, 04.

Here is a nice way to arrange this computation. If we count all the occurrences of numbers in figure 11.12, we will find that there are 31, essentially twice the number of elements in the original set. Let us suppose that we have a set of

Figure 11.15   **Addressing for tournament sort**

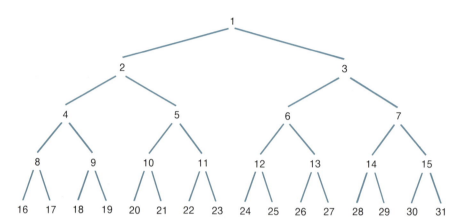

size n and that we place it originally in the top half of an array of size $2n$. For convenience, we shall assume that n is a power of 2, leaving the general case as an exercise. Now examine the addressing scheme shown in figure 11.15. Observe that in this scheme, one of the values in locations $2k$ and $2k + 1$ is promoted into location k for each value of k. This implies that if we place the original set in the top half of an array as suggested, we can easily fill the lower half, with the winning element showing up eventually in the first location. Figure 11.16 shows how this might look. (The array is shown in two rows, with initial location 0, that is always unused.)

To develop the first round of this array, for example, we examine the elements in locations 30 and 31, and place the larger one (69) in location 15. Then we compare the elements in locations 28 and 29, placing the larger one (30) in location 14. This comparison is continued until the array is fully developed. Once the first round is completed, the largest element (95) occurs in location 1. It is traced back through the array, in locations 2, 5, 11, and 22, and removed. The element with which it was compared in the first round (76) is promoted to location 11 and compared with the element in location 10 (90) to initiate the second round.

Figure 11.16   **Tournament sort, in an array**

38	37	04	47	50	90	95	76	85	22	16	87	07	30	69	12

Initial array

—	95	95	87	47	95	87	69	38	47	90	95	85	87	30	69
38	37	04	47	50	90	95	76	85	22	16	87	07	30	69	12

First round

—	90	90	87	47	90	87	69	38	47	90	76	85	87	30	69
38	37	04	47	50	90	—	76	85	22	16	87	07	30	69	12

Second round

—	87	76	87	47	76	87	69	38	47	50	76	85	87	30	69
38	37	04	47	50	—	—	76	85	22	16	87	07	30	69	12

Third round

An analysis of tournament sort shows that it is a very efficient sorting method. Think of the moves that are necessary for each element. For the element in position k, the number of moves is proportional to $\lg k$. This is most easily seen from the addressing diagram, figure 11.15, where we can see the number of moves that each element must make to reach the top. Since we must move each element in an n element set, we need at most a total of $n \lg n$ comparisons and moves. Hence tournament sort is an $O(n \lg n)$ sorting algorithm. A program using a tournament sort procedure is given in figure 11.17. Note that this procedure requires space equivalent to three copies of the set. The original set occupies the top half of the array, with the bottom half used to develop the tournament. The third piece of space is needed to store the sorted set.

(Note that the formal parameter TreeSize in the definitions of Make-Tournament and TournSort has been given the type "integer" rather than "1..MaxSize." This is because Pascal does not permit direct use of the latter type in formal parameter specifications. If we had defined another TYPE, SizeType, to be 1..MaxSize, then we could have used SizeType in the formal parameter specifications as well as wherever the specification "1..MaxSize" has been used.)

Figure 11.17, Part 1   Tournament sort program

```
PROGRAM TournamentSort (output);

{ For simplicity choose 2 ** N - 1 for the tournament size
to sort 2 ** (N - 1) elements.  }

CONST
  ListSize = 128;
  MaxSize  = 255;

TYPE
  ElementType = integer;
  ListType    = ARRAY[1..ListSize] OF ElementType;
  NodeType    = RECORD
                   Data     : ElementType;
                   Location : 1..MaxSize
                END;
  Tournament  = ARRAY[1..MaxSize] OF NodeType;

VAR
  Index      : 1..MaxSize;
  SortedList : ListType;
  Tree       : Tournament;

PROCEDURE MakeTournament (VAR TournTree : Tournament;
                              TreeSize      : integer);

  VAR
    Index : 1..MaxSize;

  BEGIN
    FOR Index := TreeSize DIV 2 DOWNTO 1 DO
      IF TournTree[2 * Index].Data >
           TournTree[2 * Index + 1].Data THEN
        TournTree[Index] := TournTree[2 * Index]
      ELSE
        TournTree[Index] := TournTree[2 * Index + 1]
  END; { MakeTournament }
```

Figure 11.17, Part 2   Tournament sort program

```
PROCEDURE TournSort (VAR TournTree  : Tournament;
                         TreeSize    : integer;
                         VAR OutputList : ListType);

  CONST
    Marker = -1;

  VAR
    Index       : 1..MaxSize;
    NextParent : 0..MaxSize;

  BEGIN
    FOR Index := 1 TO (TreeSize DIV 2) + 1 DO
      BEGIN
        OutputList[Index] := TournTree[1].Data;
        TournTree[TournTree[1].Location].Data := Marker;
        NextParent := TournTree[1].Location DIV 2;
        WHILE NextParent <> 0 DO
          BEGIN
            IF TournTree[2 * NextParent].Data >
                TournTree[2 * NextParent + 1].Data THEN
              TournTree[NextParent] := TournTree[2 * NextParent]
            ELSE
                TournTree[NextParent] := TournTree[2 * NextParent + 1];
            NextParent := NextParent DIV 2
          END
      END
  END; { TournSort }

BEGIN
  FOR Index := (MaxSize DIV 2) + 1 TO MaxSize DO
    BEGIN
      Tree[Index].Data := trunc (random (50));
      Tree[Index].Location := Index
    END;
  MakeTournament (Tree, MaxSize);
  TournSort (Tree, MaxSize, SortedList);
  writeln ('Sorted List ');
  writeln;
  FOR Index := 1 TO ListSize DO
    BEGIN
      IF Index MOD 25 = 1 THEN writeln;
      write (SortedList[Index] : 3)
    END
END. { TournamentSort }
```

11.5 Heaps and heapsort

The same type of structure that was used for the tournament sort can be used in another sorting technique. This technique, however, requires space for only one copy of the set.

We can think of tournament sorting as a method of promoting the correct element to the top of the tournament at each round. It works well because there is a simple way to decide which element to promote at each stage. For the structure we now develop, the **heap,** we have a similarly simple way to decide which element to promote each time.

The heap structure works well in any situation where we need know only which element is next to be processed. Basically, we develop a simple way of determining "who's next" which at the same time organizes the remaining elements sufficiently that, when they come near the head of the processing line, we can still easily determine "who's next." This is the basis of a method commonly used for allocating computer resources, the **priority queue.** We may think of a heap or a priority queue as having the property that the next element to be processed is at the head of the line, and all other elements are more-or-less in their proper positions but not exactly so.

There are two types of heaps, **top-heavy** and **bottom-heavy.** The organization for each is based on the relationships among the elements at locations k, $2k$, and $2k + 1$ for each value of k. In a top-heavy heap, the element at location k is larger than those at locations $2k$ and $2k + 1$; in a bottom-heavy heap, it is smaller than either of the other two. In both types of heap, we know nothing about the relationship between the elements at locations $2k$ and $2k + 1$. Finally, the heap is always organized so that the consecutive locations $1, 2, ... , n$ in the array are filled.

Again we take as our example the set

$$\{38, 37, 04, 47, 50, 90, 95, 76, 85, 22, 16, 87, 07, 30, 69, 12\},$$

which we think of as occupying the first sixteen locations of an array. Using the addressing diagram of figure 11.15, we would think of this set as shown in figure 11.18. This structure is not a heap. While the element in location 1 (38) is larger than either of the elements in locations 2 and 3 (37, 04), the element in location 2 (37) is smaller than those in locations 4 and 5 (47, 50). Suppose that we try to rearrange this into a top-heavy heap. One way is to begin at the back of the set and work toward the front. We want to compare the element at location k with those at locations $2k$ and $2k + 1$. The elements 85, 22, ... , 12, which are in locations 9 through 16, have no corresponding elements at locations 18 through 33, so we can let them be for the moment. Thus we start with the element 76, at location 8. We observe that it is larger than the element at location 16 and that there is no element at location 17. Fine: It stays where it is. Next we consider

Figure 11.18   The example set in the addressing scheme

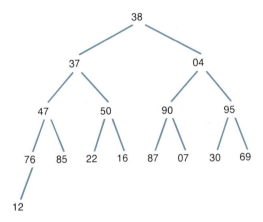

Figure 11.19   First exchange in heap formation

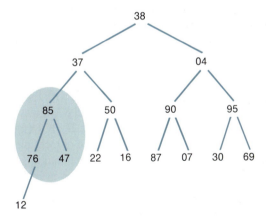

the element at location 7, which has the value 95. It is larger than the elements at locations 14 and 15, so it stays where it is. The same is true for the elements at locations 6 and 5: they each stay where they are.

Now consider the element at location 4, with value 47. When we compare this with the elements at locations 8 and 9, we see that 85, at location 9, is the largest of these. Hence we exchange the elements at locations 4 and 9 (fig. 11.19). We have moved 47 into location 9, but since there are no elements at locations 18 and 19, it is where it should be (for the moment).

Figure 11.20   Second exchange in heap formation

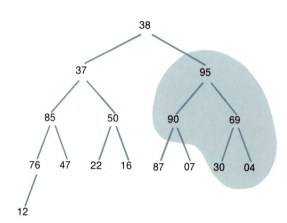

We now move to location 3, where we find the element 04. Comparing this with the elements at locations 6 and 7, we move the largest (95) into location 3 and the element from location 3 into location 7. But now we must compare locations 7, 14, and 15. We see that the 69 in location 15 is the largest, so we exchange that with the 04 that we have moved into location 7 (fig. 11.20). We continue this process with the element at location 2. This exchanges first with the element at location 4 and then with the element at location 8 (fig. 11.21).

The fourth series of exchanges for this set begins with the element in location 1, which is exchanged successively with 95, 90, and 87, always exchanging with the larger of the two elements in locations $2k$ and $2k + 1$ (fig. 11.22).

We now have a top-heavy heap. For each triple of locations $(k, 2k, 2k + 1)$, the largest element is at location k. The process of making the heap is called **heapifying** the set. The procedure for doing this is given in figure 11.23. Heapification by this method is an $O(n)$ process. A nice proof of this is given in Standish (1980, pp. 87–88).

Figure 11.21   Third exchange in heap formation

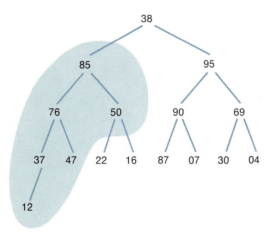

Figure 11.22   Fourth exchange in heap formation

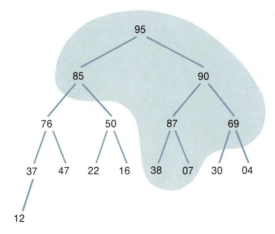

Figure 11.23, Part 1   Heap formation (top-heavy) procedure

```
CONST
  MaxSize = UserSuppliedConstant;

TYPE
  Index       = 1..MaxSize;
  ArrayType   = ARRAY[Index] OF integer;
  ElementType = integer;

PROCEDURE Swap (VAR First, Second : ElementType);

{ A procedure used to swap heap values. }

  VAR
    Temp : ElementType;

  BEGIN
    Temp := First;
    First := Second;
    Second := Temp
  END; { Swap }

FUNCTION LargePlace (VAR Heap         : ArrayType;
                         ParentPosition : Index;
                         HeapSize       : Index) : Index;

{ A function which determines the index or location of
the largest child of a parent node. Note that in some
cases the parent node may only have one child. }

  BEGIN
    IF 2 * ParentPosition = HeapSize THEN
      LargePlace := 2 * ParentPosition
    ELSE
      IF Heap[2 * ParentPosition] >
          Heap[2 * ParentPosition + 1] THEN
        LargePlace := 2 * ParentPosition
      ELSE
        LargePlace := 2 * ParentPosition + 1
  END; { LargePlace }
```

Figure 11.23, Part 2   Heap formation (top-heavy) procedure

```
PROCEDURE Heapify (VAR Heap : ArrayType; Size : Index);

   VAR
      Counter         : Index;
      LargeChildPlace : Index;
      Place           : Index;

   BEGIN
      FOR Counter := (Size DIV 2) DOWNTO 1 DO
        BEGIN
          Place := Counter;
          LargeChildPlace := LargePlace (Heap, Place, Size);
          WHILE (Heap[LargeChildPlace] > Heap[Place]) AND
                (Place <= Size DIV 2) DO

            BEGIN
              Swap (Heap[LargeChildPlace], Heap[Place]);
              Place := LargeChildPlace;
              IF (2 * Place <= Size) THEN
                 LargeChildPlace := LargePlace (Heap, Place, Size)
            END
        END
   END; { Heapify }
```

This procedure can easily be adapted to forming a bottom-heavy heap. We simply choose the smallest element at each stage rather than the largest. For our example set, the result is shown in figure 11.24.

Let us return to the top-heavy heap. As stored in an array, it will look like figure 11.25. This set is obviously not sorted, but we know that the largest element is now the first element in the array. We can sort the set by exchanging that element with the last element in the array, isolating it logically from the rest of the array, and then letting the new first element **sift down** to its proper location in the heap. But now the process is easier, since we have only disturbed the first element in the array. After the exchange, element 12 has been moved into the first location (fig. 11.26). We compare this with the elements in locations 2 and

Figure 11.24   Bottom-heavy heap

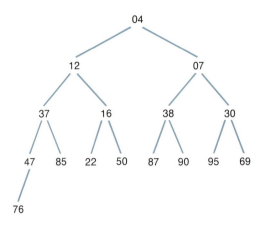

Figure 11.25   The set heapified

95   85   90   76   50   87   69   37   47   22   16   38   07   30   04   12

Figure 11.26   The first sorting exchange

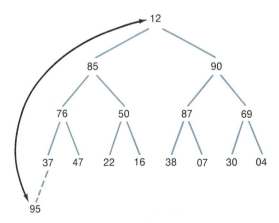

3, switching it with the 90, and then we continue to compare, switching it successively with 87 and 38 (fig. 11.27). We now exchange 90 with 04, isolating the
90, and let 04 sift down (fig. 11.28).

The next exchange and sift down moves 87 into the third position from the
end. If we look at this as an array, we see that we have begun to construct the
sorted set from the large end down (fig. 11.29) and that the next element (85)
is waiting in the first location.

Figure 11.27   The set reheapified

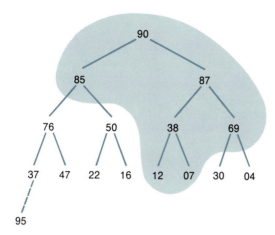

Figure 11.28   Second reheapification

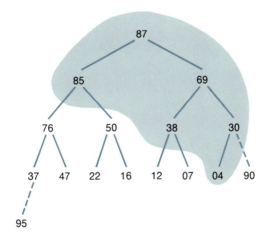

Figure 11.29   The set after the third reheapification

85   76   69   47   50   38   30   37   04   22   16   12   07   <u>87</u>   <u>90</u>   <u>95</u>

Figure 11.30, Part 1   HeapSort procedure

```
CONST
  MaxSize = UserSuppliedConstant;

TYPE
  Index       = 1..MaxSize;
  ArrayType   = ARRAY[Index] OF integer;
  ElementType = integer;

PROCEDURE HeapSort (VAR TheHeap : ArrayType; HeapSize : Index);

  VAR
    NextElement      : Index;
    Place            : Index;
    LargeChildPlace  : Index;
    IsPlaced         : boolean;

  PROCEDURE Swap (VAR First, Second : ElementType);

  { See fig. 11.23. }

  FUNCTION LargePlace (VAR Heap         : ArrayType;
                       ParentPosition   : Index;
                       HeapSize         : Index) : Index;

  { See fig. 11.23. }

  PROCEDURE Heapify (VAR Heap : ArrayType; Size : Index);

  { See fig. 11.23. }

  BEGIN
    Heapify (TheHeap, HeapSize);
    FOR NextElement := HeapSize DOWNTO 2 DO
      BEGIN

        { Repeatedly trade the top of the heap for the last heap
        element and reduce the size of the heap by 1. }

        Swap (TheHeap[1], TheHeap[NextElement]);
        HeapSize := HeapSize - 1;
        Place := 1;
        IsPlaced := false;
```

Figure 11.30, Part 2   HeapSort procedure

```
{ Let the top of the heap sift down until a heap is
re-created. }

WHILE (2 * Place <= HeapSize) AND (NOT IsPlaced) DO
  BEGIN
    LargeChildPlace := LargePlace (TheHeap, Place, HeapSize);
    IF TheHeap[LargeChildPlace] > TheHeap[Place] THEN
      BEGIN
        Swap (TheHeap[Place], TheHeap[LargeChildPlace]);
        Place := LargeChildPlace
      END
    ELSE
      IsPlaced := true
  END
END
END; { HeapSort }
```

The process we have described here is logarithmic in nature, because at each comparison in sifting down we eliminate one of the two substructures, either that at location $2k$ or that at location $2k + 1$. Since we carry out this logarithmic process n times, the process of forming the heap and then sorting is $O(n) + nO(\lg n)$, an $O(n\lg n)$ procedure. Our version of the sorting process, called **HeapSort,** is given in figure 11.30.

11.6 Exchange sorting: Quicksort

An **exchange sort** involves exchanging or switching pairs of elements, gradually moving each element closer to its final position. We had an exchange within the selection sort when we switched the lowest remaining element with the element that was in its position. But most exchange sorts do not involve such a search for the lowest or highest element; rather, they make exchanges whenever two elements are perceived to be out of order. Since these exchanges do not generally move an element to its final position, we might expect exchange sorts to be rather inefficient, and some of them are. But remember that we are not doing lots of extra work looking for the "right" elements to switch.

If we want the elements to be in increasing order, for example, with an exchange sorting technique we will search for a larger element preceding a smaller one and switch the two of them. We will keep doing this until no more elements can be switched because they are all in order. An exchange sort of our example set is shown in figure 11.31. We underline the two elements to be exchanged.

Figure 11.31   Exchange sort example

<pre>
t i f v o l u
i t f v o l u
i f t v o l u
i f t o v l u
i f t o l v u
i f t o l u v
f i t o l u v
f i o t l u v
f i o l t u v
f i l o t u v
</pre>

A well-designed exchange sort can be highly efficient. The key is to select the exchanges carefully and avoid moving any one element back and forth many times. **Quicksort** is this type of sort.

Quicksort is a **divide and conquer** technique based on the concept of splitting the set into two subsets, one of which contains all elements smaller than a given element, with the other containing all the elements larger than the given element. In this way, we can then confine our attention to each of the subsets in turn, since we already know that we do not need to compare an element from one subset with an element from the other.

A divide and conquer algorithm, such as quicksort, is implemented very elegantly as a **recursive algorithm**. In this kind of algorithm, one use of the algorithm either solves the problem or calls for another use of the algorithm on a different set of data. Quicksort either sorts the set immediately (if the set contains just a few elements) or divides the set into two smaller subsets, and then calls for another application of quicksort to each of these subsets. Each of these may be split further, so that we may at one point have a large group of these smaller subsets on which to work.

One problem in using quicksort is selection of the dividing or **pivot element**. We do it simply: pick the first element in the set.

The exchange process for this sort switches the pivot element with smaller elements, placing the smaller element to the left, and with larger elements, placing the larger element to the right. To do this efficiently, we start at the right end of the set to find smaller elements and at the left end of the set to find larger elements. We "ping-pong" back and forth, looking for larger and smaller elements. Here is our example, with the pivot element in boldface and the comparison element underlined:

17	5	34	2	6	12	28	3	7	10	13	<u>20</u>
17	5	34	2	6	12	28	3	7	10	<u>13</u>	20

Since 13 is less than 17, we switch and start looking from the left for larger elements:

switch:	13	5	34	2	6	12	28	3	7	10	**17**	20
	13	5	34	2	6	12	28	3	7	10	**17**	20
	13	5	34	2	6	12	28	3	7	10	**17**	20

Switch again, and resume comparison from the right for a smaller element. Note that we do not need to check 13 again, since we already know that it is smaller than the pivot. Similarly, on each iteration of the process we can ignore the two elements already switched to the ends of the set, as these have been checked against the pivot:

	13	5	**17**	2	6	12	28	3	7	10	34	20
	13	5	10	2	6	12	28	3	7	17	34	20
	13	5	10	2	6	12	28	3	7	**17**	34	20
	13	5	10	2	6	12	28	3	7	**17**	34	20
	13	5	10	2	6	12	28	3	7	**17**	34	20
	13	5	10	2	6	12	17	3	7	28	34	20
	13	5	10	2	6	12	7	3	**17**	28	34	20

Our final comparison of the first cycle of the sort is between the pivot element and the element adjacent to it. In this example, 3 is less than 17, so we are finished with this cycle. Note that all elements smaller than the pivot are to the left and all elements larger than it are to the right.

We now need to sort these two subsets independently of each other. For this we could recursively call on quicksort again; however, when a set becomes small enough a straight selection or insertion sort is better because of the simplicity of these sorts. Sedgewick (1978) has shown that this change to a simpler algorithm (he recommends linear insertion) is appropriate when the set to be sorted contains fewer than ten elements.

Whether we use quicksort again or a simpler algorithm, one of the two sets must be placed on a stack of unsorted sets while we sort the other one. Hoare (1962) established that placing the larger set on the stack and sorting the smaller one first keeps the stack length shorter, thus requiring less stack storage. This makes sense. Every time we process a larger set, we generate two new sets to be processed, one of which will be added to the stack. Thus we keep adding more and more sets, including some short ones, to the stack. But if we process the shorter set first, the depth of recursion is less and hence the stack does not become so deep. Note that we do not need to place each set explicitly on the stack, but can merely indicate where it begins in the array and how large it is. Thus the stack storage needed is proportional to the number of sets on the stack rather than to their sizes.

Here is a slightly different version of quicksort, used by Sedgewick. For this version, we leave the pivot element where it is, using it only for comparisons, until all other elements have been sorted with respect to the pivot element. Then one exchange moves the pivot into its correct location, and we have two subsets to sort. Note that we have two pointers to elements that we compare. First the rightmost pointer moves left to an element smaller than the pivot, then the leftmost pointer moves right to one larger. These elements are exchanged, and the pointers moved again:

17	5	34	2	6	12	28	3	7	10	13	20
17	5	34	2	6	12	28	3	7	10	13	20
17	5	34	2	6	12	28	3	7	10	13	20

Now exchange the 34 and 13, and move the pointers again. Note that immediately after the exchange, the leftmost pointer points to an element less than the pivot and the rightmost points to one greater than the pivot. Continuing:

17	5	13	2	6	12	28	3	7	10	34	20
17	5	13	2	6	12	28	3	7	10	34	20
17	5	13	2	6	12	28	3	7	10	34	20
17	5	13	2	6	12	28	3	7	10	34	20
17	5	13	2	6	12	28	3	7	10	34	20
17	5	13	2	6	12	28	3	7	10	34	20

Exchange 28 and 10, and move again. When the two pointers point to the same element, it will be the rightmost element that is less than the pivot. Exchange that with the pivot, and we are ready to sort the two subsets:

17	5	13	2	6	12	10	3	7	28	34	20
17	5	13	2	6	12	10	3	7	28	34	20
17	5	13	2	6	12	10	3	7	28	34	20
17	5	13	2	6	12	10	3	7	28	34	20
7	5	13	2	6	12	10	3	17	28	34	20

If we have failed to monitor the pointer movements correctly, we will find that they have crossed during the search. For example, we would find the "leftmost" pointer pointing at 28 and the "rightmost" at 7. This is no problem: simply exchange the pivot element with that indicated by the "rightmost" pointer.

Using this method we have the same subsets to the left and right of the pivot as we did with the first method, but we used fewer moves to accomplish this. Although the elements of these sets are not in the same order as they were with the first method, since these subsets have yet to be sorted the particular order of their elements at this point does not matter. Moreover, the pivot element is in its correct position (in both methods) and need not be moved again.

Quicksort is interesting, in that on the average it is a very good sorting method but for the worst case it is poor. In fact, it is on average an $O(n \lg n)$ sort, with a constant smaller than that of heapsort. But observe what happens when we apply quicksort to the left subset that we derived in the first example. The pivot element, 13, happens to be the largest element in the set. It is switched with the 3 and then compared with all the other elements, without any further switches. Thus the right subset generated on this cycle is the empty set, $\emptyset$, and we have only sorted out one element, the pivot. In the worst case, quicksort is $O(n^2)$.

How can we assure that quicksort works well for a given set? The trouble that we have indicated seems to arise from the fact that all the elements lie on one side of the pivot element—either all are smaller than the pivot or all are larger. In effect, when this happens repeatedly for each pivot element, we expend much effort just checking to verify that each pivot element is already in its correct position.

The idea behind avoiding this problem is to assure somehow that the pivot element is roughly in the middle of the set—a median element, with just as many set elements above it as below it. If this could be assured each time, then each subset we examine will be half the size of its parent set, which is the hallmark of a logarithmic process.

Thus, to improve the performance of quicksort, we try to choose the pivot element in a different way, one that is more likely to yield a pivot near the middle of the set. We arbitrarily chose the first element as the pivot. We could have randomly chosen an element rather than just taking the first one. One method that seems to work well is to take the first and last elements together with one from the middle and choose the middle value of these three. For our set we would use the first, the twelfth, and either the sixth or seventh elements. Observe that if we used the sixth element, we would still choose 17 as the pivot (from 17, 12, 20) but that if we used the seventh element, we would choose 20 as the pivot (from 17, 28, 20). So choosing the **median of three**, as this method is called, does not improve the first round pivot. However, in dealing with the larger subset, on the left, we would choose either 3 (from 13, 2, 3) or 6 (from 13, 6, 3) as the pivot element, thus producing a better split of the left subset. The procedure QuickSort (fig. 11.32) implements the first version that we have given, repeatedly swapping the pivot element. Implementation of Sedgewick's version and of the median of three choice of a pivot are left as programming exercises.

Figure 11.32, Part 1   QuickSort

```
CONST
  ListSize = UserSuppliedConstant;

TYPE
  ElementType = UserSuppliedType;
  ListType    = ARRAY[1..ListSize] OF ElementType;

PROCEDURE QuickSort (VAR List : ListType;
                         Start    : integer;
                         Finish   : integer);

{ This procedure implements QuickSort as first described in the
text. Start is the index of the leftmost element in the portion
being sorted, and Finish is the index of the rightmost element in
this portion. }

  VAR
    Left        : integer;
    PivotPlace  : integer;
    Right       : integer;

  PROCEDURE Swap (I, J : integer);

  { Swap is a local procedure which swaps List[I] and List[J]. }

    VAR
      Temp : ElementType;

    BEGIN
      Temp := List[I];
      List[I] := List[J];
      List[J] := Temp
    END; { Swap }

  BEGIN { Main procedure. }

    { Assert: Start <= Finish }

    PivotPlace := Start;
    Left := PivotPlace + 1;
    Right := Finish;
    REPEAT
```

Figure 11.32, Part 2   QuickSort

```
{ Find a right element less than the one at PivotPlace and
swap. }

WHILE (List[PivotPlace] <= List[Right]) AND
      (Right > PivotPlace) DO
  Right := Right - 1;
IF Right > PivotPlace THEN
  BEGIN
    Swap (PivotPlace, Right);
    PivotPlace := Right;
    Right := Right - 1
  END;

{ Find a left element greater than the one at PivotPlace and
swap. }

WHILE (List[PivotPlace] >= List[Left]) AND
      (Left < PivotPlace) DO
  Left := Left + 1;
IF Left < PivotPlace THEN
  BEGIN
    Swap (Left, PivotPlace);
    PivotPlace := Left;
    Left := Left + 1
  END
UNTIL Left > Right;

{ Assert: All elements left of PivotPlace are less than
List[PivotPlace]; all elements right of PivotPlace are greater
than List[PivotPlace]. }

IF Start < PivotPlace - 1 THEN
  QuickSort (List, Start, PivotPlace - 1);
IF PivotPlace + 1 < Finish THEN
  QuickSort (List, PivotPlace + 1, Finish)
END; { QuickSort }
```

11.7 Merging

As with our other operations, we expect **merging** of two sorted sets to maintain the sorted order. Actually, the merge operation for sorted sets can take advantage of the sorting and be very efficient. We never need to look back within either of the sets to decide which element to place next in the merged sets: the search always moves forward. Let us see how this works with two small sets. Suppose we wish to merge the sets {2, 5, 17, 34} and {3, 6, 12, 28}. Here is the process:

compare	merged set
2 and 3	{2}
5 and 3	{2, 3}
5 and 6	{2, 3, 5}
17 and 6	{2, 3, 5, 6}
17 and 12	{2, 3, 5, 6, 12}
17 and 28	{2, 3, 5, 6, 12, 17}
34 and 28	{2, 3, 5, 6, 12, 17, 28}
(end of set)	{2, 3, 5, 6, 12, 17, 28, 34}

We observe that to merge these two sets of four elements we required seven comparisons. In general, to merge two sorted sets of sizes m and n, maintaining the sorted order, is an $O(m + n)$ operation. We also observe that no further comparisons are required once we have placed all the elements of one of the two sets. Figure 11.33 is the procedure. The merging process need not be restricted to two sets at a time. Merging of several sets, or a **multiway merge,** is frequently used for efficient processing of large sets.

Figure 11.33, Part 1   Merge Procedure

```
CONST
  MaxSize = UserSuppliedSize;

TYPE
  ElementType = UserSuppliedType;
  Index       = 1..MaxSize;
  ListType    = ARRAY[Index] OF ElementType;

VAR
  List : ListType;

PROCEDURE Merge (List1Start, List1End     : Index;
                 List2Start, List2End     : Index;
                 VAR List3Start, List3End : Index);

{ Assert: List1 and List2 each have at least one element. }

  VAR
    I                                     : Index;
    List1, List2, List3                   : ListType;
    List1Element, List2Element, List3Element : Index;
    List1Empty, List2Empty                : boolean;
    List1Size, List2Size, List3Size       : Index;

  PROCEDURE MakeList (ListStart,ListEnd : Index;
                      VAR NewList       : ListType;
                      VAR Size          : Index);

    VAR
      I    : Index;
      Next : Index;

    BEGIN

      { Make List from the input parameters. }

      Next := 1;
      FOR I := ListStart TO ListEnd DO
        BEGIN
          NewList[Next] := List[I];
          Next := Next + 1
        END;
      Size := ListEnd - ListStart + 1
    END; { MakeList }
```

Figure 11.33, Part 2   Merge Procedure

```
BEGIN { Merge }

  { Initialization Section--form two lists from List to be merged.
  Name them List1 and List2. The merged list is named List3. }

  List1Element := 1;
  MakeList (List1Start, List1End, List1, List1Size);
  List1Empty := false;
  List2Element := 1;
  MakeList (List2Start, List2End, List2, List2Size);
  List2Empty := false;
  List3Element := 1;
  List3Size := List1Size + List2Size;

  WHILE (NOT List1Empty) OR (NOT List2Empty) DO

    { Assert: At least one list has elements. }

    BEGIN
      IF List1Empty THEN

        { List1 is empty; copy the remainder of List2. }

        BEGIN
          FOR List3Element := List3Element TO List3Size DO
            BEGIN
              List3[List3Element] := List2[List2Element];
              List2Element := List2Element + 1
            END;
          List2Empty := true
        END
      ELSE
        IF List2Empty THEN

          { List2 is empty; copy the remainder of List1. }

          BEGIN
            FOR List3Element := List3Element TO List3Size DO
              BEGIN
                List3[List3Element] := List1[List1Element];
                List1Element := List1Element + 1
              END;
            List1Empty := true
          END;
```

Figure 11.33, Part 3   Merge Procedure

```
{ Assert: Either both lists are empty, or both lists have
further elements. }

IF NOT List1Empty THEN

  { Copy the next element. }

  IF List1[List1Element] < List2[List2Element] THEN

    { Copy from List1. }

      BEGIN
        List3[List3Element] := List1[List1Element];
        List1Element := List1Element + 1;
        List3Element := List3Element + 1;
        List1Empty := List1Element > List1Size
      END
    ELSE

      { Assert: List2[List2Element] <= List1[List1Element] }

      { Copy from List2. }

      BEGIN
        List3[List3Element] := List2[List2Element];
        List2Element := List2Element + 1;
        List3Element := List3Element + 1;
        List2Empty := List2Element > List2Size
      END
  END; { WHILE }

{ Copy List3 back into original List and set List3Start and
List3End. So storage is not exceeded, keep moving the merged
lists to the left of List. }

List3Start := List1Start;
List3End := List1Start + (List3Size - 1);
FOR I := List3Start TO List3End DO
  List[I] := List3[I - List3Start + 1]
END; { Merge }
```

Figure 11.34   MergeSort example

$$\text{tifvolu}$$

ti fv ol u

it fv lo u   (subsets sorted)

fitv lou   (pairs of subsets merged)

filotuv   (final merger)

11.8 Merge sorting

Another group of sorting techniques, the **merge sorts,** also depend on a divide and conquer technique. For this type of sort, we divide the set into subsets of roughly equal size, sort each of these subsets, and then merge the results of all the sorts. The advantages of this method result from dealing with smaller sets. For one thing, if the base set is too large to fit into main memory, we can divide it into subsets that will fit into main memory and sort each of these without repeated access to secondary memory. Only for the merging process do we need more frequent access to secondary memory. In addition, any nonlinear process works much more rapidly on smaller sets. Hence it is advantageous to work with smaller sets, provided that we don't lose the time gained when we recombine the sets.

For our example, we divide our set into subsets of one or two elements each, sort these, and then merge them by choosing the smallest elements for pairs of subsets. The result is shown in figure 11.34.

To demonstrate the savings that can be achieved by working with smaller sets, suppose that a process takes n^2 operations (time cycles) on a set of n elements. For a set of 1000 elements, this operation would thus take 1,000,000 cycles. Now suppose that we divide this set into ten sets of 100 elements each. The operation now takes only 10,000 cycles per set, or 100,000 cycles in all. We thus have 900,000 cycles left that can be used for combining the results of the operation on the smaller sets before we start losing efficiency. The results are similar, although less impressive, for $n \lg n$ operations. Processing the large set requires 9970 cycles, and processing each of the small sets requires 665 cycles. We still have more than 3000 cycles left for combining the results.

Consider this set of twelve numbers:

$$\{17, 5, 34, 2, 6, 12, 28, 3, 7, 10, 13, 20\}.$$

We can subdivide it in a number of ways. Which should we choose? Here is an interesting idea. We can think of each element by itself as a subset which is already sorted and then concentrate on merging these sets. Noting that the sets to be merged do not need to be the same size, we can make the process efficient by thinking of the sets as being in a queue. Then we simply place each merged set at the end of the queue and continue the process until we have only one set left. It looks like this:

$$\{17\}, \{5\}, \{34\}, \{2\}, \{6\}, \{12\}, \{28\}, \{3\}, \{7\}, \{10\}, \{13\}, \{20\}.$$

Merge the first pair of subsets, and place the merged set at the end of the queue:

$$\{34\}, \{2\}, \{6\}, \{12\}, \{28\}, \{3\}, \{7\}, \{10\}, \{13\}, \{20\}, \{5, 17\}.$$

In merging these sets, we have sorted their elements into order. Continue the process:

$$\{6\}, \{12\}, \{28\}, \{3\}, \{7\}, \{10\}, \{13\}, \{20\}, \{5, 17\}, \{2, 34\}$$
$$\{28\}, \{3\}, \{7\}, \{10\}, \{13\}, \{20\}, \{5, 17\}, \{2, 34\}, \{6, 12\}$$
$$\{7\}, \{10\}, \{13\}, \{20\}, \{5, 17\}, \{2, 34\}, \{6, 12\}, \{3, 28\}$$
$$\{13\}, \{20\}, \{5, 17\}, \{2, 34\}, \{6, 12\}, \{3, 28\}, \{7, 10\}$$
$$\{5, 17\}, \{2, 34\}, \{6, 12\}, \{3, 28\}, \{7, 10\}, \{13, 20\}.$$

We have now merged all the single element sets into two element sets. We continue, merging the sets that we have formed thus far:

$$\{6, 12\}, \{3, 28\}, \{7, 10\}, \{13, 20\}, \{2, 5, 17, 34\}$$
$$\{7, 10\}, \{13, 20\}, \{2, 5, 17, 34\}, \{3, 6, 12, 28\}$$
$$\{2, 5, 17, 34\}, \{3, 6, 12, 28\}, \{7, 10, 13, 20\}$$
$$\{7, 10, 13, 20\}, \{2, 3, 5, 6, 12, 17, 28, 34\}.$$

We are now down to two sets to be merged. The fact that they are different sizes does not matter:

$$\{2, 3, 5, 6, 7, 10, 12, 13, 17, 20, 28, 34\}.$$

The data structure we use for this process is a queue of sorted sets. The skeleton for the procedure is simple (fig. 11.35). We observe that this procedure will terminate, assuming that the actual merge operation does. The reason is that we begin with at least one set in the queue, and each pass through the WHILE loop removes two sets from the queue then adds one to the queue, a net decrease of one in the number of sets. Hence the number of sets (QueueSize) must eventually reach 1. What happens if QueueSize is initially 1? Then Size has the value 1; but Size is the number of elements in the original set. Thus the original set, with only one element, is indeed sorted.

Figure 11.35   Skeleton for MergeSort

```
PROCEDURE MergeSort (List : ListType; Size : integer);

  VAR . . .

  BEGIN

    { Place each set element from List in Queue. }

    { Assert: Queue consists of singleton sets; Size is
    the number of such sets in Queue; Size >= 1. }

    QueueSize := Size;
    WHILE QueueSize > 1 DO

      { Assert: Queue consists of QueueSize sorted sets
      whose union is the original set. }

      BEGIN

        { Remove the first two sets from Queue. }

        { Merge the two sets in sorted order. }

        { Place the merged set at the end of Queue. }

        QueueSize := QueueSize - 1
      END

    { Assert: Queue consists of the original set, sorted. }

  END; { MergeSort }
```

In implementing this procedure, we must be aware of the possibility that the queue might migrate out of the available memory. Even if it does not do this, a straightforward implementation might require a very large amount of memory. For example, if we were to place the merged sets in new storage at the end of the queue, our little example with twelve numbers would require fifty-six storage cells: twelve for the original set, twelve for the merged pairs, twelve for the merged quadruples, eight for the merged set of eight, and then twelve for the final merged set. We can conserve storage by copying the two sets to be merged and keeping track of where the next merge round should start. Then we can merge the two sets for this round and store the result back in the locations from which we took the sets.

The procedure MergeSort (fig. 11.36) uses the Merge procedure that we developed as figure 11.33 in the previous section.

Both Merge and MergeSort are rather lengthy procedures. Yet by themselves they are incomplete: they are merely the "working portions" of some program. To show how these all fit together, here is a program (fig. 11.37) to generate and sort a list of integers. The value given for MaxSize is sufficient to allow as many as 1024 integers in the list.

The MergeSort procedure is a good example of the interplay among various data types. The basic structure underlying this implementation is an array. But conceptually, we have a queue of lists. Thus three different data types come into play. We could have stayed more strictly with the concepts of lists and queues, and implemented a merge sort using the operations that were defined in the abstract data types of chapters 5 and 6. Writing the program would have been simpler. For example, we would not have written explicit queue-handling routines, such as PlaceInQueue and RemoveFromQueue. Instead, we would have called on the standard Enqueue and Dequeue routines. But while this would have simplified writing the program, it would probably result in a less efficient program that required more space. We have also used global variables, rather than pass many parameters between procedures. If we are going to run the program only a few times, then the ease of writing it is important. But if the program is to become part of a standard library that is used repeatedly, then it is important to think about the details of implementation and modify the standard procedures to operate more efficiently under the specific circumstances, as we have done here.

Because our example set is so small, we cannot get a good feeling for the complexity of merge sort from it. However, we can show that merge sort is another good sorting technique, of order $n \lg n$. The reason is that each merge operation basically results in a set double the size of the sets merged. Here is the calculation.

Figure 11.36, Part 1   MergeSort

```
CONST
  MaxSize    = UserSuppliedSize;
  QueueUpper = UserSuppliedBound;     { MaxSize + 1 }

TYPE
  ElementType       = UserSuppliedType;
  Index             = 1..MaxSize;
  ListType          = ARRAY[Index] OF ElementType;
  QueueElementType  = RECORD
                        First : Index;
                        Last  : Index
                      END;
  QueueIndex        = 1..QueueUpper;

VAR
  Front : QueueIndex;
  Rear  : QueueIndex;
  Queue : ARRAY[QueueIndex] OF QueueElementType;

PROCEDURE MergeSort (VAR List : ListType; Size : Index);

  VAR
    I                     : Index;
    List1First, List1Last : Index;
    List2First, List2Last : Index;
    List3First, List3Last : Index;

  PROCEDURE SetUpQueue;

    BEGIN
      Front := 1;
      Rear := 1
    END; { SetUpQueue }

  PROCEDURE PlaceInQueue (First, Last : Index);

    BEGIN
      Rear := Rear + 1;
      IF Rear > MaxSize THEN Rear := Rear MOD MaxSize;
      Queue[Rear].First := First;
      Queue[Rear].Last := Last
    END; { PlaceInQueue }
```

Figure 11.36, Part 2   MergeSort

```
FUNCTION QueueSize : Index;

  BEGIN
    QueueSize := abs (Front - Rear)
  END; { QueueSize }

PROCEDURE RemoveFromQueue (VAR First, Last : Index);

  BEGIN
    Front := Front + 1;
    IF Front > MaxSize THEN Front := Front MOD MaxSize;
    First := Queue[Front].First;
    Last := Queue[Front].Last
  END; { RemoveFromQueue }

PROCEDURE AdjustListAndQueue (Amount, Size : Index);

  VAR
    I : Index;

  BEGIN
    FOR I := 1 TO Size DO List[I] := List[I + Amount];
    FOR I := Front + 1 TO Rear DO
      BEGIN
        Queue[I].First := Queue[I].First - Amount;
        Queue[I].Last := Queue[I].Last - Amount
      END
  END; { AdjustListAndQueue }

BEGIN { MergeSort }

  { Initialize Queue by placing one-item lists in the Queue. }

  SetUpQueue;
  FOR I := 1 TO Size DO PlaceInQueue (I,I);
  WHILE QueueSize > 1 DO
    BEGIN
      RemoveFromQueue (List1First, List1Last);
      RemoveFromQueue (List2First, List2Last);
      Merge (List1First, List1Last, List2First, List2Last,
             List3First, List3Last);
      PlaceInQueue (List3First, List3Last);
      IF List2First = 1 THEN AdjustListAndQueue (List2Last, Size)
    END
END; { MergeSort }
```

Figure 11.37, Part 1   Program using MergeSort

```pascal
PROGRAM MergeDriver (input, output);

CONST
  MaxSize    = 2048;
  QueueUpper = 2049;    { MaxSize + 1 }

TYPE
  ElementType       = integer;
  Index             = 1..MaxSize;
  ListType          = ARRAY[Index] OF ElementType;
  QueueElementType  = RECORD
                        First : Index;
                        Last  : Index
                      END;
  QueueIndex        = 1..QueueUpper;

VAR
  I        : Index;
  IsSorted : boolean;
  Front    : QueueIndex;
  List     : ListType;
  Queue    : ARRAY[QueueIndex] OF QueueElementType;
  Rear     : QueueIndex;
  Size     : Index;

PROCEDURE Merge (List1Start, List1End     : Index;
                 List2Start, List2End     : Index;
                 VAR List3Start, List3End : Index);

{ This procedure is given in fig. 11.33. }

PROCEDURE MergeSort (VAR List : ListType; Size : Index);

{ This procedure is given in fig. 11.36. }

FUNCTION Random (Count : integer) : integer;

{ This function has the purpose of generating a random
integer of size no larger than Count. It is a built-in
function in some versions of Pascal, such as Turbo
Pascal, but must be written for other versions, such as
IBM/PC Pascal. }
```

Figure 11.37, Part 2   Program using MergeSort

```
BEGIN { Driver for MergeSort }
  writeln ('Enter set size between 1 and ', MaxSize DIV 2 : 4);
  readln (Size);
  writeln ('Size of set is ', Size);
  IF (Size < 1) OR (Size > MaxSize DIV 2) THEN
    writeln ('RUN ABORTED--RETRY')
  ELSE

    { Assert: The set to be generated occupies at most half the
    space. }

    BEGIN

      { Generate random input keys.}

      FOR I := 1 TO Size DO
        List[I] := Random (50);

      { Write the original set, ten per line. }

      writeln ('Original Keys');
      FOR I := 1 TO Size DO
        IF I MOD 10 = 0 THEN
          writeln (List[I] : 4)
        ELSE write (List[I] : 4);
      writeln;

      { Sort, and write the sorted set, ten per line. }

      MergeSort (List, Size);
      writeln ('Sorted Keys');
      FOR I := 1 TO Size DO
        IF I MOD 10 = 0 THEN
          writeln (List[I] : 4)
        ELSE write (List[I] : 4);
      writeln;

      { Verify the sort. }

      IsSorted := true;
      FOR I := 1 TO Size - 1 DO
        IsSorted := IsSorted AND (List[I] <= List[I + 1]);
      writeln ('IsSorted is ', IsSorted : 7)
    END
END. { MergeDriver }
```

Assume that we are mergesorting a set of $n = 2^k$ items. For each pass through the algorithm, we have these counts:

pass number	number of merges	merge list length	number of comparisons per merge
1	2^{k-1}	1	$\leq 2^1$
2	2^{k-2}	2	$\leq 2^2$
.	.	.	.
.	.	.	.
.	.	.	.
$k-1$	2^1	2^{k-2}	$\leq 2^{k-1}$
k	2^0	2^{k-1}	$\leq 2^k$

Multiplying the number of merges by the maximum number of comparisons per merge, we get

$$(2^{k-1})2^1 = 2^k$$
$$(2^{k-2})2^2 = 2^k$$

.

.

.

$$(2^1)2^{k-1} = 2^k$$
$$(2^0)2^k \ \ \ = 2^k$$

Since k passes each require 2^k comparisons, we get $k \cdot 2^k$ comparisons (and moves); but $k = \lg n$. Hence the process involves $\lg n \cdot n$ comparisons; it is $O(n \lg n)$.

11.9 Updating

Updating a sequentially stored sorted set is more complex than updating an unsorted set, simply because the sorted order must be maintained. That affects the updating process in two ways. First, if an element is deleted, we cannot simply put the final element in its place, since that would destroy the sorted order. We must move each of the succeeding elements down one position. Second, when a new element is added, we cannot simply place it at the end, for the same reason. We must find where it belongs in order and make room for it there. Thus deletion of an element involves locating it and then moving all succeeding elements in the set to fill in the gap, while addition of an element involves locating its position and then moving all succeeding elements in the set to make room for it. For each of these operations we can use a binary search to locate the correct position and a linear element-by-element move to add or remove a position. An updating procedure using a linear search is given in figure 11.38.

Figure 11.38, Part 1   Update procedure

```
CONST
  MaxSize = UserSuppliedConstant;

TYPE
  ElementType = UserSuppliedType;
  Operation   = (Add, Delete);
  SetType     = RECORD
                  Size        : 0..MaxSize;
                  SetElement  : ARRAY[1..MaxSize] OF ElementType
                END;

PROCEDURE Update (VAR SetName : SetType;
                      Element       : ElementType;
                      AddOrDelete : Operation);

  VAR
    ElementPlace : 1..MaxSize;
    Index        : 1..MaxSize;

  BEGIN

    { Locate Element using a linear search--note the use of a
    sentinel to guarantee that Element is always in the set and
    thus the loop terminates. }

    WITH SetName DO
      BEGIN
        IF Size + 1 > MaxSize THEN
          writeln ('ERROR: No room in set for sentinel.')
        ELSE

          { Assert: (Size + 1) <= MaxSize }

          BEGIN
            ElementPlace := 1;
            SetElement[Size + 1] := Element;
            WHILE SetElement[ElementPlace] < Element DO
              ElementPlace := ElementPlace + 1;
            CASE AddOrDelete OF

              Add : BEGIN
                      IF (ElementPlace < (Size + 1)) AND
                        (Element <> SetElement[ElementPlace]) THEN

                        { Make room by moving SetElement[ElementPlace],
                        SetElement[ElementPlace + 1], ... ,
                        SetElement[Size] down one location. }
```

Figure 11.38, Part 2   Update procedure

```
                    BEGIN
                      FOR Index := Size DOWNTO ElementPlace DO
                        SetElement[Index + 1] := SetElement[Index];
                      SetElement[ElementPlace] := Element;
                      Size := Size + 1
                    END
                  ELSE
                    writeln ('ERROR: Element was already in set.');
                  IF ElementPlace = Size + 1 THEN
                    Size := Size + 1
                END; { Add }

          Delete : BEGIN
                    IF (ElementPlace = Size + 1) OR
                       (SetElement[ElementPlace] <> Element) THEN
                      BEGIN
                        write ('ERROR: Element ', Element);
                        writeln (' is not in the set.')
                      END
                    ELSE
                      BEGIN
                        FOR Index := ElementPlace TO Size - 1 DO
                          SetElement[Index] :=
                            SetElement[Index + 1];
                        Size := Size - 1
                      END
                  END { Delete }
              END { CASE }
            END { ELSE }
        END { WITH }
    END; { Update }
```

11.10. Search and retrieval

Because of the sequential structure that we are assuming for sets in this chapter,
retrieval of data from a stored set involves nothing more than traversal of the set
to locate the data. Since the set is sorted, we can use the binary search (divide
and conquer) method that we have already discussed. We make this observation.
If we had an unordered set whose elements were randomly distributed, then on
the average we could expect to search half the set before finding an element that
is in fact present; but we would need to search the entire set to determine that
a desired element was not there. On the other hand, in the best of all possible
worlds, we would find the desired element right away. Thus for an unsorted set
we have search times

$$\begin{array}{ll}
\text{best:} & O(1), \\
\text{average:} & O(n/2), \\
\text{worst:} & O(n).
\end{array}$$

Using binary search on a sorted set, the search time is proportional to the logarithm of the size of the set—and is the same whether the desired element is present or not. Our search times are

$$\begin{array}{ll}
\text{best:} & O(1), \\
\text{average:} & O(\lg n), \\
\text{worst:} & O(\lg n).
\end{array}$$

Since we cannot count on living in the best of all possible worlds, search times on a sequential sorted set are generally less than those on an unsorted set, or on a set that is sorted but stored as a linked list.

11.11 Reformatting

One process that arises frequently with an ordered or sorted set is reformatting or reorganizing it into a different order. For example, it is convenient to maintain a mailing list in alphabetical order for checking names and for updating the list. However, the post office prefers that it receive large mailings sorted into ZIP code order. One way to handle the need for two different orderings is to maintain the list in unsorted order and then sort it into whichever order is needed at any particular moment. Another way is to decide on one of the arrangements, perhaps alphabetical, as the standard one and then sort a copy of the list into the other order whenever that is needed. Note the need to sort a *copy* of the list, for otherwise we would have to resort it into the standard order. A third option is to maintain the list in one of the sorted orders, keeping track of which it is, and then resort it into the other order only when that is necessary. A fourth option is to keep multiple copies of the list, one in each of the desired orders. This option is generally highly undesirable. In addition to requiring storage for each copy, this option presents the problem of keeping all copies updated.

Any of these options demands some reworking of the list. The choice depends on the application. A personal mailing list tends to be relatively small and checked frequently for individual names and addresses. Hence alphabetical order might be the appropriate one. A large commercial mailing list, however, is rarely checked for individual addresses and is used to generate mass mailings. Thus ZIP code order might be better as the standard.

This particular reformatting problem may arise in other contexts. It is a relatively simple one, depending only on sorting a set into a particular order rather than on changing some fundamental characteristic of the data. Any of the sorting techniques that we have discussed will handle this problem, which may be thought of as sorting a complete unsorted set.

There are two other options that should be considered. We might consider maintaining the list as a linked list, with one set of pointers for each desired order. For the mailing list, we would have two pointers, one for alphabetical order and the other for ZIP code order. Note that this option does *not* gain us most of the advantages of sorted lists, since the items are not in contiguous storage locations. Thus we cannot, for example, search a sorted linked list in $O(\lg n)$ time. However, updating the list is simplified, since we need only adjust a couple of pointers rather than move large numbers of data. And whenever we want the output printed in either order, we have it ready to print, without going through a sorting operation.

The final option is to keep an **inverted index** in the list. This is simply an index telling where to find all records having a certain characteristic. For a mailing list, the index might show how to access all names beginning with a certain letter or it might show where to find all records for a particular ZIP code. It is easy to keep the index in sorted order, and as long as we can get from the index to the records, there is no need to keep the records in sorted order.

Here is a simple example. Suppose we wish to keep records of a family, including the names, ages, and food preferences of each family member. Suppose further that we need to have these records sorted on each of the three fields. We can do this by maintaining the database as a set of records, with an inverted index for each of the fields. The record structure would be

```
TYPE
   PersonalData = RECORD
                     Name : NameType;
                     Age  : 0..100;
                     Food : FoodType
                  END;

VAR
   Family : ARRAY[1..8] OF PersonalData;
```

To have a specific example, we can consider the following family:

	Name	*Age*	*Food*
Family[1]	Norman	45	Italian
Family[2]	Barbara	44	French
Family[3]	Karen	13	American
Family[4]	Jennifer	11	Mexican

For each inverted index that we need, we set up an array indicating the order in which the members of the family occur with respect to the particular characteristic:

```
VAR
   AgeIndex  : ARRAY[1..8] OF 1..8;
   FoodIndex : ARRAY[1..8] OF 1..8;
   NameIndex : ARRAY[1..8] OF 1..8;
```

For our example family, the inverted index values are

AgeIndex[1] = 4	FoodIndex[1] = 3	NameIndex[1] = 2
AgeIndex[2] = 3	FoodIndex[2] = 2	NameIndex[2] = 4
AgeIndex[3] = 2	FoodIndex[3] = 1	NameIndex[3] = 3
AgeIndex[4] = 1	FoodIndex[4] = 4	NameIndex[4] = 1

Using these indices, we find, for example, that the food preferences in alphabetical order are given by

Family[FoodIndex[1]].Food = Family[3].Food = American
Family[FoodIndex[2]].Food = Family[2].Food = French
Family[FoodIndex[3]].Food = Family[1].Food = Italian
Family[FoodIndex[4]].Food = Family[4].Food = Mexican

In a more realistic situation, each element of the inverted index array would be a list of all entries having the same value. We might find, for example, several family members with a preference for Chinese food. The numbers of their records would all be listed under the same entry in the inverted index, enabling us to find all people with the same preference easily. Notice that if we add a fifth family member, say David, age 18, with a preference for Chinese food, the inverted indices would be changed but the original data set would not be affected:

Family[5]   David   18   Chinese

AgeIndex[1] = 4	FoodIndex[1] = 3	NameIndex[1] = 2
AgeIndex[2] = 3	FoodIndex[2] = 5	NameIndex[2] = 5
AgeIndex[3] = 5	FoodIndex[3] = 2	NameIndex[3] = 4
AgeIndex[4] = 2	FoodIndex[4] = 1	NameIndex[4] = 3
AgeIndex[5] = 1	FoodIndex[5] = 4	NameIndex[5] = 1

Inverted indices thus provide an efficient way to access the elements of a set by their characteristics. And at the same time, the use of inverted indices permits us to insert new elements in the set without having to reorganize the entire set every time a new element is added. The inverted indices, in fact, provide pointers to the appropriate elements of the set.

Summary

In this chapter we have looked at a variety of basic sorting techniques. The techniques we have chosen are generally the best available for a simple set data structure.

Three of the classical sorting techniques have been relegated to exercises. One of these, the **bubble sort,** is very simple to program but very inefficient. We do not recommend its use. In the situations where we might consider a bubble sort, an insertion or straight selection sort is just as easy to program and will probably be more efficient. The second, the **Shell sort** (named for D. Shell), is better, but more complex and not as efficient as some of the other techniques we have discussed. The third technique is the **radix sort,** an extension of bin sorting that was used extensively with punched cards in the early days of computing.

We have also discussed the various other operations, merging, updating, and reformatting, that we might want to perform on sorted sets. We have observed that some of these operations are more difficult because of the need to maintain the sorted property, while others can in fact take advantage of the sorted property and actually are simpler to do.

The final observation to be made in this chapter is that we should consider the data carefully when choosing a particular algorithmic technique, such as a particular sorting method. We have noted, for example, that while quicksort is generally excellent, it can perform poorly on sets that are nearly in order. On the other hand, an insertion sort, which is generally less efficient than quicksort, performs very well when the set is nearly ordered. There is still an art to choosing a good algorithm; part of the art is matching the algorithm to the data characteristics.

Vocabulary

ascending order
bin sort
binary insertion sort
bit map
bottom-heavy heap
bubble sort
decision tree
decreasing order
descending order
divide and conquer
exchange sort
heap
heapify
heapsort
increasing order
insertion sort
inverted index
linear insertion sort
lower bound

median of three
mergesort
merging
multiway merge
pivot element
placement sort
priority queue
quicksort
radix sort
recursive algorithm
selection sort
Shell sort
sift down
stable sorting method
straight selection sort
top-heavy heap
tournament sort
tree selection sort

References

Hoare, C. A. R. "Quicksort." *Computer Journal* **5**, 1 (1962): 10–15.

Sedgewick, Robert. "Implementing Quicksort Programs." *Communications of the ACM* **21**, 10 (October 1978): 847–857.

Standish, Thomas A. *Data Structure Techniques*. Addison-Wesley, Reading, Mass. 1980.

Problems

11.1. The binary insertion sort (section 11.1) requires $O(n \lg n)$ comparisons to locate the positions of all the elements to be inserted. The linear insertion sort uses a linear scan to find the location of each new element. Show that this sort requires $O(n^2)$ comparisons to determine the locations of all the new elements.

11.2. Apply quicksort to the sequence 1, 3, 4, 8, 9, 10, 11, 14 and also to the sequence 14, 11, 10, 9, 8, 4, 3, 1. Observe what happens. From your observations show that the worst case behavior of quicksort is $O(n^2)$ and state conditions under which it can occur. Suggest a process for avoiding this worst case behavior.

11.3. In defining quicksort, we arbitrarily chose the first element as the pivot. Obviously, this could be a bad choice. Develop another method (other than median of three) for selecting a pivot that better guarantees that the choice of an element will be nearer the middle of the sorted subset.

11.4. Using the sets {2, 5, 10, 11}, {3, 6, 7, 12, 15}, and {4, 8, 9, 13}, demonstrate the merging of three sorted sets.

11.5. Suppose that a set is fully in order except that the kth element occupies the ith position, $i \neq k$. How much work is required to sort the set using the following:
   A. linear insertion sorting
   B. binary insertion sorting
   C. straight selection sorting
   D. quicksort
   E. heapsort
   Does it make any difference if $i < k$ or $i > k$?

11.6. Consider the word "alphabetical." Sort the distinct letters of this word into alphabetical order using each of the sorting techniques given in the text (insertion, selection, exchange, merge, placement). Next, label in some distinctive way each occurrence of the letters that occur more than once (for example, a_1, a_2, . . .), and repeat the sorts for all letter occurrences, noting where the various copies of the respective letters end up.

The following three sets of data are to be used for the next five problems (11.7–11.11). Assume they are given in the order listed:

set1	9	13	24	43	53	64	76
set2	76	64	53	43	24	13	9
set3	53	13	76	64	43	9	24

11.7. How many comparisons and exchanges are made when the Pascal procedure BinaryInsert (fig. 11.4) is executed on each of the three data sets?

11.8. How many comparisons and exchanges are made when the Pascal procedure StraightSelection (fig. 11.11) is executed on each of the above three sets of data?

11.9. How many comparisons and exchanges are made when the Pascal procedure HeapSort (fig. 11.30) is executed on each of the three sets of data?

11.10. How many comparisons and exchanges are made when the Pascal procedure QuickSort (fig. 11.32) is executed on each of the three sets of data?

11.11. How many comparisons are made when the Pascal procedure MergeSort (fig. 11.36) is executed on each of the three sets of data given above?

11.12. Stable sorting methods are those which do not rearrange elements that have equal value. Assume that $p_i = p_j$ for $i, j = 1, 2, 3, 4$ in the following multiset:

16   p_1 p_2 p_3 9   0 p_4.

If the final arrangement is

0   p_1 p_2 p_3 p_4 9   16,

we say that the sorting method is **stable.** Which of the following, as described in the text, are stable sorting methods?

    A. binary insertion,
    B. straight selection,
    C. heapsort,
    D. quicksort,
    E. mergesort.

11.13. How many comparisons have to be made in the best case and the worst case to merge a list of size m with a list of size n, $m \le n$?

11.14. Use the fact that two lists of size n can be merged in at most $O(n)$ work to show that mergesort does $O(n \lg n)$ work.

11.15. How many comparisons are necessary (best case and worst case) to merge k lists of sizes $n_1, n_2, \ldots, n_k$, $(k > 2)$?

11.16. Discuss which of the sorting methods in this chapter should be used if you wanted to sort a small list of, say, ten or fewer elements. Note that there is no unique correct answer. Be careful about assumptions.

Programs

11.1. Write a procedure to build a set using straight insertion sorting. Run both your program and BinaryInsert for several large data sets, and observe any differences in the time required for the two programs.

11.2. Write a program for a straight selection sort, selecting the largest element rather than the smallest each time.

11.3. Write a program for a straight selection sort, modified so that on each pass you find both the largest and the smallest elements, and move these to their proper positions. Analyze the time complexity of this program.

11.4. Write a program that will accept n sorted sets of integers ($n \ge 2$) and merge them together.

11.5. Write a procedure inplementing Sedgewick's version of quicksort.

11.6. Modify QuickSort to choose the median of three numbers as a pivot, swapping this into the first position before dividing the set.

Projects

11.1. In problem 11.1 the linear insertion sort is described. Linear insertion, binary insertion, and straight selection require $O(n^2) = \alpha n^2$ work to sort a list of size n. See if your system allows you to time a procedure accurately. If it does, try the following experiment. Generate several random sets of $n = 500$, 1000, and 1500 elements. Run and accurately time the three sorting procedures. (Apply all three to the same data set before generating a new one.) Using this information, see if you can compute the constant α in front of the n^2 term for your computer. (Note: The equality is only approximate.)

11.2. Modify the procedure QuickSort to find the kth smallest element of a set without necessarily sorting the entire set. For example, the 3rd smallest element in the set {9, 42, 22, 36, 18, 14} is 18.

11.3. One variation of the insertion sort is the Shell sort, which is basically a repeated insertion sort over selected elements of the set. A decreasing sequence of intervals is chosen, for example, 8, 4, 2, 1. In the first pass, elements that are eight positions apart are sorted by insertion sort. That is, the following groups of positions would be sorted independently:

```
1,   9,  17,  25,  33,  41, . . .
2,  10,  18,  26,  34,  42, . . .
3,  11,  19,  27,  35,  43, . . .
              .
              .
              .
8,  16,  24,  32,  40,  48, . . . .
```

For the second pass, the second increment, four, would be chosen as the interval determining the positions to be sorted:

```
1, 5,   9,  13,  17,  21,  25, . . .
2, 6,  10,  14,  18,  22,  26, . . .
3, 7,  11,  15,  19,  23,  27, . . .
4, 8,  12,  16,  20,  24,  28, . . . .
```

For the third pass, elements two positions apart would be sorted, and for the fourth and final pass, adjacent elements would be sorted.

Write a program to accept a set of integers to be sorted, together with a decreasing sequence of increments, that will sort the integers by Shell sort. Experiment with different increment choices to satisfy yourself that the sorting method works and to obtain an estimate of its order of complexity.

11.4. A radix sort is an iterated bin sort that operates from the least significant digit or letter of a set element toward the most significant. For example, consider the following set of three digit numbers:

067 726 207 553 028 061 620 018 557 292 492 002 326 360 100 122

In a radix sort these are first sorted into bins depending on the units digit, then gathered up in order and resorted into bins depending on the tens digit. This process is repeated for all (three) digits, resulting in a sorted set:

First pass:

620	061	292	553	726	067	028
360		492		326	207	018
100		002			557	
		122				

Gathered:

620 360 100 061 292 492 002 122 553 726 326 067 207 557 028 018

Second pass:

100	018	620	553	360	292
002		122	557	061	492
207		726		067	
		326			
		028			

Gathered:

100 002 207 018 620 122 726 326 028 553 557 360 061 067 292 492

Third pass:

002	100	207	326	492	553	620	726
018	122	292	360		557		
028							
061							
067							

Gathered:

002 018 028 061 067 100 122 207 292 326 360 492 553 557 620 726

The same technique can be used to sort words of varying length, if you assume that all words start in the same position, with trailing blanks to fill them out to a uniform length. Write a program that will sort a set of words of at most six characters each by radix sort. What is the complexity of this method?

11.5. A bubble sort is an exchange sort that begins repeatedly at one end of a set, exchanging successive elements with the objective of moving the highest remaining element into its correct position. For example, we begin at the left and move higher elements to the right:

53	26	41	13	18	69	27
26	53	41	13	18	69	27
26	41	53	13	18	69	27
26	41	13	53	18	69	27
26	41	13	18	53	69	27
26	41	13	18	53	27	<u>69</u>

(begin again)

26	13	41	18	53	27	69
26	13	18	41	53	27	69
26	13	18	41	27	<u>53</u>	69

(begin again)

13	26	18	41	27	53	69
13	18	26	41	27	53	69
13	18	26	27	<u>41</u>	53	69

(begin again—no more exchanges)

Write a program that will bubble sort a set of integers. What is its complexity? Compare actual running times for bubble sorting a set of 1000 integers with the times required by other techniques.

11.6. One spelling checker sorts its dictionary by word length, and within each length, alphabetically. Given this organization, what techniques would you suggest, and why, for searching and updating the dictionary?

12

Graphs

Introduction

Perhaps the most general data structure in use today is the linear graph. In its directed and undirected forms, the linear graph exhibits a degree of flexibility and adaptability that permits its use in modeling a wide variety of data organizations.

12.1 Linear graphs

A **linear graph** is defined as a set of **nodes** or **vertices,** together with a binary relation, called the set of **edges,** on the vertices. If this relation is symmetric so that $<a, b> = <b, a>$ for all vertices a and b, the graph is called **undirected.** Otherwise, the graph is called **directed.** It is customary to use the terms **graph** for an undirected graph and **digraph** for a directed graph. Also, in a digraph, it is customary to call the edges **arcs.** Three assumptions, while not required by the theory, are standard:

1. A graph or digraph has a finite number of vertices and edges.

2. A graph or digraph has no loops, that is, edges that go from a vertex back to itself.

3. A graph has no multiple edges. That is, there is at most one edge between a given pair of vertices. For digraphs, a similar assumption holds, but arcs in opposing directions are allowed.

We shall use the notation $\{a, b\}$ to refer to the edge of a graph and $<a, b>$ to refer to the arc of a digraph. Pictorially, we show an edge in a graph as a plain line joining two points and an arc in a digraph as a line joining two points with an arrowhead on the line indicating the direction of the arc (fig. 12.1). The terms **head** and **tail** are used to refer to the two ends of an arc.

From this general definition, we see that we have already been working with graphs and digraphs. Indeed, whenever we take two data items and associate them in any way, we have the beginnings of a graph. Vectors, linked lists, stacks, queues, trees, and arrays can all be interpreted as graphs or digraphs. For example, in figure 12.2 we have a matrix, A, with an associated graph. Since $A[1, 2] = 4$ and $A[1, 5] = 7$, we have a vertex, v_1, with two adjacent arcs of **weights** 4 and 7. Representing a matrix or other structure as a graph or digraph should be done only when the graph representation aids in understanding the structure.

A graph theorist, or mathematician who studies graphs, is often content with graphs and digraphs as we have defined them. However, in computing, we decorate a graph with additional properties—data values at the vertices, and weights or decision conditions on the edges. In some situations, we are also concerned about the left to right or top to bottom orientation of a graph. (We have already seen this for trees.) In other situations, the orientation does not matter.

We begin considering graphs and digraphs as abstract data types. Recall from chapter 1 that there are certain basic operations in common to all data structures: building, navigating, searching, ordering, updating, and so forth. Recall also that an abstract data type consists of a data structure together with an abstract or functional definition of basic operations. The development of fundamental abstract operations for graphs follows standard lines and is not especially revealing. However, there are operations that are specific to graphs, which we now examine.

Figure 12.1   Representations of edge and arc

Figure 12.2   A digraph corresponding to an array

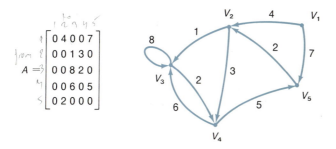

Figure 12.3   A typical graph and digraph

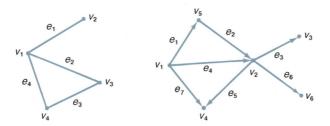

We assume that each vertex of a graph (or digraph) has an identifying label, v_i, and that each edge (or arc) also has an identifying label, e_j. Note that these labels are for identification only and are distinct from any values that may be associated with a vertex or edge (fig. 12.3).

Two key relations in a graph or digraph are **adjacency** and **incidence** relations. We define these first for a graph. A vertex and an edge are incident if and only if the vertex is one of the pair defining the edge. Two distinct vertices are adjacent if they are both incident to the same edge. Thus incidence is a relation between vertices and edges, while adjacency is a relation between vertices and vertices.

Among the functions and operations that we want to define for a graph are the following:

IsAdjacent (v, w)—returns "true" if v and w are vertices, and v and w are adjacent; returns "false" otherwise. It returns an error if either v or w is not a vertex.

IsIncident (v, e)—returns "true" if v is a vertex, e is an edge, and v and e are incident; returns "false" otherwise. It returns an error if v is not a vertex or e is not an edge.

In a digraph, the definitions of incidence and adjacency become slightly more complex because of the distinction between the arc $<a, b>$ and the arc $<b, a>$. The words "to" and "from" are sometimes used to identify the arc direction. Thus the arc $<a, b>$ is **incident from** a and **incident to** b; vertex b is **adjacent from** vertex a while a is **adjacent to** b.

In addition to these boolean functions, we need functions that return a vertex adjacent to a given one, an edge incident with a given vertex, and a vertex incident with a given edge. Let us consider a specific example to determine the type of specification we need. We shall look at a graph, leaving the analogous development for digraphs as an exercise.

Consider the graph of figure 12.4. Each vertex and each edge is labeled, and we observe a natural order (by the subscripts) among these labels. Note that this labeling order does not necessarily correspond to any ordering within the graph itself. We see that the vertices adjacent to v_3, for example, are v_1, v_4, v_6, and v_7. Many graph algorithms involve examining the vertices adjacent to a given vertex, either computing some value for all such vertices or selecting a "proper" vertex from among them. To do this in a systematic manner, we define this function:

AdjacentSet (v)— returns the set of vertices adjacent to v, or the empty set if there is no adjacent vertex, or an error if v is not a vertex.

Once we have the set of vertices adjacent to v, we can call upon the set operations we defined in chapters 4 and 5 to manipulate these vertices.

Similarly, we can define the function **IncidentSet** (v) that returns the set of edges incident to vertex v.

It is also useful to have two functions that relate vertices and edges:

Edge (v, w)—returns the name of the edge $\{v, w\}$ if the edge exists or a special value if it does not. Edge returns an error if either v or w is not a vertex.

Vertices (e)—returns the pair of vertices incident to edge e or an error if e is not an edge of the graph.

Figure 12.4   Small example graph

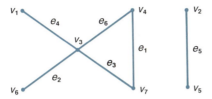

There is an analogous set of functions for a digraph. However, since the adjacency and incidence relations each split into two separate relations, the function set grows correspondingly. For example, in place of AdjacentSet we have the functions **AdjacentToSet** and **AdjacentFromSet.** The first of these is the set of vertices we can reach from the given one (following the edge directions), while the second is the set of vertices from which we can reach the given one. Specification of these is left as an exercise.

In addition to these functions that verify the inclusion of a vertex or an edge in a graph, and return specific sets of vertices and edges, there are other functions that can be defined. The main ones that concern us now are the two counting functions, **NumberOfVertices** and **NumberOfEdges,** that take as input a graph, that is, a set of vertices and a set of edges, and have as their values the number of vertices and edges of the graph, respectively.

Any other functions we need can be defined in terms of these basic functions.

12.2 Graph representations

To represent a graph in a computer, we must represent both the vertex set and the edge set, and the relationship between these sets. Among the possible representations, four are widely used and important. Two of these representations explicitly list both the vertices and the edges. As we might expect, these representations are based on the incidence relation. The other two representations are based on the adjacency relation and explicitly represent only the vertices. The edges can be inferred from the adjacency relation.

Viewed from another perspective, two of the representations are simply lists of vertices or edges. These have the advantage of compactness, at the expense of some irregularity in the data structure. The other two representations are basically matrix representations. These exhibit high regularity and permit the use of matrix operations for implementation of the graph operations. However, they are less compact than the list representations and frequently cause less efficient graph operations.

Figure 12.5   Edge list for fig. 12.4

$$\{4, 7\}$$
$$\{3, 6\}$$
$$\{3, 7\}$$
$$\{1, 3\}$$
$$\{2, 5\}$$
$$\{3, 4\}$$

To illustrate these data structures, we refer to the graph of figure 12.4. The **edge list** representation is simply a list of the edges of the graph, given as vertex pairs. We achieve some regularity in this representation by listing the edges in (numerical) order and listing the edge $\{v_i, v_j\}$ only for $i < j$. Vertex v_i is represented by the integer i in figure 12.5.

In the computer, this could be simply a list of integer pairs. The vertices are explicitly listed, and each vertex pair is an explicit representation of one of the edges. Here is a suitable set of declarations:

```
CONST
   MaxEdgeNumber    = UserSuppliedEdgeMax;
   MaxVertexNumber = UserSuppliedVertexMax;

TYPE
   Edge = RECORD
             Vertex1 : 1..MaxVertexNumber;
             Vertex2 : 1..MaxVertexNumber
          END;

VAR
   Graph : ARRAY[1..MaxEdgeNumber] OF Edge;
```

For a digraph, we use a slightly different rule for listing the vertex pairs. The direction on the arc is shown by listing first the tail, then the head. Thus $<v_1, v_2>$ represents the arc from v_1 to v_2, while $<v_2, v_1>$ represents the arc from v_2 to v_1. Note that these declarations suffice for representing a digraph with only three minor modifications. Change "Vertex1" to "Head," "Vertex2" to "Tail," and "Graph" to "Digraph."

The **incidence matrix** for a graph is a matrix representation explicitly giving both the vertices and edges. Each row of the matrix represents a vertex, while each column represents an edge. Each entry a_{ij} in the matrix is either 0 or 1, according to the rule

$a_{ij} = 1$ if vertex v_i is incident to edge e_j;

$a_{ij} = 0$ otherwise.

Figure 12.6   Incidence matrix for fig. 12.4

$$
\begin{bmatrix}
0 & 0 & 0 & 1 & 0 & 0 \\
0 & 0 & 0 & 0 & 1 & 0 \\
0 & 1 & 1 & 1 & 0 & 1 \\
1 & 0 & 0 & 0 & 0 & 1 \\
0 & 0 & 0 & 0 & 1 & 0 \\
0 & 1 & 0 & 0 & 0 & 0 \\
1 & 0 & 1 & 0 & 0 & 0
\end{bmatrix}
$$

Figure 12.7   Incidence matrix columns for two arcs

The arc $<v_3, v_7>$	The arc $<v_7, v_3>$
0	0
0	0
-1	$+1$
0	0
0	0
0	0
$+1$	-1

Since each edge has exactly two vertices, each column of the incidence matrix has exactly two 1's, with the other entries being 0's (fig. 12.6). Thus the incidence matrix for a graph with m vertices and n edges has only $2n$ nonzero entries. For most graphs, the incidence matrix is sparse. (Note that the number of nonzero entries is $O(n)$.)

For a digraph, we modify the definition of the incidence matrix, using a -1 to denote the tail and a $+1$ to denote the head. Thus each column has exactly one -1 and one $+1$. For example, instead of the third column of figure 12.6 representing the edge $\{v_3, v_7\}$ we would have a column representing the arc $<v_3, v_7>$ or the arc $<v_7, v_3>$ (fig. 12.7).

We turn now to the representations that do not explicitly list the edges. The first of these is the **vertex adjacency list.** This is simply a list, for each vertex, of the vertices that are adjacent to it. For a graph, each edge is implicitly represented twice, once in the list of each of its vertices (fig. 12.8). For a digraph, the

Figure 12.8   Vertex adjacency list for fig. 12.4

1: 3

2: 5

3: 1, 4, 6, 7

4: 3, 7

5: 2

6: 3

7: 3, 4

Figure 12.9   A digraph and its vertex adjacency list

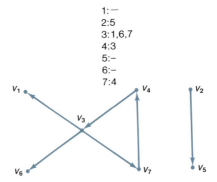

1:—
2:5
3:1,6,7
4:3
5:—
6:—
7:4

arcs are listed once, only in the list of the tail (fig. 12.9). Since each edge of a graph is represented twice the space needed is $2e$ or $O(e)$; similarly, each arc of a digraph is represented once, so the space needed is a or $O(a)$, where a is the number of arcs.

The final representation that we consider, the (**vertex**) **adjacency matrix,** has one entry for each vertex pair. The matrix entry a_{ij} has the value 1 if $\{v_i, v_j\}$ is an edge and the value 0 otherwise. Note that this implies the matrix is symmetric: $a_{ij} = 1$ if and only if $a_{ji} = 1$ (fig. 12.10).

For a digraph, the entries in the adjacency matrix reflect the direction of the arc, with $a_{ij} = 1$ if and only if the arc $<v_i, v_j>$ is in the graph (fig. 12.11).

We see that the adjacency matrix, just like the incidence matrix, is generally a sparse matrix. For an undirected graph of m vertices and n edges, the adjacency matrix contains $2n$ 1's, but only half of these are really needed. For a digraph, the adjacency matrix contains n 1's.

Representing a graph by a matrix allows us to perform matrix calculations, which may be meaningful for graphs. For example, the product of the incidence matrix with its transpose (obtained by interchanging the rows and columns) yields

Figure 12.10   Adjacency matrix for fig. 12.4

$$
\begin{bmatrix}
0 & 0 & 1 & 0 & 0 & 0 & 0 \\
0 & 0 & 0 & 0 & 1 & 0 & 0 \\
1 & 0 & 0 & 1 & 0 & 1 & 1 \\
0 & 0 & 1 & 0 & 0 & 0 & 1 \\
0 & 1 & 0 & 0 & 0 & 0 & 0 \\
0 & 0 & 1 & 0 & 0 & 0 & 0 \\
0 & 0 & 1 & 1 & 0 & 0 & 0
\end{bmatrix}
$$

Figure 12.11   Adjacency matrix for fig. 12.9

$$
\begin{bmatrix}
0 & 0 & 0 & 0 & 0 & 0 & 0 \\
0 & 0 & 0 & 0 & 1 & 0 & 0 \\
1 & 0 & 0 & 0 & 0 & 1 & 1 \\
0 & 0 & 1 & 0 & 0 & 0 & 0 \\
0 & 0 & 0 & 0 & 0 & 0 & 0 \\
0 & 0 & 0 & 0 & 0 & 0 & 0 \\
0 & 0 & 0 & 1 & 0 & 0 & 0
\end{bmatrix}
$$

a form of the adjacency matrix. We can use powers of the adjacency matrix to count the paths from one vertex to any other in the graph. However, for both of the matrix representations, the large number of 0's in the matrices wastes both space and additional processing time. We would avoid much of the space waste by using a linked list representation of the matrices, but then most of the advantage of having matrix calculations would also be lost. Since space requirements tend to be critical for large graphs and there are other ways of calculating such things as paths, we find that the two list representations are generally used more often. Of these, the vertex adjacency list is preferred unless there is some particular reason that an explicit edge or arc listing is needed.

In the remaining sections, we focus on some of the more common and useful graph algorithms. We examine the algorithms in the abstract and then discuss briefly the impact of different graph representations on algorithm efficiency.

12.3 Depth first search

Many problems that are modeled by graphs involve traversing the graph, perhaps to locate some specific information or to determine a minimum or maximum value associated with the graph. One such problem is that of finding the shortest path from one vertex to another. Another problem, if we think of the graph as representing a transportation network, is to determine the maximum amount of material that can be passed through the network in a given period of time.

In an undirected graph, a **path** from a to b is any sequence of vertices,

$$a = v_1, v_2, \dots, v_n = b$$

from vertex a to vertex b, such that $\{v_i, v_{i+1}\}$ is an edge for $i = 1, 2, \dots, n - 1$. In a digraph, a path is similarly defined, with the additional condition that we must traverse each arc in the direction of its orientation. That is, if c and d are consecutive vertices along a path, then in a graph we require that $\{c, d\}$ be an edge of the graph and in a digraph we require that $<c, d>$ be an arc of the graph. For graph traversal we are interested in **simple paths,** that is, paths that have no repeated vertices.

The problem of traversing a graph completely is rather like the problem of following all paths through a park. Unless we carry out the traversal in a systematic manner, we cannot be sure that we have really covered all edges in the graph. Generally, when we visit a vertex, we find that from that vertex there are several adjacent vertices that could be visited next. Our problem has two parts: deciding which vertex to visit next and remembering all of the vertices that we could have visited but decided to bypass temporarily. There are two widely used methods of systematically making these choices and traversing a graph.

These two methods are related closely to the way in which we store the bypassed vertices. One method, **depth first search,** stores these vertices in a *stack*; the other method, **breadth first search,** stores them in a *queue*. With either method, we always know which among the bypassed vertices is next to be visited.

Let's begin by considering depth first search. Basically, in depth first search we start at a vertex, pick a path, and follow the path as long as possible. That is, we either follow it to the end or, because we are interested only in simple paths, follow it until the next vertex choice would have to be a vertex that we have already visited. Once we reach the end of the path, we **backtrack** and pick up the vertices we have bypassed.

At our initial vertex, we have no vertices we have bypassed: the set of bypassed vertices is empty. Suppose that the first vertex is a and that the vertices adjacent to it are v, w, x, y, z. We mark vertex a as visited, and by some criterion, we pick one of these unmarked vertices to visit next. The criterion used for this choice depends on the particular problem. For example, if we are looking for a shortest path through the graph, we try to pick the vertex that is "closest" to a. (We will follow this example in section 12.8.) The remaining vertices are then placed on a stack for future visits. Thus, if our choice criterion results in visiting v next, the vertices w, x, y, z are placed on the stack.

We next visit the chosen vertex, v, and repeat the process. Suppose that the adjacent vertices are $a, b, c, \ldots, k$. Vertex a has already been visited, and we have marked it to indicate that. We choose the next vertex to visit from among the unmarked ones and stack the remaining vertices. For example, if the criterion indicates that we visit vertex b next, we stack vertices $c, \ldots, k$. Depending on the order in which we place vertices on the stack, the stack may look like

(top) c k

                .   .

                .   .

                .   .

               k or c
               w z

                .   .

                .   .

                .   .

               z w

or some other arrangement of these vertices. The important thing is that vertices $c, \ldots, k$ are nearer the top of the stack than vertices $w, \ldots, z$, and will be popped (visited) first. Some of the vertices in the stack may become marked through visits to other vertices. Hence, when we backtrack and pop vertices from the stack, we can ignore the marked ones and only visit those that are still unmarked.

When we are placing vertices on the stack, we can simply stack the unmarked vertices, since we know we will not need to visit any that are already marked. However, in the course of following a search through the graph we may visit and mark a vertex that is already on the stack. Hence we need to check the stack vertices to determine whether they have been visited, even if the only vertices we place on the stack are unmarked when we place them there.

Note that in depth first search the next vertex chosen is always one that is adjacent to the vertex currently being visited, as long as there is an adjacent vertex we have not yet visited. This is why the process has the nature of following a path as deeply as possible into the graph (and why the search is called "depth first"). When no such vertex exists, the backtracking process follows the path back to the first vertex from which we can visit a new vertex (the one at the top of the stack) and then proceeds down that side branch.

Figure 12.12   A depth first search in a graph

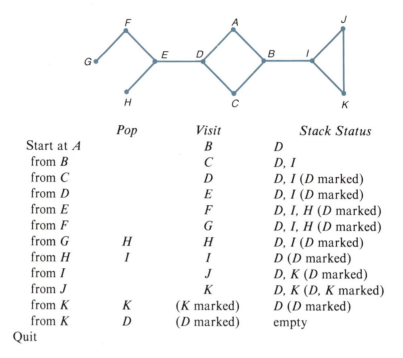

	Pop	Visit	Stack Status
Start at A		B	D
from B		C	D, I
from C		D	D, I (D marked)
from D		E	D, I (D marked)
from E		F	D, I, H (D marked)
from F		G	D, I, H (D marked)
from G	H	H	D, I (D marked)
from H	I	I	D (D marked)
from I		J	D, K (D marked)
from J		K	D, K (D, K marked)
from K	K	(K marked)	D (D marked)
from K	D	(D marked)	empty
Quit			

Here is an example showing how this works. The process is the same in either an undirected graph or a digraph, but there is frequently less backtracking in an undirected graph because of the lack of direction. Consider the graph of figure 12.12, where we have begun at vertex A and indicated a search through to vertex K. We start by visiting and marking A.

Figure 12.13 presents a procedure for depth first search. In this algorithm we have a procedure "Visit" which is intended to do whatever processing we want to do at each vertex. Note that by using recursion we avoid having to manage a stack explicitly.

We say that a graph is **connected** if there is a path from any vertex in the graph to any other vertex. Whether or not a graph is connected, a maximal connected subgraph of a graph is called a **connected component,** or more briefly, a **component.** Thus a connected graph has one component (the graph itself), while a disconnected graph has two or more components.

In a connected graph, a depth first search assures that we visit every vertex. However, if the graph is not connected, then the backtracking and stacking procedure will end with some vertices yet unvisited but no edges to pop from the stack. It is easy to show that at this stage we have visited every vertex in one of the components of the graph—the component that contained our initial vertex.

Figure 12.13   Pascal implementation of depth first search algorithm

```
CONST
  MaxDegree    = UserSuppliedDegree;
  MaxGraphSize = UserSuppliedSize;

{ Note: MaxDegree must be one larger than the actual maximum degree. }

TYPE
  VertexType    = integer;
  AdjacencyList = ARRAY[1..MaxGraphSize, 1..MaxDegree] OF VertexType;
  MarkSet       = SET OF 1..MaxGraphSize;

PROCEDURE Visit (Vertex : VertexType);

BEGIN
  writeln ('Visiting vertex ', Vertex : 2)
END; { Visit }

PROCEDURE DepthFirstSearch (Vertex   : VertexType;
                            Adjacent : AdjacencyList;
                            VAR Mark : MarkSet);

  VAR
    I : 1..MaxDegree;

  BEGIN
    Visit (Vertex);

    { Mark is initially the complete set of vertices. As each vertex
    is visited it is deleted from this set. }

    Mark := Mark - [Vertex];
    IF Mark <> [] THEN
      BEGIN
        I := 1;

        { Assert: In each row of the adjacency list, 0 indicates
        the end. }

        WHILE Adjacent[Vertex, I] <> 0 DO
          BEGIN
            IF Adjacent[Vertex, I] IN Mark THEN
              DepthFirstSearch (Adjacent[Vertex, I], Adjacent, Mark);
            I := I + 1
          END
      END
  END; { DepthFirstSearch }
```

Thus the unvisited vertices belong to other components of the graph. We can visit these by arbitrarily picking another vertex from among those that have not been visited and repeating the depth first search. This must be done once for each component of the graph, if we are to visit all of the vertices.

12.4 Breadth first search

A depth first search is associated with a *stack* of vertices that have not been explored. Similarly, the other major search technique, breadth first search, is associated with a *queue* of vertices. Placing the vertices in a queue rather than a stack yields a processing sequence that proceeds uniformly across the graph—by levels, as it were—rather than a sequence that explores very deeply along one path and then backtracks to find others.

In breadth first search we do not pick a path and follow it as long as possible. Rather, we establish a queue and when we visit a vertex, we place in the queue all of its adjacent vertices that have not been placed there already. We then pick up the next vertex from the queue and do similarly with it. Here is how it works.

At our initial vertex, the queue of vertices to visit is empty, since we are just starting the process. Suppose that the first vertex is a and that the vertices adjacent to it are v, w, x, y, z. We mark vertex a as visited, and by some criterion for ordering them, we place its adjacent unmarked vertices on the queue and mark them. The criterion used for this choice depends on the particular problem; frequently the order is not important, and we place them just as they occur in our graph representation. Thus, if order is not important, we place vertices v, w, x, y, z on the queue in that order and mark them.

We next visit the first vertex in the queue, v, remove it from the queue, and repeat the process. Suppose that the adjacent vertices are $a, b, c, \ldots, k$. All of these vertices that have not been marked as visited are placed on the queue also. Note that vertex a has been visited (since we started here). Hence it will not be placed on the queue. At this point our queue has the form

(front) w

                 x

                 .

                 .

                 .

                 z

                 b

                 c

                 .

                 .

                 .

(rear) k

Figure 12.14   A breadth first search in a graph

	Dequeue	*Visit*	*Queue Status*
Start at *A*		*A*	*B, D*
from *A*	*B*	*B*	*D, C, I*
from *B*	*D*	*D*	*C, I, E*
from *D*	*C*	*C*	*I, E*
from *C*	*I*	*I*	*E, J, K*
from *I*	*E*	*E*	*J, K, F, H*
from *E*	*J*	*J*	*K, F, H*
from *J*	*K*	*K*	*F, H*
from *K*	*F*	*F*	*H, G*
from *F*	*H*	*H*	*G*
from *H*	*G*	*G*	*empty*
Quit			

Depending on the criterion used, some other arrangement of these vertices may constitute the queue. The important thing is that vertices $w, x, \ldots, z$ are nearer the front of the queue than vertices $b, c, \ldots, k$, and will be dequeued (visited) first.

In breadth first search the next vertex chosen is not always one that is adjacent to the vertex currently being visited. Instead, we first visit all vertices adjacent to the initial vertex. Following that, we visit all vertices (not already visited) that are adjacent to the first neighbor of the initial vertex, then all vertices adjacent to the second neighbor of the initial vertex, and so forth. Because of this order of visitation, breadth first search tends to be useful for processes that relate to small portions of a graph, in contrast to those such as path finding that go from one end of a graph to the other. Using the graph of figure 12.12, let us see how breadth first search works (fig. 12.14). We begin again at vertex *A*.

Figure 12.15 presents a procedure for breadth first search. Note that in this algorithm we have a procedure "Visit" which is intended to do whatever processing we want to do at each vertex visited. Observe that a breadth first search relies on a queue to hold vertices not yet visited, while a depth first search uses a stack. As with depth first search, if the graph is connected, then eventually all vertices will be visited.

Figure 12.15, Part 1   Pascal implementation of breadth first search algorithm

```
CONST
  MaxDegree     = UserSuppliedDegree;
  MaxGraphSize = UserSuppliedSize;

{ Note: MaxDegree must be one larger than the actual maximum degree. }

TYPE
  VertexType    = integer;
  AdjacencyList = ARRAY[1..MaxGraphSize, 1..MaxDegree] OF VertexType;

PROCEDURE BreadthFirstSearch (StartVertex : VertexType;
                              Graph       : AdjacencyList);

  TYPE
    ElementType  = integer;
    MarkSet      = SET OF 1..MaxGraphSize;
    QueuePtr     = ^QueueElement;
    QueueElement = RECORD
                     Element : ElementType;
                     Next    : QueuePtr
                   END;
    QueueType    = RECORD
                     Front : QueuePtr;
                     Rear  : QueuePtr
                   END;

  VAR
    Mark        : MarkSet;
    NextVertex  : VertexType;
    VertexQueue : QueueType;

  PROCEDURE Create (Var Queue : QueueType);

    BEGIN
      Queue.Front := NIL;
      Queue.Rear := NIL
    END; { Create }

  FUNCTION Empty (Queue : QueueType) : boolean;

    BEGIN
      Empty := Queue.Front = NIL
    END; { Empty }
```

Figure 12.15, Part 2   Pascal implementation of breadth first search algorithm

```pascal
FUNCTION Full (Queue : QueueType) : boolean;

{ Note: This is a theoretical implementation, that assumes
that a linked list queue can never be full. }

  BEGIN
    Full := false
  END; { Full }

PROCEDURE Enqueue (QueueIn    : Elementtype;
                   VAR Queue : QueueType);

{ Note: This procedure has the effect of increasing the queue size. }

  VAR
    Temp : QueuePtr;

  BEGIN
    IF NOT Full (Queue) THEN
      BEGIN
        new (Temp);
        Temp^.Element := QueueIn;
        Temp^.Next := NIL;
        IF Queue.Rear <> NIL THEN Queue.Rear^.Next := Temp;
        Queue.Rear := Temp;
        IF Queue.Front = NIL THEN Queue.Front := Temp
      END
    ELSE
      writeln ('Error on enqueue: queue full.')
  END; { Enqueue }

FUNCTION Dequeue (VAR Queue : QueueType) : ElementType;

{ Note: This function has the effect of reducing the queue size. }

  VAR
    Temp : QueuePtr;

  BEGIN
    IF NOT Empty (Queue) THEN
      BEGIN
        Temp := Queue.Front;
        Dequeue := Temp^.Element;
        Queue.Front := Temp^.Next;
        dispose (Temp)
      END
    ELSE
      writeln ('Error on dequeue: queue empty.')
  END; { Dequeue }
```

Figure 12.15, Part 3   Pascal implementation of breadth first search algorithm

```pascal
PROCEDURE MarkAndQueue (Vertex            : VertexType;
                        VAR Adjacent      : AdjacencyList;
                        VAR VertexQueue   : QueueType;
                        VAR Mark          : MarkSet);

  VAR
    I : 1..MaxDegree;

  BEGIN
    Mark := Mark + [Vertex];
    I := 1;
    WHILE Adjacent[Vertex, I] <> 0 DO
      BEGIN
        IF NOT (Adjacent[Vertex, I] IN Mark) THEN
          EnQueue (Adjacent[Vertex, I], VertexQueue);
        I := I + 1
      END
  END; { MarkAndQueue }

PROCEDURE UnMark (MarkList : MarkSet);

  BEGIN
    Mark := []
  END; { Unmark }

PROCEDURE Visit (Vertex : VertexType);
  BEGIN
    write (Vertex : 3)
  END; { Visit }

BEGIN { BreadthFirstSearch }
  Create (VertexQueue);
  UnMark (Mark);
  Visit (StartVertex);
  MarkAndQueue (StartVertex, Graph, VertexQueue, Mark);
  WHILE NOT Empty (VertexQueue) DO
    BEGIN
      NextVertex := DeQueue (VertexQueue);
      IF NOT (NextVertex IN Mark) THEN
        Visit (NextVertex);
      MarkAndQueue (NextVertex, Graph, VertexQueue, Mark)
    END
END; { BreadthFirstSearch }
```

Figure 12.16   Digraphs with and without a cycle

One process for which breadth first search is useful is determining the cycles in a graph. A **cycle** in an undirected graph is a path that is simple, except that the final vertex in the path is the same as the initial vertex. In a directed graph a cycle is similarly defined, with the added condition that the arcs must be consistently directed. Thus, in figure 12.16, the first digraph has a cycle but the second does not, due to inconsistent arc directions. Note that if we ignore the directions and consider the graphs as undirected, then both have a cycle. Because of the sequence of visiting vertices in breadth first search, short cycles tend to be found quickly. Whenever we examine the vertices adjacent to a given vertex and find that one of these has been visited (is marked), we are likely to have found a cycle in the graph. Thus short cycles are found almost as soon as they are detectable. In contrast, in depth first search short cycles tend not to be found until most of the graph has been explored, because the edge closing the cycle may be bypassed and not noticed until the backtracking process worked its way back to that edge.

12.5 Minimal spanning trees

In this section we shall use undirected graphs. One common problem associated with a connected graph is to find a minimal spanning tree. A **spanning tree** for a graph, G, is a tree whose vertices are exactly the vertices of G and whose edges are all among the edges of G. We leave it as an exercise to show that G has a spanning tree if and only if G is connected.

Spanning trees arise in the solution of electrical circuit problems and in many problems that involve the traversal or search of a graph. In many of these problems some value is associated with each edge of the graph. We may use either depth first search or breadth first search to find a spanning tree. We illustrate both approaches with an example.

We have already discussed the concept of a tree as a computer professional sees one—replete with data, decision criteria, and full orientation. As we mentioned in chapter 10, the usual graph theoretical definitions of a tree are not the best for many computing purposes. However, in discussing spanning tree problems, the best starting point is one of these definitions:

A tree is a connected acyclic graph.

Figure 12.17   A dag that is not a directed tree

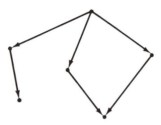

Figure 12.18   Paths in a tree

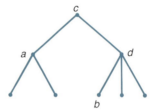

An **acyclic graph** is one with no cycles. For digraphs, we require, as for any path, that the arcs of a cycle be consistently traversed, in the direction in which they point. Directed acyclic graphs are sufficiently important in computing that the acronym **dag** is a commonly used term. While a directed tree is a dag, not all dags are directed trees (fig. 12.17).

The definition of a connected acyclic graph says, first, that we can find a path from any one vertex in the graph to any other and second, that we cannot return to the starting point of any path without retracing our steps. This implies that a simple path between any two vertices exists and is unique. For example, in the tree of figure 12.18, (*a, c, d, b*) and (*a, c, d, c, d, b*) are paths between a and b, but only the first of these is simple.

Suppose we are given a graph. Arbitrarily pick a vertex in the graph, and start following a path from that vertex. If the path is simple, then ultimately one of three things must happen:

1. We may be able to follow the path through all of the vertices of the graph.

2. We may reach an endpoint, where the only thing left to do is to turn back to the previous vertex.

Figure 12.19   Possible path terminations

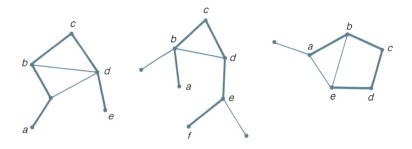

Figure 12.20   Taking a branch off a path

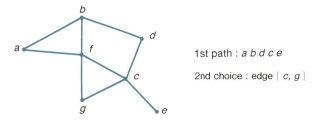

1st path : *a b d c e*

2nd choice : edge | *c, g* |

3. We may reach a point where there is no next step, except to return to some vertex that we visited earlier in the path.

These three possibilities are illustrated in figure 12.19.

    In the first of these situations, it is obvious that the graph is connected: we have a single path along which we can move from any one vertex to any other. In the second and third situations, we may or may not have visited every vertex. If we have visited every vertex, then again the graph is connected. If not, then we must see if the other vertices can be reached from those we have already visited.

    Recall that a depth first search has the characteristic of following one path as far as possible and then backtracking to find alternative paths. If we use this technique, we find that as we follow a path through the graph, we have stacked vertices that we have not yet visited. Each of these vertices represents a potential branch off the path we have traversed.

    Let us find a spanning tree for the graph in figure 12.20. Suppose that we start at vertex *a* and follow the indicated path to vertex *e*. Along the way we have stacked vertex *f* (from *a*), *f* (from *b*), *f* (from *c*), and *g* (from *c*). Backtracking,

Figure 12.21   Depth first spanning tree for G

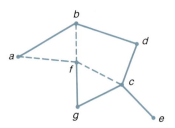

Figure 12.22   Nonspanning and spanning trees

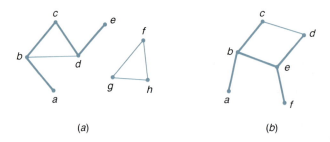

(a)   (b)

we pop vertex *g* from the stack and take the path from *c* through *g* to *f*. At vertex *f* we find that all adjacent vertices have already been visited. Further back-tracking will pop vertex *f* from the stack three times, but since it has already been visited, no further paths will result. Hence we develop the spanning tree of figure 12.21.

Suppose that we iterate this process. We develop a path as far as possible and then explore all possible branches off the path, branches off the branches, and so forth, until we have reached every vertex that we can possibly reach from our starting point. One of two things happens. First, there may still be some unreachable vertices. In this case, the original graph is not connected (fig. 12.22*a*) and has no spanning tree. Second, we may have reached every vertex in the graph. In this situation, the graph is connected and the branched set of paths that we have generated is a spanning tree of the graph (fig. 12.22*b*).

Suppose now that we use a breadth first search technique to generate a spanning tree for this same graph (fig. 12.20). Starting at vertex *a*, we place the adjacent vertices in a queue, mark them, and then proceed to visit these vertices. Because a vertex will be adjacent to several others and we are interested in generating a tree, we also retain the vertex which caused a given vertex to be placed

Figure 12.23   Breadth first spanning tree for G

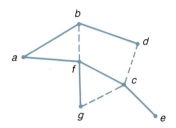

in the queue. The notation that we use is $b(a)$, meaning that vertex b is in the queue because it was adjacent to vertex a. This enables us to recover the edges. The sequence is this:

> Visit and mark a, queue and mark b and f.
>> Queue: $b(a)$, $f(a)$.
> Visit b (edge from a), queue and mark d.
>> Queue: $f(a)$, $d(b)$.
> Visit f (edge from a), queue and mark c and g.
>> Queue: $d(b)$, $c(f)$, $g(f)$.
> Visit d (edge from b).
>> Queue: $c(f)$, $g(f)$.
> Visit c (edge from f), queue and mark e.
>> Queue: $g(f)$, $e(c)$.
> Visit g (edge from f).
>> Queue: $e(c)$.
> Visit e (edge from c).
>> Queue: empty.

Figure 12.23 shows the spanning tree that this generates. Observe that it is different from that generated by the depth first search.

If the original graph is a tree, then the spanning tree that we find by this process will be unique—just the original tree itself. However, if the original graph is connected and has one or more cycles, then there will be several spanning trees, depending on where we break each cycle (fig. 12.24).

When several spanning trees exist for a graph, the process of generating one involves choices. For example, if we start at vertex a of the graph in figure 12.24, then when we reach vertex b we have a choice of two possible branches. A good algorithm for generating a spanning tree must provide a means of making these choices. A common means is to assign values to the edges of the graph. We may think of these values as weights, times, or distances. For any spanning tree, we

Figure 12.24   Possible spanning trees

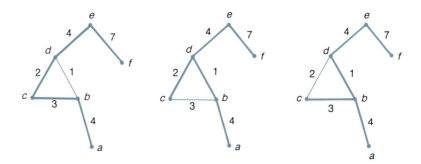

can easily total the values along the edges chosen for the tree, giving a value for the entire tree. A **minimal spanning tree** for a given graph is one whose value is the least possible. Thus, in figure 12.24, the middle choice is the minimal spanning tree, with a value of 18. In the next two sections we develop two algorithms for finding a minimal spanning tree.

12.6 Prim's minimal spanning tree algorithm

Minimal spanning trees arise in a number of situations when it is important to minimize costs. For example, suppose that we are developing a communication network for a group of cities. We could run communication lines between each pair of cities, but that obviously involves far more lines than is necessary. We could also run a line loop through all cities. But if this line is a cycle, that is, returns to the city from which it started, it too involves more lines than is necessary: we could remove one segment and still have connections between all cities (fig. 12.25).

Clearly, we need at least a spanning tree to have a communication network that involves all the cities, and anything more than a spanning tree will include communication lines that are not absolutely necessary. If our measure of "distance" between cities is the cost of putting in the communication lines, then we minimize the line costs by finding a minimal spanning tree.

Similarly, in laying out roads between cities, we minimize the amount of concrete required by using a minimal spanning tree. In wiring a house, we minimize the amount of wire needed by finding a minimal spanning tree. (Note that in all these applications, other considerations may dictate a different solution that does not involve a minimal spanning tree.)

One difficulty that sometimes arises in designing an algorithm is that the obvious thing to do may produce the wrong result. For example, if we are in hilly country and want to reach the top of the highest hill, the obvious thing to do is to look around and climb to the top of the highest hill we can see. But once on

Figure 12.25   Communication networks

Figure 12.26   Starting a minimal spanning tree

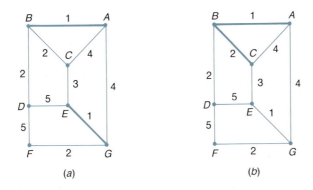

(a)   (b)

top, we may discover another, higher hill, so we must climb down again: the obvious move has been the wrong one. There is, however, a class of algorithms known as **greedy algorithms,** for which the obvious move is always the correct one: it produces the desired result. The two minimal spanning tree algorithms that we describe are examples of greedy algorithms.

We want to find a minimal spanning tree, that is, one with the total value of its edges as small as possible. If we are "greedy" about this, the obvious starting point is to choose an edge which has a minimal value. (If there are several of the same value, list them in some specific order and choose the first one in the list.)

Having chosen the first edge, we now delete it from the set of available edges and look for the second one. One possibility is to use the same rule: choose an edge with minimal value. The only problem is that this edge might not be connected to the first one (fig. 12.26a). We'll follow this line of reasoning in the next section and choose a different rule for now.

Since we are trying to generate a tree, let's make sure that we have a tree at each stage of the development. Obviously, the first edge by itself is a tree. If we choose a second edge that has a vertex in common with the first one, we still have a tree. Thus let's choose the second edge this way, with the condition that its value be the least among all edges adjacent to the original one (fig. 12.26b).

Figure 12.27   Minimal spanning tree generation

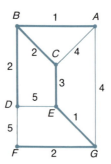

This greedy approach guarantees that we have a tree, but we have already ignored a low value edge. As we shall see, however, we ultimately pick the low value edges for inclusion in the tree.

Let us continue with this method. Having two edges in the tree, we look for another edge to join to it, one having the least possible value. In figure 12.26*b* we choose {*B, D*} to join to the tree {*A, B*}, {*B, C*}. Note that this edge could join the tree at either of its endpoints or at the midpoint. Continuing this development by choosing {*C, E*}, {*E, G*}, and {*F, G*} in that order, we ultimately generate a minimal spanning tree for the graph. (fig. 12.27).

This method of generating a minimal spanning tree is known as **Prim's algorithm.** The rule is:

> Choose any vertex. Note that this is a tree. At each step, choose an edge with minimal value *that can be added to the developing tree.* If the process involves all vertices of the graph, then a minimal spanning tree has been found; if it stops before involving all vertices, then the graph is disconnected and no spanning tree exists. However, in the latter situation, we have found a minimal spanning tree for one piece, or connected component, of the graph. We can then do the same for every other connected component, developing a minimal **spanning forest** for the graph.

Let us examine briefly the contention that Prim's algorithm actually produces a minimal spanning tree for a connected graph. If it does not, that means that there is some low valued edge {*v, w*} that should be in the tree. Observe that, if we were to add this edge to the tree, we would create a cycle containing the new edge and that the value of this edge would be less than that of some other edge in this cycle. Now suppose that vertex *v* was included in the tree before vertex *w*. When we added *w* to the tree, we had a choice between the edge {*v, w*} and the edge that was actually chosen—and we chose the edge with the lower

Figure 12.28   Proof diagram for Prim's algorithm

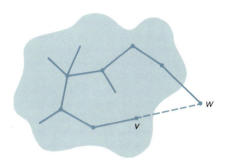

value (fig. 12.28). Thus $\{v, w\}$ cannot have a value lower than any other edge in the cycle it generates. Hence, using $\{v, w\}$ in the tree will *not* produce a spanning tree of lower value. We have a proof by contradiction: assuming that $\{v, w\}$ should be in the tree has led to the conclusion that it should not be; therefore, the edges chosen by the algorithm are the correct ones.

To implement Prim's algorithm we must first choose a data structure representation. Since the basis of this algorithm is the edge values, it would seem that a representation that explicitly lists the edges, sorted in increasing value order, is most appropriate. However, we also need to know what is included in the developing tree and what can be added at each stage. It turns out that this is easier to track if we focus on the vertices rather than the edges.

Here is the reason. Suppose we have a vertex, v, that is not yet in the tree. We *really* are interested in the shortest distance from this vertex to the tree—that is, in the edge of least value joining v to a vertex in the tree. There may be many edges incident to v, but at any one time we are interested in only one of them. A good idea is to focus on this vertex and the particular edge value. The value may change every time we add another vertex (edge) to the tree; but if it does so, the change is due to the newly added vertex and is simple to monitor.

Let us follow this process through for the graph of figure 12.26, using the edge $\{A, B\}$ as the initial tree. For each vertex not in the tree, we must track its nearest neighbor in the tree and the distance (value of the edge joining them). For vertices that are not adjacent to the tree, we take the distance to be either infinite or an extremely large positive value. Thus, initially, only vertices C, D, and G are adjacent to the tree. The data being kept are these:

Vertex	A	B	C	D	E	F	G
Distance	—	—	2	2	—	—	4
Nearest Tree Vertex	B	A	B	B	—	—	A

(For the initial vertices, A and B, we have listed each other as the nearest tree vertex.)

We also need the vertex adjacency list:

A	B, C, G
B	A, C, D
C	A, B, E
D	B, E, F
E	C, D, G
F	D, G
G	A, E, F

We see that the shortest distance is 2, and that we can choose either vertex *C* or vertex *D*. Let us choose vertex *C*. Looking at the adjacency list, we see that only vertex *E* is adjacent to *C* and not in the tree. Hence only its distance value will be affected:

Vertex	A	B	C	D	E	F	G
Distance	—	—	—	2	3	—	4
Nearest Tree Vertex	B	A	B	B	C	—	A

We have removed the value for *C*, since that vertex is now in the tree. Repeating the process, we choose *D*, observing that vertex *F* is now adjacent to the tree:

Vertex	A	B	C	D	E	F	G
Distance	—	—	—	—	3	5	4
Nearest Tree Vertex	B	A	B	B	C	D	A

Next, choose vertex *E*, noting that this is adjacent to *G* (not yet in the tree) and hence may affect its distance from the tree:

Vertex	A	B	C	D	E	F	G
Distance	—	—	—	—	—	5	1
Nearest Tree Vertex	B	A	B	B	C	D	E

Vertex *G* is now the closest vertex not yet in the tree. Adding it changes the distance from vertex *F* to the tree:

Vertex	A	B	C	D	E	F	G
Distance	—	—	—	—	—	2	—
Nearest Tree Vertex	B	A	B	B	C	G	E

We finally gather in vertex *F*:

Vertex	A	B	C	D	E	F	G
Distance	—	—	—	—	—	—	—
Nearest Tree Vertex	B	A	B	B	C	G	E

By canceling out the distances but keeping the nearest tree vertex data, we have retained the spanning tree but destroyed its value. If it is also important to keep the value, then the algorithm can be modified for that purpose. A Pascal implementation of the algorithm is given in figure 12.29. The process executed in this algorithm is a minor modification of that which we used in our example.

Figure 12.29, Part 1   Pascal implementation of Prim's algorithm

```
CONST
  MaxGraph    = UserSuppliedGraphSize;
  Marked      = 0;
  LargeValue = UserSuppliedLargeValue;
```

{ *MaxGraph is the largest acceptable number of vertices in a graph. LargeValue is a very large real number, used to indicate that two vertices are nonadjacent.* }

```
TYPE
  Graph = ARRAY[1..MaxGraph, 1..MaxGraph] OF real;

PROCEDURE Prim (N : integer; VAR Distance : Graph);
```

{ *Computes a minimal spanning tree. N is the number of vertices in the graph, and Distance is a matrix of distances between vertices. If vertices I and J are not adjacent then Distance [I,J] has the value LargeValue.* }

```
  VAR
    Closest          : 1..MaxGraph;
    I                : 1..MaxGraph;
    J                : 1..MaxGraph;
    MinDistance      : ARRAY[1..MaxGraph] OF real;
    NearestNeighbor : ARRAY[1..MaxGraph] OF 0..MaxGraph;
    NewMinimum       : real;

  BEGIN
```

{ *Assert: The graph is connected.* }

{ *Begin the tree at vertex 1. Initialize the MinDistance and NearestNeighbor arrays. When a vertex is added to the tree, its NearestNeighbor will be marked and removed from consideration.* }

```
    FOR I := 2 TO N DO
      BEGIN
        MinDistance[I] := Distance[1, I];
        NearestNeighbor[I] := 1
      END;
```

Figure 12.29, Part 2   Pascal implementation of Prim's algorithm

```
{ Run the algorithm for the remaining vertices. }

FOR I := 2 TO N DO
  BEGIN

    { Find the vertex not in the tree nearest to some vertex in
    the tree. }

    Closest := 2;
    NewMinimum := MinDistance[2];
    FOR J := 3 TO N DO
      IF MinDistance[J] < NewMinimum THEN
        BEGIN
          NewMinimum := MinDistance[J];
          Closest := J
        END;

    { Having the closest vertex not in the tree, add it to the
    tree and adjust the minimum distances. }

    writeln ('Adding edge ', NearestNeighbor[Closest], '-',
             Closest, ' at cost ', NewMinimum : 4 : 1);

    { Mark the vertex just added to the spanning tree and remove
    it from the table of candidates to be considered. }

    NearestNeighbor[Closest] := Marked;
    MinDistance[Closest] := LargeValue;

    { Update the table of candidates to reflect the vertex just
    added to the spanning tree. }

    FOR J := 2 TO N DO
      IF (NearestNeighbor[J] <> Marked) AND
         (Distance[J, Closest] < MinDistance[J]) THEN
        BEGIN
          MinDistance[J] := Distance[J, Closest];
          NearestNeighbor[J] := Closest
        END
  END
END; { Prim }
```

On each iteration, rather than move a vertex from the set that we have not added to the set that we have added, we mark it as added by setting its nearest neighbor to a vertex not in the graph (Marked = 0) and its distance to the tree to LargeValue. Then we can search among all vertices rather than check each time to make sure the vertex is not one that we have already added to the tree. Note further that the procedure uses a vertex adjacency matrix and not a vertex adjacency list as in the explanation above.

12.7 Kruskal's minimal spanning tree algorithm

We turn now to a second method of generating a minimal spanning tree. This is also a greedy algorithm, based on the idea of grabbing the lowest value edge not yet chosen and adding it to the developing tree. We noted in the previous section that we may have more than one tree under development at any one time: these trees will eventually grow together. The only other caution is that we must not add an edge that would form a cycle. Here, for the graph of figure 12.26, is how the method would work.

First, choose edges $\{A, B\}$ and $\{E, G\}$. Note that we can always choose the first two edges without worrying about forming a cycle (why?) and that in this example we have chosen the only two edges with value 1. There are three edges of value 2, so we have a choice again. As it happens, none of these edges will form a cycle, so we can add them all: $\{B, C\}$, $\{B, D\}$, and $\{F, G\}$. At this stage we still have two trees under development. The one edge of value 3, $\{C, E\}$, joins these two trees into a single tree. If we were smart, we might now recognize that we have a spanning tree and stop the algorithm. If not, then we observe that each of the edges $\{A, C\}$ (with value 4) and $\{D, F\}$ (with value 5) forms a cycle, and hence cannot be added to the tree.

This method is known as **Kruskal's algorithm.** It happens for our example that both Prim's and Kruskal's algorithms produce the same minimal spanning tree, but this is not generally the case, as problem 12.7 shows.

The focus in Kruskal's algorithm is more directly on the edges of the graph than is the focus in Prim's algorithm. We choose the next edge without regard to its relationship to the tree and then check to see whether it can be added. Remember that with this algorithm we generally have several trees under development at any one time. Four different situations arise. First, the newly chosen edge may not be adjacent to any of the current trees, and hence it starts a new tree. This is shown by the fact that neither of its endpoints is in any of the trees. Second, the new edge may be adjacent to exactly one of the trees, as indicated by the fact that one endpoint is listed in a tree but the other is not. In both of these situations the new edge can be added to the developing structure (fig. 12.30a, b).

The other two situations arise when both endpoints of the new edge are listed in the current tree structures. If one endpoint is in one tree and the other in another tree, then the new edge can be added to the structure and will combine

Figure 12.30   Adding edges, Kruskal's algorithm

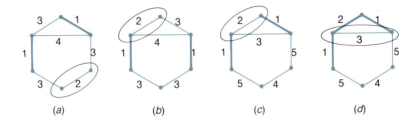

(a)	(b)	(c)	(d)

the two trees into one (fig. 12.30c). However, if both endpoints of the edge are listed in the same tree, then the new edge would form a cycle within that tree, and hence it cannot be added to the structure (fig. 12.30d).

Thus the crucial check, once an edge has been chosen, is to determine whether its endpoints have already been listed and, if so, whether both of them are listed in a single tree.

Because of the focus on edges in Kruskal's algorithm, an edge list ordered by increasing value is an appropriate data structure. We also need a list of the vertices in each tree and a method of merging these lists when two trees are joined by an edge. For our example graph, we have this result:

Edge	*Vertices*		*Value*
1	A	B	1
2	E	G	1
3	B	C	2
4	B	D	2
5	F	G	2
6	C	E	3
7	A	C	4
8	A	G	4
9	D	E	5
10	D	F	5

First edge choices, edges 1 and 2:

Tree #1:   A   B

Tree #2:   E   G

Second edge choice, edge 3. With *B* in Tree #1 and *C* in no tree, this edge joins Tree #1:

Tree #1:   A   B   C

Tree #2:   E   G

Third edge choice, edge 4. Again, this edge joins Tree #1:

Tree #1:   *A   B   C   D*
Tree #2:   *E   G*

Fourth edge choice, edge 5. This edge joins Tree #2:

Tree #1:   *A   B   C   D*
Tree #2:   *E   F   G*

Fifth edge choice, edge 6. This edge has one vertex in Tree #1 and the other in Tree #2. Hence the two trees are merged into one:

Tree #1:   *A   B   C   D   E   F   G*

At this point we have all seven vertices included in one tree. Hence this is a minimal spanning tree of the graph. If we were to examine the remaining edges (7, 8, 9, and 10), we would find for each of them that both endpoints of the edge are already in the tree, so that adding it would form a cycle.

Proving that Kruskal's algorithm results in a minimal spanning tree for a connected graph is simple. The edges that have been omitted are either further down the list, and thus have higher values than those used, or would form cycles when added to the tree, and hence cannot be used. We can easily keep track of the specific edges that have been included in the tree, since they are already in the list. We need only delete (or mark) the edges that have been bypassed because of cycle formation, and delete or mark all edges beyond the number necessary for a spanning tree. Observe that since at each stage we need know only the next edge to consider, it is more efficient to organize the edges into a priority queue or heap (see section 11.5) rather than into a fully sorted list.

There are two keys to efficient implementation of this algorithm: knowing which edge to examine next, and being able to manipulate the tree fragments that contain the vertices of a new edge. For the first of these we could sort the edges by length, but this is not necessary. A heap or priority queue contains all of the information necessary to choose the next edge. Efficient manipulation of the tree fragments depends on having a pair of algorithms to find the fragment whose vertex set contains a vertex of the new edge and to merge the new edge into the tree fragments. This latter task may involve creating a new fragment, adding the edge to a given fragment, or merging two of the given fragments and the new edge into a single fragment.

A Pascal implementation of Kruskal's algorithm is given in figure 12.31. By placing each vertex in a separate fragment initially, we assure that whenever we examine an edge each of its vertices will be listed in some fragment. Initially the number of fragments will be the number of vertices; the algorithm is finished when the number of fragments has been reduced to one, the minimal spanning tree.

Figure 12.31, Part 1　　Pascal implementation of Kruskal's algorithm

```
CONST
  MaxVertices = UserSuppliedMaximumNumberOfVertices;
  MaxEdges    = UserSuppliedMaximumNumberOfEdges;

TYPE
  EdgeRange    = 1..MaxEdges;
  VertexRange  = 1..MaxVertices;
  EdgeType     = RECORD
                    Ends   : ARRAY[1..2] OF VertexRange;
                    Weight : real
                 END;
  GraphType    = ARRAY[EdgeRange] OF EdgeType;
  TreeType     = SET OF EdgeRange;

PROCEDURE Kruskal (NumberVertices : VertexRange;
                   NumberEdges    : EdgeRange;
                   VAR Graph      : GraphType;
                   VAR TheTree    : TreeType);

  TYPE
    FragmentType = ARRAY[VertexRange] OF SET OF VertexRange;
    HeapElement  = RECORD
                      EdgeIndex : EdgeRange;
                      Weight    : real
                   END;
    HeapType     = ARRAY[EdgeRange] OF HeapElement;

  VAR
    End1            : VertexRange;
    End1Fragment    : VertexRange;
    End2            : VertexRange;
    End2Fragment    : VertexRange;
    Fragments       : FragmentType;
    HeapSize        : EdgeRange;
    IsPlaced        : boolean;
    NumberFragments : VertexRange;
    Place           : EdgeRange;
    SmallChildPlace : EdgeRange;
    TheHeap         : HeapType;

  FUNCTION FragmentNumber (EndPoint        : VertexRange;
                           NumberFragments : VertexRange;
                           VAR Fragments   : FragmentType) : VertexRange;
    VAR
      Number : VertexRange;
```

Figure 12.31, Part 2   Pascal implementation of Kruskal's algorithm

```
BEGIN
  Number := 1;
  WHILE NOT (EndPoint IN Fragments[Number]) AND
            (Number < NumberFragments) DO
    Number := Number + 1;
  FragmentNumber := Number
END; { FragmentNumber }

PROCEDURE FormFragments (NumberVertices : VertexRange;
                         VAR Fragment   : FragmentType);
  VAR
    Index : VertexRange;

  BEGIN
    FOR Index := 1 TO NumberVertices DO
      Fragment[Index] := [Index]
  END; { FormFragments }

PROCEDURE FormPriorityQueue (VAR Graph            : GraphType;
                             NumberOfEdges        : EdgeRange;
                             VAR ThePriorityQueue : HeapType);
  VAR
    Index : EdgeRange;

  BEGIN
    FOR Index := 1 TO NumberOfEdges DO
      BEGIN
        ThePriorityQueue[Index].Weight := Graph[Index].Weight;
        ThePriorityQueue[Index].EdgeIndex := Index
      END
  END; { FormPriorityQueue }

PROCEDURE Swap (VAR First, Second : HeapElement);

{ A procedure used to swap heap values. }

  VAR
    Temp : HeapElement;

  BEGIN
    Temp := First;
    First := Second;
    Second := Temp
  END; { Swap }

  { Swap from figure 11.23. }
```

Figure 12.31, Part 3   Pascal implementation of Kruskal's algorithm

```
FUNCTION SmallPlace (VAR Heap         : HeapType;
                         ParentPosition : EdgeRange;
                         HeapSize       : EdgeRange) : EdgeRange;

{ A function which determines the index or location of the
smallest child of a parent node. Note that in some cases
the parent node may only have one child. }

  BEGIN
    IF 2 * ParentPosition = HeapSize THEN
      SmallPlace := 2 * ParentPosition
    ELSE
      IF Heap[2 * ParentPosition].Weight <
           Heap[2 * ParentPosition + 1].Weight THEN
        SmallPlace := 2 * ParentPosition
      ELSE
        SmallPlace := 2 * ParentPosition + 1
  END; { SmallPlace }

{ SmallPlace adapted from LargePlace in figure 11.23. }

PROCEDURE Heapify (VAR Heap : HeapType; Size : EdgeRange);

  VAR
    Counter         : EdgeRange;
    SmallChildPlace : EdgeRange;
    Place           : EdgeRange;

  BEGIN
    FOR Counter := (Size DIV 2) DOWNTO 1 DO
      BEGIN
        Place := Counter;
        SmallChildPlace := SmallPlace (Heap, Place, Size);
        WHILE (Heap[SmallChildPlace].Weight < Heap[Place].Weight) AND
              (Place <= Size DIV 2) DO
          BEGIN
            Swap (Heap[SmallChildPlace], Heap[Place]);
            Place := SmallChildPlace;
            IF (2 * Place <= Size) THEN
              SmallChildPlace := SmallPlace (Heap, Place, Size)
          END
      END
  END; { Heapify }

{ Heapify adapted from figure 11.23. }
```

Figure 12.31, Part 4   Pascal implementation of Kruskal's algorithm

```pascal
PROCEDURE MergeFragments (Fragment1              : VertexRange;
                          Fragment2              : VertexRange;
                          VAR NumberFragments : VertexRange;
                          VAR Fragments          : FragmentType);
   VAR
     Temp : VertexRange;

   BEGIN
     IF Fragment1 > Fragment2 THEN
       BEGIN
         Temp := Fragment1;
         Fragment1 := Fragment2;
         Fragment2 := Temp
       END;
     Fragments[Fragment1] := Fragments[Fragment1] + Fragments[Fragment2];
     FOR Index := Fragment2 TO NumberFragments - 1 DO
       Fragments[Index] := Fragments[Index + 1];
     NumberFragments := NumberFragments - 1
   END; { MergeFragments }

BEGIN { Kruskal }
   FormPriorityQueue (TheGraph, NumberEdges, TheHeap);
   HeapSize := NumberEdges;
   Heapify (TheHeap, HeapSize);
   FormFragments (NumberVertices, Fragments);

   { Initialize the spanning tree. }

   TheTree := [];
   NumberFragments := NumberVertices;
   WHILE NumberFragments > 1 DO
     BEGIN
       End1 := TheGraph[TheHeap[1].EdgeIndex].Ends[1];
       End2 := TheGraph[TheHeap[1].EdgeIndex].Ends[2];
       End1Fragment := FragmentNumber (End1, NumberFragments, Fragments);
       End2Fragment := FragmentNumber (End2, NumberFragments, Fragments);
       IF End1Fragment <> End2Fragment THEN
         BEGIN
           MergeFragments (End1Fragment, End2Fragment,
                           NumberFragments, Fragments);
           TheTree := TheTree + [TheHeap[1].EdgeIndex]
         END;
       TheHeap[1] := TheHeap[HeapSize];
       HeapSize := HeapSize - 1;
```

Figure 12.31, Part 5   Pascal implementation of Kruskal's algorithm

```
{ Let the top of the heap sift down until a heap
is recreated. }

Place := 1;
IsPlaced := false;
WHILE (2 * Place <= HeapSize) AND (NOT IsPlaced) DO
  BEGIN
    SmallChildPlace := SmallPlace (TheHeap, Place, HeapSize);
    IF TheHeap[SmallChildPlace].Weight >
        TheHeap[Place].Weight THEN
      BEGIN
        Swap (TheHeap[Place], TheHeap[SmallChildPlace]);
        Place := SmallChildPlace
      END
    ELSE
      IsPlaced := true
  END
END
END; { Kruskal }
```

Because of the different orientations of Prim's and Kruskal's algorithms, we might expect that their performances differ also. This is the case. Prim's algorithm, which operates on the vertices of a graph, has worst case complexity $O(n^2)$, while Kruskal's algorithm, which operates on the edges of a graph, has worst case complexity $O(e\lg e)$, where n is the number of vertices and e is the number of edges. This implies that Kruskal's algorithm can be expected to work better for graphs with relatively few edges, whereas Prim's algorithm is faster for graphs with a relatively large number of edges.

The reasoning for the complexity values is this. In Prim's algorithm (see fig. 12.29) the dominating factor is the second FOR loop. This loop is executed $n - 1$ times, but each execution includes two $O(n)$ inner loops: one to find the closest vertex not in the tree and the other to update the distance values. In Kruskal's algorithm (fig. 12.31) the dominating factor is forming the priority queue of edges, which takes $O(e\lg e)$ time.

12.8 Shortest paths

A typical problem associated with a digraph is that of finding the **shortest path** from one point to another in the graph. Recall that in a path in a digraph all arcs must be consistently directed: we must traverse the arc from its beginning vertex to its end vertex. Thus, even though a digraph may be "connected" if we were

Figure 12.32   Directed graph with no path from *A* to *B*

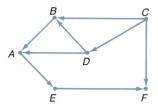

to ignore the directions on the arcs (look at the graph as undirected), it may not be possible to find a path from vertex *A* to vertex *B*, because of the arc directions (fig. 12.32).

If we are able to find a path from *A* to *B*, there may be a choice of several such paths. One criterion to use in choosing a path is to find the shortest one—that is, the one with a minimal sum of edge values. In finding the shortest path from *A* to *B*, we do not know which other vertices we must traverse. **Dijkstra's algorithm** finds the shortest path from a given vertex (such as *A*) to every other one in essentially the same time the algorithm would take to find the shortest path from vertex *A* to any other specific vertex (fig. 12.33).

Dijkstra's algorithm is another example of a greedy algorithm. At each stage, we choose the arc that will result in the shortest partial path for the next stage. This is also an example of the influence of data structure choice on algorithm efficiency. We observe that the algorithm involves nested loops. Since we are interested in distances or values along arcs, it is appropriate to use a data representation that displays the arc values explicitly—either an adjacency matrix or an adjacency list, with values inserted. When we chose the adjacency matrix the nested loops required examination for each vertex; hence they resulted in complexity $O(n^2)$. However, if we had chosen the adjacency list, ordered by the "to" vertex, then we would have needed to execute the inner loop for arcs into vertex *w*. Since we do this for all vertices, we examine each edge just once. Hence the total time for all executions of the inner loop is $O(e)$. The other major contribution to execution comes from "Locate vertex *W* in $V - S$ such that Short-Distance[*W*] is minimal." By organizing the vertices in $V - S$ as a priority queue (see chapter 11), this choice takes $O(\lg n)$ time for each iteration of the loop. Thus, with the adjacency list representation, the time complexity of this implementation would be $O(e \lg n)$. For graphs with a small number of edges, this can be considerably better than $O(n^2)$.

We must point out that Dijkstra's algorithm is valid only for non-negative edge values and will generally fail if negative edge values are introduced. Problem 12.9 explores this difficulty.

Figure 12.33, Part 1   Pascal implementation of Dijkstra's shortest path algorithm

```pascal
CONST
  LargeNumber = UserSuppliedLargeNumber;
  MaxVertices = UserSuppliedMaximumNumberOfVertices;

TYPE
  VertexRange    = 1..MaxVertices;
  DistanceMatrix = ARRAY[VertexRange, VertexRange] OF real;
  DistanceType   = ARRAY[VertexRange] OF real;

PROCEDURE Dijkstra (NumberVertices     : VertexRange;
                    VAR Distance       : DistanceMatrix;
                    VAR ShortDistance  : DistanceType);
  VAR
    Index       : VertexRange;
    MinDistance : real;
    S, V        : SET OF VertexRange;
    Vertex      : VertexRange;
    W           : VertexRange;

  BEGIN

    { Initialize list of shortest distances so far. }

    ShortDistance[1] := 0;
    FOR Index := 2 TO NumberVertices DO
      ShortDistance[Index] := LargeNumber;
    S := [1];
    V := [2..NumberVertices];

    { Compute distances from vertex 1 to its neighbors. }

    FOR Index := 2 TO NumberVertices DO
      ShortDistance[Index] := Distance[1, Index];
    WHILE (V - S) <> [] DO
      BEGIN

        { Enumerate the vertices in V - S. }

        MinDistance := LargeNumber;
        W := 2;
```

Figure 12.33, Part 2   Pascal implementation of Dijkstra's shortest path algorithm

```
FOR Index := 2 TO NumberVertices DO
  BEGIN
    IF Index IN (V - S) THEN
      IF ShortDistance[Index] < MinDistance THEN
        BEGIN
          MinDistance := ShortDistance[Index];
          W := Index
        END
  END;

{ Locate vertex W in V - S such that ShortDistance[W]
is minimal. }

S := S + [W];

{ Update shortest distances by examining those through W. }

FOR Vertex := 2 TO NumberVertices DO
  IF Vertex IN (V - S) THEN
    IF ShortDistance[Vertex] >
      ShortDistance[W] + Distance[W, Vertex] THEN
        ShortDistance[Vertex] :=
          ShortDistance[W] + Distance[W, Vertex]
  END
END; { Dijkstra }
```

Summary

Graphs, undirected and directed, play a major role in data structures, both because they can be used to represent a very broad array of data structures, and because the theory of graphs is well developed and forms a sound basis for a theory of data structures. In this chapter we have introduced some of the basic ideas and looked at two types of problems that arise in the use of these structures. There are many other properties that graphs have and many other algorithms that apply to these data structures. Not all of the algorithms are "greedy." In fact, for determining some of the major properties of graphs, there are no good algorithms. All known algorithms for such properties involve work that grows exponentially, or worse, with the number of vertices.

Vocabulary

acyclic graph
adjacency
adjacency matrix
adjacent from
adjacent to
arc
backtrack
breadth first search
component
connected
connected component
cycle
dag
depth first search
digraph
Dijkstra's algorithm
directed graph
edge
edge list
graph
greedy algorithm

head
incidence
incidence matrix
incident from
incident to
Kruskal's algorithm
linear graph
minimal spanning tree
node
path
Prim's algorithm
shortest path
simple path
spanning forest
spanning tree
tail
undirected graph
vertex
vertex adjacency list
weight

Problems

12.1. Give an abstract data type definition for the function **IncidentSet** for undirected graphs.

12.2. Give abstract data type definitions for the functions **IsAdjacentTo, IsAdjacentFrom, IsIncidentTo, IsIncidentFrom, AdjacentTo, AdjacentFrom, IncidentTo, IncidentFrom, Arc** (analogous to **Edge**), **VerticesTo,** and **VerticesFrom** for digraphs.

12.3. For the graph in fig. 12.26, compute a minimal spanning tree using Prim's algorithm starting from the edge $\{E, G\}$.

12.4. We can think of a minimal spanning tree algorithm based on the idea of locating cycles in a graph and deleting the highest valued edge in each cycle. Develop such an algorithm, and compare its efficiency with that of Prim's and Kruskal's algorithms.

12.5. Prove that the "tree" defined by the recursive definition is also a "tree" according to the definition given in this chapter.

12.6. Plot the graphs of ke lg e, with $k = 1, 5, 10$ and e ranging from 0 to $n(n - 1)/2$, where e is the number of edges in a graph and n is the number of vertices. Note where each of these graphs crosses the value n^2. (The value k represents the ratio of the time necessary for one application of Kruskal's algorithm to the time necessary for one application of Prim's algorithm.)

12.7. For the graph in figure 12.34, show that Prim's and Kruskal's algorithms can produce different minimal spanning trees.

12.8. Apply both Prim's and Kruskal's algorithms to the graph in figure 12.35.

Figure 12.34

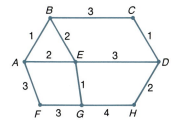

Figure 12.35

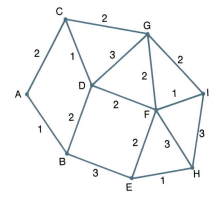

Figure 12.36

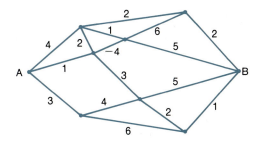

12.9. Show that Dijkstra's algorithm will not work for the graph in figure 12.36.

12.10. In section 12.2 we claim that the powers of the adjacency matrix count the paths from one vertex to another. How is this done? Hint: If there are p paths of length s from vertex i to vertex k, and q paths of length t from vertex k to vertex j, how many paths are there from i to j which are of length $s + t$ and go through vertex k?

12.11. Suppose that we use boolean arithmetic (i.e., $1 + 1 = 1$) in computing the powers of an adjacency matrix, A. What does each 1 in A^k represent? Show that the graph is connected if and only if $A + A^2 + \ldots + A^{n-1}$ has no zeros in it, where n is the size of A (the number of vertices in the graph).

Programs

12.1. Modify the Pascal program for Prim's algorithm to calculate also the value of the minimal spanning tree and print it out.

Projects

12.1. If your system permits you to determine run times, compare implementations of Prim's and Kruskal's algorithms. Use sample graphs of about fifty vertices, some with 70–100 edges and others with 1000 or more edges. (You can try this with smaller graphs, but the differences in timing may not be as evident. You should devise a subsidiary algorithm that will generate sample graphs for you rather than try to enter them by hand.)

Appendix A
ASCII and EBCDIC Codes

Two standard computer codes for data are in almost universal use. They are ASCII (American Standard Code for Information Interchange) and EBCDIC (Extended Binary Coded Decimal Interchange Code). Here we present the code for the letters, numerals, and publication marks. Other codes are used for control characters, graphic characters, italic characters, or special alphabets.

The table below gives each character, together with the ASCII and EBCDIC values expressed as decimals and as hexadecimal (base 16) numerals. The ordering used is that for ASCII, the more commonly used code.

Character	ASCII		EBCDIC		Character	ASCII		EBCDIC	
	dec.	hex.	dec.	hex.		dec.	hex.	dec.	hex.
(space)	032	20	064	40	0	048	30	240	F0
!	033	21	090	5A	1	049	31	241	F1
"	034	22	127	7F	2	050	32	242	F2
#	035	23	123	7B	3	051	33	243	F3
$	036	24	091	5B	4	052	34	244	F4
%	037	25	108	6C	5	053	35	245	F5
&	038	26	080	50	6	054	36	246	F6
'	039	27	125	7D	7	055	37	247	F7
(	040	28	077	4D	8	056	38	248	F8
)	041	29	093	5D	9	057	39	249	F9
*	042	2A	092	5C	:	058	3A	122	7A
+	043	2B	078	4E	;	059	3B	094	5E
,	044	2C	107	6B	<	060	3C	076	4C
−	045	2D	096	60	=	061	3D	126	7E
.	046	2E	075	4B	>	062	3E	110	6E
/	047	2F	097	61	?	063	3F	111	6F

Character	ASCII dec.	ASCII hex.	EBCDIC dec.	EBCDIC hex.	Character	ASCII dec.	ASCII hex.	EBCDIC dec.	EBCDIC hex.
@	064	40	124	7C	`	096	60		
A	065	41	193	C1	a	097	61	129	81
B	066	42	194	C2	b	098	62	130	82
C	067	43	195	C3	c	099	63	131	83
D	068	44	196	C4	d	100	64	132	84
E	069	45	197	C5	e	101	65	133	85
F	070	46	198	C6	f	102	66	134	86
G	071	47	199	C7	g	103	67	135	87
H	072	48	200	C8	h	104	68	136	88
I	073	49	201	C9	i	105	69	137	89
J	074	4A	209	D1	j	106	6A	145	91
K	075	4B	210	D2	k	107	6B	146	92
L	076	4C	211	D3	l	108	6C	147	93
M	077	4D	212	D4	m	109	6D	148	94
N	078	4E	213	D5	n	110	6E	149	95
O	079	4F	214	D6	o	111	6F	150	96
P	080	50	215	D7	p	112	70	151	97
Q	081	51	216	D8	q	113	71	152	98
R	082	52	217	D9	r	114	72	153	99
S	083	53	226	E2	s	115	73	162	A2
T	084	54	227	E3	t	116	74	163	A3
U	085	55	228	E4	u	117	75	164	A4
V	086	56	229	E5	v	118	76	165	A5
W	087	57	230	E6	w	119	77	166	A6
X	088	58	231	E7	x	120	78	167	A7
Y	089	59	232	E8	y	121	79	168	A8
Z	090	5A	233	E9	z	122	7A	169	A9
[	091	5B	173	AD	{	123	7B	139	8B
\	092	5C			|	124	7C		
]	093	5D	189	BD	}	125	7D	155	9B
^	094	5E			~	126	7E		
_	095	5F	109	6D					

Appendix B
Pascal Program Format and Style

Pascal imposes very few rules for program format and style. The choice of how to indent, or even whether to indent at all, is left to the programmer. Any letters may be capitalized or left in lowercase at the discretion of the user, the choice having no impact on how the program runs. (A few compilers, however, are designed to refuse uppercase letters.) A program could be written as one long continuous line of text, with statements separated only by semicolons. However, such a program is very difficult to read, understand, debug, and modify.

A number of different writing styles have been adopted by various authors. We feel that the format and style used in this text is clear and consistent, and close to that which a programmer can use at a keyboard. The only difference between the text style and what a programmer would use lies in the fact that we have italicized the comments in the text, for emphasis. Here, then, are the rules that we have followed, and that we believe to result in a good, highly readable program style.

Identifiers used in a Pascal program fall into three categories: reserved words, predefined identifiers, and user defined identifiers. See any Pascal text or programmer's manual for the list of reserved words and predefined identifiers. The distinction between these is that the reserved words (e.g., PROGRAM, BEGIN, WHILE, FOR, ...) have fixed meanings and cannot be interpreted in any other way, whereas the predefined identifiers (e.g., read, writeln, integer, sqrt, ...) have meanings that are defined for a particular implementation, but can change in different implementations. These can conceivably be overridden by the user. For example, if you write your own WriteLn procedure, Pascal uses it and ignores the predefined one.

In the programs within the text we have used one special class of identifiers. Any identifier beginning "UserDefined ..." or "UserSupplied ..." must be replaced by a specific constant value or type identifier, appropriate to the user's particular implementation and need.

Capitalization

We distinguish among the three categories of names by this convention:

Reserved words are fully capitalized;

Predefined identifiers are fully lowercase;

User defined identifiers have the first character, and the first character of any imbedded word capitalized, but all other characters are lower case.

Examples: BEGIN, END, REPEAT, UNTIL
read, write, abs, integer, real
I, Index, Count, SkipBlanks, TestForPositive

Spacing

Spacing involves the use of blanks and blank lines to separate names and portions of the program. Our conventions are these:

i Blanks separate operators, and names in a list.

Comments: {ƀ ... ƀ}   `{ This is a comment. }`
Colons: ... ƀ:ƀ ...   `Number : real;`
Assignment statements: ... ƀ:=ƀ ...   `Leftmost := 17;`
Arithmetic operators: ... ƀ+ƀ ...   `Next * (I - 17)`
Equivalence and inequivalence: ... ƀ=ƀ ...   `IF Left <> Right`
Function and procedure calls with parameters:
  DoThisƀ(...)   `FindSlope (Line);`
Read and write statements: readƀ(...)   `writeln (Next);`
Lists:
  (FirstName,ƀSecondName,ƀ ...)   `write (I * J, Center, '42');`

ii Blank lines segregate major program structures.

Declaration blocks, LABEL, CONST, TYPE, VAR, PROCEDURE and FUNCTION headers are followed by a blank line.

iii Blank lines set off each comment.

Indentation

Indentation should be consistently applied to indicate the levels of structure within a program. We recommend indenting two columns at a time, although indenting 3 columns at a time is also reasonable for smaller programs. Paired reserved words, such as BEGIN . . . END or REPEAT . . . UNTIL should be at the same level of indentation. Specifically, the following indentation structures are recommended:

Compound Statements:

```
Statement #0;
BEGIN
  Statement #1;

  .

  .

  .

  Statement #N
END;
Statement #N+1;
```

Conditional Statements:

IF-THEN statements:

```
IF Condition THEN
   Statement;
```

IF-THEN-ELSE statements:

```
IF Condition THEN
   Statement #1
ELSE
   Statement #2;
```

Chained IF statements:

```
IF Condition #1 THEN
   Statement #1
ELSE
   IF Condition #2 THEN
      Statement #2
   ELSE
      Statement #3;
```

CASE statements:

```
CASE Variable OF
   Value1 : Statement #1;
   Value2 : Statement #2;
      .
      .
      .
   ValueN : Statement #N
END;
```

Repetition loops:

WHILE-DO loops:

```
WHILE Condition DO
   Statement;
```

```
WHILE Condition DO
   BEGIN
      Statement #1;
      Statement #2;
         .
         .
         .
      Statement #N
   END;
```

REPEAT-UNTIL loops:

```
REPEAT
   Statement #1;
   Statement #2;
      .
      .
      .
   Statement #N
UNTIL Condition;
```

FOR-DO loops:

```
FOR Variable := LowerLimit TO UpperLimit DO
   Statement;


FOR Variable := LowerLimit TO UpperLimit DO
   BEGIN
      Statement #1;
      Statement #2;
        .
        .
        .
      Statement #N
   END;
```

Within the main program structure, the reserved words PROGRAM, LABEL, CONST, TYPE, VAR, PROCEDURE, FUNCTION, the first (main) BEGIN, and the final END. are all aligned at the left margin.

All declarations under CONST, TYPE, and VAR are indented two columns. All identifiers are left justified, and the equal signs or colons are aligned.

Within any procedure or function, all reserved words and statements are indented two columns with respect to the position that they would normally occupy in the main program or an enclosing procedure or function.

There is *never* more than one statement on a line.

Comments

Comments are included in a program to help inform and guide anyone who reads the program as to its intent and operation. Comments, therefore, should be informative and not merely reiterate obvious code.

It is good practice to include a comment immediately after a PROGRAM, PROCEDURE, or FUNCTION declaration, stating the purpose of the program, procedure, or function, and any unusual conditions that the programmer might not otherwise catch.

Comments related to code segments should precede the segments. Comments describing user defined identifiers may follow the declaration, on the same line:

```
VAR
   StartCount : integer; { Initial size. }
   EndCount   : integer; { Final size. }
```

Each procedure or function should be closed with a comment consisting of its name:

```
PROCEDURE MyProc (X : integer);

{ Comment on purpose. }

   BEGIN
      .
      .
      .
   END; { MyProc }
```

For comments occupying separate lines, the opening left brace should be at the same level of indentation as the code segment within which the comment occurs. The closing right brace may immediately follow the comment, or may be placed at the righthand margin. While some authors prefer to make each line of a multiline comment a separate comment, we believe it is better practice to use only one pair of braces to enclose the entire comment.

Whatever style is chosen for comments, it should be used consistently.

Multiple Line Structures

Frequently a logical line within a program will occupy more than one physical line. Our conventions are these:

For comments, additional lines begin at the same level of indentation as the original left brace:

```
{ This comment began at a fairly deep level of
  indentation, and its subsequent lines all begin
  at exactly the same level. }
```

For statements involving parameter lists, such as procedure and function calls, and read and write statements, continuation lines are begun one space to the right of the opening parenthesis:

```
PROCEDURE MyFunnyValentine (BoysName  : NameType;
                            GirlsName : NameType;
                            VAR Card  : AddressType);


{ procedure call }  MyFunnyValentine (FirstGradeBoy,
                                       SecondGradeGirl, Where);


              writeln ('The quick ', Color, ' ', Animal,
                       'jumped over the ', Structure);
```

Two points should be noted. In the procedure header the colons are aligned, whereas in the procedure call there is no attempt to align the commas. In write and writeln statements, quoted segments such as 'jumped over the ' cannot be broken across lines with this form of indentation, since extra spaces will be introduced. Hence the line breaks always occur between quoted segments.

For assignment statements with lengthy righthand sides, the break between lines is made between major portions of the righthand side wherever possible, and subsequent lines are aligned slightly to the right of the assignment operator:

```
NewValue := 2 * (MyProc (OldValue, Twist) + 3)
                + (Difference / OldValue);
```

Similarly, in conditional statements with lengthy conditions the break is made between major portions of the condition, and alignment is made to the right of the opening parenthesis:

```
IF ((NewValue > OldValue) AND (Name = KnownName))
   OR NOT GoodAddress THEN
      . . .
```

Finally, "good style" is a human judgment. The computer does not care about style, and will compile and execute a sloppily written program with the same ease that it handles one that has been well written. The programmer or user, however, will fully appreciate any effort to make a program clear and readable. A significant part of this is developing a good style and using it consistently.

Index

Index for Abstract Data Type Implementations

Function, Procedure, and Program Index